LIVING WITH ANIMALS

Ojibwe Spirit Powers

Within the nineteenth-century Ojibwe/Chippewa Medicine Society, the Midewiwin, and in Ojibwe societies in general, Michael Pomedli contends that animals as symbols demonstrated the cultural principles of these nations. In *Living with Animals*, he presents over one hundred of these images from oral and written sources – including birch bark scrolls, rock art, stories, games, and dreams – in which animals appear as kindred beings, spirit powers, healers, and protectors.

Pomedli explains that the principles at play in these sources are not just evidence of cultural values. They are unique standards brought to treaty signings by Ojibwe leaders and norms against which North American treaty re-interpretations should be reframed. The author provides an important foundation for ongoing treaty negotiations and for what contemporary Ojibwe cultural figures corroborate as ways of leading a good, integrated life.

MICHAEL POMEDLI is an emeritus professor of Philosophy at St Thomas More College, University of Saskatchewan.

Living with Animals

Ojibwe Spirit Powers

MICHAEL POMEDLI

UNIVERSITY OF TORONTO PRESS
Toronto   Buffalo   London

ISBN 978-1-4426-4701-5 (cloth)
ISBN 978-1-4426-1479-6 (paper)

Library and Archives Canada Cataloguing in Publication

Pomedli, Michael, author
Living with animals : Ojibwe spirit powers / Michael Pomedli.

Includes bibliographical references and index.
ISBN 978-1-4426-4701-5 (bound)   ISBN 978-1-4426-1479-6 (pbk.)

1. Midéwiwin.   2. Ojibwa Indians – Religion.   3. Ojibwa Indians –
Medicine.   4. Ojibwa Indians – Rites and ceremonies.   5. Animals –
Religious aspects.   I. Title.

E99.C6P68 2014   299.7'8333   C2013-906085-5

University of Toronto Press acknowledges the financial assistance
to its publishing program of the Canada Council for the Arts
and the Ontario Arts Council.

Canada Council   Conseil des Arts
for the Arts   du Canada

University of Toronto Press acknowledges the financial support of the
Government of Canada through the Canada Book Fund
for its publishing activities.

This book has been published with the help of a grant from the
Canadian Federation for the Humanities and Social Sciences, through
the Awards to Scholarly Publications Program, using funds provided by the
Social Sciences and Humanities Research Council of Canada.

To all Ojibwe/Chippewa/Anishinaabeg

Contents

Preface

Some years ago I presented a research paper at a Canadian Philosophical Association (CPA) conference, a paper examining whether thinking was involved in the formation of oral discourse, including Aboriginal stories, and whether any sophistication was evident in this process. I was new to formal presentations on this topic, and some conference participants thought that indigenous stories and rigorous philosophy were a strange juxtaposition. When I presented my paper for publication, the editor of the CPA's journal, *Dialogue*, did not consider it a serious philosophical article; instead, he told me to try journals with a religious content. "No offence intended," he remarked.

Challenging Western Thought

During that CPA presentation, I asserted that Native stories, oral and written, did have cultural importance for Natives and non-Natives alike, and even more forcefully, I maintained that thinking was involved in these and other cultural forms. The West generally holds that the prized forms of philosophical expression are the essay and the book, and conference papers and discussions; there are precedents, however, for other forms of Western philosophical presentation, such as Plato's dialogical discussions, Friedrich Nietzsche's aphorisms and music, and Gabriel Marcel's journals and dramas. My arguments, apparently, were not too compelling. While all we philosophers met, and we engendered some understanding, by and large there was no meeting of philosophies![1]

On this continent, meetings between Europeans and the radically different other – that is, Aboriginal peoples – presented mutual challenges in early contact times and still present challenges today. To really *meet* the other, one has to begin by acknowledging the legitimacy of the other, a legitimacy whereby the other has validity as an individual and as a group. In a moral process advocated by the eighteenth-century Prussian philosopher Immanuel Kant, one then affirms the other as an end and not merely as a means and accepts responsibility for preserving and even enhancing the freedom and autonomy of the other.[2] This Kantian ideal, in this conference context, should go beyond snap judgments about the worth of the other based solely on one's own cultural norms; it should go beyond labelling the others' stories as superstitious and naive; it should go beyond relegating the other to a lower level on the evolutionary ladder. Other persons and groups are entitled to legitimacy and worth in themselves. Acknowledging the other can and should lead to acknowledging the legitimacy of a diversity of cultures, a diversity of values and interpretations, and it should lead, furthermore, to the granting of legitimate rights to the other. This legitimacy may be readily acknowledged in theory, but a new non-colonial disposition is necessary that may well prove difficult in practice. Judgments may be made about the inherent incommensurability between the norms of the more powerful on the one hand, and of those with contrarian claims on the other.

Many reasons have been offered for the clash of civilizations on the North American continent. Explanations such as greed and aggressiveness on the part of Europeans and naivety and passivity on the part of Aboriginal peoples have been advanced. In this book, I will not be examining these notions; rather, I will be proposing one that seems to underpin all of them – that Europeans and Native peoples held different perceptions of the world and found it difficult to enter the world of the other in an understanding way. I will focus on the difficulty – or perhaps impossibility, given outlooks at the time – that Europeans faced with regard to understanding radically different indigenous approaches to life.

The Power of Bear Grease

We begin with a short Ojibwe story to illustrate the diversity of cultural expressions and values. It is titled "Nanabozho and the Bear's Grease" and comes from northern Minnesota:

Nanabozho killed a bear, and Nokomis cut off the fat from the meat. Then Nanabozho got Nokomis to boil the fat and dump it in a hollow. He started singing and called the birds and animals. "Here is a puddle of bear grease. Do whatever you want to do with it. You can swim in it or drink it or take as much as you want of it."

The rabbit came and dipped his paws in the bear grease and put the fat on his neck and shoulders. He said, "I'll only put it on my neck and shoulders, so I won't be too heavy." That is why the rabbit has two strips of fat on his shoulders.[3]

Immediately obvious in this charming story, and in many others like it, is a quest for causal explanations. The story appears to answer the question, "Why are there strips of fat on rabbits' shoulders?" Such an approach assumes a relationship of causality or non-causality between bear grease and the two strips of fat on a rabbit's shoulders. So, according to this assumption, the conclusion might be that this supposed relationship between bear grease and the strips of fat is based on a fetish and reflects a superstitious attitude. But that line of reasoning presupposes a normative regulatory function of causality from a Western perspective – a function that is being applied here to another cultural context. But should one cultural context always – indeed, ever – become the standard for another? Shouldn't we allow for a measure of incommensurability in this instance? Do we not have to relativize the Western cultural context and say that it is understandable to employ causality and to judge the truth or falsity of causal connections within a specific cultural framework, and that it is problematic at best to use that framework as a basis for judging another quite different framework?

Eurocentric and mono-centric perceptions were applied, perhaps unconsciously, by explorers, historians, entrepreneurs, anthropologists, missionaries, and even philosophers. The results included harsh judgments about indigenous cultures, as well as attempts to eradicate peoples and practices that did not approximate the assumed norms of "civilization," which was generally conceived of in the singular. Of course, enlightened philosophers and others today know better and would never fall into that trap! Or, conversely, are we continuing to argue that these norms are universal for all societies and not merely for the dominant one?

We suggest in this book that while causality captures universal notions, the Ojibwe and post-contact worlds were and still are quite different. There are similarities, of course, but we will be examining some aspects of that indigenous difference, which is a legitimate difference with its own reasons, logic, and coherence. Indigenous cultures still work today and have done so for a long time.

How is it possible to enter an Ojibwe world? How can any outsider say anything meaningful and intelligent about that world? First, as already noted, we have to accept that Ojibwe cultures are different and are valuable and meaningful in those differences, at least to their practitioners. This sympathetic, empathetic approach preserves the legitimacy of both cultures: the Western, which prides itself on precision, scientific investigation, and quantity of output; and the Ojibwe, which prizes values and relationships on many levels. The outsider then asserts that another approach has value and is meaningful in itself even though he or she does not necessarily comprehend it. In this small step, the other is acknowledged as equal and not as inferior.

But to say more than that about Ojibwe cultures, we must do more than sympathize – we must venture into the culture itself. With regard to the story of bear grease recounted above, it takes an imaginative and inquiring mind to ask what kind of world view makes possible a coherent conjunction between bear grease and strips of fat on a rabbit's back. And this imaginative effort cannot generally proceed along the lines of nineteenth-century evolutionary theory, which attached so much importance to science and technology. Perhaps the Ojibwe approach is as good as any other! For the Ojibwe, all animals are kin to one another; the bear is supreme among animals, and bear grease has salubrious medicinal and other properties. Also, instead of applying the principle of the unicity in the literal sense, we might entertain the possibility that the story has multiple subtexts generating multiple meanings.

Bears as Persons

Let us see if we can enter this new cultural world, with a focus on the bear itself instead of on its grease and the effects of that grease on the rabbit. We offer here another narrative, for in Ojibwe culture, narratives have a natural hegemony, whereas the focus in the West is often on understanding causal connections and amassing vast quantities of information. The bear was a privileged animal in nineteenth-century Ojibwe societies and was prominent in the performances of the Grand Medicine Society known as the Midewiwin.[4] That society had, and still has, earth membership on four levels, as well as sky membership on four additional ascending levels, according to some traditions. One of the highest earth levels is typified by the bear. Here we examine some characteristics of the bear, beginning with an anecdotal account from Rock Cree and Ojibwe culture in northern Saskatchewan and Manitoba:

> B.L. cached his clothing and food on a rack for three days before going out to lift his traps. He was worried about bears or wolverines getting into his stuff, so he barked[5] the upright poles on the rack and rubbed them real smooth so no animal could climb up there. When he returned, he was dismayed to find that a bear had been there during his absence. Although the bear couldn't get at the food because it was in the middle of the platform, the bear hooked his claws up over the edge and pulled down all of B.'s clothes. All of his clothes were ripped up into shreds except one new suit of long underwear from the Bay. This suit was spread out on the ground with arms and legs outstretched. It had been carefully arranged. And right on the seat of the underwear, the bear had left a large pile of scats [dung]. B. said, "What next?" He said that the bear had gotten mad about the food and gotten even with him on purpose. He said he'd heard about smart bears but he'd never seen one that smart.[6]

This anecdote illustrates the perception that the bear is very close physically, intellectually, and temperamentally to humans. Bears have physical characteristics akin to humans. They walk on the soles of their feet, "not on their toes, as most other carnivores do."[7] Black bears have a highly adaptable nature and can coexist with humans when given the chance.[8] Cree and Ojibwe often think that bears have an intelligence equal to or exceeding that of humans. There are stories where bears understand human languages. By contrast, non-Aboriginal peoples might admit to a loose analogy between bears and humans, but not to close affinities and definitely not to near identities or to reciprocal transformations.

In this bear story the Ojibwe understand the affinity between animals and humans in the context of origin or ancient stories. According to those stories, animals in old times had characteristics that today we consider specifically human. As time passed, however, animals lost most of these characteristics. Animals in the past, then, were human or human-like; the animal–human separation came later – an idea quite different from Western evolutionary theories.

With this cultural world as a backdrop, B.L. quite easily recognizes human-like qualities in the bear. Hunters and the hunted often were or became much the same, with the same characteristics. They had similar physical and intellectual powers, inhabited the same territory, ate the same foods, shared many Ojibwe-like characteristics, and had both individual and group needs. It is not known whether the bear aspired to be a human being and consciously adopted human qualities, but the Ojibwe admired many features of the bear, especially its ability to survive the winter through hibernation – an admirable attribute that might keep starvation at bay.[9] So, although we do not know whether bears try to become human, we do know that the Ojibwe try to become bears.

In addition to the physical and intellectual kinship of bears and humans, which we will examine later in greater detail, contemporary Woodland artist Norval Morrisseau notes the sacred nature of the bear arising from its human-like form. "If Indians meet a bear, in fear they address it as 'Our grandfather to all of us' and start to talk to it. It is a great sight to see a bear's ears and head moving as you speak to it."[10] According to Morrisseau, a bear "understands the Indian language and will never attack or fight any Indian if he is addressed properly."[11] Morrisseau writes and paints from his and his father's very close experiences with bears. Bears figure prominently in his paintings; he depicts them as part of a headdress, as a clan animal, as medicine persons, as integral to the Grand Medicine Lodge, and as "sacred bear" who moves between the water world and the forest world.[12] Morrisseau attempted to demonstrate this near-identity between humans and animals in his original version of a mural at the Indian Pavilion at Expo 67 in Montreal. According to Morrisseau/Copper Thunderbird, in that original piece, "Earth Mother and Her Children," a human mother was breastfeeding both a small boy and a bear cub. However, in the revised (sanitized?) version that most people viewed at this world event, Morrisseau "depicted a white-haired mother figure nursing a boy while the bear cub watched."[13]

From art, stories, and observations, we can conclude that humans and bears have close affinities.

Impersonating the bear. Birch bark scroll picture. The third degree candidate "personates the bear," as the benevolent animal/person is present during the medicine ceremony. Hoffman, "The Midê'wiwin," 169–169a.

Transformative Possibilities Make Definitive Judgments Difficult

We noted earlier that it is possible for non-Natives to take a sympathetic stance toward Native worlds and to enter those worlds in order to understand them. Westerners, however, often find it difficult to do so. One impediment may be the sensitivities arising from a form of logical thinking.

Those of us who have taught courses in critical thinking are well versed in informal fallacies, and in one of those fallacies in particular: ambiguity. When we consider examples of that fallacy, we may relativize the fallaciousness that is evident, for ambiguities are not always considered noxious; after all, they pervade our lives and have the charm of being the stuff of jokes. Yet teachers are directed not to relativize and trivialize ambiguity, for to do so would display a lack of seriousness about critical thinking. In their textbook, Ed. L. Miller and Jon Jensen take a decidedly non-joking attitude toward the fallacy of ambiguity, writing that ambiguity and informal fallacies reflect a "carelessness with respect to the clarity and consistency of our language ... Mastery of [this and other fallacies] will ... prevent many unnecessary blunders in philosophical discussion and, for that matter, any discussion whatsoever."[14]

How, then, are we to view cultures – including Western ones – in which ambiguity, metaphorical thinking, and mythical images are the very bedrock of culture. What about cultures in which mathematical certainties are not always the ideal, in which the criteria of truth and falsity and the principle of identity are somewhat puzzling at best, in which belief systems are neither explicitly explored and expressed nor consciously espoused? Do we again fall into the evolutionary pit and label these cultures as lower in intellectual attainment and therefore as uncivilized?

Let us examine an example of writing that strives to be utterly unambiguous. Early twentieth-century novelist and poet Gertrude Stein wrote: "Rose is a rose is a rose is a rose."[15] Stein here is employing a style and content based on bare experiential evidence that displays scant interest in metaphors or allegories. Richard Kostelanetz tells us that Stein was an empiricist whose style was "declarative and descriptive, rather than symbolic and allusive."[16] But according to Selwyn Dewdney, an anthropologist who has explored the sacred scrolls of the Midewiwin, instead of writing that "a rose is a rose is a rose," an "Indian would be more likely to say, 'A bird is a loon is an eagle is a man is a manitou.'"[17]

What are those of us schooled in Western philosophy to make of this "Indian approach"? Are we to be dismissive of it, as Westerners were in earlier contact times? Or are there many valid ways of perceiving the world? Is it possible to accord validity to the seemingly more ambivalent portrayal of animal and human identities, as Dewdney suggests? Is it possible to accord validity theoretically and sympathetically, that is, without understanding completely or even in part the implications of doing so? Thomas W. Overholt and J. Baird Callicott offer us an orientation to these seemingly mixed – puzzlingly so – identities of a bird, a loon, an eagle, a man and, a Manitou: "What would I have to believe about reality, in order to make the circumstances which the story describes seem plausible?"[18]

We might accord validity to ambiguity in novels and movies, and in informal situations such as joking around; in this same manner we might also view ambiguity as acceptable in Ojibwe narratives.

In Ojibwe worlds there are ambiguities on several levels. On the general level, Ojibwe maintain that it is not always possible – indeed, may never be possible – to make judgments about individuals or their powers. One is never completely sure which direction a human or animal may take – that is, toward the more beneficent or toward the more harmful.[19]

Also, as we noted earlier, Ojibwe origin stories do not establish neat categories between animals and humans, for animals in the past were human in some way and perhaps retain some of those originary dispositions. Or perhaps those origin stories actually depict stable animal essences, so that subsequent generations are merely variations and deviations from that norm.

Many of us are inconsistent in both our arguments and our perceptions. That inconsistency can be rooted in ambiguities, real or fictitious, regarding what we perceive. In Ojibwe life, the presumption is that the world outside the perceiver is not consistently of the same cloth; as cognitive anthropologist Mary Black has observed, there are variables in that world that lead to "instability" in their taxonomy.[20]

This variability has two possible sources: the person perceiving, and the object perceived. On the personal perceptual level, many relativities contribute to perception: one's disposition, one's cultural context, variations in the light intensity at the perceived location, and the strength of one's perceptual powers. All of these affect the ways one perceives even the same objects in different circumstances and at different times. These variations in personal perception can be called subjective.

On the level of the object perceived, Ojibwe maintain that the object presents itself in different ways on different occasions. Here, variations in perception are generated largely by the object, so one must be cautious about making definitive judgments about anything. At the very least, one must hold off making fixed determinations while one is actually doing the perceiving. Thus, when you perceive what appears to be a bear, you may act on the basis of that perception, and it may well be prudent to do so, but you do not know for certain during the act of perceiving whether that really was a bear or, for instance, a human being. Guy Lanoue speculates that the reason for postponing such judgments is that it is more difficult to ascertain the identity of that being than to wait and see the practical consequences of the bear's action on social relations and then definitively label it a bear. Waiting for the practical implications of what the bear does leads to more consistent pronouncements. Lanoue accounts for these slow judgments partly in terms of an Ojibwe world view that seems to lack aggression and that allows "events to unfold without actively participating in the process."[21]

We think there is another reason – perhaps a more foundational one – for the Ojibwe belief in the impermanence of all forms. That reason focuses on the Ojibwe belief in the possible transformation of all forms of being. A. Irving Hallowell has stated: "So far as appearance is concerned, there is no hard and fast line that can be drawn between an animal form and a human form because metamorphosis is possible. In perceptual experience, what looks like a bear may sometimes *be* an animal and, on other occasions, a transformed human being."[22] For Hallowell, the Ojibwe concepts of transformation and power "underlie the entire Indian mythology, and make sensible the otherwise childish stories of culture heroes, animal husbands, friendly thunders, and malicious serpents. The bearwalker idea fits at once into this dream world – literally a dream world, for Ojibwa children go to school in dreams."[23] This power of metamorphosis links humans to other-than-human persons. More on the "bearwalker idea" later.

A Cree or Ojibwe or any non-Aboriginal person who is steeped in this cosmological view might be perplexed when confronted with an animal: Is the animal that I perceive really an animal, or is it a human that has appeared as an animal? If one perceives a being who appears to be human, the question might be: Is this really a human being or is it an animal that has appeared as a human, perhaps even deceiving the perceiver? Does the human perceive a fellow human as human or as animal because he or she is enchanted with this being as either human or animal? Still other questions can be asked of the perceiver: Is he or she deluded, and faulty in this delusion, or is he or she involved in self-deception? Or, are the animals deluding us? Or, does the perceiver see deeper, as those in many Ojibwe traditions do, to the heart of the animal, seeing human characteristics, more than ordinary humans can perceive?[24] Does this cultural tradition, then, admit of an expansion of sensory awareness beyond fixed identities?

Robert Brightman suggests further questions that follow from this expansive sensitivity: Are the differences between humans and animals in large part a matter of perception? If so, are those differences merely in appearances, that is, in surface characteristics? Does the reality or essence of both humans and animals transcend these appearances?[25] Do animals put on a disguise for humans, an outfit they strip off when in their own world?[26]

What are we to conclude about the relationship between humans and animals? The following are some possibilities:

1. For pragmatic reasons, for reasons of the hunt, Ojibwe have to maintain an essential difference, a difference in kind, between humans and animals. They have to transcend the notion that animals speak and use cultural objects, and they also have to transcend an evolutionary perspective of close kinship between animals and humans. Although animals speak in stories, visions, and dreams, these renditions are for practical reasons generally a matter of metaphorical and comparative reality. Animals are hunted, not humans.

2. But pragmatic relationships are merely one type – albeit a natural type that ensures human survival. Appearances suggest that there are reasons for ambiguous interpretations of whether this specific being is human or an animal. Also, transformations are possible, from human to animal and back to human. Stories, visions, dreams, and clan structures indicate that humans and animals are innately the same. If we move beyond appearances, we notice continuities in the actions of humans and animals; we notice the possibility of relationships that give evidence of a common background and other common properties. Too rigid distinctions between humans and animals are artificial; they will not do.

Even if Ojibwe label a specific being as an animal, as a human, or as an object – stone, sun, moon – there is still a suspicion, a mental reservation, that this does not tell it all. This hesitation is founded on the belief that while so-called inert, inanimate objects such as stones may be regarded as rather fixed, they can also be regarded as dynamic.

If today we label a stone as having a fixed nature, tomorrow we may have to see it as fluid, as changing, and as having a memory. If reality is dynamic, if it is actually changing or possibly changing, we have difficulty granting it a fixed essence, a permanence.

For Ojibwe, the meanings of the terms *human* and *animal* seem less than fixed. Each of these terms, or nouns, has two meanings, and each meaning *involves* the other: the term *human* has the meaning of *human* but also, in varying forms, *animal*; the term *animal* has the meaning *animal* but also, in varying forms, *human*. One meaning may be stressed more than the other.

Morrisseau and his fellow Ojibwe artists in the Woodland School of Art paint this dual relationship in the form of humans within animals and animals within humans. External power lines connect humans and animals and other parts of the cosmos. Humans wear animal masks. Powwow songs and dances have imitative animal actions and sounds involving the crow, bear, eagle, chicken, and turkey.[27] Advance runners in the buffalo hunt use female buffalo skins to entice male buffalo over the steep jumps. Ojibwe adopt their proper names from animals.

We have asked a lot of questions; let us, as a penultimate conclusion, ask another: Humans see animals as possibly human. Do animals see humans as possibly animal?

Dennis McPherson and Douglas Rabb suggest that a transformation in orientation is necessary in order for individuals and societies to understand and to begin to appropriate other world views such as the Aboriginal. In the same way that Ojibwe on vision quests employ the appropriate means to gain insight into themselves and the cosmos, outsiders need similar exercises in "transformative philosophy" in order to "get in touch with, and learn to respect, the living world of other-than-human persons whom our technological society is in danger of destroying."[28] Then, although we might not be able to catch the bear, human–animal ambiguities might not be an impediment to cross-cultural understanding.

Water Manitou. Song scroll: "You are a spirit, my Mide brother; you are prepared, my Mide brother." "The person addressed is represented as a manido, in form like those that appear in the water." Densmore, *Chippewa Music*, 1:115.

Introduction

Scope of This Book

This book is about the Ojibwe peoples of the Great Lakes region (Minnesota, Michigan, Wisconsin, and Ontario) and parts of Manitoba and Saskatchewan. In the examination of the Ojibwe/Chippewa Medicine Society, the Midewiwin, and of Ojibwe societies in general, we focus on the animals that "inhabit" the ascending rungs on that society's ladder. We conclude that the animals used as symbols in the medicine rituals express the cultural principles of the various Ojibwe nations. In this sense, Ojibwe songs, words, and drawings on birch bark scrolls embody cultural ideals.

While the nineteenth-century Medicine Society had a formative influence on Ojibwe lives and on their treaties, other accounts of animals from stories, as well as moral injunctions, petroglyphs, petroforms, pictographs, and material cultural representations, corroborate Midewiwin cultural principles. In all of these depictions, performances, and sounds, animals are pervasive and predominant (indeed pivotal) symbols and keepers[1] of Ojibwe values. We will be broadening our investigation even further than the Ojibwe in general to include other Algonquian-related and some non-Algonquian sources when they shed light on animal symbolism.

The cultural norms we will uncover are more than mere evidence of cultural values; they are unique standards that Ojibwe leaders brought to treaty signings, and when North American treaties are being reinterpreted and reframed, it should be in terms of those norms. This account provides an important foundation for such pursuits.

This book relies on many sacred stories, *aadizookanag*, that is, traditional stories; these stories are "seasonally restricted and ... somewhat ritualized," A. Irving Hallowell notes. The Ojibwe regarded the characters in these stories as living beings who "have existed from time immemorial ... [These stories] are thought of as conscious beings, with powers of thought and action"; hence the Ojibwe called these stories "our grandfathers"; they were "true accounts of events."[2]

We will utilize stories from both oral and written sources. Some of the main written ones will be those of William Jones,[3] who was born on the Sauk and Fox Reservations in Oklahoma and who received the name Megasiawa or Black Eagle. He was cared for by his tribal grandmother, who had the gift of healing. After obtaining a doctoral degree from Columbia University, he recorded hundreds of Anishinaabeg[4] stories from Fort William in Ontario, Bois Fort and Leech Lake in Minnesota, Turtle Mountain in North Dakota, and other reserves/reservations.[5] A mixed blood anthropologist, he reveals in his notes that his "work is to be taken largely as an attempt to get at the religious ideas of the people from their own point of view ... The language of most of the material is conversational [and the sentences are] colloquial, seldom sustained, and often loose and incoherent. Vagueness of reference is common."[6] In this volume we will be using Jones's early-twentieth-century stories provided by five narrators and published in the original Ojibwe and its translations.

The early Anishinaabeg or Ojibwe did not write and thus did not have books to read. Instead, according to missionary Jerome Lalemant, the Anishinaabe leaders themselves were "living books" who contained many stories.[7] We will strive to establish a geographical, cultural, and temporal context for both oral and documentary stories; we will indicate where possible the names of the storytellers.[8]

There are at least three important traits of stories, both indigenous and others: they house spirits; they can heal; and their power of healing is dependent on their interpretation and application.[9] The Ojibwe stories often arise in an oral tradition and are then written down and passed along, some only slightly polished into a literary form. They bear a lively spoken character, and even when translated into English, they retain their original/Aboriginal flavour, ideas, and literary constructions.

In addition to sacred stories, this book relies on petroglyphs, picto-graphs, and petroforms.[10] These voices in line drawings, stone forma-tions, and incised stone speak of performances that were vital to the Ojibwe peoples of the Great Lakes region in the nineteenth century. These performances and visions are continued in many cultural rep-resentations – for example, on clothing and utensils, as images carried or tattooed on the person, and in contemporary art. Cultures that are immersed in sounds that emanate from visions and from the worlds above, below, and in between treasure the drum and other instruments. We have included these illustrations to give meaning to our written text, and also as another and sometimes parallel articulation of Ojibwe cultures.

How can one savour this past, these cultures perhaps strange to most ears and eyes, strange to non-Aboriginals, and mysterious and chal-lenging to many Aboriginals as well? Those of us who are attempting to understand these cultures must engage in some form of transformation from or out of present-day technical and post-European formulations. We need to acquire a sense of wonder whereby the old becomes new, the past is understood in the present, the strange and unfamiliar are accepted on their own terms. We must immerse ourselves in a setting other than the twenty-first century. We must put things, events, and experiences together to form a whole; try to accept terms and situations that are sometimes vague and ambiguous; hear sounds in seemingly the same but different ways; and let references be, instead of analys-ing completely and discarding the incomprehensible. A measure of comprehension demands an acceptance of presentations that may not immediately make sense, that are at first mysterious and remain so, that are piecemeal like life itself.[11]

This book lives with animals, and with humans too, but as part of an inherently interrelated world. "Living with" has many meanings ranging from a mere juxtaposition or geo-positioning of one being with another, to a co-mingling and near identification of one being with another. On the psychological and dispositional level, "living with" can range in meaning from despising or hating the other, to varying ways of being-with, of showing affection, love, and care. "Living with" can be viewed on the level of social and political structures ranging from the sometimes extreme differences between leaders and followers, to much smaller differences among those who assume certain leadership roles while retaining more or less equal status to others.

Our book focuses on the varied experiences that humans have while living with animals and on the interpreted experiences of animals living with humans. We refer to the latter experiences as "interpreted," for humans can often only guess what animals think and feel. But we do surmise that animals speak and act and have emotions and thinking patterns that humans often only dimly recognize. Animals relate to their surroundings in ways both strange and clear; they *are* their surroundings. They are beings from several different but interrelated worlds, those of the sky, the earth, and the waters. Animals are creatures of mystery both in themselves and in their relationships. According to Ojibwe Lawrence Martin, animals bless human beings; they are power spirits who are connected to and are mutually dependent on other spirit powers.[12]

Animals have disclosed themselves to the Ojibwe in many forms. Animals are visible and tangible. They have entered humans through vision, song, and sound quests. They have been prized, and their presence has been continued in many patterns and designs. They have helped humans realize who they are as animals, and helped humans realize who they are as humans. They have given themselves to humans on their own terms, especially in the hunt.[13] With humans, animals are engaged in a "cosmic economy of sharing."[14]

Animals are beings in themselves, but they are conceived and expressed in terms of humans and in a human language. In this way, they are like humans, but also different; they are "other-than-human persons."[15] These persons people a world in common with humans, move more within that world than upon it, and share that world without being separated from it. Like stones, trees, and clouds, animals work in recognizable but not fully understandable ways. But stones, trees, clouds, and animals are not merely physical and passive; they are active agents in the world.[16] Places, objects, animals, and people are channels for harmful or beneficent spiritual agents. All of these beings act according to a time and momentum, not necessarily (if ever) regulated by mechanical–technical means, but rather ordered by the rhythms of the seasons. It is the cosmos that establishes meanings for everyone.[17]

Aboriginal peoples have been studied extensively, if not always intensively. They have endured many external forces, many of them not to their advantage. They have often been regarded as victims, as passive beings, as objects for investigation. Yet like animals, they are beings in themselves with powers to disclose who they are. Through their stories, ceremonies, and other cultural forms, Aboriginal peoples (in this book, the Ojibwe/Anishinaabe in particular) reveal who they are. As Ojibwe historian William Warren wrote in mid-nineteenth-century Minnesota: "There is much yet to be learned from the wild and apparently simple son of the forest, and the most which remains to be learned is to be derived from their religious beliefs."[18]

These religious beliefs have more than one form of expression and activity: they encompass the whole Ojibwe world. Ojibwe cultures have flourished in the past and continue to empower the present in a variety of ways. Our interpretations of these tough and resilient cultures endeavour to present Ojibwe points of view that have been corroborated or corrected by Ojibwe such as Lawrence Martin and Cecil King, by Aboriginal leaders, and by the general populace, both Aboriginal and non-Aboriginal.

Geography of the Ojibwe

The cultures we consider in this book began to expand geographically in the early seventeenth century, from north of present-day Lake Huron (the Chippewa–Ojibwe) toward eastern Lake Superior and the Michigan Peninsula. In the nineteenth century there was further expansion into southeastern Ontario and western Saskatchewan, as well as from northern Ontario into western Michigan, Wisconsin, Minnesota, and North Dakota. This expansion resulted in four major geographical and cultural groups: (1) the Southeastern Ojibwe in southeastern Ontario and southern Michigan; (2) the Northern Ojibwe or Saulteaux in regions north of the Great Lakes and west to Lake Winnipeg;[19] (3) the Southwestern Chippewa/Ojibwe in northern Wisconsin and the northeastern corner of Minnesota; and (4) the Western/Plains Ojibwe of southern Manitoba and Saskatchewan and northern North Dakota.[20] The Ojibwe in these various locales developed in somewhat different ways culturally; hence we often use the plural form – Ojibwe cultures – and strive to point out the specific locales in which these cultures occurred.

Map of the range of the Anishinaabe in North America in the early nineteenth century as given by Hickerson. Brown and Peers indicate in Hickerson's work that the Anishinaabe "also extended farther into Saskatchewan and Alberta than older writers recognized. Fur trade documents show that Ojibwa were then residing, at least in small numbers, along the North Saskatchewan River as far as Edmonton and Lesser Slave Lake; they later withdrew from these areas as trading conditions deteriorated." "The Chippewa and their Neighbors," ii, 135.

The Ojibwe worlds we will be inhabiting in this volume are flat, "like a thick pancake," in Fred K. Blessing's words. According to the Medicine Society's spiritual cosmological perspective, the earth floats in the air, with evil spirits hovering near its distant edge and inhabiting its thickness. Theoretically, then, it would be possible to travel to the

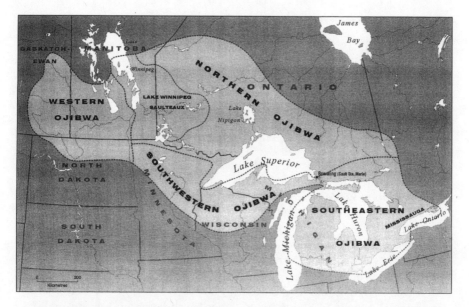

Ojibwe/Chippewa cultures in the mid-nineteenth century. Wayne Moodie and Michael Angel, *Preserving the Sacred*, 8.

earth's edge and fall off. This precipitous plunge is unlikely, however, since it would take a lifetime to traverse the world and no one has ever done so; but spirits have journeyed there. In the Midewiwin teachings, these spirits found powers on the earth's dangerous perimeter and returned safely because they were protected by the Midewiwin lodge.[21]

"Spirits above." Copway, *The Traditional History*, 135.

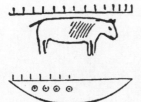

"Animals under ground." Copway, *The Traditional History*, 136.

"Spirits under water." Copway, *The Traditional History*, 136.

Goals and Methodology

Goals

As we examine Ojibwe cultures generally in the Great Lakes/Boundary Waters region, we focus on the nineteenth century, often with the Midewiwin or Grand Medicine Society as a focus. Inescapable under this approach are the animals that, in a multitude of ways, symbolize the ascending and advancing steps in this Medicine Society. The Midewiwin becomes a window onto the Ojibwe worlds, since it often provided solid nourishment for Ojibwe cultures generally and nurtured many of their leaders. These Midewiwin leaders and other Ojibwe had to find ways to survive the onslaughts of disease and white settlement, a declining land base, displacement to unfamiliar surroundings, and the loss of much autonomy, with consequent struggles to regain independence and control over their resources in the aftermath of treaty negotiations and signings.[22] We present the role of kinship, as well as a sense of Ojibwe heritage and identity.

To elucidate the Midewiwin, its stages of medicine, and the animals/cosmos that represent those stages, we required a cultural hermeneutic. What has emerged from our search for one is a perspective forged in pre-contact communities, forged anew in contact with colonizers, and thought through with stories and ceremonies; together, these provide an enriched framework for interpreting Ojibwe cultures. From the mosaic of two cultural orientations has sprung a new story that is expressive of hopes and dreams.

This book takes a unifying approach that weaves together the ceremonial/symbolic and the practicalities of survival. The foundation for this bringing together of the symbolic and the practical is a belief in Manido/Spirit whereby relations do not depend solely on the initiatives and power of humans and indeed transcend a predominantly anthropocentric approach; thus, actions proceed not from human autonomy alone. The spirits in the world shape a people. An interdependent world, a web of relationships, is the source of cultural norms.

Aboriginal cultural norms and rights, then, are not merely human and do not flow from human reason alone. The Aboriginal world view posits – radically, from some perspectives – that the inquiring subject can be (and perhaps for the most part *should* be) relatively passive – a listener and receiver, a resonating board of the cosmos. It is the world (as surround) with which he or she is a kindred being, the active world, that gives. The inquirer, then, does not take a pre-eminently calculating perspective; rather, he or she is receptive, letting what is there enter on its own terms. This is a truly objective approach: humans respond to the world's beckoning.

Aboriginal cultural traditions are in accord that the natural world is both complex and interdependent and that all peoples are an integral part of it. This perspective is not mere primitive or magical thinking; it has been crafted in the context of daily life and is based on thousands of years of empirical observation. Indeed, this approach is consistent with the advanced biological sciences, which underscore that cosmic/individual relationships are both complex and interdependent.

This book is informed by written literature on Ojibwe heritages and the Midewiwin. There are general comments on medicine societies in the seventeenth-century *Jesuit Relations,* in nineteenth-century texts, in twentieth-century notes on Midewiwin lodges and curing rituals, and in writings by Midewiwin leaders and contemporary scholars. In this book, various sources of songs, texts, and cultural forms are compared; for instance, the words and paintings of the contemporary Woodland artist Norval Morrisseau support past writings about Ojibwe cultures. Significant here are songs from the Boundary Waters treaty time, available in modern forms, and also Frances Densmore's 1907–9 wax cylinder recordings of 340 Ojibwe songs that highlight animals' contributions to society.

The Midewiwin ritual promoted general precepts under the rubric of *bimaadiziwin* – leading the good life of integration in all possible ways: moral, spiritual, medicinal, social, and political. That integration was founded on relationships with animals and spirits. The Midewiwin performances, while somewhat separated from people's everyday concerns, were nevertheless much at home with that life. Those performances involved stories, symbols, songs, drums, scrolls, ritual actions, and games. The ceremonies created an aura conducive to empowerment and to becoming animals, and spirits.[23]

The animals on the ascending rungs of the healing society's ladder signified the general values the Ojibwe cherished. There are more animals in Ojibwe cultures than we consider in this volume; we will be focusing on the ones that were commonly encountered in the Medicine Society and that were significant in Ojibwe lives. Otter, owl, bear, and creatures of the water- and sky-world were in varying interpretations the animals on the initial ascending levels of the Midewiwin. To the extent that this book mirrors Ojibwe cultures, it has received authoritative empowerment and confirmation from these and other animals and from the Ojibwe themselves.

A backdrop to this investigation is a comparison of Ojibwe and mainstream cultures regarding their treatment of animals. We will not make this investigation thematic, but there is a growing rapprochement between the two cultures now that investigators are abandoning the notion that there is a wide gap between animals and humans and are positing close relationships, as first delineated by Charles Darwin.[24]

Methodology

Since there are notable differences between Ojibwe cultures and mainstream ones, it is logical to use a special form of investigation. There are two ways to approach research into nineteenth-century Ojibwe cultures:

1. Return to or retrieve an *ur*-Ojibwe thinking, that is, the thinking of pre-contact cultures uninfluenced by Judeo-Christian and Western European approaches. Something pure, foundational and really Ojibwe.

2. Translate nineteenth-century Ojibwe cultures into Western European philosophy, interpreting them in that context. One problem with this approach is that there are many Western philosophies, from the early Greeks to the contemporary. What counts as Western European can range from early Greek poetic and rather undeveloped forms, to Plato's Dialogues, to thesis dialectics in the Middle Ages, to Kantian and Hegelian systems, to Marcel's journals, to Sartre's romantic rationalism, to logical positivism.

We had decided not to apply any specific Western philosophical system. Instead, we approach nineteenth-century Ojibwe cultures, and the Mide-wiwin in particular, with as few presuppositions as possible. Whenever possible, we let the phenomena themselves reveal both the form and the content of these cultures. Granted, we are a product of Western European philosophy, science, and technology and cannot as interpreters stand aloof from that influence. But our approach is quite different from translating Ojibwe cultures into a specific Western philosophy.

Also, we do not mean to suggest that we are retrieving *ur*-Ojibwe cultures, whatever those may be. Rather, we are setting out to disclose what is there. Clearly, Ojibwe perspectives have been influenced by a number of factors, including Christianity, so we will be considering the influence of Judeo-Christianity on Ojibwe thinking and morality and distilling what appear to be its impacts. Another author may one day research and further elucidate this influence, but it is not our focus, nor is it our intention to explore that influence. Also, we do not enter into an explicit intersubjective dialogue with Ojibwe cultures.

More specifically, what is the methodology at work in this book?

Ojibwe cultures emerge through oral and written stories, dreams, ceremonies, designs, depictions, birch bark scrolls, and the stratagems of war and peace. There is little about Ojibwe cultural forms that is philosophically "Western." Those forms are not cast in Western scientific, mathematical, quantitative, analytical, or syllogistic ways. Rather, they are descriptive, poetic, celebratory, and metaphorical. Hence, we have let descriptions – indeed, an abundance of them – prevail, for these are a primary embodiment of Ojibwe cultures.

To summarize so far, we do not attempt to retrieve *ur*-Ojibwe values, philosophies, or lifestyles. Nor do we adopt any specific philosophical system as providing linguistic and normative ways of thinking. However, we use the English language, which is laden with its own heritage. In this regard, we try to select the words and concepts that suit Ojibwe cultures and are careful not to destroy the uniquely Native. There is a subjectivity involved here, but less than in adopting a system a priori. Since the English language is used in Ojibwe oral and written discourses and also in this book, translations from Ojibwe linguistic and non-linguistic sources remain approximate, limited, proportional, emergent, and subject to alternative interpretations.

In general, our method is to return to embodied, experiential meanings and descriptions of Ojibwe phenomena as they were lived in the nineteenth century, comparing these with Ojibwe life today. We strive to unfurl and be faithful to world relations in all their indeterminacy, ambiguity, complexity, obscurity, richness, and novelty. In doing so, we try to refrain from importing external frameworks and try to set aside judgments about the truthfulness of the phenomena. This sort of evidence-based research needs to consider the context in which the phenomena occurred, their history, and the authors and creators who lived that history; we will do this, relying on data that relate to the phenomena without making this thematic. We acknowledge that to give a complete picture, any examination of nineteenth-century Ojibwe peoples should include an exploration of pre-contact, early-contact, treaty, and post-treaty historical contexts. Perforce, then, our project remains open to more ample and extensive development and more generalizations from our specific investigations.

Our method reflects the phenomena being investigated. It involves subjects – human beings – who have universal characteristics but who are also significantly different from mainstream Canadians. This is evident in Canada's Constitution Act, which "recognizes and affirms" the "existing" Aboriginal and treaty rights in Canada. These Aboriginal rights protect the activities, practices, and traditions that are integral to the distinctive cultures of Aboriginal peoples, including Aboriginal title to land used for traditional practices.[25] Our methodology is at the service of this unique difference. So we will stay close to what is given in all its distinctiveness and diversity. We will investigate everyday experiences, verbal and non-verbal expressions, actions, artworks, and stories. We will give priority to Ojibwe stories, unfolding them without judging their relative worth and without trying to slot them into categories.

Linda Finlay has described approaches that take their force from the phenomena at hand as "disciplined naïveté, bridled dwelling, disinterested attentiveness, and/or the process of retaining an empathic wonderment in the face of the world."[26] Such an approach is necessary in order to transcend previous positions that adopted European and post-European ways of thinking and acting as the sole norms. In our method we bracket past assumptions, understandings, and information about phenomena so as to focus on their appearing. Avoiding the privileging of one authority over another can free the researcher to discover reality claims outside his own cultural limitations.

P.D. Ashworth suggests that in phenomena-centred investigations, at least three specific areas of presupposition need to be set aside: first, scientific theories, knowledge, and explanation; second, the truth or falsity of claims being made by the participant; and third, the personal views and experiences of the researcher, which would cloud descriptions of the phenomenon itself.[27]

Other researchers deny that this setting aside – this neutral attitude – is possible or even desirable. Instead, they make explicit their pre-existing beliefs, vested interests, and assumptions and how these may affect the research process and its findings.[28] On the basis of the researcher's biases and presuppositions, a conversation can then take place in which new and interrelated perspectives can emerge, for such an intersubjective horizon of experience allows access to the experiences of others. This method is commendable and perhaps even necessary; it is not the one we follow in this book.

We have not abandoned the scientific method, especially the emphasis on facts; but we do expand its general field of investigation to include artistic and literary prose. Our investigation is data-based, but in a way that allows imaginative variation and an internal validity check to determine which are essential features and which are merely incidental. In this way we seek to retain the "concrete, mooded, sensed, imaginative, and embodied nature" of the phenomena, as Finlay outlines.[29]

Our methodology differs from that of many academic research programs. By exposing the differences between Ojibwe and mainstream cultures, it is possible to challenge and unsettle conventional methods and beliefs. Again, our approach adheres to Ojibwe cultural foundations, which differ from eighteenth-century modernist philosophies, which are based largely on anthropocentric concerns. An attunement that is sympathetic to unique Aboriginal cultures,[30] and that does not entail objective distancing, is necessary to retrieve what is there. A scientific apparatus with preset, systematic questions that attempt to generate numerical and quantitative tallies would likely miss, for instance, the essence of Ojibwe ceremonies. A less formalized approach that is open to radically different cultures seems more appropriate when the goal is to generate insights into unique differences. Granting the legitimacy of the metaphorical and the symbolic, of stories and ceremonies, and of the role of the five senses can lead to understandings – not necessarily quantifiable ones, but meaningful and rigorous ones nevertheless. It has been necessary to relativize modernist perspectives as far as possible in order to provide a window through which Ojibwe orientations might shine; had we not done so, these distinctive perspectives might have been lost or viewed solely through a Western lens.[31] An Aboriginal lens will let the light from the world of nature guide us to Ojibwe cultural norms. The source for approval and affirmation of such norms will then be outside the self and even outside the community. Ultimately, it will be the cosmos that approves.

Dale Turner reserves the term "word warriors" for tough-minded Aboriginal deliberators who have lived Native philosophy, know it, and have performed it and who are now engaging political structures and their representatives in order to recover Aboriginal rights.[32] These warriors are aided necessarily by Aboriginal philosophers, who, in addition to living their culture, are adept at using the correct words to convey that knowledge. We see ourselves as attenuated word warriors or servants, bringing to light and making explicit Aboriginal meanings and values and making a case for protecting and defending their legitimacy in a "Western" book. As non-Aboriginals, we can aid the warrior strategy by uncovering an understanding of Native ways and highlighting essential Native values; we can also speak/write from a European framework and help dispel the myths that colonizers have propagated.

We, with Turner, indigenous intellectuals, and the general Ojibwe population, want to engage colonialism and overcome its pervasive thrust. We also want to preserve, protect, and defend indigenous ways of knowing so that they are "not devalued, marginalized, or ridiculed in the marketplace of ideas."[33] We hope this book will help provide a foundation for understanding Ojibwe cultures, and beyond that, for understanding North American treaty negotiations and for reframing those treaties and reimplementing them. But that on its own will not be enough. For Aboriginal voices to be heeded in North America, there must be an attitude shift among the general populace and among Canada's political, spiritual, cultural, and social leaders, a shift that the *Report of the Royal Commission on Aboriginal Peoples* strongly promotes.[34]

While researching this book, we took both an informal and an academic/formal approach to gathering information about the nineteenth-century Grand Council/Midewiwin. Regarding the informal, we identified keepers of Midewiwin knowledge and gained the confidence of Ojibwe leaders and consultants who had knowledge of and experience with Midewiwin ceremonies. We respected Ojibwe choices regarding how much they were willing to disclose. Regarding the more formal approach, we read the literature on the Midewiwin and consulted other materials – symbols, birch bark scrolls, biographies, pictographs, petroglyphs, petroforms, songs, and paintings. Again, Ojibwe leaders, consultants, and community members guided the interpretation of these documents to help us understand the Grand Council's principles and standards.

Our methodology followed research ethics protocols[35] to ensure that the parties involved had a clear and full understanding of the goals, methods, and intended results of the research and that they would be its primary beneficiaries. Ojibwe consultants and community members made sure that the research was respectful of their cultures, observant of local meanings and values, and in accord with Ojibwe cultural understandings. We strove to be sensitive to and respectful of oral, archival, and published materials and to use them properly. Aboriginal leaders read our entire manuscript and gave helpful critiques.

As noted earlier, there are differences between Ojibwe cultures and mainstream ones. But while those differences are significant, they are not absolute. During this project, various forces brought these two historical, factual, and observational elements together. First, there was the common humanity that brought together many values and meanings. Second, there were expressions held in common: some of these were linguistic, such as ideas and stories, while others were artistic, such as images and sounds. The tool that mediated between these seemingly incommensurable elements, the Ojibwe and the mainstream, was often the English language. That language is not neutral and has the texture of the mainstream, yet paradoxically, it is the vehicle for the stories and accounts of Ojibwe cultures themselves. It is common to both enterprises, and although it bears European and other influences, it can be tailored and refined to suit Ojibwe perspectives. These two cultural approaches, therefore, are not incommensurable. They are comparable and analogous provided that the differences are not erased, as was attempted in earlier colonial times. One thrust can understand the other; but while there are comparable common values and meanings, this focus on commonness will remain mostly latent in this book. Instead of developing these similarities, we will highlight the values, expressions, and actions that for individual and communal Ojibwe existence hold a special place and status[36] indicative of "artful" thinking. For the Ojibwe, however, reflection generally does not adopt explicit Western European frames of reference or systems. The symbols in Ojibwe cultures do not resist articulation; they do, however, invite and even compel thinking that is logical and coherent.[37]

Notwithstanding the extensive documentation (i.e., notes and references), we have tried to write in language that is comprehensible first of all to Aboriginal peoples and then also to the average person, who often greatly enjoys stories. The illustrations should be compelling as well.

Use of Terms, Spellings, and Illustrations

In this book we will use the terms Midewiwin and Mide interchangeably; in its strict usage, Mide is an abbreviation and an adjectival form of Midewiwin and denotes its practitioners.[38] The word Mide is often translated as shaman, priest, conjurer, sorcerer, spiritual leader, or psychologist; all of these translations, however, contain cultural and historical orientations; consequently, we will generally retain the term Mide or translate it as "traditional healer" or "medicine man/woman."[39]

The general term we will use for Aboriginal peoples is sometimes Native, but also Indian, a loaded term but one that is preferred by many

Native peoples themselves. In his *Handbook of Indians of Canada,* F.W. Hodge provides more than 100 different names and spellings for the Chippewa/Ojibwe.[40] For the specific peoples considered in this book, we use Ojibwe, a very common spelling, and the Ojibwe linguistic referents, Anishinaabe and Anishinaabeg (plural). Another common name is Saulteaux, a name given them by the French.[41] Variations of these terms will be retained as used in written sources.

In his brief analysis of the name of his people, Anishinaabeg, Warren concludes that the best translation is "original man."[42] The inclusiveness of the name, however, does not mean cultural and linguistic homogeneity. We point out here that throughout this volume, there is no monolithic Ojibwe culture. The sacred stories and other cultural forms emanate from different encampments and have varied expressions, meanings, and sacred medicine adaptations. Consequently, we do not use the name Ojibwe in a univocal way, but will indicate variables with the plural form: Ojibwe *cultures.* Nurit Bird-David uses an analogy to demonstrate both the separateness of and the differences between various communities, as well as their cohesiveness and unity. These communities can be likened to individual drops of oil floating on the surface of a pool of water; when the drops come together they combine into smaller and larger pools. But those drops can also split into smaller ones and remain separate or coalesce with other drops.[43] This process applies to Ojibwe cultures.

The name of the Ojibwe's cultural hero has variant spellings, but we will use Nanabush, except where variants occur in the narratives. Other spellings are used for the same being: Nanabozho, Nannebush, and Winabojo. Michigan and Wisconsin Ojibwe often use the name Manabozho or Menapus.[44] Another term, *bimaadiziwin,* has several spellings, including *pimadiziwin.* However it is spelled, the word means "life," "a good life," "a life of harmony," or "the right way to live."[45]

Nanabush. "Song for medicine hunting": "Who is a spirit? He that walketh with the serpent, walking on the ground; he is a spirit." Tanner, *A Narrative,* 356–7.

Many Anishinaabeg use Manitou for spirit being and Manitouk for the plural form. For the plural we will use Manitous. Generally, we will follow the spellings in Nichols and Nyholm, *A Concise Dictionary of Minnesota Ojibwe*.

On many occasions we will use the past tense in describing Ojibwe life since the primary focus of this book is the nineteenth century. This use of the past tense does not imply that references to an earlier period exclude the existence of present forms and practices.

We asked a former student, an Anishinaabe, to apply her artistic skills to the book's illustrations. She declined because they involved the Midewiwin. Other Anishinaabe have strongly encouraged us to use all resources possible in a respectful way. So we have provided many illustrations from written and other cultural sources. We have identified the artists where possible. The line drawings may not always be clear in themselves, even in their word and song interpretations, and at least some are adaptations by non-Native hands; however, they do form a consistency in interpreting Ojibwe cultures, even though specific images may not reflect the immediate written narrative. Maps are included, as noted above.

The title elder/Elder has multiple implications, especially for the Midewiwin. We will not use this term in writing that originates with us. We will retain it, however, when it appears in quotations and in titles of source material.

Acknowledgments

The author gratefully acknowledges the following for their contributions to this volume: Lawrence Martin, Eau Claire, Wisconsin, and Cecil King, Saskatoon, Saskatchewan; Monte Keene Pishny-Floyd, James Youngblood Henderson, Dennis McPherson, J. Douglas Rabb, Mary Lou Rabb, Joan Halmo, Tom Deutscher, Len Husband, Wilfrid Denis, Bruce Morito, Braj Sinha, Kathe Harder, William Cowan, Claire Martin, Stephen Pomedli, Rachel Pomedli, Cath Oberholtzer, Frances Mundy, and Matthew Kudelka; and the Information Technology Services Division, University of Saskatchewan, Help Desk Services.

The author also gratefully acknowledges the following fellowships and grants:

Social Sciences and Humanities Research Council of Canada (SSHRC)
  Standard Grants, 1992–5, 2005–9
Saskatchewan Heritage Foundation Grant, 2004
Rockefeller Foundation Humanities Fellowship, Native Philosophy
  Project, Lakehead University, Thunder Bay, Ontario, 1996–7
Research Publication grants: St Thomas More College, and Univer-
  sity of Saskatchewan, Saskatoon, Saskatchewan, 1998
Research grants in lieu of salary: St Thomas More College, 1999–2004
St Thomas More College, University of Saskatchewan, SSHRC grants,
  1999, 2000, 2004
Intergovernmental and Aboriginal Affairs grant, Regina, Saskatch-
  ewan, 2002

Genesis of This Book

Many of the chapters in this book had their beginnings as conference
presentations; two were journal articles. We have made revisions to all
previous presentations and publications.

The Preface began as "'Catch Me If You Can': Animals as Ambiguous
in an Ojibwa Perceptual World," a paper presented at the 40th Western
Canadian Philosophical Society Conference, University of Lethbridge,
2003.

The Introduction is largely new.

Chapter 1, "'Paths of the Spirit': Moral Values in the Writings of Four
Nineteenth-Century Ojibwa," appeared, in part, as papers at the 38th
Algonquian Conference, University of British Columbia, 2006, and at
the Canadian Congress of the Arts and Humanities, University of Saskatchewan, 2007.

Chapter 2, "The Grand Medicine Society: The Midewiwin," is new.

Chapter 3, "Otter: The Playful Slider," originated as a paper, "The
Otter: Laughter and Treaty Three," presented at the Trente-deuxième
congrès des Algonquinistes, McGill University and McCord Museum,
Montreal, 2000, and appeared with the same title in John Nichols, ed.,
Actes du Trente-deuxième congrès des Algonquinistes (Winnipeg: Univer-
sity of Manitoba Press, 2001), 359–73.

Chapter 4, "Owls: Images and Voices in the Ojibwe and Midewiwin
Worlds," was originally presented as a paper, "Ojibwa Owls: Giving a
Hoot or Giving a Scare?," at the Thirty-Third Algonquian Conference,
University of California, Berkeley, 2001; it was published as "Owls:

Images and Voices on the Ojibwa and Midewiwin Worlds," *American Indian Culture and Research Journal* 26 (2002): 45–62.

Chapter 5, "Omnipresent and Ambivalent Bears," is new.

Chapter 6, "Water Creatures," was presented, in part, as a paper at the 40th Algonquian Conference, University of Minnesota, 2008.

Chapter 7, "Thunderbirds," is new.

Permissions

Alethea Helbig

Human Studies Film Archives / National Anthropological Archives, Smithsonian Institution, Museum Support Center

Joan and Romas Vastokas

St John's Abbey Archives

Johns Hopkins University Press; Tracy Thomas of the Wolf Clan of the Mohawk Nation, illus.

Thunder Bay Historical Museum Society

University of Chicago Press and Wilfrid Laurier University Press

University of Manitoba Press

Wayne Yerxa

LIVING WITH ANIMALS

Ojibwe Spirit Powers

1

The Grand Medicine Society, the Midewiwin

There was one society or gathering at the heart of Ojibwe life: the Midewiwin, whose members were called Mide. It was also referred to as the Grand Medicine Society, and it had been given to the Ojibwe by the Great Spirit. Central to the Midewiwin were ceremonial and song scrolls and performances.

There are other names that describe the Midewiwin: mystic rite, mystic rite of the sacred paint, mystic rite of the ghost, mystic rite of the serpent, mystic rite of the attendants. Fred K. Blessing writes that "the correct Ojibwa name for the Mide Lodge was Mah nee doo wigi wahm (Spirit Lodge)" and that following this righteous path would lead to a wholesome life.[1]

Midewiwin ceremonies vary greatly depending on the locale and on the needs, skills, and world views of the practitioners.[2] In many Ojibwe stories, the Mide ritual is necessary for healing and well-being and to ward off evil Manitous. In those stories, the good Manitous make a concerted effort to heal sickness and to keep everything in well-being. As an illustration, Wasagunachank and Midasuganj from the Bois Fort/Nett Lake Reservation in Minnesota gave an early-twentieth-century story about Mighty-One, grandfather, who asked his grandson to promise to look after his grandmother, Nokomis. The boy learned from grandfather how to make medicine using a bear. The provident bear, the "big animal folk," helped stave off hunger. Mighty-One gave his grandson the knowledge of songs to accompany the medicine.[3] One scroll song and its illustration are about desiring the place where bear dwells; there is a representation of a bear pouch as well as a flame to give light. There is also a prayer that identifies the body of the self with the body of the bear. This prayer is sung to procure bears in the hunt and to invoke the powers that are latent in the mystic pouch

of the black bear.[4] The bear/human person is further transformed into
a spirit: "The body in which I dwell is a spirit. The body in which you
dwell is a spirit."[5]

Sickness. Song scroll: "The spirit has put
away all my sickness." "He has received new
life, and is, henceforth, free from the disturbing influences of evil manidos." Hoffman,
"The Midê'wiwin," 203a, 219.

Membership

Both non-members and members often regarded the Midewiwin as a
secret society; they feared and respected it and often remained silent
about it. Membership in the Midewiwin generally demarcated more
traditional Ojibwe from those who espoused Christianity and from
those who were neutral about religious/spiritual concerns. Such
distinctions were apparently not always made, however. Lucy Bigay
from the Lac Courte Oreilles Reservation (Big Drum Lodge in Round
Lake Community), Wisconsin, stated that the condition of her becoming a member of the Midewiwin was a dream she had when she was
a little girl. Although becoming a member was quite involved, "a lot
to it," "all the people in [New] Post [Reservation] were Midewiwin,
and Signer, Round Lake, Chief Lake, Whitefish [communities]," even
Roman Catholics. "No they never let go. Some of these that are Catholic
now still belong to that Indian way."[6] In her 1930s study of the White
Earth Reservation, Minnesota, M. Inez Hilger states that "of the parents
in the one hundred fifty families, thirteen (4.7%), six men and seven
women, were members of the Midewiwin."[7]

A woman. Song scroll: "Signifies that women may also be
admitted to the Midewiwin." Song on birch bark from Red
Lake. Hoffman, "The Midê'wiwin," 186.

Among some of the Ojibwe, there was and continues to be a taboo against speaking about the Midewiwin, for to speak about it directly might conjure up evil spirits. This medicine society has been regarded as quite esoteric and beyond the comprehension of the average person – indeed, its members often use unconventional language in its ceremonies – so it is generally not part of common conversation. While many Ojibwe regard the Midewiwin as special and traditional, both past and present practitioners regard the "ordinary way" – that is, non-Midewiwin ways – as commendable also.[8]

Robert Ritzenthaler tabulates the "price to be paid" for initiation into each of the four Midewiwin degrees among the Wisconsin Ojibwe, especially on the Lac Courte Oreilles Reservation: first degree, 7 blankets and 2 galvanized pails; second, 11 blankets, 2 pails; third, 17 blankets, 2 pails; fourth, 21 blankets, 2 pails. Clothing is sometimes substituted for blankets.[9] On the basis of their experience as fourth-degree members of the Midewiwin on the Long Plains and Swan Lake reserves in Manitoba, Kennahmodi/Moose-Bell and Jim Beatty state that "the masters who know all the Midéwin songs often charge a neophyte the value of two horses for teaching a single song."[10]

Lodge and gifts. Song by Gegwedjiwebinun: "My Mide brethren, I walk in a circle, The bear, Goes on before, To the Mide lodge, Telling, The old Indian, What gifts to give." "On a pole are hung blankets and other gifts, which are to be distributed according to the directions of the bear. The person to be initiated appears in the drawing, also the bear, which is entering the Midewigan. Curiously, the bear's footprints precede him, indicating the path he is to travel." Densmore, *Chippewa Music*, 1:112.

Records of Lac Vieux Desert (Wisconsin) ceremonials in the 1930s reveal differences in the lodge performance compared to both earlier records and Ritzenthaler's. For instance, John Pete stated that there was no secrecy in the rite and that there were no fees (although there were some offerings), no sweat baths, sacred stones, posts, or funeral ceremonies. Also, there were no great authority figures; only part of the lodge was enclosed, and wine or whiskey was introduced.[11]

Blessing adds further details from his experience in the mid-twentieth century: "One basic feature of the Medicine Lodge, which can easily be deduced after a brief acquaintance with scrolls, is the association of minor animal species with the lower degrees, and a succession of increasingly dominant species in the higher degrees."[12] Membership in the Midewiwin was granted to both females and males and was also open to sick persons or to family members who had experienced a vision. A deterrent could be the cost of the many gifts required to ascend the ladder.

Alanson Skinner observes of the Eastern Cree and Northern Saulteaux in the early twentieth century that "the badge of membership [in the Mide] was the skin of some small animal, such as beaver, mink, muskrat, owl, or even snake, highly ornamented with porcupine quills and containing personal charms and medicine." Mide members honed their natural abilities and accumulated skills during their initiation into the ascending degrees. James Stewart describes a feast at Berens River where the sick were being tended: four or five Mide were often present at a bedside. Skinner notes: "They [the Mide] make use of ermine (weasel), mink, otter, and young bearskins ornamented with beads and ribbons. These are considered to be actually embodied with power to perform various acts."[13] Practitioners became more adept at using various instruments, signs, and songs to influence the success of hunting or love making. A condition (often unstated) for practising medicine was leading an upright life.

Ascending the Midewiwin initiation ladder, whether four, eight, or sixteen rungs, entailed acquiring various proficiencies: use of herbal remedies and medicines; knowledge of the origins and history of the people; and the memory and ability to sing a repertoire of songs. In this way, personal proficiency was grafted onto traditional knowledge. Along with this individual knowledge and proficiency came the responsibility to use power wisely.[14] Practitioners could transcend the first four "earth grades" to the more powerful and effective "sky grades"; here they might be tempted to use their newly acquired ability for personal and/or harmful effects. In the higher degrees, the Great Spirit replaced the megis [shell] Manitou, and the eagle replaced the bear Manitou, according to Landes.[15] James Redsky of the Shoal Lake Reserve, Ontario, identifies the four earth phases of the Midewiwin with coloured trees: red for the first phase, green for the second, blue for the third, yellow for the fourth. "Right at the last we find happiness and everlasting life if we are righteous in the eyes of the Great Creator. That is our reward."[16]

Gitche Manitou. Song from White Earth: "He who sees me, he who sees me, stands on the middle of the earth." "The human figure symbolizes Kitshi Manido; the magic lines cross his body, while his legs rest upon the outline of the Midewigan [Lodge]. His realm, the sky, reaches from the zenith to the earth, and he beholds the Mide while chanting and conducting the Midewiwin." Hoffman, "The Midê'wiwin," 244, 268a.

Wabeno, Jessakkid, and Midewiwin

Joan M. and Romas K. Vastokas and others do not examine the temporal origins of the Midewiwin; they do, however, suggest that the Mide grew out of the early informal practices of curers such as the Wabeno and the visionary Jessakkid. The Mide then came to occupy a place between those seeking and attaining individual visions and a public agricultural society.[17] Curers and visionaries continued to exist independent of the Mide and alongside Mide ceremonies.[18] Some viewed the Midewiwin as harmful and disreputable and as a blight on Ojibwe traditions.[19] When surveyed, however, according to its results – success in hunting, longevity, group solidarity, and well-groomed leaders – it was undeniable that the Midewiwin had positive effects.

Animal and hunter. Song by Becigwiwizans: "Out of the woods, We will bring, Even as we are telling you." "The animal is seen approaching the hunter." Densmore, *Chippewa Music*, 1:83.

Other sources point to some animosity between the Wabeno and Jessakkid, on the one hand, and between them and the Midewiwin, on the other. Christopher Vecsey describes the Wabeno as a simplified and degenerate form of the Midewiwin. The first written references to the Wabeno are in *The Jesuit Relations*, where they are referred to as jugglers (*jongleurs*).[20] According to Vecsey, the "Wabeno complex" began around 1796 in the Lake of the Woods region. By the early twentieth century, its songs, dances, and other ceremonies were no longer being practised by individuals or by groups. Wabeno men (women were generally excluded) showed their power by using herbal preparations to protect their skin and then juggling or taking red-hot coals and stones in their hands or mouths. These fire handlers then rubbed their heated hands over their patients while chanting vision songs. There are accounts of naked Wabeno engaging in boisterous dancing around the ailing patient; some of their words, songs, and actions had erotic connotations.[21] Their mnemonic prayer boards demonstrated the hunting purposes of the Wabeno complex.[22] The Wabeno had powers to cure and made charms for success in war, love, and especially the hunt.[23] Members of the Wabeno used images from fire or reflections from a bowl of water to interpret dreams and to guide the people in contacting and communicating with helping spirits who would heal the sick.[24] Some Ojibwe, however, referred to the Wabeno as an evil group that inflicted disease and that prevented good luck for hunters and success in war.[25]

Individual Ojibwe, mostly young men, sought the help of animal spirits through vision quests; members of the Jessakkid sought and apparently received even more power from Manitous and helping spirits. These individuals then used their greater powers to direct those spirits in various ways; one way was to capture the soul of a sorcerer and force him or her to cease all malevolent acts. Another action the Jessakkid performed was prophesying; still another was the removal of foreign bodies by sucking on a tube made of bone. The Jessakkid, however, were best known for their divination ritual, the Shaking Tent Ceremony. A member of the Jessakkid, referred to as a conjurer, enclosed himself in a tall and very narrow tent that was open to the sky. The Jessakkid then called forth spirits, who announced their presence inside the tent by violently shaking the tent poles. According to one tradition, a prophetic power was then bestowed on the Jessakkid by a thunderbird. The principal mediator was the turtle spirit, who answered questions posed by people outside the tent; this spirit used different voices and often a different language from the common one. Thus the Jessakkid were regarded as three types of medicine persons: prophet, healer, and conjurer.[26] The Wabeno and the Jessakkid somewhat resembled the Midewiwin; however, members of the former generally did not belong to the Medicine Society. Hoffman indicates, however, that members of the Wabeno and Jessakkid could sometimes gain admission.[27]

Origins of the Midewiwin

There are two principal theories about the origin of the Midewiwin. According to one, it was founded in pre-contact times; according to the other, it is more recent. Felix M. Keesing describes the Midewiwin as a nativistic cult or revitalization movement that arose in response to the encroachment of Europeans.[28] A notable proponent of this post-contact theory is Harold Hickerson, who views the Midewiwin as part of a larger social organization among the Ojibwe in the latter part of the seventeenth and early eighteenth centuries. In *The Chippewa and Their Neighbors* he relies – as he did during his testimony regarding Native land claims – on published sources alone, including trapping records and seventeenth-century Jesuit writings.[29] For Hickerson, there is no evidence of the Mide prior to the seventeenth century; Midewiwin ceremonials "represented and reflected new modes of organization, not ancient ones." With the termination of the Feast of the Dead and the beginning of the Mide there came a shift in the social organization of the Ojibwe that saw the establishment of village communities such as Sault Ste Marie. In Hickerson's view, the Mide served as a solution to the problem of authority in this new tribal group. The Mide were a hierarchical organization that took the place of a more or less egalitarian one and that permitted the accumulation of wealth in the hands of a minority.[30]

Land of the dead. "This figure represents Mokwa [bear] coming by a mountain in the land of the dead." Chief Moses Day Daybwaywaindung's Medicine Bark (History Chart) Parchment, Reagan, "A Ritual Parchment," 235, 242.

Yet the Ojibwe themselves and those authors who rely on oral sources generally consider the Midewiwin to be a pre-contact Aboriginal society. Among the latter are several Aboriginal writers such as William Warren[31] and Fred K. Blessing, but also William J. Hoffman[32] and W. Vernon Kinietz.[33] These authors emphasize that Ojibwe origins involve migrations, with each community having a variant history. We have already noted this tradition from the pen of William Warren. According to Blessing, the original people lived on the shores of the great saltwater sea, the Atlantic Ocean, and then migrated west.[34] Selwyn Dewdney suggests that it is possible to interpret the Mide on the basis of the symbolic re-enactment of this westward migration. The direction indicated by the scrolls – from east to west – represents this migration. The four lodges found along this path represent not only the four degrees of initiation but also four geographical stopping points on the path of that migration.[35] For Dewdney, then, and for Thomas Vennum, this migration is more than symbolic; it also depicts the historical journey of the Ojibwe from the eastern seaboard to the west of Lake Superior during the seventeenth century.[36]

Those who rely on oral sources, and some recent archaeologists, emphasize the pre-contact origins of the Midewiwin. Robert Hall uses the same sources as Hickerson but comes to a different conclusion – that elements of the Midewiwin ceremony pre-dated contact with Europeans.[37] Adding credence to this theory is Kenneth Kidd's discovery of scroll fragments dating to 1560 that are comparable to more recent Midewiwin scrolls intended for ritual use. These vestiges of scrolls, found in a cave in Quetico Provincial Park, Ontario, suggest that the Midewiwin may in fact pre-date the contact period.[38] William Hoffman states that he discovered in the late nineteenth century in Red Lake, Minnesota, "an ancient chart which, according to the assurances of the chief and assistant Mede priests, had never before been shown to a white man."[39] Archaeologist James B. Bandow of the University of Western Ontario has noted that recent digs at Birch Bay on Lake Temagami and Witch Bay on Lake of the Woods, both in Ontario, unearthed dog remains indicating a pre-contact Mide lodge. Also, digs at Hope Bay on Georgian Bay, Ontario, unearthed bear remains also associated with the lodge and dated 1500 or earlier.[40]

Most scientists are very concerned about precise times, locations, and causes of events. The Ojibwe use a different approach – stories. A recurring and detailed albeit varied story of the origin of the Midewiwin features a young boy, Ode'imin. In one version from the U.S. Upper Midwest, a plague struck the people and killed, among others, this boy of fifteen. When he arrived in the other world, Ode'imin pleaded with Gitche Manitou to save his people from the ravages of this affliction. Since Ode'imin asked nothing for himself, Manitou agreed to provide "a message of hope" if Ode'imin agreed to live again. "You will tell them that I will send Nanabohzo to teach them and watch over them; and he will establish and set in motion the Great Laws that will rule the sky and the earth; and the plague will be ended and the People saved." It happened, however, that Ode'imin not Nanabohzo/Nanabush brought the redeeming message. "Each spring and each summer Ode'-imin is remembered and celebrated, for the blossom of the strawberry is Ode'imin's first life and the berry itself his second."[41] George Hamell writes that berries are generally signs "of the soul's liminal state-of-being, betwixt the here and there, and the here and the here-after ... Berries are also the substance by which these threshold states-of-being are positively resolved."[42]

Another block of stories concerns the origin and purpose of the Midewiwin; these stories highlight healing experiences but also deal with an ordering of the cosmos. In a healing story, the principal character, as in the above story, is male with several names; he is referred to generally as a young boy or a young man,[43] or as Ode'imin, Strawberry, or Heartberry,[44] but more commonly as Cutfoot. Born to two older parents who lived on the shore of a large body of water, Cutfoot as he grew up became strongly attached to his brother. After his brother became ill (or died), Cutfoot had an eight-year series of visions in which Manitou instructed him on methods of curing his brother. In one version, Cutfoot returned to his parents with a water drum, herbs, and the Mide lodge, and, according to Edward Benton-Banai, with seven gifts.[45] Cutfoot was thus the medium through which the Great Spirit worked to bring a healing performance to the Ojibwe. This ceremonial, believed to have originated before contact with Europeans, became a focal point of identity for the many Ojibwe groups. While many Ojibwe were not privy to Medicine Society ceremonies, the moral tone and injunctions of the Midewiwin pervaded all aspects of Ojibwe life.

Sikassige from White Earth, Minnesota, and Hoffman add details to their version of the Cutfoot story. On a birch bark scroll, the origin of the medicine lodge and the origin of the Anishinaabe are intertwined so as to depict the stratified terrestrial origins of the Anishinaabeg and their healing symbols. In Charles Clelland's paraphrased story, "the Great Spirit called upon four lesser spirits to accompany the original people to the earth ... A lodge was built on the earth, and the first child was produced by the *Anishnabeg*. The child, however, soon died but was returned to life with the help of the Sun and Bear Spirits. Through a series of three gifts to the spirits ... the *Anishnabeg* learned the healing mysteries of the Grand Medicine Society, or *Mide-wi-win*." Illustrated below is the lodge guarded by the bear spirit with Midewiwin power that invigorates the bristling earth.[46]

Sikassige and Hoffman add details to the above story. A bear ministered to the deceased brother, uttered "hu, hu, hu, hu," and walked around his body four times as its quivering increased; then "the body came to life again and stood up" and the bear spoke to his father. The bear transferred his powers to the boy, and the boy became a bear, called "a little bear boy. [He] taught them the mysteries of the Grand

Medicine ... He told his adopted father that as his mission had been fulfilled he was to return to his kindred spirits, for the Indians would have no need to fear sickness as they now possessed the Grand Medicine which would enable them to live."[47]

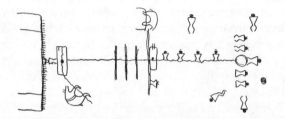

Origin of the Anishinaabeg. From right of chart: creation of two men and two women; four lesser spirits on the line moving left; four winds on the periphery; bear/bear-boy in centre and entering the lodge; left part: candidate personating bear spirit and entering another lodge; left: earth's bristling surface. Hoffman, "The Midê'wiwin," 172–4, 172a.

Blessing notes that "according to tribal historians within the Mide priesthood," the Ojibwe had a spiritual life before the advent of the Midewiwin healing society. In their earlier rites, the Ojibwe prized "the individual clan's fauna identity" and fasted and took sweat baths in preparation for visions. In the Midewiwin ritual, celebrations were more organized, and "each volunteer spirit form provided ritualistic aspects and songs pertinent to a certain degree. Consequently each of these forms became the symbol of the degree for which it had interceded."[48]

The Midewiwin ritual incorporates the most ancient Ojibwe songs and migratory traditions. "In this rite is also perpetuated the purest and most ancient idioms of their language, which differs somewhat from that of the common every-day use," Warren writes. "And if comparisons are to be made between the language of the Ojibways and other languages, it must be with their religious idiom." He believes there is a similarity between this ceremony and that of the Hebrews, with certain rules to guide Ojibwe lives that "are represented in hieroglyphics."

For Warren, the Mide arose in the context of stages in the Ojibwe migrations: "While our forefathers were living on the great salt water toward the rising sun, the great Megis (sea-shell) showed itself above the surface of the great water, and the rays of the sun for a long period were reflected from its glossy back. It gave warmth and light to the

An-ish-in-aub-ag (red race). All at once it sank into the deep, and for a time our ancestors were not blessed with its light. It rose to the surface and appeared again on the great river which drains the waters of the Great Lakes, and again for a long time it gave life to our forefathers, and reflected back the rays of the sun. Again it disappeared from sight and it rose not, till it appeared to the eyes of the An-ish-in-aub-ag on the shores of the first great lake." Origins through the guidance of the megis shell are noted here. However, Warren acknowledges another tradition of origin that focuses on the otter (a more detailed account is given later).[49]

Medicine knowledge. Song scroll: "Yes, I see there is plenty of it." "The Mide has knowledge of more than he has imparted, but reserves that knowledge for a future time. The lines of 'sight' run to various medicines which he perceives or knows of." Mallery, *Picture-Writing*, 1:237.

Blessing presents an amplified account of the genesis of the Midewiwin ceremonies. "The Creator met with his four main assistants, the four wind spirits, and discussed the presentation of a religion to the Indian. It was decided to give them the Medicine Lodge. The Creator called for volunteers to transmit the religion to receptive individuals on earth. The white otter (albino) was the first spirit form to volunteer and so he assumed leadership of the intercessory Mide spirit forms. The white otter also became a symbol of the candidate's 'true life' or 'spiritual birth.' Other volunteers came forth from the reptile, bird and animal kingdoms. As assistants to the Creator they appeared to men on earth in dreams and began to transmit the rites of the Midewiwin."[50]

One of the "Four Elders of God's House with their Credentials [otter bags]." James Redsky, "Unpublished Manuscript." Thunder Bay Museum.

Mide songs and symbols become more explicit as otter and bear become agents in bringing life to the Ojibwe. Otter breaks through the sandbar while bear penetrates "successively each of the four layers of the earth with his tongue."[51] From the song scrolls, we note repeated references to the lodge, bears, and spirits: "My lodge is the source of life." And the spirit of humans is the bear: "My namesake spirit (i.e., the bear)." "I am the spirit's mouth." "My heart lives; it is full of strength (like a bear)." "Am I mistaken, or have I found the chief (spirit master) in my heart?"[52] Mide member Tom Badger from Lac du Flambeau notes in a general way that all members of the lodge are Manitous or spirits.[53]

Christopher Vecsey sketches the many stories in the Ojibwe traditions regarding the origin of the Midewiwin. In one tradition, recorded by William Jones, Nanabush and his brother created everything in the world. Special animals such as bird-hawk, owl, and otter became the helpers of human beings. In another origin story, the Manitous, sometimes four and sometimes sixteen, met in council and appointed an agent to bring the Midewiwin to the Ojibwe. As controllers of the winds, Manitous from the four corners of the cosmos felt that the people were in a deplorable condition and that they needed the Midewiwin and its plan for long life and health, abundance of food, and comfort. According to various accounts, these Manitous "delegated Bear, or Nanabozho, Eagle or Otter, Sun or the East Manito to travel to earth, and either to deliver the saving medicines or to become incarnate in a little boy born to an old, childless Indian couple ... After overcoming barriers, the agent delivered Midewiwin to various geographical locations. Otter, Megis, or Bear travelled by water, usually from east to west, carrying a message and making it possible for local manitos to help Indians with their cures, since all local manitos derived their powers from the agent of the manito council."[54]

Otter-skin sack. Song by Sikassige: "When I come out the sky becomes clear." "When the otter-skin Mide sack is produced the sky becomes clear, so that the ceremonies may proceed." Mallery, *Picture-Writing*, 1:237. Fulford translates the song as "How shall I carry it (the otterskin medicine pack) away?" "Ojibwa Picture Writing," 194.

Day Dodge and Saycosegay relate the provenance and characteristics of the lodge as they touch on healing. In the beginning, the top layer of the earth was bare. Trees and stones were on the second layer of the earth. While the Manitous were talking about the plight of the Anishinaabe, the trees and stones heard them and surfaced. Then they scattered everywhere. Thereafter, stones and trees played a role in Midewiwin lodge performances. Near the entrance to the Mide lodge was a stone that was believed to have the power to draw disease from the body of a sick person. At a further distance was a painted post representing a tree: an emblem of life and strength. For healing, the sick person would lean against the post.[55]

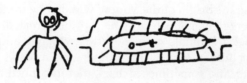

Song scroll: "You shall now behold, They of the Mide." "This drawing shows the Midewigan, the medicine pole, the stone, and the assembled members of the Midewiwin. The candidate for initiation sees and hears the ceremony mentally before entering the lodge. Note the eyes and the ear of the candidate." Densmore, *Chippewa Music*, 1:67.

A "pictomyth" described by Vizenor shows that the spiritual power of the Midewiwin gave a man strength to live to an old age. "The old man praises his age as spiritual power."[56] On the theme of old age and death, Densmore recorded a Midewiwin burial song to be sung after the composer's death. One of the Midewiwin spirits is present.[57]

We have examined the healing ritual involving Cutfoot/Ode'imin. In one version, bear brought the Midewiwin ceremony to cure a dead boy.[58] Vecsey refers to two variant healing stories featuring "a girl, either so sick that she stank and had to be isolated, or so abused by her adoptive parents that she ran away from home."[59] In the first case, bear engaged in a shooting initiation of the sick girl by piercing her body with megis shells and a bow and arrow; the girl then took bear's Mide pack[60] for herself. In most cases, the shooting action results in general body penetration; however, for the Lac des Bois Ojibwe, the neophytes "put the migis in their mouths and make a vomiting noise in their throats."[61]

In the second story, a woman took the sick girl across the water in a canoe that turned out to be the serpent, Mishi Ginabig. Grandmother Old Vermilion introduced the sick girl to the Mide lodge poles, gave her paints from her aged skull, and prophesied that she would marry South Wind. The girl returned on the canoe-like serpent and taught the Midewiwin performances to her people. On the basis of this account, women can become members of the Midewiwin.[62] Relying on at least one female Mide member and collaborator, Nawajibigokwe, Densmore wrote: "Respect toward the Midewiwin is emphasized, and respect toward women is enjoined upon the men."[63]

"Mede curing sick woman." "A Mede, named Newikki, curing a sick woman by sucking the demon through a bone tube." Hoffman, "Pictography," 221.

According to the Three Fires Society (Ojibwe, Odawa, Potawotomi), the petroform site in Whiteshell Provincial Park in Manitoba is where the Midewiwin actually began. This site is called "where Manito sits," which is the meaning of Manito Ahbee (Manitoba). One of the society's spokespersons, Katherine Pettipas, describes this Mide location as comprising "boulder mosaics," "boulder art," and "boulder temples." At this site are found the tools for religious leaders from many nations to impart important spiritual and practical lessons. The instructions given to Original Man are "written in stone," and as members ascend the sixteen steps of the Midewiwin, they hear more of the sacred teachings. Only initiates may enter. "No one would think of going there," Pettipas writes, "as it was said anyone crossing the 'ground' would not live long afterwards."[64]

Cosmic Ordering

Cutfoot served as a mediator in two ways. First, as already noted, he brought the Midewiwin to his people in order to effect physical and moral healing. Second, he brought cosmic order for individuals in the form of waking and sleep and by structuring day and night for the earth. According to Hole-in-the-Day, this story of Cutfoot is told by a senior member during Midewiwin ceremonies at the close of every night session, just before everyone leaves the lodge. In this narrative, Cutfoot is portrayed as a lame and tottering old man and as the first Ojibwe to sleep. This story is not simply about the advent of sleep for the people, that is, about restoring body and mind; it also deals explicitly with the rhythmic relation between day and night as caused by the rising and setting of the sun.[65]

Structural anthropologist Claude Lévi-Strauss envisions mythological beings who are lame, sick, or deformed like Cutfoot as having positive significance. Limping, he writes, is a "reflection, or more accurately ... a diagramatic expression, of the desired imbalance" between climatic periods like dry and wet seasons, and between winter and summer. A normal gait could be a symbolic representation of the regular periodicity of seasons, while a desire to change this periodicity in order to extend one season and shorten another could be represented by a limping gait.[66]

The Ojibwe could relate to an earlier quasi-normal life as well as to nineteenth-century imbalances. The influx of traders, changes in political structures, diminishing food supplies, loss of resources and control over them, and European attempts to Christianize them were some of the forces battering Ojibwe populations. Creative adaptation and innovation was possible for them – indeed, it would be necessary if they were to maintain their identity. So there was a movement back to origins, toward what was uniquely Ojibwe, to stories, songs, and ceremonies. That movement inspired them to cope by radically inverting destructive forces. Cutfoot was depicted as young, blissfully innocent, and receptive to Manitou, but also as old, wise, and skilled at resolving tensions. Midewiwin members brought with them to treaty signings both this originality of vision and this wisdom to adapt. Cutfoot symbolized the resolution of these differences in the past and the present.

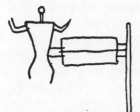

Medicine Lodge. Song scroll: "I am going into the medicine lodge." "The Midewigan is shown with a line through it, to signify that the precepter is going through it in imagination, as in the initiation." Mallery, *Picture-Writing*, 1:238. Fulford translates the above song scroll as "I go straight home;" "Ojibwa Picture Writing," 180.

The Cutfoot stories can also be interpreted as encompassing even more fundamental differences than those presented by European peoples and cultures. The challenge for the Ojibwe was twofold, just as were the stories representing Cutfoot as both young and old. Their first challenge was to forge a relationship with the Europeans, to live in peace and fellowship with them, to heal wounds and provide balm for the future. Their second challenge was to re-create a world order that would maintain regularized patterns such as the reciprocity of day and night and the four seasons even while allowing them to cope with imbalances such as the ones expressed by Cutfoot's limping. The Ojibwe themselves sought to interrupt some patterns in nature, using ceremonials to prolong the growing and maturing seasons and to extend the times available for hunting and gathering. Taking much the same tack, they hoped to address the imbalance of their lives in ways that would preserve the differences between Aboriginals and Europeans and that would help them find creative resolutions to conflicts.

There is a similarity as well between the Desana in the South American rainforest and the Ojibwe and other North American Aboriginal peoples with regard to both the retention of traditions and adaptation to change. For the Desana, a balance is always maintained as the cosmos goes about depleting and replenishing itself. Mitch Albom writes that the Desana "see the world as a fixed quantity of energy that flows between all creatures. Every birth must therefore engender a death, and every death bring forth another birth. This way, the energy of the world remains complete. When they hunt for food, the Desana know that the animals they kill will leave a hole in the spiritual well. But that hole will be filled, they believe, by the souls of the Desana hunters when they die. Were there no men dying, there would be no birds or fish being born."[67] The details in this process differ from one nation to another, but this give-and-take, be it through degeneration or reincarnation, remains a constant.

When they negotiated with Europeans in the nineteenth century, the Ojibwe fully expected that the cosmic order as established in stories and in the Mide healing rites would be maintained in the treaties that resulted. For example, since wood and water were gifts of the Great Spirit and were necessary for their livelihood as well as for ceremonials, those treaties would ensure that these staples would remain in place. Aboriginal peoples would not mindlessly and irreligiously have given up trees, for they provided material for their sacred pipes; nor would they have forfeited lands, for that is where they grew tobacco to be used in ceremonies. And they would not have ceded rights to their animals,[68] for they were their relatives and were necessary for livelihood and ceremonies. Financial gain and agricultural implements provided by the treaty did not supersede the ritual demands of the drum, rattle, birch bark scrolls, songs, and the lodge, all of which had been validated by their stories.

The Creator gave earthly beings for human sustenance; all beings have interrelated roles to play. Harold Cardinal writes:

"As long as the Sun shines, the Grass grows, and the Rivers flow." These words have a symbolic meaning to Indian people, because the water, the grass, and the sun are all basic elements of life. In the Indian religion, they have a special role to play in human life. In naming these elements, our people were saying that they would not give up any elements basic to their religious practices. Our people were calling upon the sun, the water, and the grass as witnesses to the fact that they were not surrendering, by those treaties, either their sovereignty or their relationship with the Great Spirit …

If we are told that we gave up all the timber by the treaties, we say that that cannot be accurate, because if we had given up the forests, we would have sacrificed a material basic to our religious practices. Our pipes are an integral part of our religious ritual. The pipe stem is made of wood. Our elders would never have agreed to give away the forests because they would have been giving away part of the responsibility they had to their religious ceremonies.

In our religious rituals, we use sweet grass as incense in our prayers. If our elders had given up the grass that grew on Mother Earth, they would have been surrendering an important adjunct of their religious beliefs to outsiders who did not understand these beliefs. This they would not, and did not, do. Water, fire, and other natural elements play a role in our ritual. From a religious standpoint we never intended the surrender of any of those things to be a part of any treaty-making process.

I don't think that the white people ever thought that religion was any part of the treaty-making process.[69]

For Cardinal, Aboriginal peoples did not give up their identities as nations, and did not give up their relationship with the Great Spirit and animals, nor did they give up their religion and ceremonies.[70]

During the negotiation and signing of Treaty Three[71] in 1873 in Ontario and Manitoba, Chief Mawedopenais referred indirectly to the continuance of the Great Spirit's cosmic ordering and traditional government: "We think where we are is our property. I will tell you what he said to us when he planted us here; the rules that we should follow – us Indians – He has given us rules that we should follow to govern us rightly."[72]

The origin stories relate that the Great Spirit had a design for the cosmos, one that was embodied in certain laws and directives. Acting according to those laws and directives would result in harmonious relationships among all peoples, animals, and plants. Warren suggests another way of conceiving these directives. Writing about the Great Lakes Ojibwe in the mid-nineteenth century, he placed the origin of the Midewiwin in a context of offence and retribution. The Ojibwe "fully believe that the Red man mortally angered the Great Spirit which caused the deluge, and at the commencement of the new earth it was only through the medium and intercession of a powerful being, whom they denominate Man-ab-o-sho, that they were allowed to exist, and means were given them whereby to subsist and support life; and a code of religion was more lately bestowed on them, whereby they could commune with the offended Great Spirit, and ward off the approach and ravages of death. This they term Me-da-we-win."[73] For others, the "code of religion" and the name of the Great Spirit did not arise in the context of retribution, of punishment and reward.

Having immersed herself in Ojibwe cultures, Frances Densmore came to deny that the Mide ceremonies had as their main purpose the appeasement of the spirits of the offended Manitous. Instead, she proposed a more positive goal for these rites. Given that her background and interest was music, she was sensitive to the important role played by singing and instruments in the ceremonies and in Ojibwe life as a whole. From her perspective, as Angel describes it, the Ojibwe tried through songs to free themselves from debilitating diseases and from revenge and war. For the Ojibwe, according to Densmore, harsh occurrences in nature and in wars were not the result of the Great Spirit's punishment. She also downplayed aspects of the Midewiwin as well as those parts of its performances "that dwelt with the temptation by high-degree Mideg to use their power for evil purposes." She chose not to include any examples of "bad medicine" in her descriptions. This perspective may have been influenced by the many female collaborators she consulted.[74]

"A Mitsha Mide or Bad Mide, one who employs his powers for evil purposes."
Such an individual can assume any disguise he wants; here it is that of a
bear. In this drawing, bear has made footprints, sometimes near the lodges of
his victims. The trees are a forest, the habitat of these Mide. Hoffman, "The
Midê'wiwin," 168–169a; see 238.

Nanabush

In another story, the puzzling character, Nanabush, brings the
Midewiwin to the Ojibwe. Basil Johnston recounts that Nanabush was:

> born of a human mother, [and] sired by a spirit, Epingishmook (The
> West). Like his older brothers, Mudjeekawis, Papeekawis, and Chibiabos,
> Nanabush possessed supernatural powers and was a spirit in nature. Of
> all the powers he possessed, none was more singular than his power of
> transformation ... Nanabush [could] assume at will, and in an instant, a
> new form, shape, and existence ... As pure incorporeal being he would be
> neither accepted, nor understood ... Were he to become a man or woman,
> he could be as courageous or fearful as a man or woman could be; he
> could be generous or miserly; he could be true or he could be false, loving
> or hating. As an Anishnabe, Nanabush was human, noble and strong, or
> ignoble and weak. For his attributes, strong and weak, the Anishnabeg
> came to love and understand Nanabush. They saw in him, themselves ...
> For his teachings, they honoured Nanabush.[75]

Nanabush was a multifaceted person – a human, a "wolf, demigod,
hero, trickster and buffoon."[76] In Denmore's words, Nanabush was
"the master of life – the source and impersonation of the lives of all sentient things human, faunal, and floral. He endowed these with life and
taught each its particular ruse for deceiving its enemies and prolonging
its life."[77] It is fitting that as a master and prolonger of life, and as the
active quickening power of life,[78] Nanabush was so intimately involved
with the Midewiwin. But his actions are not always consistent in these
stories: he is the bringer of death in some versions.[79]

Nanabush. Helbig, *Nanabozhoo*, title page.

As a trickster, Nanabush assumes any guise he chooses. Tomson Highway writes that this comic and clownish character teaches "about nature and the meaning of existence on the planet Earth; he straddles the consciousness of man and that of God, the Great Spirit."[80] Nanabush relies on the help of many animals in order to survive, for they have superior hunting abilities and can disclose the weaknesses of adversaries. Stories featuring Nanabush are a pragmatic way to judge reality through observation and dreams.[81] Nanabush gives us "a more complete insight into their [the Ojibwe's] real character, their mode of thought and expression, than any book which can be written concerning them," Warren writes.[82]

Nanabush is a central character in many Ojibwe stories. When Sister Bernard Coleman asked the Chippewa, "'Who is Nanabozho?' they looked at us perplexed. They accept Nanabozho and his characteristics, inconsistent as they may be, and thus they found it difficult to reply. Most of them said that he is a powerful manido or spirit being ... One woman said, 'He is both human and super-human.' One of our youngest informants spoke of him as 'a superman,' and still another said, 'Nanabozho is an ordinary Indian and an Indian extraordinary.'" Almost unanimously Nanbozho was mentioned as a brother to the animals, the plants, the trees, and the many different aspects of nature. As the legends show, Nanabozho has all of these characteristics and still others.

"The Ojibwa beliefs about Nanabozho," Sister Coleman adds, "need to be viewed in relation to the traditional belief in a large number of manidos or spirit beings (good and evil) that were thought to exist everywhere in nature – in the animals, birds, trees, an odd-shaped rock, the waterfalls, thunder and lightning, the winds and the cardinal directions. The heavens and the earth and the layers above and below the earth were all the abode of the manidos. The entire concept rested on the belief that the natural and the supernatural were inseparable. Thus it can be seen how the natural world would be considered a source of spirit power."[83]

Animals especially had spirit power and the ability to change into many different forms. Nanabush as a large animal hearkens back to an earlier time when animal spirits were believed to be of great size and power. In some stories, Nanabush had the greatest power, but he also had formidable opponents, especially the underwater manidos. Aiding Nanabush generally were the thunderbirds, who "helped Nanabozho chase the big snakes."[84]

Health and the Midewiwin

The following story indicates the powers ascribed to the Midewiwin: A son died and the parents searched for a way to restore him to life. They summoned the Mide, and four of them prostrated themselves on the dead boy and repeated chants. The son's recovery was gradual as parts of his body began to move. At first he seemed dazed, but then he recovered his speech and told of his trance-like condition in the spirit land where he learned of the "grand medicine." The boy prophesied about the future Mide practitioners: "The Mide spirit taught us to do right. He gave us life and told us how to prolong it. These things he taught us, and gave us roots for medicine. I give to you medicine; if your head is sick, this medicine put upon it, you will put it on."[85]

Medicinal root. Song scroll: "See what I am taking." "The Mide has pulled up a medicinal root. This denotes his possessing a wonderful medicine and appears in the order of an advertisement." Hoffman, "The Midê'wiwin," 292–292a.

One goal of the Midewiwin was to achieve *bimaadiziwin*, or a long, productive, and healthy life. Benton-Banai writes that "the Midewiwin religion taught the people how to use the powers of the Spirit World to treat their sicknesses. The Midewiwin gave the people a sense of spiritual strength to be balanced with its twin – the physical side of life. The people were no longer frail and began to live longer."[86]

Suffering. Song scroll: "I cause to look like the dead, a man I did. I cause to look like the dead, a woman I did. I cause to look like the dead, a child I did." "The lines drawn across the face of this figure indicate poverty, distress, and sickness; the person is supposed to have suffered from the displeasure of the medicine man." Tanner, *A Narrative*, 342–3.

Ojibwe concern for health and well-being was intensified during epidemics of new diseases. Included in the armoury of the Ojibwe generally, and specifically in that of the Mide, were an "impressive array of both disease concepts and native curative rattle devices" necessary for a hunting people whose livelihood and indeed survival depended on mentally and physically healthy hunters.[87] Densmore recounts this Ojibwe focus on physical health: "Health and long life represented the highest good to the mind of the Chippewa, and he who had knowledge conducive to that end was most highly esteemed among them. He who treated the sick, by whatever means, claimed that his knowledge came from *manido* (spirits), and those who saw a sick man restored to health by that knowledge readily accepted its origin as supernatural."[88] Robert Ritzenthaler concurs that the Ojibwe were preoccupied with health: "deep concern for health was present in the Chippewa before white contact; this concern was sustained and deepened during the first part of the contact period due to the introduction of new diseases, particularly smallpox."[89]

According to André Thevet, the sixteenth-century cosmographer, one finds all kinds of treasures when one studies nature.[90] The early Ojibwe were better versed than Europeans with the healing powers of plants.[91] To ensure that their various communities had healthy hunters, the Ojibwe (largely their women) used more than 140 different plants to produce more than 300 different medicines. Densmore notes that the ingredients in these medicines included roots,[92] bark, leaves, and minerals, in both powder and liquid form. Herbalists stored these medicines in bags made of buckskin, yarn, or bark. The herbs were not simply remedies; they were also preventatives, and defences against diseases.[93] The power of these medicaments came not merely from the natural ingredients but also from the presence of potent spirits. "It is a teaching of the Midewiwin that every tree, bush, and plant has a use," Densmore writes. "A country of such bountiful vegetation as that of the Chippewa presents a great amount of this material."[94]

Rattles. "The four human forms ... are the four officiating Mide priests whose services are always demanded at an initiation. Each is represented as having a rattle." Hoffman, "The Midê'wiwin," 167, 169a.

During performances of the second degree of the Midewiwin, initiates were taught the "magical properties of plants," powers that would "influence men" rather than animals (to use plants to influence animals was the mandate of the first-degree medicines).[95] A rock art painting depicts the Mide as a bear who holds a medicine bag and stands on the ground radiating with the power of plants.[96] The administering of different potions and the giving of advice depended on the needs of individuals and communities; apparently the Mide of the Lac des Bois Ojibwe from Kenora, Ontario, needed "four kinds of love medicine."[97] Jane Ash Poitras writes that the "names by which plants are designated by the Chippewa are usually compound nouns indicating the appearance of the plant, the place where it grows, a characteristic property of the plants, or its principal use."[98]

Yet hunters and gatherers could not simply abandon themselves to the spirit power in herbal medicines; they also had to apply their own skills and ingenuity. E.E. Carpenter writes of hunter-gatherers who, because of their relatively powerless position in nature, had to closely observe evolving and uncontrollable nature if they hoped to obtain the desired goods from it. Each piece of information received from plants had to be examined both individually and in a wider context. The significance of a certain wind, for example, emerged in the broader context of a particular season of the year, the time of day, and the individual locale.[99]

For the Ojibwe, all diseases had personal causes, explicit meanings, and (often) specific cures. Every disease had a prescribed treatment of plants and herbs, which was administered by an individual healer, commonly within the framework of the Midewiwin. European diseases, however, often rendered the Ojibwe defenceless, in that traditional medicines and techniques could not always treat these new maladies.[100]

The Ojibwe believed that a healthy person had a healthy body. Moral rectitude was also necessary, however; a long and healthy life

required upright living and humble behaviour. There were directives
for both physical and moral development on the ascending levels of
the Midewiwin. Mide members were required to have a large body
of knowledge: of tribal and Mide stories, instructions for initiation,
medicinal recipes, and the songs used in rituals. Some ritual performances required a means for recording the information, besides a good
memory. In addition to the medical performances recorded on the
authoritative scrolls, there were medicine bags, rattles, and drums.[101]

Functions of the Midewiwin

Accounts of the origins of the Midewiwin constitute a rich tapestry
that blends many representations of animals. The general function of
the Midewiwin was to ensure a healthy way of life, but it had other,
more specific functions as well. Regarding the spiritual purpose of the
Midewiwin in early times, Ojibwe historian William Warren wrote that
"the rites of the Me-da-we-win (their mode of worshipping the Great
Spirit), [secure] life in this and a future world, and [conciliate] the lesser
spirits."[102]

Another function of the Midewiwin was to gather stories about
the origins and migrations of the Ojibwe, thereby maintaining self-
knowledge. An early-nineteenth-century ritual parchment from Lake of
the Woods and Rainy Lake gives a "talk dance" in which Chief Moses
Day/Daybwaywaindung narrates the stories of migration.[103] According to Thomas Vennum, a researcher from the Smithsonian Institution,
the Midewiwin served as a "tribal historian"[104]; according to Mide
member Nicholas Deleary, those initiated into the Midewiwin were
"the main keepers of this cultural knowledge."[105] For M. Inez Hilger,
the Midewiwin was "the custodian of the traditional religion of the
Chippewa."[106] One Ojibwe story relates that bears had once recorded
their own deeds, thoughts, dreams, and prayers on wampum sashes.
Concerning the Anishinaabe, however, bears entrusted the task of
record keeping to Maudjee-kawiss, Winonah's first-born son, which is
why today bears and males are the guardians and keepers of records.[107]
A memory of the past ensured a sense of identity. "During the services
or ceremonies of the Mide Lodge, there was considerable preaching
by the various priests in attendance," Blessing asserts. "Some of this
preaching concerned the history of the receiving and developing of the
Mide religion."[108]

The Midewiwin also provided ceremonies of word and song during which new members were initiated (according to Warren, "a costly ordeal")[109] and instructed about important events. During these rituals, performers relied on totemic[110] figures on birch bark scrolls. In addition, Mide members of the Grand Council, both women and men, were responsible for medical tradition and practice.

"Ojibwa birch bark scroll figure." Peterborough petroglyph. Vastokas and Vastokas, *Sacred Art*, 57.

The Midewiwin also functioned as a judicial body that arbitrated disputes and acts of retaliation. Warren recounted three ways of responding to the homicide of a fellow Ojibwe. One was to retaliate immediately; another was to wait until the spirits of the dead cried out for vengeance and determined its mode and duration. In the third way, the perpetrators of the crime covered the bodies of the dead with presents. Warren furnishes a fourth way (really the primary one that he himself proposes): that of immersing oneself in the Mide performances. He seems to think that although murder leads to war – understandably so – and although it satisfies feelings for revenge and renown, immersing oneself in the Midewiwin and/or covering the dead with presents or showering them on relatives is an excellent alternative, morally speaking.[111]

Another function of the Midewiwin, and part of its historical role, was that of moral instruction. Yet another role of the Grand Medicine Society, though not necessarily directly intended, was economic and involved dealing with changing community and inter-nation relationships through trade. Initiation into the Midewiwin required gifts, fees, or trade goods acquired through hunting and trapping. "The influx and ceremonial distribution of wealth entailed by the ceremony reconfigured social relationships and created new social groups," Larry Nesper writes.[112]

Benton-Banai notes that the Creator gave his people a clan system that carried out many functions of the Midewiwin. This clan framework, especially that of the bear, provided the Ojibwe with an orderly government. The bear clan used its knowledge of plants "to treat the ailments of the people."[113] Danny Musqua notes that the bear clan were "warriors, the army, the police societies, and they were the most numerous because everybody was an honourary member ... The bear clan was supposed to maintain all of the stories of all the clans. We were supposed to keep the stories of all the clans intact."[114]

A twentieth-century Ojibwe from Minnesota, Fred K. Blessing, highlights the special medicinal aspects of the Mide society. "The word 'medicine' ... does not denote cures for ailments. It refers to the great mystery of spiritual horizons which lie beyond the understanding of the average individual. It is this area of spiritual mystery to which the French were referring as they failed to comprehend the complexities of Midewiwin." Members of the Midewiwin celebrated rituals that were central to life itself by focusing on "the mysterious beating of the human heart. They believed that the mortal heartbeat duplicated the beat of the Creator's heart. They knew that when the heartbeat ceased mortal life was gone." The Midewiwin's ceremonial regimen was "to influence the member to live in such a way that his life span would be increased. Through deference to the Creator's teachings, which the priesthood dispensed through the Midewiwin, the heart would be kept beating as long as possible."[115]

Sound of the Drum

Nicholas Deleary writes about the role of sounds in the Midewiwin ceremony. The water drum[116] accompanies the human voice: "Without the drum to accompany the Mide, his or her voice would be inaudible, powerless, and hence ineffective in prolonging life. The sound of the Water drum carried its voice loud and clear, the sound of the water drum goes everywhere. Sound itself is the essence of the Midewiwin – Mide-wi-win. Mideway in one translation means Sounding voice; Wi-win, translates as Good all over; hence, sounding good all over. The Mide would add to this interpretation that Midewiwin means, the Way of the Heart beat, the good heart sound of Life."[117] According to J. Richard Haefer, the drum is "a materialization of a vision as an artifact."[118]

Regarding the pervasive presence of animals in this performance, especially that of the drum, Vecsey writes: "It is informative to observe the nature symbolism in the origin of the Mide drum: Otter, whose skin stretched across the top; Snake, who coiled around the drum, holding Otter's skin tightly; Turtle, who formed the base of the drum; Loon, who formed a stick from its beak; Rattlesnake, who fashioned the rattles; and the elder Tree, whose body makes the body of the drum ... When the drum is played, it communicates with the natural world, and through that the supernatural world ... to promote human life through that communication."[119] The Midewiwin was in part reactionary, in the sense that when disease and pandemics affected a society's providers, the healing society's concerted action was needed. The Midewiwin, however, served many preventative and enhancing functions as well.

Drum and drum sticks. Birch bark song by Eshbigoga/Nanabush from Red Lake, Minnesota. Hoffman, "The Midê'wiwin," 186.

Medicine Bags

A pivotal symbol of healing in the Mide ceremonies was the medicine bag. Blessing writes that "the degree skins (Mide bags) were filled with assortments of sacred shells (megis), sacrificial tobacco, and small packets and pouches of dried roots and herbs. Informants presented two specific reasons for the dried parts of a variety of plants being included in the contents of the Mide bags; many plants have special spirit forms of a tutelary nature [as guardians, protectors] rather than a medicinal value and are carried in the bags because of their supernatural influence; actual medicines used for the curing of ailments were often carried into the Medicine Lodge in the Mide bags because the spiritual contact experienced during the rituals was believed to enhance the curing properties of the substances."[120]

Deleary describes the medicine bundle as "a living, animated object that contains our beliefs, history, identity, strength, faith, generosity, and kindness. Our bundle also contains our frustrations in the face of adversity and denial; our collected tears and sorrows as we watch continual ethnocide and warfare destroying our way of life."[121]

The Mide bags served as a spiritual housing or a storage place for medicines and guardians, but they were also "symbols or badges denoting an individual's advance in the degrees of the Mide lodge." They were of greatest significance and possessed the "ultimate in spiritual power," according to Blessing. Shaker drums, rattles, and sucking tubes of bone, copper, or brass might also be included in the bags.[122]

Birch Bark Scrolls, the Lodge, Teachings, Ceremonies

The Mide were the main keepers of Ojibwe words and cultures.[123] Birch bark scrolls depicted and directed in stylized words, pictures, and songs the complex ceremonies of the Midewiwin. For the Southwestern Ojibwe, the scroll's symbols functioned on several levels and served as visual memory aids for the performance of ceremonies. The scroll was a means of communication, guiding the celebrants to utter appropriate words and sing the customary songs. Blessing believes that the hieroglyphic line drawings on the scrolls, however, were more than a mnemonic support for songs and words; they were the initial phases of a written language, for generalizations of form were "steadily taking place and would have continued but for the arrival of the white man in North America."[124] According to Christopher Barry-Arredondo, the writings on the scrolls were the quasi-universal language of signs and were both functional and aesthetic. This picture writing was a means of communication, combining, sometimes, several ideas at once; it served as a map of the Ojibwe's political and religious universe.[125] Adept Mide practitioners did not need the scrolls for ritual performances, for they knew the songs and texts from memory; nevertheless, unopened scrolls continued to be present at ceremonies because of the spiritual powers they possessed.

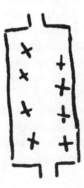

Lodge. Song by Little Frenchman: "They are sitting in a circle ('around in a row')." "Mide lodge; Mide sitting around. The crosses represent the persons present." Mallery, *Picture-Writing*, 1:242.

In addition to using picture writing, the Ojibwe began communicating by writing texts. There are documents written in Ojibwe by Southeastern Ojibwe chiefs during the period 1823 to 1910. The Anishinaabeg "used Ojibwe writing to communicate various matters to a diverse audience," Alan Corbiere writes.[126]

The spirits on stone in the petroglyphs continued the same sentiments and ideas as the birch bark pictographs. Emmanuel Desveaux writes that there is a "continuity between river bank art [petroglyphs] and birch bark scrolls. In the scrolls, the symbols support the connection of the mnemonic technique with the definite discourse, with the chant texts and the vision recitals."[127]

Fine-day/Dedate Bange/Fast Flutter of Wings suggests that song "texts" and drawings on birch bark provide music-like and earthy contexts for members of the Midewiwin; these members appear standing on a lily pad, "shouting and skipping" on a riverbank, or singing, playing, and frolicking in the woods, and relating to a snake.[128]

Midewiwin and Rock Art

The pre-eminent visual and acoustical forms of the Midewiwin are line drawings and song "texts" or representations on birch bark scrolls. We have noted, however, that representations on rock formations are quasi-equivalent in importance to those on the scrolls; or, we could conclude that one artistic medium informs another. We could also view rock art as a text or a musical score awaiting words and performance; or, in a less static way, we could assert that rock art is already a performance. Pictographs, like icons, are more than mere images; as Barry-Arredondo states, they are also a presence.[129] In *Painted Dreams: Native American Rock Art*, Thor Conway notes that "rock art comes from vision and instinct more than intellect ... [And, we may add, that it comes from sound also.] Three environments are often depicted on the rock walls: the personal, often directed inward through vision questing or the shaman's journey; the community, where rock art is part of an established sacred site; and ultimately, the intertwined landscapes of the natural world."[130]

Sah-Kah-Odjew-Wahg-Sah/Fred Pine calls the markings on rocks "true teaching," "a map for your mind," and "the path to travel in the spiritual world."[131] According to him, "rock art contains a familiar record of the dreamscape – a perception as real to aboriginal nations as that gained from the outward world." Contemporary Midewiwin followers attest that the pictograph sites in northwestern Ontario conform to Midewiwin symbols and performances.[132]

Since rock art can give directions for life, what insights might it furnish? Having examined rock art in the Great Lakes region, Guy Lanoue argues that there is a direct albeit subtle relationship between art in general and society. Symbols in art mirror society and can imply frustrated aspirations, "fundamental paradoxes," or even great hopes that may lead to incomplete actions or none at all.

Lanque notes that animals are symbolic mediators of many paradoxes that confront hunter and gatherer societies. Animals play these roles because they embody characteristics common to humans; for example, both are mobile and territorial, with some physical resemblances and similar social bonds. "It is no wonder that a strong identity develops between people and the animals they hunt and consume,"[133] he writes. Also, humans and animals are regarded as having common origins and natures. Human cultural models are often based on animal characteristics. Therefore, animals are obviously important for human survival and form a basis for bonds, including the totemic, as noted in stories, ceremonials, and artworks. Lévi-Strauss observes this affinity of humans and animals, especially in the life of birds. "[Birds] build themselves homes in which they live a family life and nurture their young; they often engage in social relations with other members of their species; and they communicate with them by acoustic means recalling articulated language." Thus, the Ojibwe think that the bird society is metaphorically or even actually a human society, and vice versa.

But animals are also different from humans. Animal lives do not intersect completely with those of humans but can exist in a parallel fashion. Specifically, birds have a relationship with humans based on many differences, including in physical characteristics. "They are feathered," Lévi-Strauss writes, "winged, oviparous and they are also physically separated from human society by the element in which it is their privilege to move."[134] Although birds' communities are independent of human associations, this very independence can mirror that of humans.

The opposing beneficial and the adversarial aspects of the Ojibwe hunt affirm the similarities and differences between humans and animals.[135] In the hunt, humans and animals benefit each other; the human benefits are obvious, but animals also benefit in that they are offered gratitude and reverence for their giving. Animals, however, can and do resist giving their lives in the hunt – an adversarial relationship. Ojibwe art reflects this paradox.

Lanoue acknowledges that most people in primal societies distinguish between "two systems of knowledge – totemism, which is designed to simultaneously rationalize and hide paradoxes of human relations, and instrumentality, which is designed to enable humans to survive."[136] Artworks by early humans echo these twin thrusts. One representation (or the same representation with two modalities) relates to the instrumentality between humans and animals and to art's attempt to influence the outcome of the hunt; the other, that of totemism, relates to the conception that animals are superior to humans. The first relationship to animals is economic, the second is social.[137]

The characteristics that humans prize in animals are chosen almost arbitrarily. Lanoue notes that early peoples were fascinated by animals for their own sakes. The Ojibwe knew the physical properties of animals but portrayed them differently in their art. It is as if these people experienced two worlds of animals: one corresponded to that of the hunter-gatherer experience; the other seemed to be more objective and corresponded to the more scientific classifications of biologists and zoologists. Thus, Ojibwe representations of animals verged on the abstract and were stylized and symbolic.[138]

Totems are paramount in Mide lives. The owl is a protector who provides shelter, food, and warm wind, even while harbouring the possibilities of being a predator and bringing death. As protector and provisioner, owl enacts a bond with humans. Although its instrumentality for survival and sharing is noted in some stories, owl can furnish, at best, only emergency food. Thus, animals such as owls become in large part symbols for the expectations of signatories and for the outcome of treaties. In a vision context, bear is the hunted, but bear also takes on trappings of the hunter. Bear is also the means to healing – mending even broken bones – and aids successful war parties and the hunt.[139] While instrumentality and totemism connect many facets of bear's personality and activities, bear eclipses these categories. Representations of bear, then, transcend the particularities of the hunt; they have an almost timeless and spaceless applicability. Such is the petroglyphic image that Dewdney and Kidd examined in Devil's Gap, near Kenora, Ontario; they conclude that this example of lithic art relates to the Mide birch bark scrolls. "The sacred bear stands above a rectangular structure beside a horned figure, who might represent a powerful Miday leader. A line leads directly to the typical drawing of a Miday lodge."[140]

 Impersonating the bear. Song scroll (with contemporary notation) from Baiedzik, Mille Lacs: "I have tried it, My body is of fire." "He likens himself to the Bear Manido, and has like power by virtue of his migis, which is shown below the lines running downward from the mouth. He is represented as standing in the Midewigan – where his feet rest." Hoffman, "The Midê'wiwin," 267–268a.

For indigenous people, and for the Ojibwe specifically, rock art provides an instrumentality and symbolism analogous to that of line drawings and songs in Midewiwin ceremonies. Humans are related to animals as hunter and hunted. This relationship, however, can be reversed: humans can become the hunted. In addition to pragmatic considerations, rock art houses symbolic dimensions that can relate to accepted human–animal origins and that are often paradoxical, social, and somewhat abstract, at least in representation.

Birch bark scrolls are specific to the Midewiwin and their cere-monies; petroglyphs and riverbank art have a broader and more public audience.[141] They are an ancient art gallery, spirits on stone, painted dreams.[142]

Bear, the "Guiding Spirit of the Midewiwin"

The salutary haven that the lodge provided for the Ojibwe was often localized in several animals, but in one especially: the bear. Sikassige of the Mille Lacs Mide from Minnesota told Hoffman that the Mide and candidates "must personate [sic] the Makwa Manido – Bear Spirit – when entering the Midewiwin."[143] Mainans narrated to Densmore similar instructions, and Densmore recorded a song about it: "The ground trem-bles / As I am about to enter / My heart fails me / As I am about to enter / The spirit lodge."[144] Fulford connects the words "bear" and "lodge" both linguistically and homophonically – the Ojibwe word for bear is *makwa*, and the word for spirit lodge or box is *makak*.[145] Thus, lodge is a symbol of the bear and bear's being carries the meaning of the lodge.

Lodge members. "They think me unworthy, My Mide brethren, But look and see, The length of my wigwam." "The oblong represents the Mide-wigan; the two larger figures are manido and the smaller ones members of the Midewiwin." Densmore, *Chippewa Music*, 1:111.

Megis/Shell

In an origin story, bear carried the gift of life or the Mide pack, including the megis shells, to the Ojibwe through the four worlds or under the water.[146] We have already noted these Mide bundles or packs and the megis shells. Shells or megis live deep within the earth, are native to salt water, and have a smooth, white upper surface and a long, narrow opening on their underside. They have been used extensively as ornaments in general and on the garb of the Mide, and as currency. To become a Mide, a candidate was required to purchase a shell.[147] Warren maintains that since megis "gave warmth and light" to the Ojibwe, it was a symbol of the Midewiwin itself. Megis played a central role in the instruction for the ascending levels of the Midewiwin.[148] The poles in the Mide lodge were sometimes partly or completely covered with dots of paint or clay imitating shells.[149] Representations of shells on song scrolls were also covered by dots or cross-hatching. Both in the scrolls and on the poles, shells carried details of the origin story. In the Midewiwin ceremony, shells or medicine sacks containing megis were shot into the initiate and then extracted from his body, for megis had life-giving and healing powers. As noted earlier, the megis or sea-shell played an important part in the origin of the Ojibwe; it reflected the geographical origins of the Ojibwe, in that it bore "reference to the shores of the ocean whence their religious doctrines and rites came to them from the East."[150] Megis also defined early human characteristics: humans were believed to have been originally covered with enamel or scales; when they shed these scales, they lost the power and protection the scales provided.[151] The otter seemed to be the main symbol for the Midewiwin in northern Minnesota, and megis was the main symbol in the southern part of that region.[152] Because we now know that bear was also a weighty symbol, we now have several symbols vying with one another in importance, or complementing one another.

Hand covered with megis. Song scroll: "I too have taken the medicine he gave us." "The speaker's arm, covered with migis, or magic influence, reaches toward the sky to receive from Kitshi Manido the divine favor of a Mide's power." Hoffman, "The Midê'wiwin," 203a, 219.

Hoffman recounts the use of megis: "The power with which it is possible to become endowed after passing through the fourth degree is expressed by the outline of a human figure ... upon which are a number of spots indicating that the body is covered with the migis or sacred shells, symbolical of the Midewiwin. These spots designate the places where the Mide priests, during the initiation, shot into his body the migis and the lines connecting them in order that all the functions of the several corresponding parts or organs of the body may be exercised."[153] Those who had been initiated in the Mide rites could accomplish great feats in contacting the dead and predicting the future. It was believed that they could read the thoughts and intentions of others and that they could cast out demons that had entered the sick.

Mide presiders and initiates acted in accordance with their powers and knowledge. The candidate was instructed in Ojibwe traditions, stories, songs, and Mide plants. He or she learned to identify and prepare various vegetable substances. Hoffman indicates that the candidate was pragmatically and systematically "taken into the woods where it is known that a specified plant or tree may be found, when a smoke offering is made before the object is pulled out of the soil, and a small pinch of tobacco put into the hole in the ground from which it was taken. This is an offering to Nokomis – the earth, the grandmother of mankind – for the benefits which are derived from her body where they were placed by Kitshi Manido."[154]

According to Ojibwe collaborator Will Rogers, shell and bear, or bear covered with shells, were responsible for the origin of the Midewiwin itself, for shells lifted this ceremony from its birthplace in the bowels of the earth and delivered it to the Ojibwe.[155] In one version of this origin story, bear pushed through several layers of earth with a cedar tree and then crossed a huge body of water to a large island. When he emerged from the water, bear was covered with Manitou-empowering shells. In another version of the origin story, the island itself was a large shell.

When bear climbed onto the island, he was then covered with shells.[156] In one of Norval Morrisseau's paintings, "Mother Earth," earth has the qualities of a woman. She is life giving and nurturing. Her breasts hang heavy with milk and her vagina is swollen, open to give birth. Her children are present: bear (representing land), sturgeon (water), and bird (air) as well as human figures. Circular forms in the painting seem to suggest a union of earth's vagina and the sun. The painting implies the interdependence of life-giving and life-sustaining forms. In another painting with the same title, "Mother Earth," Morrisseau fuses the vagina of Mother Earth (and its yellow dots covering the red shape) with the power of shell in the origin story. The fertile vaginal opening echoes the contours of the megis shell. In the painter's vision, earth and shell become the passageway through which life emerges.[157]

Contact with megis. Song by Sikassige: "The spirit is in my body, my friend." "The migis, given by Kitshi Manido, is in contact with the Mide's body, and he is possessed of life and power." Hoffman, "The Midê'wiwin," 203–203a. Fulford translates the song as "I am a spirit, my brother." "Ojibwa Picture Writing," 191.

In his juxtaposition of twenty song scrolls from White Earth, Fulford points out a salient depiction of the multiple transformations of the megis. A heart is substituted for the megis (cowrie shell) in one scroll, and heart replaces the megis in another scroll, thus indicating their similarity, at least speculatively. On another song scroll, both heart and shell are then represented by circles.[158] This association and intertwining of the scroll, ceremony, and shell are reflected in song: "I roll up the birch bark so that he may feel the migis in him (i.e., it's time for the 'shooting ceremony.')"[159]

Megis. Song scroll: "Who is it, who?" "The migis shell, the sacred emblem of the Midewiwin." Hoffman, "The Midê'wiwin," 192a, 193.

The connections among lodge, bear (and other animals), and shell are featured in the following words of songs on the scrolls that Fulford put into concordances and retranslated from Hoffman: "I unroll the birch bark scroll to perform magic." "He (i.e., the spirit) gives us the Midewiwin." "Let's eat like the bear (i.e., have a feast)." "My heart is as strong as the bear's." "When I skin the bear I promise to keep a claw for him." "The white bear is coming, spirit of my heart." "My mide spirit-brother." "My migis spirit burns (i.e., shines) for a little while." On a pictograph on Scroll A (Fulford's ordering), bear, who is a bringer of knowledge, returns to his place in the sun once his task on earth is complete.[160] Shingwauk, a Mide at Sault Ste Marie, told Henry Schoolcraft that "the Sun was formerly worshipped by the northern Indians,"[161] for the megis shell reflected its rays.

Joy. Song scroll from Baiedzik, Mille Lacs, Minnesota: "This is the way I feel, spirit." "The speaker is filled with joy at his power, the migis within him, shown by the spot upon the body, making him confident." Hoffman, "The Midê'wiwin," 244a, 261.

Ojibwe Lawrence Martin notes today that from his experience, "people who are being initiated into the Midewiwin wear a megis shell pinned to their shirt all the time, not just in ceremonies."[162]

Midewiwin and Leadership

One objective of the Midewiwin was to promote long life; another was to receive from the Manitous the power to achieve that goal. Michael Angel writes that the Grand Lodge provided an alternative way of obtaining power that did not depend on visionary experience but did not displace them, either.[163] The study and practice of Ojibwe traditions, including healing remedies, provided a solid grounding during treaty negotiations for all Ojibwe leaders, not just for the members of the Midewiwin; these Mide leaders represented all groups of Ojibwe, including Christians.

In addition to noting the healing properties of the Midewiwin ceremony, Angel highlights the spiritual and social goals, as well as the leadership roles of the rite. "In one sense, individual members of the society sought and received 'blessings' which gave them power to ensure that their well-being would be guaranteed. While individuals received special powers, the communal nature of Ojibwa society meant that these powers would normally be used to contribute to the welfare of the band in general. Thus, it was natural that individuals who had received considerable power through Midewiwin ceremonies would also be seen as people with socio-political power. It is no surprise, then, that Ojibwa political leaders such as Eshkebugechoshe (Flat Mouth) [Leech Lake, Minnesota], Pizhiki (Buffalo) [La Pointe, Wisconsin], Shingwaukonse (Little Pine) [Sault Ste Marie, Ontario], Powasang (Powassan), Mawedopanais [both from the Treaty Three area, Ontario], and Ogimauwinini [Brokenhead Reserve, Manitoba] were also high-ranking Mideg, since the survival of the community depended upon the ability of these leaders to deal with the environmental and political challenges that faced them. Many Midewiwin rituals were concerned not only with the acquisition of blessings, but also with the use of these powers for the benefit of the people as a whole."[164]

Kitagiguan/Spotted Feather: "A turn at eating and smoking, indicated by the pipe and the dish." Kohl, *Kitchi-Gami*, 292–5.

But the type of leadership exercised by Mide leaders and others was quite different from the European. As Angel states: "Rather than being based on the direction of a single individual, Anishinaabe leadership was more consensual in approach. Individuals who had received 'blessings' from the manidoog, giving them specific powers, who knew the narratives of their people, and who had lived through numerous experiences in their lifetime were generally revered as 'elders,' whom others relied on for advice when important decisions concerning the entire band had to be made. Gatherings of all those concerned were held, the participants smoked their pipes so that their thoughts would mingle with those of the manidoog, and all present were given a chance to speak, although weight was given to the opinions of the elders. As in other aspects of Anishinaabe life, religious concepts and ceremonies played an integral role in socio-political organization and leadership."[165]

Cary Miller writes of the two main sources for Ojibwe leadership in the early nineteenth century:

Charismatic individuals, who led war parties or emerged from the ranks of the Midewiwin Society, and the hereditary ogimag [chiefs, leaders]. Those who exerted the strongest influence in Anishinaabeg society were those who combined hereditary and charismatic leadership. Only ogimag from hereditary patrilineal lineages held authority to designate land usage rights and mediate disputes concerning resources. Age, spiritual authority, and chiefly medals played an important role, but were not determining factors. Yet, reputation and ability formed the basis for the degree of chiefly influence, particularly outside their home communities, and successful leadership could only be achieved through access to manidog assistance.

The scholarly characterization of charismatic leadership as aberrant, irrational, and unstable ignores the many societies that maintained orderly charismatic leadership structures over long periods of time. In societies like that of the Anishinaabeg and other Native American peoples, we must accept charismatic authority as a stabilizing institution. Charismatic avenues to leadership through the Midewiwin Society and war leadership democratized access to prestige and authority otherwise attainable only through heredity lineage. Anishinaabeg society evaluated the quality of candidates for hereditary chiefly offices according to their ability to obtain and hold charismatic offices. As a result, charismatic leadership provided stability and authority rather than chaos to Anishinaabeg governance.

As Christianity expanded into Ojibwe communities, some Ojibwe leaders sought to join the church and use its authority in a similar manner. This meant that the choice between Midewiwin and Christianity opened up a new field for the contestation of chiefly authority. Because Anishinaabe communities made no distinction between religious and political power, missionaries not only challenged the religious authorities of Anishinaabe communities, but its political authorities as well. Missionaries lived in these communities oblivious to the temporal responsibilities their claims to religious authority entailed. While charismatic leadership positions provided some individuals in the community a chance for advancement, authority, and prestige, charismatic credentials alone could not trump those of local hereditary ogimag. At least among the Ojibwe, all leaders employed ceremony, ritual and religious symbols to promote unity and enhance their authority.[166]

Michael Angel summarizes James G.E. Smith's and E.S. Rogers's thesis that the Anishinaabeg formed groups of patrilineal bands in which leadership passed to the senior male in the group. These leaders or *ogimaas* came together at different times of the year to celebrate civil and spiritual events. During the contact period, Europeans called those Ojibwe who seemed to be in charge, "chiefs." However, the

Ojibwe referent had a different significance than the European one: Ojibwe chiefs were not merely powerful as individuals; they also brought powers given them by the Manitous as well as the consensus of the Anishinaabe.[167]

For the Ojibwe, leadership took many forms. In addition to becoming guides, individuals among the Ojibwe also became supporters, defenders, and guardians of the people, their families, and their clans. Such leaders, according to Louis Bird, "were always looked up to, because they have accumulated a lot of knowledge how to survive on the land." They had a lot of "mitewiwin power" and became "automatically" advisers, decision makers, and protectors "because they have a wisdom."[168]

Shingwaukonse or Little Pine (1773–1854), from Garden River First Nation east of Sault Ste Marie, Ontario, was one of these wise leaders and a former member of the Midewiwin. He "set precedents which profoundly affected the course of Canadian Indian policy," Janet Chute writes. Between 1820 and 1840 he established links with missionary organizations and government agencies, thereby earning sympathy and respect from dynamic individuals deeply involved in Canadian nation building. Through these liaisons, Shingwaukonse ensured that Ojibwe values and organizational structures would survive in a changing world. After 1840, Shingwaukonse proved to be a principled policy maker as he mitigated the heavy-handed role of Indian Agents and attained some degree of independence and proprietorship for the Ojibwe over resources on Aboriginal lands. He did not act alone, however; he rallied the support of other Aboriginal leaders, maintaining "reciprocal responsibility" with his followers, Chute remarks.

After 1845, when discoveries of copper, iron, gold, and silver made Native-designated lands the richest for mining in the Canadian West, Shingwaukonse hoped that his people would reap rewards from these. He could be stalwart against "developers," as evidenced by his people's takeover of the Mica Bay mine in 1849. His approach, though, was even-tempered; he was not against resource exploration and development, but he wanted a fair share for his community. In addition, he sought to preserve Ojibwe community structures; he had been involved in the Midewiwin and remembered the values it espoused. But at the same time, he was not a rigid traditionalist: he welcomed cooperative ventures to meet new economic and political challenges, even while demanding a voice for his people in the regulation of logging, fishing, and mining. All in all, Shingwaukonse was shrewd, calculating, and far-sighted. He remained faithful to traditional group norms and values while recognizing that present-day challenges demanded new responses.[169] Chute concludes: "For almost a century and a half, Shingwaukonse's goals inspired decision-making in the Sault region for the collective past as well as for the present."[170]

Although Shingwaukonse seemed to act as an individual leader, he really acted in concert with his community and with a sensitivity to past ideals. Leadership needed to be exercised with regard to the "developers of resources" but also with regard to formalized relationships with relatively new governments. An examination of treaty consultations, negotiations, and signings will offer us insights into the types of Ojibwe leadership.

Practitioners of the Midewiwin were prominent leaders in their communities. Midewiwin members gathered knowledge over a lifetime; they were advisers and decision makers.[171] At least two of the signatories to Treaty Three in Ontario and Manitoba were Mide. Most of the negotiators and signatories to the treaties in the Great Lakes region were from the bear clan/totem, who inhabited the region encompassing Cass Lake, Leech Lake, and Lake Winnipeg. As early as 1671, Pierre Gaultier de Varennes, Sieur de La Verendrye, had noted charismatic Ojibwe leaders who resided at Sault Ste Marie just east of Rainy Lake; according to Joan Lovisek, those leaders had achieved ascendancy through hereditary descent and totemic association. Midewiwin members were signatories to the Selkirk Treaty of 1817 and the Robinson Treaty of 1850; they were "the acknowledged war chiefs and warriors of the tribe, and [were] keepers of the war-pipe and war club, and [were] often denominated the bulwarks of the tribe against their enemies."[172]

Ceremonial pipe. Song scroll. "I wish to smoke." "The pipe used is that furnished by the promoter or originator of the war party, termed a 'partisan.' The Mide is in full accord with the work undertaken and desires to join, signifying his wish by desiring to smoke with the braves." Hoffman, "The Midê'wiwin," 228a, 240. Fulford translates the song scroll as "He hides from me." "Ojibwa Picture Writing," 195.

Midewiwin leaders exerted great influence in their communities and in external affairs. According to Lovisek, "although the political organization of the Boundary Waters Ojibwa is reflected in the documents through personal characteristics, military skill, hereditary and totemic association, during the early 19th century, a close link developed between religion and politics manifested through participation in the Midewiwin or Grand Medicine Society. The Boundary Waters region, particularly along the Rainy River, became the centre for mide-wiwin and other aboriginal practices in the 19th century."[173] "There is a Midewiwin connection to almost all of the historically identified leaders present at Treaty #3 negotiations."[174]

After 1840 the Mide used its power to enforce authority in civic and foreign matters. Ojibwe spiritual ceremonies and political meetings, often on a large scale, became closely linked. These ceremonies were appealing because they displayed charismatic leadership and ritual and oratorical finesse. While the Ojibwe continued to make decisions in a consensual way, influence through rank also became acceptable in this egalitarian society.[175] Mawedopenais, a prominent Mide civil chief who was closely associated with the general rejection of Christianity, became the principal spokesperson and negotiator for Treaty Three. Another leader who spoke during the negotiations was Chief Sakatcheway. The first signatory to this treaty, Lovisek writes, was a very aged hereditary chief, Kektapaypinais, "a Rainy River chief whose role in the negotiations appears to have been one of traditional status through age and descent."[176]

The Midewiwin mixed politics and religion. Its members leveraged their status to achieve goals both for themselves and for their society. As noted earlier, Midewiwin medicine and healing offered not only cures for diseases but also preventative measures to ensure a wholesome life for individuals and for the community. Healing also addressed moral and spiritual concerns, as we will outline in our discussion of four nineteenth-century Ojibwe leaders. Lodge members who had received many blessings recounted how those blessings were used to bring about the prosperity of the entire people. Extending this holistic advantage even further, the Manitous empowered members of the Midewiwin to take on various roles in the community, including social and political leadership roles. As problems arose that threatened Ojibwe survival – the scarcity of fur-bearing animals, the encroachment of settlers, the waning of autonomy as a result of treaties – Midewiwin members emerged among the recognized leaders.[177]

Prior to the signing of treaties in the nineteenth century, Ojibwe leaders represented the sum of Ojibwe performances and beliefs. They carried in their consciousness the presence and power of animals, which were felt especially in the lodge ceremonies. The values represented by these animals were in the leaders' thoughts and hearts as they negotiated and signed treaties with Europeans. These leaders brought their own charisma and therefore much diversity, but they also represented traditional values and practices. The Midewiwin leaders conveyed a certain exclusivity, for they were explicitly carriers of Ojibwe identity; they were among the ones who made it a point to understand their history. Although attunement to the Manitous was based on individual visions, the Midewiwin represented an additional social approach through its cultural performances.[178]

Let us summarize this chapter on the Midewiwin. Among the nineteenth-century Ojibwe, the various heritages of the Midewiwin were both respected and feared, for they could harness powerful spirits either for good or for evil. But in general, their purpose was to ensure the well-being of the Ojibwe. Membership in the Grand Medicine Society was open to both men and women, and various animals typified its ascending levels.

Those who rely mainly on written sources claim that the Midewiwin arose as a response to contact with Europeans, as a means to marshal all Ojibwe resources to deal with radical changes in their societies. Other critics, relying mainly on oral sources, contend that the Medicine Society pre-dated European contact. Archaeological digs and carbon dating of ceremonial artefacts support their claims.

Ojibwe stories offer varying accounts of the origins of the Midewiwin. Many animals, the trickster Nanabush, and men and women both young and old helped bring this healing regimen to the people. Mide performances were determined in part by cosmic orderings, the sun, the four winds, and dreams; the stagings, songs, and traditions of those performances were founded in part on the phases of Ojibwe migrations to the West. The purpose and design of the lodge stemmed from the Great Spirit who ordered the cosmos through laws and directives. Ojibwe leaders, who were often members of the Midewiwin, strove to honour these directives during treaty negotiations.

Related to but not identical with the Midewiwin were the Wabeno and Jessakkid. These movements also involved service to the people but focused more on individual visions and prowess than the Midewiwin. In the Wabeno and Jessakkid movements and in the Midewiwin, there was a preoccupation with *bimaadiziwin* – that is, with health, with cures for diseases through the use of plants, and with a holistic approach to a prolonged life. Thus the Mide served many functions, from medicine to memory and from the prevention of maladies to the enhancing of health. Mide ceremonial bags were symbols of that healing: these animal-skin bags housed specific animal spirits and signified a member's status in this medicine society. Birch bark scrolls, believed to be on the way to a written language, were a practical mnemonic tool indicating specific performance songs and words. These scrolls were also the presence of spiritual forces and teachings.

Overcoming death. Song scroll (with contemporary notation) from Baiedzik, Mille Lacs: "My migis spirit. I overpower death with." "His body is covered with migis as shown by the short lines radiating from the sides, and by this power he is enabled to overcome death." Hoffman, "The Midê'wiwin," 268–268a.

Rock formations were somewhat similar in importance to Mide birch bark scrolls. Both were the homes of spirits. The hopes and frustrations of Ojibwe society were mirrored in rock art. Animals were the predominant lithic representations since there was a similarity between humans and animals (as well as differences). Some representations commanded economic benefits through the hunt, while others symbolized social and totemic values in quasi-abstract forms.

Bear loomed large in daily and ceremonial life. In fact, there was a near identity of bear with the lodge, and of bear with the Ojibwe. Bear was a guiding spirit throughout life and into death.

Another important part of the Midewiwin ceremonial was the megis or shell, which was shot into the candidate. It was a symbol of origins along water routes, for it arose from the water and shone, giving warmth and light. Indeed, the Mide was believed to have originated from these shells.

European leadership was largely compartmentalized; by contrast, Ojibwe leadership – especially that which emanated from the Midewiwin – fused religious, political, and social elements. The Midewiwin had a formative influence on Ojibwe leaders, as did stories, songs, and rock art. Requirements for leaders were varied. Although some involved hereditary claims, charisma and demonstrated ability were predominant.

Spirited power. Song scroll: "I hear the spirit speaking to us." "The Mide-singer is of superior power, as designated by the horns and pointer upon his head. The lines from the ear indicate hearing." Mallery, *Picture-Writing*, 1:238.

The Grand Medicine Society (Midewiwin) was important in Ojibwe cultures, although it often was (and still is) a mysterious and taboo subject. There are several accounts of its origins, all of which, however, involve the Great Spirit bringing healing and ordering to the people. The Midewiwin became an encompassing context for understanding how cosmic forces such as megis shells, elements of nature, and dream songs together ensured wholesome living. During Midewiwin performances, bear was a guide for right living, a guardian of the portals to spiritual power, and a companion to the the cosmic Manitous. Women were included in Midewiwin ceremonies, where they merited respect. In some stories, the ambivalent figure, Nanabush, using animals as volunteers, carried the Midewiwin from the Great Spirit to the Ojibwe. Other Ojibwe stories intertwined Nanabush's activities with those of bear.

The Midewiwin became the focus of many Ojibwe cultures. It outlined a spiritual direction for living and dying. It also served as a keeper of tribal history, especially of Ojibwe migrations. With bear clans leading the way, the Midewiwin functioned as a keeper of cultural knowledge and records. Mide members celebrated important events, were keepers of medical tradition and practice, acted as judges, and provided moral instruction. Bear was the leader for many Midewiwin tasks, particularly those of policing and ordering (e.g., guarding the doorways to the Midewiwin lodge) and of healing, health being essential in a hunter society.

During Midewiwin lodge performances, the water drum stood in for the Creator's heart, which through its rhythmic pulsations kept human hearts beating and transformed them. The medicine bundle/bag served as a guardian against harm and carried the people's hopes and trials.

In the Midewiwin lodge, song scrolls as visual aids and Manitou presence furnished directives for each performance's ascending degrees. Among other things, those directives provided incentives to moderate living, encouraged reverence for the spirits, protected people from harm, and enjoined them to be considerate of others. Bear personified the lodge itself and was its pre-eminent salutary animal. In fact, bear became a transcendent symbol of the people themselves: both bear and Ojibwe walked as bears on "bear's path" within and outside the lodge, hibernating in the winter and emerging with new life in the spring.

Bears were often allied with the ceremony's megis shells. In line drawings, bear is covered with shells, and it is bear that provides protection, enables contact with the dead, predicts the future, reads others' thoughts, and casts out demons.

Since members of the Midewiwin and the bear clan played many leadership roles in their communities, they often acted on behalf of their communities when it came to, for example, negotiating and signing treaties. Empowered by Manitous and the consensus of the Ojibwe, these members represented the sum of Ojibwe traditional values, which were often expressed in this somewhat exclusive Midewiwin context.

2

"Paths of the Spirit": Moral Values in the Writings of Four Nineteenth-Century Ojibwe in the Spirit of the Midewiwin

From an examination of the Ojibwe Medicine Society, we learn about the meaning and value of life both for individuals and for communities. The society's lodge was open to the sky, to specific seasons of the year, and to the winds; songs, words, and events revealed the proper ways to think and act. In the lodge performances, the world was a kindred being to humans; the world gave to and beckoned humans. In the Medicine Lodge ceremonies, however, humans were not alone; there was a symbiosis of humans and animals, who shared the same space; at many times and in many ways, humans and animals were inter-beings, in near identity with each other. What the cosmos and its animals spoke and how they acted were important for the Ojibwe. The world and animals disclosed norms and principles for living long and healthy lives, individually and communally. Since the world and animals were so important, nineteenth-century Ojibwe listened to them and sought their images and voices in dreams and in vision and sound quests; they also crafted these images and voices on many items, such as bags, utensils, knife sheaths, moccasins, and rocks.

"Medicine Lodge. The lodge is represented with men in it; the dots above indicate the number of days." Copway, *Traditional History*, 135, 137.

The content of Mide teaching during the ceremonials indicated the values the Ojibwe espoused. On the basis of scrolls, teachers recalled the history of the Midewiwin. "The candidates were informed that the Medicine Lodge represented the house of the Great Spirit and that the

Great Spirit was omnipresent in the universe," Blessing states. "It was taught that if one walked the right path that led through the home of the Great Spirit he would have a good life."[1] In each of the four ascending degrees of the Midewiwin, there were specific exhortations and directives. In the first degree, for instance, the "candidate is exhorted ... to cast aside temptations and live moderately. He is taught that reverence of the Great Spirit and consideration of others is expected of him. His reward will be an extended life."[2]

We will be using a wide lens to examine Ojibwe cultural ways in order to find directives for right living; to this end, we will focus on the evidence provided for moral rectitude by four Ojibwe writers in the early and mid-nineteenth century in the Great Lakes region. These Aboriginal writers had been influenced by Christianity and espoused a post-European Christianity and Canadian–American ways; nevertheless, they retained indigenous roots and values. Our exploration examines the moral values that were in the minds and hearts of Ojibwe leaders and of their peoples in general. (In a later volume we will explore these moral values in the minds and hearts of nineteenth-century treaty negotiators and signatories.) Many of these values were embedded in their Medicine Society and reflected a general Ojibwe orientation: *bimaadiziwin*, a healthy and good life. We will seek to develop a perspective on moral orientations from the Aboriginal side, from primary sources and tribal memories.

Peter Jones: Like the "Red Squirrel" Who Stores Nuts, Store Works of the Great Spirit

Peter Jones/Kahkewaquonaby/Sacred Feathers (1802–1856) wrote extensively about his personal vision quest,[3] which led to his embrace of Methodism.[4] While he did not use the term Midewiwin explicitly in his writings, he recounted many feasts as well as the activities of learned "powwows" who were spiritual practitioners. He noted that there were general councils for peace and friendship, for making and renewing treaties, and for establishing boundaries, all of which involved peace pipes and council fires; these pipe and fire councils, he thought, were derived from the Oneida, for he had observed them during his residence among the Mohawk. Among his own peoples, he encountered a medicine society in each tribe, comprising men and women, "an order of priesthood consulted and employed in all times of sickness ... [who perform] extraordinary cures, either by the application of roots and herbs, or by incantations." He was amazed by the variety of medicines and their efficacy; "Indian doctors" were on occasion more effective than "regular physicians."[5]

Jones, a long-time Methodist missionary, sometimes ridiculed his previous Indian beliefs, such as the ones that linked the thunderers with rains and storms, and the "sacrifice [made] to the god of the waters."[6] Although he wrote a description of the Mide lodge and the role of "an order of priesthood," and noted the activities of the powwows or medicine men in treating sickness, he seemed not to accept traditional Ojibwe views.[7] Yet he did not unequivocally embrace Christian Methodism. While he espoused a European/Canadian Methodism, for he found a personal resonance and benefit in it, he also worked for indigenous causes and did not abandon his Ojibwe roots. In his writings he indicates that he adopted a pragmatic position between his Native ancestry and Methodism.

The benefits of Christianity were obvious to Jones, and so was the need to embrace some aspects of Western culture and technology. But he was selective in this and was suspicious about Western religion, science, and technology, for he was well aware of Westerners' ruthless commercial spirit, which manifested itself especially in the blight that alcohol had brought to the Indians. He was well aware, also, of the destructive example of lax Christians and of the ruin caused by drunkenness, blasphemy, and deception. He wrote in his *History*: "The diseases most common among the aborigines of America before the landing of the Europeans were few, in comparison with those now debilitating their constitutions, and so rapidly thinning their numbers."[8]

Jones's suspicions about Western civilization were hardly unique to him; they were pervasive among Aboriginal women. Many Indian women looked askance at the colonizing culture and compared it unfavourably with their own. They preferred to wear customary clothing, unlike the men, who were happy to dress in Western garb; also, they often preferred their Native spirituality and its practices.[9] In *Countering Colonization: Native American Women and Great Lakes Missions, 1630–1900,* Carol Devens writes that Indian women in the Upper Great Lakes region were rigid when it came to shaping their encounters with Europeans. While many Indian men readily adopted the trappings of Western culture, these women endured torture and hardships in defence of their lifeways. They refused to wear non-Indian dresses, "generally did not participate in prayer sessions," and were reluctant to accept girls' schools. Indian men routinely regarded school education, European languages, and conversion to Christianity as advantageous; Indian women often considered these things a threat to their autonomy and prestige.[10]

A female "empowered to cure with magic plants." Chart from Red Lake. Hoffman, "Pictography," 216–17.

During and after the fur trade, Jacqueline Peterson writes, "Indian women and their métis daughters after them played key economic roles as provisioners, fur dressers, moccasin and snowshoe makers, canoe and lodge builders, as well as occasional hunters, guides, transporters, diplomatic agents, spies, and traders ... [They] served as cultural and often political liaisons between their male kin and Euro-American husbands. Teachers, advisers, and interpreters, they helped to set the norms of an emerging society."[11]

Although Jones did not provide a catalogue of precepts, we will examine his writings in order to compile some of his moral directives. These are of two types: some are Methodist in formulation, and others seem to be more Ojibwe in character. Among the latter is the following, from his *History of the Ojebway Indian:* "In their heathen state they very seldom cut down green or living trees, from the idea that it puts them to pain; and some of the pow-wows have pretended to hear the wailing of the forest trees when suffering under the operation of the hatchet or axe."[12] While Jones was not against the use of trees, the "heathens" – that is, the Ojibwe – had clear views about their abuse.

Jones's Ojibwe character was also evident in his preaching; his moral precepts blended past Ojibwe values with contemporary Christian ones. He preached so that his Indians could receive the benefits of the whites. He was a man of action, and his prayers were always short; he wanted to construct a better Indian culture, one that the Ojibwe could control and that would encompass essential ingredients of their past way of life.[13]

His autobiography, a conversion narrative, is a mosaic of his struggles and includes many cultural negotiations and questions and answers, as well as a tally of his successes and failures. For him, authentic Christianity was not wrapped in European clothes; it was not a way of assimilation but a new mode of survival. Christian teaching was not coterminous with European civilization but rather preceded it.

Jones's first moral orientation was rooted in his traditions; his second flowed from his Methodism. Many of the practices propounded by the Methodism he had adopted made sense to the Ojibwe people: caring for the sick, building schools, obeying the Creator, and doing good works. All of these activities reflected a certain pragmatism, a survival strategy, but they were also a bridge to the future. Methodism resembled Ojibwe ethics, and conversely, Ojibwe culture resembled the Christian one, for both counselled human service, fasting, and vision quests (such as those practised by Moses and Jesus).

Jones' moral project was selective. Regarding the Ten Commandments, he accepted the second tablet, which emphasized human service, rather than the first, which emphasized monotheism. Because white people often failed to observe the Commandments, he called them heathen and wicked, reversing the usual name calling. He blended the moral wisdom of Native and Newcomer, savouring the best of both, and produced a comprehensible faith.

Communing. Song scroll: "We are talking to one another." "The Mide communes with Kitshi Manido; he is shown near the sky, his horns denoting superior wisdom and power, while the lines from the mouth signify speech." Hoffman, "The Midê'wiwin," 203a, 209.

There were some Methodist precepts that did not directly contradict Ojibwe rules of behaviour, though neither were they clearly part of Ojibwe traditions. John Wesley's eighteenth-century revival of faith within the Anglican communion had laid out a methodical, disciplined path, a series of rules and behaviours to which strict adherence was demanded. In "Advice to the People Called Methodists," Wesley had stated: "[Make] it a rule to abstain from fashionable diversions, from reading plays, romances, or books of humour, from singing innocent songs, or talking in a merry, gay, diverting manner; your plainness of dress; your manner of dealing in trade; your exactness in observing the Lord's day; your scrupulosity as to things that have not paid custom; your total abstinence from spirituous liquors (unless in cases of necessity); your rule 'not to mention the fault of an absent person, in particular of Ministers or of those in authority' ... With respect, therefore, both to your name, principles, and practice, you may be considered as a new people."[14] Here was an appealing moral system that sanctioned social and financial controls[15] and that accorded the leadership Peter Jones and his brother John felt they needed in order to deal effectively with other missionaries, with settlers around the Credit River, Ontario, and beyond, and with the federal Indian Department. This form of methodical Christianity was necessary to a settled way of life, Jones believed, for now it was "the Son of the Great Spirit who protected them from freezing, disease, and starvation just as the Indians' guardian spirits once did."[16] The hymns composed by Wesley's brother Charles taught noble values – right dealing, honesty, general uprightness – that the Mississauga Indians had also learned from childhood. Jones had not witnessed this rigorous moral approach among the Roman Catholics.[17]

Other aspects of Methodism attracted Jones. He admired the fervour of its practitioners, their zeal and community spirit. They often worshipped near their dwellings and on hillsides, not in stodgy, hierarchically laid-out churches. It is no accident, then, that Jones embraced this earlier form of Methodism.[18]

Even so, Jones retained many external signs of his Indianness: he treasured the eagle feathers that Chief Wahbanosay had given him at his naming feast as well as his decorated buckskin suit and his shot bag[19] with its eagle totem. He believed that many Ojibwe medicines were superior to European ones. And he retained various internal Ojibwe-like dispositions, including moral orientations: before beginning his translations of the Bible into Ojibwe, he fasted; he loaned money liberally to Indians in need; he made business arrangements by word of mouth; he accorded freedom to his children to make decisions, much to the consternation of his English-born wife. An Indian identity remained.[20] But it was a new identity, a symbiosis of two different traditions. Was this a new Ojibwe moral theology, an amalgam of Ojibwe and Methodist traditions? Was Jones proposing an Ojibwe liberation theology, a liberation from colonialist impositions? His was a creative response to crises in which a new form of Christianity was born. As James Axtell writes: "Christianity (and its attendant culture) offered answers to their [Native Americans'] most urgent questions, balm to their frayed emotions, and techniques of prediction and control to replace those they had lost."[21]

In his *Life and Journals*, Jones borrowed an image from another successful Indian preacher, John Sunday, who urged his Indian Christians to be a red squirrel who wisely provides food for the winter. Christians should store works of the Great Spirit, thus imitating the red squirrel, which gathers nuts from any source – a task Jones fulfilled both personally and collectively.[22] In his life and beliefs, Jones had a clear attachment to Christianity. But this was coupled with some degree of detachment and independence from Christianity, with at least some unconscious adherence to past Ojibwe values and observances. According to Karl Hele, "Sault-region Anishinabeg, while nominally Christian by the mid-nineteenth century, perceived their conversions and Christianity from within their cultural framework."[23] As a missionary, however, Jones seemed to regard himself as more than a nominal Christian. According to Catherine Stoehr, he was one of the Methodist missionaries who "adopted Christianity as new wisdom suitable for refitting their existing cultural traditions to a changed cultural environment ... Methodist teachings ... promoted *bimadziwin*, or health and long life, for their communities ... Many Anishinabe people believed that the basic moral injunctions of their own traditions compelled them to adopt Methodism because of its potential to promote *bimadziwin*."[24]

Andrew J. Blackbird: "The Great Spirit is looking upon thee continually"

Andrew J. Blackbird/Macketebenessy (1810–1908),[25] who had two identities, Chippewa and Odawa,[26] gave an account "of the Indians who formerly occupied the straits of Mackinac and Mackinac Island" and of others he encountered during his travels in Michigan and around Fort William.[27] In *History of the Ottawa and Chippewa Indians of Michigan*, Blackbird described a medicine society and its code of conduct. He did not provide specific descriptions of the lodge, its song and ceremonial scrolls, and its initiation ceremonies; but he did write about decision-making councils, song and dance gatherings, and the retention of oral cultural records; and he often recounted his communings with animals.[28] He wrote that besides parental and other personal guides in the moral formation of children, there was an "Instructor of the Precepts" at every feast and council both for the council itself and for the people in general.[29] The history of the Grand Councils and of his people, however, was in danger of vanishing from memory, along with the practices attached to it; hence, he wrote his personalized *History* to remind readers of the values of past times and as a code of conduct. His expectations for normative action were based on his reminiscences as well as on practical education to ensure that Indians "have equal rights and privileges with American Citizens ... We must educate! We must educate!! or sink into the vortex of destruction. We are like minerals covered in the dust of ignorance and superstition, and we shall remain there ... unless a different course shall be pursued."[30]

Blackbird descended into poverty as a consequence of his educational pursuits, and died in a white man's home for the aged. But before then, from the beginning, he promoted a clear agenda of cultural independence: "When the white man took every foot of my inheritance, he thought to him [*sic*] I should be the slave. Ah, never, never! I would sooner plunge the dagger into my beating heart and follow the footsteps of my forefathers, than be slave to the white man."[31]

Blackbird wrote poetically of a yearly custom in the spring to put winter garments on a long pole during "festivals and jubilees to the Great Spirit." The purpose of this festival was to implore the Great Spirit to have compassion "on his red children."[32] "The worship of the Great Spirit consisted mostly in songs and dancing accompanied with an Indian drum, which has a very deep and solemn sound ... I used to think that the sound of it must reach to the heaven where the Great Spirit is."[33] He wrote of the spring celebrations at Arbre Croche, Michigan, a "prolonged merriment and another feasting of the dead and peace offerings. Grand medicine dances, fire dances, and many other jubilant performances my people would have before they would go to work again to plant their corn."[34]

Drummers. "At the sound of the drum all the Mide rise and become inspired, because Kitshi Manido is then present in the wigiwam." Hoffman, "The Midê'wiwin," 185.

In his attempt to bestow a proper memory on his people, Blackbird undertook a historical moral retrieval by searching for their ancestry "towards the west, even as far as to the Rocky Mountain." There, the Ottawa took "prisoners of war," later adopting them. He singled out this "underground race of people" for "their exploits and bravery" and for "being great hunters" and "best counselors, best chieftains and best warriors."[35]

In Blackbird's account of the genesis of Aboriginal morality, the Ottawa nation was "always considered the oldest and most expert on the warpath and wise councilors [*sic*]." Such a reputation among fellow Algonquians[36] made them arbiters of disputes since "every tribe of Indians far and near ... deposited their pipe of peace with the head chief of the Ottawa nation as a pledge of continual peace and friendship." Their ancestral "symbolical ensign," a small hawk, Pepegwen, empowered them "in a grand council" to review cases, ascertain causes of disputes, effect "reconciliation," and thereby ensure friendly relations.[37]

In chapter 14 of his *History*, Blackbird enumerates "twenty-one precepts or moral commandments of the Ottawa and Chippewa Indians, by which they were governed in their primitive state, before they came in contact with white races in their country." His knowledge of and belief in the Ten Commandments[38] with its "thees" and "thous" is apparent. Blackbird was a Roman Catholic and then a Protestant, but he granted equal if not pre-eminent importance to his ancestral heritage.

Blackbird's twenty-one "uncivilized precepts"[39] follow. That is more than double the number of commandments tabled in the Decalogue of Moses:[40]

> 1st. Thou shalt fear the Great Creator, who is the over ruler of all things.

Blackbird notes that the "moral commandments" taught were akin to the Decalogue, except for the sabbath observance.[41] The author and ruler of all is the Great Creator.

> 2d. Thou shalt not commit any crime, either by night or by day, or in a covered place: for the Great Spirit is looking upon thee always, and thy crime shall be manifested in time, thou knowest not when, which shall be to thy disgrace and shame.
> 3d. Look up to the skies often, by day and by night, and see the sun, moon and stars which shineth in the firmament, and think that the Great Spirit is looking upon thee continually.

Comments that Blackbird makes in his *History* are relevant to Precepts Two and Three. The "eye of this Great Being" is the sun and moon, and therefore "God or the Great Spirit sees all things everywhere, night and day ... Even the very threshold or crevice of your wigwam will be a witness against you, if you should commit any criminal action when no human eye could observe your criminal doings."[42]

There are "certain deities all over the lands who to a certain extent govern or preside over certain places ... over this river, over this lake, or this mountain, or island, or country."[43] Celestial bodies are the visual organs of the Great Spirit. Things – the threshold or the crevice of a wigwam – are standards and witnesses to right and wrong conduct even when there are no human witnesses.

Mide on a mountain. Song scroll. "There is a mountain, there is a mountain. There is a mountain, my friends." "The upright outline represents a mountain upon which a powerful Mide is seated, symbolical of the distinction attained by a Mide." "The Midê'wiwin," 238a, 250. Fulford translates the song scroll as "There is a mountain, my brother." "Ojibwa Picture Writing," 196.

4th. Thou shalt not mimic or mock the thunders of the cloud, for they were specially created to water the earth and to keep down all the evil monsters that are under the earth, which would eat up and devour the inhabitants of the earth if they were set at liberty.

This precept follows from the authority and omnipresence of the Great Spirit and echoes Odawa and Chippewa traditions. One group of cosmic spirits, the thunderers, has special power both to nurture the earth and to restrain the ravishing appetites of the second class of cosmic spirits, the underwater creatures. These cosmic spirits exist in addition to the Great Spirit.

5th. Thou shalt not mimic or mock any mountains or rivers, or any prominent formation of the earth, for it is the habitation of some deity or spirit of the earth, and thy life shall be continually in hazard if thou shouldst provoke the anger of these deities.

Blackbird's *History* contains many sentiments of love and reverence for the land in general and for specific spirits who dwell on it. "O my destiny, my destiny! How sinks my heart, as I behold my inheritance all in ruins and desolation. Yes, desolation; the land the Great Spirit has given us in which to live, to roam, to hunt, and build our council fires, is no more to behold. Where once so many brave Algonquins and the daughters of the forest danced with joy, danced with gratitude to the Great Spirit for their homes, they are no more seen. Our forests are gone, and our game is destroyed ... O, my father, thou hast taught me from my infancy to love this land of my birth; thou hast even taught me to say that 'it is the gift of the Great Spirit,' when yet my beloved mother clasped me close to her peaceful breast while she sang of the warlike deeds of the great Algonquins. O, my father, our happiest days are o'er, and never again shall we enjoy our forest home. The eagle's eye could not even discover where once stood thy wigwam and thy peaceful council fire."[44]

6th. Honor thy father and thy mother, that thy days may be long upon the land.

7th. Honor the gray-head persons, that thy head may also be like unto theirs.

8th. Thou shalt not mimic or ridicule the cripple, the lame, or deformed, for thou shall be crippled thyself like unto them if thou shouldst provoke the Great Spirit.

9th. Hold thy peace, and answer not back, when thy father or thy mother or any aged person should chastise thee for thy wrong.

10th. Thou shalt never tell a falsehood to thy parents, nor to thy neighbors, but be always upright in thy words and in thy dealings with thy neighbors.

11th. Thou shalt not steal anything from thy neighbor, nor covet anything that is his.

12th. Thou shalt always feed the hungry and the stranger.

White-haired spirit. Song scroll: "They have taken pity on me, The white-haired ones." "One of the white-haired Mide spirits." Densmore, *Chippewa Music*, 1:60.

Precepts Six to Twelve extend the Decalogue's "honour" beyond parents to encompass the aged and wise; these commands foster respect for specially challenged people and advocate peaceful listening and truthfulness. They are universal Golden Rules that provide reciprocal recompense to the practitioner. "And we always rested in perfect safety at night in our dwellings, and the doorways of our lodges had no fastenings to them ... But we were not afraid for any such thing to happen us [sic], because we knew that every child of the forest was observing and living under the precepts which their forefathers taught them, and the children were taught almost daily by their parents from infancy unto manhood and womanhood ... [The Ottawas and Chippewas] were strictly honest and upright in their dealings with their fellow-beings. Their word of promise was as good as a promissory note, even better ... This was formerly the character of the Ottawa and Chippewa Indians of Michigan. But now, our living is altogether different."[45]

> 13th. Thou shalt keep away from licentiousness and all other lascivious habits, nor utter indecent language before thy neighbor and the stranger.

Blackbird recounts: "I never heard any boy or any grown person utter any bad language, even if they were out of patience with anything. Swearing or profanity [was] not even found in their language." One of the drawbacks to learning the English language and culture, according to Blackbird, was that "every one of the little Indian urchins" learned profanity "like the white children." For Blackbird, something has obviously been lost in the history of his people, and therefore, records "of their ancient legends and their traditions" should be preserved.[46] In chapters 9 and 10 of his *History*, he engages in this preservation by including stories of Nenawbozhoo and the Odawa/Chippewa traditions.   ·

> 14th. Thou shalt not commit murder while thou art in dispute with thy neighbor, unless it be whilst on the warpath.
> 15th. Thou shalt chastise thy children with the rod whilst they are in thy power.

Precept Fifteen is more in accord with the Hebrew book of Proverbs – "Spare the rod and spoil the child" – than with general directives of non-interference in the raising of children that Ojibwe such as Peter Jones, for instance, practised.[47]

16th. Thou shalt disfigure thy face with charcoals, and fast at least ten days or more of each year, whilst thou are yet young, or before thou reachest twenty, that thou mayest dream of thy future destiny.

17th. Thou shalt immerse thy body into the lake or river at least ten days in succession in the early part of the spring of the year, that thy body may be strong and swift of foot to chase the game and on the warpath.

18th. At certain times with thy wife or thy daughters, thou shalt clean out thy fireplaces and make thyself a new fire with thy fire-sticks for the sake of thyself and for the sake of thy children's health.

19th. Thou shalt not eat with thy wife and daughters at such time, of food cooked on a new fire, but they shall be provided with a separate kettle and cook their victuals therein with an old fire and out of their wigwam, until the time is passed, then thou shalt eat with them.

In Precept Nineteen, Blackbird refers to two specific pages of Elias Boudinot's book, *A Star in the West*.[48] In this and in an earlier work, Boudinot – a political leader of the American Revolution and an apocalyptic Episcopalian – contended that Indian languages, traditions, and customs were similar to the Mosaic law with its attendant religious beliefs and practices. This likeness pointed Boudinot toward the conclusion that the Indians were one of the ten lost tribes of Israel. The conversion of the Indians and Jews to Christianity would mark the end of the world, he prophesied.

The specific parallel that Boudinot and Blackbird highlighted in the Hebraic and Indian religions was the Feast of Harvest. In both traditions there is an end to the old and a beginning of the new. The old, whether grain or clothes, is collected and burned; houses, hearths, and wigwams are cleansed, and even the old fire is extinguished to make a clean break with the past. For three days there is abstinence "from food and passion," and a general amnesty is proclaimed. In both Hebrew and Ojibwe rituals, a new fire is kindled by rubbing dry sticks together, which produces a pure flame; new corn and fresh fruits are shared with all. As the inhabitants don new clothes, they rejoice, dance, and sing.[49]

Feasting. Song scroll: "They are feasting with me, The outside medicine-bag, You are the spirit, You will be called." "This drawing suggests the square bag used by the Chippewa for storing and carrying rice." Densmore, *Chippewa Music*, 1:114.

Regarding Precept Eighteen, it is unclear what causal links there are between cleansed fireplaces, a new fire, and better health conditions. In his *History of the Ojibway People,* William Warren mentions this cleansing practice: "if a person died of some virulent disease, his clothing, the barks that covered his lodge, and even the poles that framed it, were destroyed by fire."[50] Is this an oblique reference to the invasion of pestilence and hence to drastic means to prevent or curtail it through yearly purgings? It is also unclear why a husband would prohibit his wife and daughters from cooking and eating from the new fire until a certain time has passed. Is this an Indian taboo the purpose of which is to preserve past or present values? Is it a gloss on Boudinot's teaching? Is it a prohibition involving menopause?

What expectations is Blackbird implicitly voicing in Precepts Eighteen and Nineteen, which advocate revitalization? A revival of his people's traditions and land holdings? A new life in the land of the spirits? A New Jerusalem? A new Little Traverse? A return to an earlier idyllic morality? In another section of the *History,* he writes: "I thought my people were very happy in those days, when they were all by themselves and possessed a wide spread of land, and no one to quarrel with them as to where they should make their gardens, or take timber, or make sugar. And fishes of all kinds were so plentiful in the Harbor [Harbor Springs]. A hook anywheres in the bay, and at any time of the year, would catch Mackinaw trout, many as one would want. And if a net were set anywheres in the harbor on shallow water, in the morning it would be loaded with fishes of all kinds. Truly this was a beautiful location for the mission. Every big council of the Indians was transacted in the village of Little Traverse."[51]

These prohibitions and purgings have some parallels with the commands of Tenskawatawa, a Shawneee prophet who in the early nineteenth century unequivocally forbade present practices, both Western and indigenous, in an attempt to halt the progress of American domination. He admonished Shawnees and other Aboriginal peoples to return to the foods, implements, and clothing of their ancestors. He advised his followers to destroy all dogs and to avoid eating the unclean domestic meat of cattle, sheep, and hogs; instead, they were to eat their accustomed meats of deer, bear, and other wild animals, and fish. He also forbade bread since it was the "food of Whites"; instead, he encouraged Shawnees to cultivate corn, beans, and other traditional crops and to gather maple sugar. And he instructed his followers to relinquish European/American technology. Although they might use guns for self-defence, warriors were to hunt solely with bows and arrows. Stone or wooden implements must replace metal ones.[52]

Blackbird did not advocate this radical departure from the dominant culture, nor are his suggestions entirely in tune with those of Boudinot. He does, however, assert the value of some traditional practices.

20th. Thou shalt not be lazy, nor be a vagabond of the earth, to be hated by all men.

Among the twenty-one precepts, there is not one against imbibing alcohol to excess. Perhaps this echoes the custom of drinking in moderation among Blackbird's earlier fellow Roman Catholics! "Scarcely any drunkenness, only once in a great while the old folks used to have a kind of short spree; particularly when there was any special occasion of a great feast going on."[53] But elsewhere he does inveigh against alcoholic excess; he may even be considered a teetotaller: In earlier times, Indians "were very strict in their religion." There was zero tolerance for "intoxicating liquors" "within the Harbor," and in Little Traverse, the old war chief, Aupawkosigan, "would order him [sic] men to spill the whisky on the ground by knocking the head of a barrel with an ax."[54] Blackbird later "caused" a pledge against drinking any alcohol to be signed in every village, for he had noticed that in Cheboygan, a former Indian reservation, "there are about 40 whiskey shops and vile places, but only 9 churches."[55] He also worked for citizenship and suffrage for the Indians; and he negotiated treaties, including the one of 1855, which established a large home reservation.[56]

Blackbird advocated industriousness in procuring an American education that would lead to a higher standard of living: "There is no other method [than education] by which our people can obtain true enlargement of mind, and become acquainted with the arts and sciences, language, manners and customs of the white man."[57] Literacy and knowledge would help avert being "taken advantage of," and indeed, there are many examples of exploitation in his From the Indian's Standpoint.[58] He pursued this educational plan himself, travelling outside his community to study and then returning to positions of leadership.

21st. Thou shalt be brave, and not fear any death.

We have already noted that in war the Ottawa took prisoners and adopted them. While these war exploits provided opportunities to show bravery and compassion, hunting, counselling, and leadership were also occasions for virtuous actions.

Blackbird offers other positive admonitions that are not specifically mentioned in the precepts. He made education – as advanced as possible – a personal moral imperative. On the basis of that ideal, he worked hard to procure treaty funds for the education of all Ojibwe.[59] He also made strong efforts to ensure that the terms of treaties were thoroughly reviewed and understood before his people signed them. He sought to redress many injustices: the Treaty of 1836, for instance, was made "not with the free will of the Indians, but by compulsion," a fact he mentions several times.[60] Other injustices were related to unfulfilled promises of annuities and to deceptions, direct or indirect, concerning the removal of Ojibwe peoples from their ancestral lands.[61] The Ojibwe "voice was to be recognized in the ballot box in every election; and I thought, this is what ought to be, for the same God who created the white man created the red man of the forest, and therefore they are equally entitled to the benefits of civilization, education and Christianity."[62] Grace Walz notes that "a series of letters in the National Archives in Washington, D.C. shows [Blackbird's] extensive correspondence concerning land ownership, pensions, and other legal issues among the Indians at Little Traverse."[63]

Blackbird concluded his twenty-one precepts with this advice: "If thou shouldst observe all these commandments, when thou diest thy spirit shall go straightway to that happy land where all the good spirits are, and shall there continually dance with the beating of the drum of Tchi-baw-yaw-booz, the head spirit in the spirit land. But if thou shouldst not observe them, thy spirit shall be a vagabond of the earth always, and go hungry, and will never be able to find this road, 'Tchi-bay-kon,' in which all the good spirits travel."[64]

Blackbird's Chippewa/Odawa heritage – a heritage that he had lived – was the basis for his later-in-life moral formulations as found in the twenty-one precepts.[65] Those precepts flowed from Grand Council deliberations, from communal celebrations and stories, and from individual parental admonitions;[66] they were rooted in his own and his people's belief in the Great Spirit and in the many spirits who provide moral regulations. For them, some places, such as places that house special spirits, were more hallowed than others. In many ways, the past could provide wisdom and guidance for the good life and for wise counsel in treaty negotiations. In his *History*, published near the end of his life, he noted that the past provided much wisdom; in his *Education*, an earlier writing, he considered the past as of only relative importance and was optimistic that the tools provided by education would ensure that Indian youth "may be fitted for usefulness among our people."[67] Toward the end of his life, however, when that earlier confidence was strongly challenged, he fell back upon his roots, as evidenced by his twenty-one precepts and by "The Lamentations of the Overflowing Heart of the Red Man in the Forest." In that lamentation, as he scanned his past, especially his ancestral past, he grieved the many losses: "the land that the Great Spirit has given us," the spirit of joy and gratitude, the forests, "hills, groves and dales once clad in rich mantle of verdure and blooming on every mountain side, where the shouts of freemen rang," But he had to face reality: "It is gone; gone forever, like a spirit passed."[68]

Many times he reiterated that the only hope (which he referred to as a "war-song") was "side by side" education with white children. This new education was to be pursued "face to face ... with refined, intelligent, well-cultivated people, in order to be taken out of natural barbarism into true civilization." The result would be "a new generation, who will be civilized, intelligent and cultivated, [who] will represent the old race of America, once the home of their forefathers. In this way the difficulty of bringing the Indians into civilization will be done away with, as they will know how to live and work."[69] Yet there was more to Blackbird's moral agenda than an imitation of contemporary Americans. The past should not be abandoned, but should provide at the very least a corrective to American moral excesses. More powerfully and persuasively, that past should furnish wise lessons for the future.

In Blackbird's life and death, the tensions between two world views were eradicable. Walz suggests that he was a misfit both among his own people and among the immigrants – that is, the Americans. He tried hard to adopt the newcomers' ways and attained positions in government, but he remained secure only until settlers moved in and filled those offices. His wife had "white friends and tried to rear her children as white children," Walz writes, "but Andrew seems to have had no dependable friends whatever among the white population of Harbor Springs."[70] Despite his strivings, the new culture remained "strange to his nature." His once elegant English, which included "Indian phrasing,"[71] left him in old age and he fell back on his childhood language.[72] His writings narrate and promote his ancestral traditions, expressing hope – to paraphrase Ruth Phillips – that the Anishinaabeg would secure their future without losing their past.[73]

George Copway: "I am one of Nature's children"

We query another Ojibwe author about the moral teachings that his people and the Midewiwin espoused. George Copway/Kagegagah-bowh/Firm Standing (1818–1869) was an Upper Great Lakes Ojibwe who later moved more permanently to the Lake Superior region. He opposed the education of his people in their traditional language, for that language perpetuated "errors" and did not embrace the new civilization. Copway not only propagated the English language but also quoted liberally from Shakespeare, Pope, and other English authors.[74] He was the first Canadian Indian to publish a book.[75]

The English language and its literature were formative for Copway, who believed they could also be formative for his people. In his recommendations to the federal government, Copway wrote and spoke about the needs of his people: for a rational moral training, for an immersion in literature and the arts, and for a mechanical and agricultural education.[76] In *Indian Life and Indian History*, he wrote: "Our language [English] perpetuates our own ideas of civilization."[77] This approach to English literature and language was in contrast to that of Frederick Baraga, a contemporary of Conway in the same region. Baraga founded schools that instructed in the Ojibwe language, and he promoted Ojibwe literacy by translating the Roman Catholic catechism and prayers so that the Ojibwe could read, pray, and sing in their own tongue.[78]

Copway was aware of the influence of the Midewiwin. Its members engaged in "medicine worship"; its moral code he called "a path made by the Great Spirit," and its records "are written on slate rock, copper, lead and on the bark of birch trees." The Grand Council of the Midewiwin was concerned with the origins of disease and death,[79] and the Ojibwe nation's laws were "enacted with a view to the health of its subjects."[80]

Nanabush using plants to heal. Song scroll from Red Lake. Hoffman, "The Midê'wiwin," 187.

Copway's autobiographies reveal a great sensitivity toward his past, his parents, and his land; in them, he offers reflections on nature and traditional Ojibwe stories. His father was from the crane clan, his mother from the eagle, "sole proprietors of this part of Ojebwa land."[81] "When the sun is sinking in the western sky, I think of my former home; my heart yearns for the loved of other days ... I was born in *nature's wide domain!* The trees were all that sheltered my infant limbs – the blue heavens all that covered me. I am one of Nature's children; I have always admired her; she shall be my glory; her features – her robes, and the wreath about her brow – the seasons – her stately oaks, and the evergreen – her hair-ringlets over the earth, all contribute to my enduring love of her; and wherever I see her, emotions of pleasure roll in my breast, and swell and burst like waves on the shores of the ocean, in prayer and praise to Him who has placed me in her hand. It is thought great to be born in palaces, surrounded with wealth – but to be born in nature's wide domain is greater still!"[82]

Robe. "Central Great Lakes before 1880. Tanned, smoked hide; embroidered with porcupine quills ... in simple line and zigzag band stitches ... The geometric motifs are drawn from the common vocabulary of Great Lakes imagery referring to the great cosmic spirits. The robes may have been worn by shamans and used in the ritual instruction of Midewiwin Society initiates." Phillips, *Patterns of Power*, 48, 88.

Specific places were the habitats of powerful spirits and evoked past events and disclosed directions for life. The telling of stories of these realities began in October and concluded in late May. "There is not a lake or mountain that has not connected with it some story or delight or wonder, and nearly every beast and bird is the subject of the story-teller ... The characters [in stories] would haunt me at every step, and every moving leaf around seem to be a voice of a spirit ... These legends have an important bearing on the character of the children of our Nation."[83] His memories about his homeland became still more poignant when he recalled that almost two million acres had been surrendered to the British in 1818.[84] He later sought to correct this injustice with a bold plan for relocating all Indians to a separate state where they would be self-governing.

Copway gleaned truths and general precepts from traditional Ojibwe stories and sayings, some of these in the context of his views on the Midewiwin. One such truth is recorded in *The Traditional History and*

Characteristic Sketches of the Ojibway Nation: "There is not a flower that buds, however small, that is not for some wise purpose. There is not a blade of grass, however insignificant, that the Indian does not require. Learning this, and acting in accordance with these truths, will work out your own good, and will please the Great Spirit."[85]

Copway accepted the strictures of Methodism but was also moved by visions and dreams. He recalled the drinking habits of his father, "a medicine man,"[86] before his father's conversion to Christianity, and also the alcoholic habits of other Ojibwe. On one of his tours, he spoke to the British public: "It was temperance that lifted ... the great curtain of ignorance from before the eyes of the people, the sun poured in his rays of light from the skies, man rejoiced and received the benefits thereof. (Applause). It was intemperance that had fettered and retarded the progress of Christianity in the earth."[87] In one of his writings, he noted that Methodists did not drink and likened "fire-water" to "devil's spittle!"[88]

Once, while they were on a hunt, his father offered him these words: "The Great Spirit would bless me with a long life if I should love my friends, and particularly the aged ... If you reverence the aged, many will be glad to hear of your name ... You must never laugh at any suffering object, for you do not know how soon you may be in the same condition: never kill any game needlessly."[89]

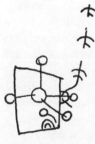

Success. Song scroll: "I myself, Will test my power." A man's song after he had successfully used his medicine to kill a bear. Densmore, *Chippewa Music*, 1:98.

In *The Life, History, and Travels of Kah-ge-ga-gah-bowh (George Copway): A Young Indian Chief of the Ojebwa Nation*, Copway recorded some "sayings of our medicine men," which also emanated from the "Me-tae-we-gah-mig or Grand Medicine Lodge":

If you are a good hunter, warrior, and a medicine man, when you die, you will have no difficulty in getting to the far west in the spirit land.

Listen to the words of your parents, never be impatient, then the Great Spirit will give you a long life.

Never pass by any indigent person without giving him something to eat ... The spirit that sees you will bless you.

If you see an orphan in want, help him; for you will be rewarded by his friends here, or thanked by his parents in the land of the spirits.

If you own a good hunting dog, give it to the first poor man who really needs it.

When you kill a deer, or bear, never appropriate it to yourself alone, if others are in want; never withhold from them what the Great Spirit has blessed you with.

When you eat, share with the poor children who are near you, for when you are old they will administer to your wants.

Never use improper medicine to the injury of another, lest you yourself receive the same treatment.

When an opportunity offers, call the aged together, and provide them venison properly cooked, and give them a hearty welcome; then the gods that have favored them will be your friends.

These are a few specimens of the advice given by our fathers, and by adhering to their counsels, the lives, peace, and happiness, of the Indian race were secured.[90]

The moral values Copway describes flowed from his Christian background and from his life as a Methodist preacher. Unlike his fellow preacher, Peter Jones, he rarely quoted the Hebrew and Christian scriptures in his writings. Yet his values and those of his fellow Ojibwe Methodists were in tune with Hebrew–Christian writings and echoed a universalist morality, that of the Golden Rule. His directives reflected the give-and-take nature of both self-interest and altruism. They set a standard by which the practitioner desired to be measured, a foundational morality for all peoples and for all times. Cathy Rex insists (arguably) that there was no foundation or standard in Copway's approach, at least not in his *Life, History, and Travels*; rather, that narrative was an instance "of infinite process and [the] unstable, malleable nature of identity."[91]

Methodism provided Copway with a firm schematic base for his life, his teaching, and his preaching. Clearly, though, his moral scheme had an additional anchor to the Christian–Methodist one. His "sayings of the medicine men" flowed from a past that reverenced all of nature and found it alive and enspirited; indeed, each part of nature was a "voice of a spirit" that gave moral commands both implicit and explicit. In Copway's description, the land and specific places were eloquent storytellers. His attachment to the land was personal, and he viewed that attachment as a favour, a blessing. His moral prescriptions, a "path made by the Great Spirit," highlighted the practice of sharing with everyone, in imitation of the spirits who shared with humankind. The flowers and blades of grass, however small and insignificant, had been placed there by the Great Spirit for a purpose – to fulfil people's needs. Copway and his Ojibwe believed that if they lived in accord with the land and its stories with the precepts of the Midewiwin, they would be protected from disease and live a good life.[92]

William Whipple Warren: "There is much yet to be learned from the wild and apparently simple son of the forest"

William Whipple Warren (1825–1853) was another nineteenth-century Ojibwe writer who was challenged by the tensions between two cultures. Some of those tensions were rooted in his ancestry, for his mother was Ojibwe, a "part-French-part-Chippewa woman,"[93] while his father is said to have descended from a Mayflower pilgrim. All of their children were baptized as Roman Catholics.[94] In his *History of the Ojibway Nation/People,* Warren documented the histories of the Ojibwe, relying on the voices of the Ojibwe themselves and not on the short-term and superficial experiences and writings of missionaries and travellers. His history is "an account of the principal events which have occurred to the Ojibways within the past five centuries, as obtained from the lips of their old men and chiefs who are the repositories of the traditions of the tribe." In a subsequent volume, he had hoped to give an account of Ojibwe beliefs, an "Indian Bible."[95] Warren was an interpreter, an intermediary, who moved in a relatively easy manner between the Ojibwe people and the new society. He often spent long winter nights with the local Indians, many of whom were his relatives. He wanted to collect their stories and write them down so "that they might last forever."[96]

Warren wrote down the history of his people not in the first person singular or plural but in the third person. There were several reasons for this detachment and non-identification with his own people. One was that he did not regard himself as totally Indian, but of "mixed blood," a "quarter (or half) breed," "a half Indian." Another was that he had spent his formative years in distant schools, especially at the Oneida Institute in Whitesboro, New York, which he attended from age twelve to fifteen. He felt he could be an authority on Ojibwe history only if he was a full-blooded Indian, had lived his culture continuously, and had some accomplishments. He judged that he did not qualify on those counts and that he had to rely on those who were.[97] Nevertheless, the Ojibwe saw him as one of their own: "Buffalo considered him his grandson and Hole-in-the-Day called him his elder brother. They relied on him for his counsel and honesty." Indeed, the La Pointe band asked him to accompany them as a delegate to Washington.[98]

Warren's *History* is vast in scope. The Midewiwin or Grand Medicine Society recounted the Southwestern Ojibwe's earliest history, a story of their migration from the east, corroborated by their birch bark scrolls. The Ojibwe's "aged men ... are the initiators of the grand rite of religious belief which they believe the Great Spirit has granted to his red children to secure them long life on earth, and life hereafter; and in the bosoms of these old men are locked up the original causes and secrets of this, their most ancient belief."[99] He was certain he was capturing very early performances: "From some of their sacred traditions, derived from their Me da we rite, I am enabled to trace their position and course for five hundred years back."[100] Warren held the Grand Medicine rites and beliefs in high esteem. Those rites, he declared, were "not yet fully understood by the whites. This important custom is still shrouded in mystery, even to my own eyes." He had "taken much pains to inquire, and made use of every advantage, possessed by speaking their language perfectly, being related to them, possessing their friendship and intimate confidence ... and yet I frankly acknowledge that I stand as yet, as it were, on the threshold of the Me-da-we lodge."[101]

Like other contemporary Indian writers, Warren sensed the impending dissolution of his culture and the consequent responsibility both to capture its history on paper and to "make a vast change for the better in [the] present Indian policy."[102] He was convinced that if he and others did not respond, they would have to answer to "the voice of the Great Creator demanding 'Cain, where is Abel, thy brother? What hast thou done? the voice of thy brother's blood crieth unto me from the ground.'"[103]

Human Manitou. Coleman, *Decorative Designs*, 9.

Ojibwe traditions had much to offer both Natives and newcomers, Warren believed. "There is much yet to be learned from the wild and apparently simple son of the forest, and the most which remains to be learned is to be derived from their religious beliefs."[104] Ojibwe leaders pointed Warren to the Mide rites as the storehouse of their ancient songs and traditions. These rites were "granted them by the Great Spirit in a time of trouble and death, through the intercession of Man-ab-osho, the universal uncle of the An-ish-in-aub-ag. Certain rules to guide their course in life were given them at the same time ... These great rules of life ... bear a strong likeness to the ten commandments revealed by the Almighty to the children of Israel."[105] Warren recounted important Ojibwe customs that were analogous to those of the Hebrews: "their faith in dreams, their knowledge and veneration of the unseen God, and the customs of fasting and sacrifice."[106] In considering these resemblances, Warren referred to Elias Boudinot, an American politician and eschatological writer, for support. Boudinot offered "many able arguments to prove [that] the Red Race of America [are] descendants of the lost tribes of Israel."[107] According to this genealogy, the Ojibwe were genetically and spiritually Semites, just as many early Christians were; the Ojibwe, then, had a close and natural relationship with Christians.

Warren drew parallels between Ojibwe beliefs and the first three Mosaic laws pertaining to Yahweh or God, since he was writing mostly for people in the Judeo-Christian tradition: "Ke-che-mun-e-do (Great Spirit) is the name used by the Ojibways for the being equivalent to our God. They have another term which can hardly be surpassed by any one word in the English language, for force, condensity, and expression, namely: Ke-zha-mune-do, which means pitying, charitable, overruling, guardian and merciful Spirit; in fact, it expresses all the great attributes of the God of Israel. It is derived from Ke-zha-wand-e-se-roin [sic], meaning charity, kindness – Ke-sha-wus-so expressing the guardian feeling, and solicitude of a parent toward its offspring, watching it with jealous vigilance from harm; and Shah-wau-je-gay, to take pity, merciful, with Mun-e-do (spirit). There is nothing to equal the veneration with which the Indian regards this unseen being. They seldom even ever mention his name unless in their Me-da-we and other religious rites, and in their sacrificial feasts; and then an address to him, however, trivial, is always accompanied with a sacrifice of tobacco or some other article deemed precious by the Indian. They never use his name in vain, and there is no word in their language expressive of a profane oath, or equivalent to the many words used in profane swearing by their more enlightened white brethren."[108]

Warren wrote that "the rites of the Me-da-we-win (their mode of worshipping the Great Spirit, and securing life in this and a future world, and of conciliating the lesser spirits, who in their belief, people earth, sky, and waters) was practiced in those days in its purest and most original form." These national yearly Mide gatherings celebrating past traditions united members with one another.[109] Since the spirit of the Ten Commandments infused initiated council members, Warren noted, there "was consequently less theft and lying, more devotion to the Great Spirit, more obedience to their parents, and more chastity in man [*sic*] and women, than exist at the present day, since their baneful intercourse with the white race ... In former times there was certainly more good-will, charity, and hospitality practiced toward one another; and the widow and orphan never were allowed to live in want and poverty."[110]

From an early contact story, Warren recounted the centrality and virtues of the Ojibwe's two prominent clans, the crane[111] and the bear: "When the white man first came in sight of the 'Great Turtle' island of Mackinaw, they beheld walking on the pebbly shores, a crane and a bear who received them kindly, invited them to their wigwams, and placed food before them." These Ojibwe extended to the Europeans sentiments and actions of welcome natural to these clans; these dispositions endeared them especially to the "old French discoverers."[112]

Water. Song scroll: "I am able to call water from above, from beneath, and from around." "The segment of a circle with dots in it, represents the water, and the two short lines touching the head of the figure, indicate that he can draw it to him." Tanner, *A Narrative*, 342–3.

Part of the tradition that Warren committed to writing was that of the totems or dodems. He confessed to some personal incomprehension about this tradition, for some of it remained "vague and unsatisfactory." According to Theresa Schenck, "the totem ... was originally the family or clan name of the people who lived in a given village and was the most important feature of identification of the group. Later, [it served] in much the same way as a person's family name."[113] Warren noted a strict moral imperative flowing from the totemic tradition, "known only to their chief Medas, or priests": "The badge or Dodaim (Totem, as it has been most commonly written), descends invariably in the male line; marriage is strictly forbidden between individuals of the same symbol. This is one of the greatest sins that can be committed in the Ojibway code of moral laws, and tradition says that in former times it was punishable with death."[114]

In addition to the Ojibwe moral precepts that bear a likeness to the Decalogue, Warren delineated some that arose more strikingly from the Ojibwe themselves. In 1760, after the English defeated the French at Quebec in "the disastrous war," Chief Mihnehwehna met the wandering British trader Alexander Henry. Henry thought he would be able to trade freely since all previous French territory was now English. But he was wrong to believe that all allegiances changed with military conquest. The Ojibwe of Michilimackinac remained resolutely on the French side and also took pride in their patrimony. As the "Ojibway chieftain" (Mihnehwehna/Le Grand Sauteur) narrated: "Englishman, although you have conquered the French you have not yet conquered us! We are not your slaves. These lakes and these woods and mountains were left to us by our ancestors. They are our inheritance, and we will part with them to none. Your nation supposes that we, like the white people, cannot live without bread – pork – and beef! But, you ought to know that He – the Great Spirit and Master of Life, has provided food for us, in these spacious lakes, and on these woody mountains."[115]

Since Henry carried no arms and was interested in trade, not war, the chief bore no hatred toward him, instead giving his hand in friendship, regarding him as a brother, and presenting him with a pipe to smoke. Some conflicts, however, did not end so peacefully. According to Mihnehwehna, there were three ways of dealing with warfare and killings. Ojibwe wars with the Dakota and with the English aroused feelings of revenge and led to acts of retaliation; this was the first way. In Henry's presence, Mihnehwehna recalled a second way, a variation of the first, that of the Ojibwe's sometimes prolonged retaliatory custom, which continued "until such time as the spirits of the slain are satisfied." It was the spirits of the dead, not the living, who cried out for vengeance and determined its duration. The chieftain, however, noted a third way, that of appeasing the spirits of the slain in a way other than "by spilling the blood of the nation by which they fell," that is, "by *covering the bodies of the dead,* and thus allaying the resentment of their relations. This is done by making presents." The feelings of vengeance among the victim's family and friends could be sublimated and the dead spirits could be pacified by this third approach through a ritual in which the perpetrators of the killing(s) covered the bodies with appropriate cloths and presents, or gave presents outright. In the judgment of Mihnehwehna, the English in general and Henry in particular were woefully unaware of this ritual and negligent in giving presents![116] While Warren did not indicate a preference for one way of satisfying the spirits of the dead over the others, giving presents instead of vengeful killing seems a more humane and morally enlightened way of acting.

Warren presented other virtues he had observed among prominent Ojibwe leaders. He highlighted the life of Waubojeeg of La Pointe, now Wisconsin, born about 1747, who acted pragmatically for his people – at times, when necessary, learning the stratagems of warfare and at other times the ploys of peace. Warren relied on the narration of Henry Rowe Schoolcraft to describe Waubojeeg's courage and his initiation "in the arts and ceremonies pertaining to war ... [At a young age, he listened to the fighters'] war songs and war stories, and longed for the time when he would be old enough to join these parties, and also make himself a name among warriors ... He also early learned the arts of hunting the deer, the bear, the moose, and all the smaller animals ... [He] took the ordinary lessons of Indian young men in abstinence, suffering, danger, and endurance of fatigue. In this manner his nerves were knit and formed for activity, and his mind stored with those lessons of caution which are the result of local experience in the forest. He possessed a tall and commanding person, with a full, black, piercing eye, and the usual features of his countrymen. He had a clear and full-toned voice, and spoke his native language with grace and fluency. To these attractions he united an early reputation for bravery and skill in the chase, and at the age of twenty-two, he was already a war leader."[117] Thus, Waubojeeg's physical characteristics complemented his moral ones, or perhaps they flowed from his moral demeanour.

Warren continued with his enumeration of Ojibwe virtues: "Expeditions of one Indian tribe against another require the utmost caution, skill, and secrecy." He noted the action or inaction required when interpreting "the breaking of a twig, the slightest impression of a footprint ... The most scrupulous attention is also paid to the signs of the heavens, the flight of birds, and above all to the dreams and predictions of the jos-so-keed, priest or prophet ... [War requires] secrecy and stratagem ... intimate geographical knowledge of the country ... knowing every prominent stream, hill, valley, wood, or rock, but ... [also] the particular productions, mineral and vegetable, of the scene of operations ... This species of knowledge, shrewdness, and sagacity is possessed on both sides, and ... the nations at war watch each other as a lynx for its prey ... Seldom ... a close, well-contested, long-continued hand battle is fought. To kill a few men, tear off their scalps in haste, and retreat with these trophies, is a brave and honorable trait with them, and may be boasted of in their triumphal dances and war-like festivities."[118]

Cultural ceremonials were occasions for both the expression and the transmission of honoured virtues. "At [the] annual returns of warmth and vegetation, they also engage in festivities and dances, during which the events and exploits of past years are sung and recited: and while they derive fresh courage and stimulus to renewed exertion, the young, who are listeners, learn to emulate their fathers, and take their earliest lessons in the art of war."[119]

Warren again relied on Schoolcraft to add to the qualities of a civic leader. Since the rigours of winter precluded pursuing war, encampment time was spent procuring the means of subsistence and clothing:

> In this ample area, the La Pointe, or Chagoimegon, Indians hunted. It is a rule of the chase, that each hunter has a portion of the country assigned to him, on which he alone may hunt; and there are conventional laws which decide all questions of right and priority in starting and killing game. In these questions, the chief exercises a proper authority, and it is thus in the power of one of these forest governors and magistrates, when they happen to be men of sound sense, judgment, and manly independence, to make themselves felt and known, and to become true benefactors to their tribes. And such chiefs create an impression upon their followers, and leave a reputation behind them, which is of more value than their achievements in war.
>
> Waub-o-jeeg excelled in both characters; he was equally popular as a civil ruler and war-chief; and while he administered justice to his people, he was an expert hunter, and made due and ample provision for his family ... He is represented as of a temper and manners affectionate and forbearing. He evinced thoughtfulness and diligence in the management of his affairs, and the order and dispositions of his lodge. When the hunting season was over, he employed his leisure moments in adding to the comforts of his lodge ... Waub-o-jeeg ... possessed ease and dignity of manners. He was a ready and fluent speaker, and conducted personally the negotiations with the Fox and Sioux nations.[120]

Warren concluded his exposition of Waubojeeg's virtues by noting that he was so courageous and single-minded in his efforts that he "impaired his health in the numerous war parties" and died at the early age of about forty-five.[121]

Warren commented on another leader, Waubojeeb or White Fisher, namesake of the previous celebrated chief: he "was a warrior of some distinction [and had] much influence with, and was loved and respected by his people.'" His peaceful, civic virtues were noteworthy: "His lodge was ever filled with the fruits of the successful chase, to which the hungry were always welcome. His social pipe was ever full, and the stem often passed around among his fellows. He was always foremost in defence of his people, when, as it too often happened, the startling war-whoop of their enemies fearfully broke on the morning stillness of their sleeping encampment! [He was] a successful and adventurous hunter, a brave and daring warrior."[122]

One who possessed many warrior virtues, but who was also less than an ideal example, was Mukimduawininewug/Men Who Take by Force, one of the Pillagers, the "bravest band of the tribe." In his battles with the Dakota for hunting grounds, Mukimduawininewug and his warring party were "filled with a daring and independent spirit, and no act was so wild, but that they were ready and disposed to achieve it." Some wild Pillagers at Leech Lake, Minnesota, seized a sick trader's goods, relished the spoils, and neglected the ailing merchant, who subsequently died. For these vicious acts, the conduct of the pillaging party (hence their name, Pillagers) "was generally censured by their more peaceful fellows as foolish and impolitic, as it would tend to prevent traders from coming amongst them for fear of meeting with the same treatment." The war party had to make reparation for the seized goods with beaver skins in order to regain "good will and friendship." The British gave to the Pillager leader "a medal, flag, coat, and bale of goods," requesting that they not unfurl the flag and open the bale of goods until they were back in their territory. The Pillagers complied, and were subsequently stricken with smallpox. Warren questioned whether the British purposely inflicted the contagion on them as punishment for their pillaging; from his investigation, he concluded that these warriors had been afflicted with smallpox in some other way.[123]

Hero. Explanation by Loon-foot: "The three [four] strokes cut into the board, painted of a red colour ... [are] the three bloody hero deeds the deceased had performed, or three enemies he had killed. The three figures holding each other's hands were his relatives mourning his loss or celebrating his funeral feast, and the inverted animal – a bear – was his family sign or name." Reading of board: "Here lies the chief of the Bear clan. His relatives and friends mourn for him. But he was a hero, for he killed three of our mortal enemies." Kohl, *Kitchi-Gami*, 159.

Warren described at length the process and wholesome consequences of peacemaking: smoking the pipe of peace at a meeting, creating a comfortable ambience, *"pin-dig-o-daud-e-win* (signifying, 'to enter one another's lodges')," and sharing ceremonies, all of which resulted in the pursuit of "the chase in one another's vicinity, without fear of harm or molestation ... And when once the 'good road' had been broken in this manner, interchanges of friendly visits would become common, and it often happened that during the winter's intercourse of the two camps, a Dakota chief or warrior taking a fancy to an Ojibway, would exchange presents with him, and adopt him as a brother. This the Ojibways would also do." Warren recalled the many breaches of this peaceful protocol, however, and the telling of corrective "lodge tales ... to teach the rising generation never to do likewise."[124]

To illustrate additional Ojibwe virtues, Warren considered Babesigaundibay or Curly Head, who attracted "the bravest warriors and hunters of the Mississippi Ojibways [to] his camp and ... soon formed a formidable body of hardy and fearless pioneers, who, ever wary against the advances of their enemies, were never attacked by them with impunity." Curly Head, a member of the crane family, "was much respected and loved by his people. In the words of one of their principal warriors, 'He was a father to his people; they looked on him as children do to a parent; and his lightest wish was immediately performed. His lodge was ever full of meat, to which the hungry and destitute were ever welcome. The traders vied with one another who should treat him best, and the presents which he received at their hands, he always distributed to this people without reserve. When he had plenty, his people wanted not.'"[125]

Warren envisioned himself as part of this caring Ojibwe tradition: "Instead of living on their scanty means which even they cannot live on, I have even divided with the hungry the last morsel of food in my home. An Indian has never come to me starving and naked, but I fed and clothed him to the utmost of my limited means ... I have carried this practice so far that I have sacrificed for my own children, many of the comforts of life ... sacrificed my personal interests for the general interests of the tribe ... I but follow the example of my fathers for three generations back."[126]

For Warren, the implicit or explicit precepts to care for others were realizations of the Ojibwe's inner nature and were ultimately freeing: "There treds not the earth a freer *man* than the aborigine of America in his native state! He is emphatically his own master, moving and acting as he lists; but seldom guided by the wishes of his chief or tribe,

and never forced. Living and acting thus, they seldom consider themselves bound by the contracts of peace or sale of lands made by their
chiefs; and this will account for many acts of the red man which look
to the eyes of civilized and law governed society as treacherous and
false."[127]

Warren's robust Ojibwe moral code, which flowed from the Midewiwin repository, had two sources: one of these pointed to a parallel
with the Ten Commandments and even to the Great Spirit as mono-
theistic, the other to indigenous virtues and directives that emanated
from contextual Ojibwe settings of war and peace, from stories depicting virtuous people, and from ceremonials that celebrated brave deeds.
Civic and war leaders inspired their fellow Ojibwe (including women,
although little is written about them) with heroic virtues while also
recounting vicious acts not to be imitated.

Warren believed that the American way of life was destined to supersede that of the Indian; also, that since Indians as Indians would soon be
extinct, written historical records would be necessary to preserve their
past. He hoped that the worth of his culture would be preserved so that
past Anishinaabeg values could continue to fashion Ojibwe destinies.

Each of the four Ojibwe writers discussed in this chapter made unique
contributions to his culture, but they had attributes in common as well.
Peter Jones embraced Methodism, but selectively. He considered its
disciplinary practices necessary for a settled way of life, but he also
remained suspicious of the newcomers' activities and pointed to the
threat those activities posed for the Ojibwe. This man of action shaped
a new identity for his people in which the son of the Great Spirit protected his people as the guardian spirits did in the past. His form of
Christianity was rooted in Ojibwe values, in the service of *bimaadiziwin*,
a healthy and long life, and in the caring service of all.

Andrew J. Blackbird presented moral injunctions within the framework of the Mosaic code. But he emphasized the second part of that
code, that of right relations with one's neighbour. He believed that
cosmic spirits at particular times and places continued to guide and
protect his people. He revered his ancestors and hoped that the past
would infuse and transform the present. He lamented the treatment
of his people, especially when treaties were broken. In his early life, he
advocated mainstream education both for himself and for his people –
indeed, he pursued it himself. In his later years, however, he returned
fervently to traditional ways. Thus, he embodied the tensions between
two world views.

George Copway, who lived in the Great Lakes region, was the first Canadian Indian reputed to have published a book. He enjoyed the English language and quoted from its literature even more than he did from the Bible. While he believed that books could be a formative influence on Ojibwe lives, he also revealed in poetic and nostalgic terms a great sensitivity to his past, to his parents, and to the land. The Great Spirit had given a path, a moral direction, for the Ojibwe, a path reinforced through the medium of stories. He advocated a gathering and relocation of all Ojibwe peoples to an area where they could regain their self-governance. The rigours of Methodism provided a framework within which the Ojibwe could curb their excessive drinking of alcohol and be of service to all. The sayings he recounted from the Ojibwe tradition indicated a universalist, Golden Rule morality.

A renowned historian, interpreter, and intermediary, William Warren, "a half Indian," relied on Ojibwe leaders as a source for an account of his people. He felt a deep responsibility to write a history of them now that they were being assimilated. He drew parallels between the Mosaic code and that of the Ojibwe, while noting that there were some unique indigenous virtues. Various historic figures exemplified outstanding virtues, which included forgiveness in the form of covering the dead with gifts, moral uprightness among the leaders of the warrior and peace societies, virtues in the hunt, and virtues recalled in the form of stories and songs to provide direction for the young. Distinguishing the Ojibwe, he thought, were their intertribal relations and peace accords.

All four writers were Ojibwe, and all of them, implicitly or explicitly, held the Midewiwin performances in high esteem. And all four emphasized *bimaadiziwin*: if individuals and groups lived in agreement with the Great Spirit's precepts, they would enjoy a long life. They all saw Christianity and modern approaches as offering some advantages, but they also revered traditional Ojibwe ways and hoped that future generations would not forget them. Finally, all four writers lived in tension between two worlds.

3

Otter, the Playful Slider[1]

We have noted the reciprocal and quasi-identical nature of human–animal relationships in Ojibwe cultures: humans are like animals and can be transformed into animals; animals are like humans and can be transformed into humans. Because of this kinship and near identity, animals have played a significant role in the consciousness of the Ojibwe in general and in that of their leaders. This close relationship with animals has often regulated their experiences. As noted earlier, otter was one of the animals involved in stories of origins and in bringing the Midewiwin to the Ojibwe. In that Medicine Society, otter was often the main one associated with the first stage in initiation rites.

We will describe otter initially in a physical, external way through its habits, characteristics, and relationship to the Ojibwe. We will then consider otter as portrayed in representational ways and as thought of, spoken of, and heard; otter is present in stories, pictographs, birch bark scrolls, and other artistic works. It is intriguing how otter is portrayed in non-figurative, non-representational ways. We will conclude by showing otter's relevance to our understanding of Ojibwe religious, political, and social life.

Physical Otter[2]

The otter *(nigig)*, a member of the weasel family, is a highly successful animal. It has survived for 35 million years and is still numerous.[3] Otters are crafty and cunning;[4] they are protective of themselves and their kin and are ferocious and even menacing to others.[5] They have a wide-ranging diet, eating "fish, crayfish, rabbits, ducks, frogs, salamanders, muskrats, and aquatic insects."[6]

Besides being resourceful, the otter has acute senses of smell, hearing, and sight. Because of these qualities, and because it lives so "efficiently," it has time for what appear to be leisure activities, including play. Delphine Haley describes river otters as "delightful clowns of the kingdom ... tumbling and tobogganing down snow-covered hillsides or sliding down muddy riverbanks." These magical moments, with lots of play, are apparently pursued for the "sheer joy of sport and frolic."[7]

The otter plays alone, "in groups, with other animals, or with people. It spends much time rolling in the grass, somersaulting underwater, frolicking in the snow, chasing its tail, or playing hide and seek. It will juggle a pebble in its paws or balance a stick on the end of its nose like a trained seal. Sometimes, in larger rivers, it will shoot the rapids, riding along with head erect on the watch for rocks and snags."[8] Emil Liers writes that "they're as good at log-rolling as experienced lumbermen, and so friendly that they'll play with dogs and bears – even children!"[9] Otters often help one another and manipulate objects to pull them apart. They learn how to do things by observing.

The otter displays great versatility both on land and in water. On land it runs with a rippling motion in a rapid, inchworm fashion; its footprints are of a diamond form – an imprint copied on Ojibwe garments and utensils. In the water it uses its tail as a rudder.[10] Grace Rajnovich writes about the zigzag pattern of the otter's path: "When chased, [it] tries to deceive its enemies by varying its course ... The otter's tracks form a long hexagon between diamonds; the animal rises on its haunches to jump, forming the diamonds, then as it leaps it drags its tail making the hexagon."[11] The track the otter makes "with its tail when it crosses the ice in the spring ... is the common design used on long narrow bead chains and borders ... The design is frequently called otter's tail."

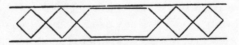

Otter's track and tail. Coleman, *Decorative Designs*, 3–4.

The emotions and intellectual traits an otter displays are similar to those of humans. Its playfulness and cunning have already been noted. Part of its intellectual display takes the form of informational coding.

An otter spends considerable time and uses elaborate techniques to produce fecal pellets, which it then coats with scent and positions carefully. Its signs – known as "spraint" – which also take the form of trenches, and urine on bushes and trees, provide individualized information, including age, sex, status, breeding condition, and the time elapsed since deposition.[12]

When alarmed or angry, an otter may emit a mustelid scent and use a series of calls, "a snort or cough in alarm, a scream in anger, sometimes a friendly chirp. One common group sound is a low-keyed chuckling noise that seems to be associated with pleasant feelings while grooming, copulating, or communicating at close range."[13] This sound can be imitated by closing the lips and saying "huh-huh-huh" explosively and as deeply and rapidly as possible. We sometimes hear public figures make that sound; one who did was Canada's former prime minister, Joe Clark. C.J. Harris mentions additional sounds: a low humming or growling, signalling a threat or apprehension; an intimidating raucous scream, accompanying an attack; bad temper or frustration, voiced as a querulous, moaning wail; and screaming and whistling when wounded or when a mate or its young (referred to as whelps) are lost. There are also various conversational noises displaying emotions other than fear, anger, or distress; these include a bird-like twittering and chirping; chuckling, whiffling, or chittering; and the sounds that a "soprano motor mower" would make. Contrasting forms of conversation-like sounds are grunts or rumbling noises in a low key, with the last syllable sometimes emerging suddenly an octave higher in a sort of questioning tone. The latter noise, which seems multi-purpose, can be emitted above or below water.[14]

Otter as Representational

So far we have been describing the otter's physical characteristics. Hunters and trappers, who were usually men, experienced otter's vivid physical presence. But they experienced more than a bodily presence, in that they believed the otter's guardian spirit had led them to where they were. Thus the representations of otter that follow these experiences partake not only of this animal's concrete physical determinants but also of otter's spiritual power. These figurative depictions become even more limited and circumscribed as concretized images of otter become the foundation for a movement toward the abstract and geometrical. This movement toward the non-figurative involves predominantly the work of women.[15] Here, as in almost every facet of Ojibwe life, women were resourceful, dynamic, and creative.[16]

A representational consideration of animals, and that of otter in particular, is found in stories. According to Julia Harrison, "in all myths concerning the Midewiwin, the messenger who brings the rituals to the Ojibwa has the ability to travel over land and through water."[17] As we have seen, the otter, with other animals, possesses this amphibious adeptness, a quality the Anishinaabe also displayed as they travelled from the "big sea," along a great river, and finally to the land surrounding Lake Superior. The events of travelling, of entering and exiting, observed in otter's life are telescoped into the image and reality of the medicine lodge. Lake Superior and its environs become a vast lodgescape, which the Ojibwe enter and exit, with the Sault as its eastern entrance, as noted when we examined bear as the "guiding spirit of the Midewiwin."[18]

In the verbal artistry of stories, otter is the aide of Nanabush.[19] William Hoffman and others narrate a legend of the place of the otter in the Midewiwin story of Nanabush. The Ojibwe were helpless, and Nanabush desired to give them the means of warding off diseases, and to provide them with animals and plants as food. As Nanabush was hovering thoughtfully over the centre of the earth, he heard something laugh, and perceived a dark object on the surface of the water to the west, and then in all four directions as a creature brought the directions together in the centre. It was otter. Nanabush instructed otter "in the mysteries of the Midewiwin, and gave him at the same time the sacred rattle[20] to be used at the side of the sick; the sacred Mide drum to be used during the ceremonial of initiation and at sacred feasts, and tobacco, to be employed in invocations and in making peace."[21]

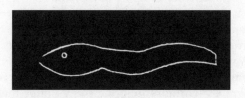

Water spirit. Coleman, *Decorative Designs*, 9.

In addition to appearing in stories, otter is a prominent Manitou figure on birch bark scrolls and has several other roles in the Midewiwin lodge, such as healing. A scroll song states: "I bring life to the people," with Hoffman's interpretation: "The speaker, as the impersonator of the sacred Otter, brings life. The Otter is just emerging [a line drawing indicates this] from the surface of the water, as he emerged from the great salt sea before the Âni'shi-nâ'beg, after having been instructed by Mi'nabo'zho to carry life to them."[22] Additional representations of otter occur on song scrolls of the third and fourth degree of the Midewiwin. The otter Manitou appears with a diagonal line across its body signifying the spirit character of the animal, and states: "I answer my brother spirit."[23] George Fulford notes that on the White Earth Reservation song scrolls, 16 percent of the seventy-four pictographs he recorded depict otters. "Otters appear in seven of the eight song scrolls," according to Fulford's concordance. On Sikassige's origin–migration scroll, otters are associated with the Mide lodge.[24]

Otters. Song scroll: "Now and then there will arise out of the waters, My Mide brethren, The otters." "The circle represents a lake from which two otters rise." Densmore, *Chippewa Music*, 1:66.

Maria Seymour and Grace Rajnovich consider similar song records from northern Minnesota that depict the spirit powers of otter; the song for the otter medicine bag is "I am helping you." There are pictographs of otter with power lines emanating from its body at Agawa Rock on Lake Superior and at Deer Lake in northwestern Ontario. Such rock paintings are associated with picture writing, and both are linked to medicine, dreams, and songs. Different media convey the same message differently.[25]

The origin–migration songs of the Midewiwin also contain otter's actions. According to Thomas Vennum, the Medicine Society's sweat bath songs "convey various images of emergence" while referring to events in their stories, including those involving otter. Nanabush "hears the laughter of Otter each time he emerges from the water; Otter emerges from the first medicine lodge to begin his trek; wherever Otter emerges from the water, *mitewiwin* is established ... In the *mite* initiation ceremony, the candidate's reenactment of Otter's journey begins upon the completion of the ritual sweating, when he exits, or emerges from the sudatory [sweat lodge] (the dot 'in the center of the earth'). His movement from the sweat lodge westward to the medicine lodge represents Otter's journey along the water route as well as the candidate's own 'path of life,' which ends symbolically when he leaves by the west exit of the *mitewikan* [medicine lodge] at the conclusion of the ceremony."[26]

In some stories, otter is the originator of the medicine bag, giving its body to form the container as it utters healing sounds from that receptacle.[27] Thomas Shingobe from Minnesota states that everything in the Medicine Lodge is "a living thing."[28] Norval Morrisseau also testifies to animals coming alive during the performances: "These hides were seen to come alive. The bearskin began to growl and the fox skins began to bark."[29] Otter gives its hide, utters therapeutic sounds for initiates and members of the lodge, and touches candidates, but also engages in cosmic changes. In a Mille Lacs depiction by Sikassige, Hoffman's collaborator, and also on Red Lake song scrolls, interpreted by Little Frenchman and Leading Feather, the otter spirit clears the sky so that ceremonies can begin.[30]

There are other depictions of otter – particularly as part of the chieftain clan of marten – as warrior, hunter, and strategist.[31]

Thus otter appears in stories, on scrolls, in songs, in pictographs, as birch bark bitings,[32] and as medicine bags. In addition, Fred K. Blessing gives a line drawing of a bowl game, a seniors' game with a bone carving of otter as one of the players. He notes that the style of bowl depicted "seems preferred by the old men, especially those closely associated with the Grand Medicine Lodge."[33] This game, with its image of the otter, recounts and reinforces the animal's playfulness.

Otter as Patterned

As the visionary and acoustic experiences derived from otter were given representational form, they retained the blessings of this Guardian Spirit. One challenge, the Ojibwe believed, was to keep the visions and sounds private lest they be lost if diffused among the populace. To overcome this cultural difficulty, the Ojibwe and others exhibited an inventive adaptability when portraying these experiences: on the one hand, the Ojibwe desired to see and feel the power and presence furnished by a visual representation of the animal; on the other, they had to portray some ambiguity in this portrayal in order to protect the animal's necessarily private manifestation. Public concrete representations would diffuse the animal's power. Creative ingenuity came to the rescue, Ruth Phillips asserts – a combination of the manifest and the hidden, a portrayal based on concrete animal forms but rendered in line drawings and designs. Spirits could then transform themselves or be transformed into both representational images and geometrical patterns, with the representational as more concretely revelatory and the abstract as more ambiguous and hidden.[34] Both of these forms rendered visions, sounds, and reality in multiple ways – a "combinatory variant principle," Desveaux notes.[35]

The otter was the sign and sound of the first stage in the incorporation of individuals into the Midewiwin. But the patterned otter had ramifications for the entire nation, a type of corporate personality; otter was an "owner" or spiritual boss.[36] By resort to an abstract patterned style, the otter's meaning was transferred onto costumes, ornaments, weapons, utensils, and sacred objects. In these cultural forms, otter took on a more spiritualized and universal outreach. Through these creations – particularly by women, who made various abstract art forms – the power of otter was multiplied.[37] The form of the otter, concretized in the skin of the medicine bag, but detached from the species in symbolic form, carried the life and power of that species. Otter was still localized and specific in megis bag shootings, but in this symbolic form it also had greater flexibility, for now many individuals and the Midewiwin itself were participants in and recipients of its power.

The zigzag movements of the otter inspired a stylized form derived from its swift, inchworm-like progressions and from its tail-swaying attempts to avoid pursuers; hence the zigzag form pertained to both its tail and its trail. Sister Bernard Coleman singles out the zigzag designs based on otter's trail or path. This design element "consists of a continuous series of broken straight lines of equal length forming equivalent angles." Some Ojibwe called it a lightning pattern. When doubled or tripled, the pattern could form a number of diamonds, also based on otter's movements. This type of design occurred in Ojibwe quill and bead work, which we will examine shortly.[38]

Another design closely related to the otter's tail and trail was the otter track. "In this design," notes Coleman, "there are two elements, a diamond and an elongated hexagon about three times as long as the diamond." This represented the otter's track, made "with its tail when it crosses the ice in the spring ... [It] is the common design used on long narrow bead chains and borders ... The design is frequently called otter's tail."[39] Menomini quilled otter-skin medicine bags from the late nineteenth century show consecutive vertical diamond shapes.[40]

Phillips asserts that these stylized and patterned movements embodied not only the otter's gait and physical meanderings but also its extended power; these patterns could also be those of sky spirits – lightning and thunder.[41] To depict these insights, women used creative styles and techniques, aided by the increasing supply of coloured trade yarns in the eighteenth century. The geometric designs they created were not degenerate forms of the representational, nor were they purely aesthetic images, nor were they merely marks of prestige for themselves and the owner; rather, they captured primarily the Guardian Spirit's power and presence as derived from visions and dreams, and presented them in a relatively immaterial form. According to Phillips, these outlined forms also displayed moods or feelings in the weaver's life and were symbolic as well as decorative.[42]

Ojibwe abstract designs were not degenerate and relatively valueless developments; neither were the floral designs based on European influence. Phillips writes that the transcultural genesis of Great Lakes floral art translated "into the new medium of floral representation the four directional quadrants of Woodlands and Plains cosmology that are expressed in the ancient, sacred, and abstract motifs of the equal-armed cross and the quartered circle." In this creative cross-cultural process, Great Lakes and European women shared the same designs but not necessarily the same meanings. "The two groups shared a belief in a spiritually empowered natural world ... The cycles of growth and the transitoriness of flowers became metaphors for human destiny, underlining the fragility of life but also offering proof of a caring providence."[43]

Song scroll: "The sky I tell you." "The otter skin medicine sack, and arm reaching to procure something therefrom." Hoffman, "The Midê'wiwin," 192a–193.

We have considered medicine bags that had significance for the craftsperson, for the owner, and for the spiritual performances in which they were used. Another type of flexible container – one with perhaps less ceremonial and more personal significance – was bandolier bags. Marcia Anderson and Kathy Hussey-Arntson describe these as colourful beaded bags with "a shoulder strap sewn to a rectangular lower section made of cloth, usually with a beaded pocket. The beadwork may consist of a separate, loom-woven panel, which is then sewn to the bag or the beadwork may be embroidered directly to a cloth section of the bag, creating an elaborate geometric or floral design." Bandolier bags appeared in the Great Lakes region during the second quarter of the nineteenth century. These early cloth and hide bags or pouches were worked with quills rather than beads, which were acquired later;[44] they were adorned with otters, thunderbirds, underwater panthers, and other Grand Medicine Society decorative motifs and served as banners of personal prestige on special occasions; the pouches could also carry personal items such as tobacco. In the Royal Ontario Museum is a pouch with two thunderbirds outlined in red, facing each other, and two small otters attached to one side of each. On the top part of the pouch are long, bold, wavy lines in red, black, yellow, and white.[45] According to Andrew Hunter Whiteford, these bandolier bags were known as friendship bags because they signified interpersonal and intertribal relationships, an early aspect of the Midewiwin.[46]

On permanent display in the Minneapolis Institute of Arts are several bandolier bags that were created in the late nineteenth century and the early twentieth; they have floral designs that reference the natural environment. An earlier bag, from 1870, of silk, wool, cotton, and beads, has a beaded design that "refers to the otter, who plays an important role in Anishinaabe stories and clan system. The series of diamonds followed by straight lines, then diamonds [alone], refer to the otter tracks. The diamonds symbolize footprints, and the straight lines the otter's tail." So reads the identifying caption. There are five sets of diamonds and lines on the top of the rectangular frontal surface of the bag and three sets of them on the sides.[47]

G. Constantino Beltrami's early-nineteenth-century "Upper Mississippi" collection, now in Bergamo, Italy, displays a birch bark container with wavy lines and horizontally positioned diamond forms, a drum with a spirit shape that is quite striking, and a birch bark purse with handle and wavy line designs.[48] It is quite possible that abstract and stylized nineteenth-century forms were based on the animals that were part of the Midewiwin performances. Two bandolier bags in the Minnesota Historical Society Museum, one from the early and the other from the mid-twentieth century, feature wavy bands and squares and rectangles of geometric patterns, seemingly in imitation of abstract animal forms. Such patterns are also apparent on an "Ojibwa Loom-woven Beadwork Band" of uncertain date. An "Ojibwa Birch Bark Cutout Pattern" has a long edge cut in a scalloped and zigzag pattern. Were these figural images and designs crafted merely for aesthetic reasons? Are they indeed stylized vestiges of otter tail and otter trail and thunderbirds?[49]

Otter's zigzag trail. According to Elizabeth Rock, "When an otter is pursued, it tries to deceive the enemy by changing its course," and consequently the zigzag lines. It is also called a lightning pattern occurring "very frequently on Ojibwa quill and beadwork articles." Coleman, *Decorative Designs*, 2–3.

Otter and Ojibwe Standards of Life

We have noted three modes of presence for otter: first, the physical otter; second, the representational one; and third, the patterned one. All three had an impact on Ojibwe lives.

The Ojibwe people and their Midewiwin leaders were immersed in these manifold depictions of otter. They did not "collect" these images as artworks; rather, they appropriated them and were empowered by them. The following characteristics of otter were core aspects of Ojibwe lives and leadership, including in relation to treaty negotiations: craftiness, adaptability, economic responsibility, an autonomous and adventurous spirit, efforts to unite sky, water, and land, an atunement to the power of the four directions and the centre, a defensiveness and elusiveness necessary for survival,[50] and playfulness. George Fulford notes that "in Sikassige's story about the origin of the Midewiwin, the otter is the carrier of sacred knowledge."[51]

Otter and snakes. Song scroll: "I am swimming – floating – down smoothly." "The two pairs of serpentine lines
indicate the river banks, while the character between them
is the Otter, here personated by the Mide." Hoffman, "The
Midê'wiwin," 292–292a.

In its representational form, otter can be multiplied and can manifest
its power in many ways. Its skin was a membrane for the Mide drum.
"As a container for the medicines, paints, and other elements of
power belonging to the shaman, the otter *pinjigosaun* [medicine bag]
functioned in the same way as the original otter of myth," Harrison
writes. "In conveying the knowledge of the Midewiwin, it protected
the essence of what it meant to be an Ojibwa."[52] The otter as physically
embodied in the medicine bag was a living being and served to prolong
and restore life.[53]

Otter was the servant of Nanabush and "the master of life," Densmore
writes, "the source and impersonation of the lives of all sentient things
human, faunal, and floral." Like the trickster, Nanabush, otter also
endowed sentient things with life and taught "each its particular ruse
for deceiving its enemies and prolonging its life."[54] According to Blessing, otter was "the most important skin in the life of a Mide member."
Today, the otter-skin bag or its counterpart leads the first-degree candidate "onto the spiritual path or his 'true life,'" a "spiritual birth."[55]

Otter. Nanabush said to otter in the first-
degree lodge: "You shall own it always." Hoffman, "The Midê'wiwin," 174b, 176.

Blessing tells us that because of the high regard in which the Ojibwe
held otter, his pelt was elaborately decorated to include "a beaded tail
and brass trade bells on the hind legs and end of tail. The bells when
shaken serve to keep harmful spirits from approaching."[56] In this way,
otter's power was merged with European artefacts such as beads to
create a new synthesis. As the otter-skin membrane vibrated, its sound
was amplified and blended with those of the singers and dancers to

become an acoustic representation of otter. As noted earlier, the drum – both its presence and its sound – was necessary in Midewiwin ceremonies. For Deleary, the essence of the medicine lodge's life-giving performance was in sound, in the drum, and – in the case at hand – in otter's representational utterances.[57]

Otter and those impersonating otter received blessings that gave them the power to ensure well-being for everyone. While that power was individual, the communal nature of Ojibwe society meant it would be used for the common good. All of Ojibwe life, then, was an extension of otter's power.[58] Otter's influence could be extended ever further to revive Midewiwin performances and to inspire reapplications of nineteenth-century treaties. Otter's laughter, then, could be heard again in many varied relationships.[59]

"On a symbolic level," Harrison writes, "the otter partakes in the most basic element of Midewiwin power, the ability to integrate the worlds that the Ojibwa see in opposition: that of the land and that of the water; that of the traditional hunting bands and that of the European fur trader or settler. The Ojibwa were striving to lessen the tensions which abounded in the world that surrounded them, both in the spiritual world and the encroaching world of European civilization, and in the powers which exercised control over them. Just as the Ojibwa drew on the resources of both land and water to survive, so too the otter lived in both environments. For a people who had traveled over land and water to reach the area that was to become their home and had been subjected to the hardships and the rewards of both, a creature who moved through both with ease and playfulness was to be respected and revered. The otter as used in the Midéwiwin was one attempt to structure and retain the ideology of the Ojibwa ancestors in order to confirm the continued existence of this Native American group."[60] For Desveaux, it was not otter's gift of laughter that was most important, but his singular propensity for irony, which dominated all that was hidden and mysterious.[61]

The otter was one of the mediators of Ojibwe cultures and the Midewiwin. A Mide ceremonial chant recounts how Nanabush received powers and assistance from various Manitous. Nanabush sat in the lodge and reflected on "how he should further be enabled to obtain necessary powers to aid his uncles and their descendants." Animals came from the various directions, bringing with them their powers. Otter came from the south and said to Nanabush: "My brother, I come to give you the konapamik [shell]; you will find it on a rock in the waters of the lake; there you will find it and give it to your mita brothers."[62] It was otter who broke through the sandbar at Fond du Lac.[63] As a mediator, he served as a rallying call to thwart disintegration. He represented traditional values now celebrated in ritual and in stories. Otter was like a flag, a hymn, like sacred writings, a symbol full of meaning, empowering and leading. [64]

Otter entering the lodge. Song scroll: "Spirit I am, I enter." "The otter, which Manido, the speaker, professes to represent, is entering the sacred structure of Mide lodge." Mallery, *Picture-Writing*, 1:236.

Otter symbolized new life. During the Mide performance, the neophyte was shot with shells from an otter-skin medicine bag. Alanson Skinner describes this ritual shooting of cowrie shells from the bag as "the most spectacular, and one of the most important, parts of the ceremony."[65]

In Fulford's analysis of Midewiwin scrolls, otter "is an equally powerful symbol" to the cowrie shells. The following epithets from the scrolls are associated with pictographs of the otter: "earth's grandchild," "sky," "my brother," "he that I hear (laughing)." Otter was associated with the dish used in Mide feasts and with the medicine pack.[66]

We have noted two patterned forms of otter. The first is that of otter as coterminous with the person of Midewiwin practitioners. The second is otter in stylized, abstract, and geometric forms.

Otter had many relations with the Midewiwin and indeed nearly shared its identity. Otter was more than merely one of the emissaries who brought to the Ojibwe the Midewiwin performances;[67] its spirit permeated the ritual's songs and words. Otter's physical presence was apparent in the medicine skin pouch,[68] and the Midewiwin itself and the lodge were often regarded as coterminous with the otter Manitou. This affinity with the healing society meant that the lodge's performances were akin to those of the otter. For instance, the appendages of several animals, including that of otter, could reveal deceit and ensure fine weather.[69] In Vizenor's account of the origins of the lodge, otter, the embodiment of comfort and joy (*swangideeshkawed*), worked in conjunction with the four winds and megis shell to provide this healing ritual.[70] Thus otter was not just a being in the world like any other, but a special being, a unique member with distinctive characteristics who was coterminous with the lodge and its performances.[71]

In addition to being incarnated in the Midewiwin, otter took various non-figurative forms. Thus, otter was displayed in abstract and geometric forms in ways that extended his power and influence into both ceremonial and everyday life. Women, as the bearers and transmitters of culture, created patterns of the otter's tracks and trails on garments and medicine bags as well as on ornaments, utensils, and ceremonial objects. These women were the originators and often the distributors of spiritual energy, using new techniques and expressions in response to changing lifeways and materials. The responses of Native men were more utilitarian than enhancing; according to David W. Penney, it was women who succeeded "in defining culture amidst the complex mosaic of post-contact Native American history."[72]

Again, these non-figural motifs were not merely decorative or aesthetic, nor were they primarily marks of prestige; rather, they crafted otter's voices and were the embodiment of special powers from dreams, sometimes imaging moods and feelings from the weaver's life – moods and feelings now given abstract expression. These symbols spoke a universal message in voices both muted and articulate, to the Ojibwe but also to settlers, traders, government officials, missionaries, and geographers.[73] The artists attempted to embody the spiritual in immanent form – as Phillips asserts, to give "visual expression to experiences which were mystical and elusive, and which, being secret, could not be fully divulged even to the wife or mother who embroidered and wove the designs he described. The artists sought, furthermore, to capture in static form qualities of light, movement and sound that were an integral part of his dream." The designs "symbolize[d] the energies unleashed by the manitos."[74]

4
Owls: Images and Voices in the Ojibwe and Midewiwin Worlds

In the previous chapter we focused on otter, the animal on the first level of the Midewiwin healing society. For the Great Lakes Ojibwe, otter was present in many ways: as an experienced corporeal reality in nature; as represented in stories and on scrolls and medicine bags; and in non-figurative patterns. We contended that otter had a vivid and expansive presence and was a powerful force not only in Ojibwe life generally but also in the ritual and life of Mide practitioners. Since otter informed the spiritual practices of the Midewiwin so thoroughly, Mide leaders brought with them the values this animal embodied.

In this chapter, we ascend the Mide ladder to the next ritual rung and examine the role another animal played in the life of the Ojibwe and in the Midewiwin. It is difficult to ascertain which animal is/was on the second step in the Midewiwin ceremonies. Robert and Pat Ritzenthaler, for instance, for the Woodlands Ojibwe, list the second-degree Mide bags as those of owl or hawk skins.[1] For the Minnesota and Great Lakes Ojibwe, Fred K. Blessing and Julia Harrison give hawk as a second-degree bag and owl as a third-degree one.[2] For northern Minnesota, William Hoffman states that the pouch of the initiated of the fourth degree contained an owl.[3] For the more eastern Ojibwe, Ruth Landes places weasel and mink as second and third bags respectively.[4] In a description from Lac Vieux Desert, John Pete tells us that twelve different skins were used in the Midewiwin ceremony: in ascending order they were "otter, mink, owl, snakeskin, bear paw, cub hide, grizzly claw, part of a big bear hide, skin and feathers from the breast of a turkey, grey squirrel, and weasel."[5] In these reports, bird seems to be the most constant focus. Based on its importance in many scrolls and stories, we will consider the owl for the second degree.

Although we will not examine in any detail the degrees beyond the fourth, some Ojibwe do. Fred K. Blessing labels the beings that typify the fifth to eighth Midewiwin degrees as "mythical spirit animals." His descriptions of these spirit animals in the upper degrees are largely negative and fit into two classes: (1) dangerous spirits that can give up their efforts to do harmful things and can become guardians, and (2) evil spirits. For Blessing, "the evil spirit influenced people to do evil at all times," whereas merely dangerous spirits were flexible and could change their orientation from evil to good.[6]

Stories, images, and voices of the owl offered a window onto the Ojibwe world. The impressions provided in these ways signified the prized qualities of the owl, qualities that the Ojibwe appropriated. Animals, however, were not merely objects to be heard, viewed, and prized; they were also agents who had voices and who were fellow subjects with human beings on life's path. Their power was multifaceted in that they could protect, guide, and mediate. But they could also frighten and molest. They were like human beings; indeed, they were guardians who were sometimes indistinguishable from human persons, and they often reciprocally exchanged places, features, and roles with humans.

Although Ojibwe stories give visions of the owl, they also and perhaps pre-eminently give voices – voices articulated by the storyteller, by the sonority of owls' names, by the vocalizations of owl itself, and by the human songs attributed to owl. The Midewiwin ceremonies themselves were owl-like in that they provided soothing medicines but also featured the sound of the evil-thwarting shaker/rattle together with other ritual reverberations.

Classification and Characteristics of Owls

We will briefly examine, mostly from non-Ojibwe sources, the two types of owls that figure prominently in Ojibwe stories, although the Ojibwe did not generally classify owls in this way. The following information sometimes conflicts with subsequent stories and with pictographic and representational forms.[7]

The first type is the Northern Hawk Owl (*Surnia ulula*). It does not regularly migrate, but moves as it follows food sources. This species is atypical of most owls in that it hunts during daylight hours and uses sight more than hearing to locate its prey. It is of medium size, and in flight its pointed wings, long tail, and swift nature appear hawk-like;

hence its name. Among its various calls is a repeated hawk-like chattering. It generally inhabits coniferous and deciduous forests but can also be found in areas of open tundra where there are tree-lined watercourses. It is not afraid of people and will nest close to human settlements.[8] Humans often have an eerie feeling about these birds, which exhibit human-like characteristics such as binocular vision and acoustic projections within the range of the human voice.[9]

The second type is the Boreal Owl or Tengmalm's Owl (*Aegolius funereus*). It is mainly nocturnal, and its most common call is the territorial song of the male, which varies widely from individual to individual. "It is a series of 'Poop' notes followed by a 3-4 second break, then another series ... The male will emit a low 'Wood' or 'Wood-whoohd' to contact a breeding female."[10] The Boreal Owl will scan the ground by moving its head slowly from side to side, listening for the movement of potential prey as it hunts, using primarily its excellent directional hearing. It inhabits a range of forests from pure coniferous to pure deciduous.[11]

Following are some general considerations of owls. There are 134 living species.[12] They have seventy-degree, three-dimensional binocular vision, with a total field of 110 degrees. By bobbing and pivoting their heads, they are able to get several perspectives (a parallax method).[13] Ornithologists theorize about this evolutionary ability in birds, while Ojibwe stories offer their own explanation: for disobeying Nanabush, owl had his eyes fixed so that he could stare only straight ahead. If he wanted to look to the side, he would have to turn his whole head. Since the other animals laughed at him because of this peculiarity, he felt foolish and hid deep in the woods and only appeared in the evenings after the sun had gone down.[14]

Owls' ears, which are positioned quite far apart, give these birds clues about the direction and distance of prey. With their powerful talons and beaks and their ability to fly silently, they are formidable predators.[15] Their relatively large wings covered with feathers and velvet pile dampen the sounds of air movement, enabling them to hunt by stealth in complete darkness using sound alone to guide them.[16]

As noted earlier, owls and other animals among the Ojibwe are more than "creatures out there"; they are independent but also interconnected agents. Our considerations of the owl will highlight their formative power; they influence not only individuals but also – indeed, especially – cultural locales and specifically the Midewiwin, which some Ojibwe have designated as their political arm. In an earlier chapter, we examined the religious/political interstices of Mide leaders; in this one we examine the cultural role that owl played in Ojibwe life.

Song scroll: "We are following the bear path, My Mide brother." Densmore states this is the "oldest Mide song known." The bear path is one of several in the Midewiwin ceremony. "Birds are closely associated with the second, third, and fourth degrees." Densmore, *Chippewa Music*, 1:106–7.

Owl as Bad Luck, Bad Medicine

For the Ojibwe, the owl had a multifaceted personality. They often recounted its negative characteristics, and its sinister powers were often used to frighten children into obedience. Ojibwe parents taught their children that if they did not go to sleep, or behave, an owl would carry them away.[17] Howard Corbiere recalls an Ojibwe–Odawa story that illustrates this parental ploy. "The Ojibwe people call the owl Ko-Ko-Ko, because that is the kind of sound he makes. They believed that he possessed magical powers, which were not always used for the good."[18] A specific story involves a young boy, his father, Nanabush, and an owl. The boy observed the owl's strange action of turning its head in a full circle, while he could turn his head only halfway around. He wondered whether it was magic that enabled the owl to turn its head so far. To account for this magical procedure, the father told the story of an owl. As we will observe later, owl's onomatopoetic expression can alter many natural processes.

The father began his narration by recalling kind and helpful Nanabush. Like the boy, Nanabush also "decided to go for a walk in the forest":

He often did this, for it was one of his favorite pastimes. It was a nice day – but the forest was thick and dark.

While Nannebush was walking along the trail, something struck him from behind. It kept striking at him, over and over again. It was an owl – and a very bold one, for he challenged Nannebush to a fight.

The two struggled together for some time. Each one tried to outwit the other. Then, Nannebush suddenly grabbed owl's head with a firm grip. With all his strength, he twisted the head of the owl all the way around.

Ever since then, the owl has been able to turn his head all the way around. He can look in front of him and see where he is going. Then he can turn his head backwards and see where he has been.

Ojibwe children are warned by their parents never to act like an owl, because the same thing might happen to them. To Ojibwe people the owl is a sign of bad luck – even to this day.[19]

Owl's ability to turn its head completely around, or almost completely, is strange and unsettling and serves as a warning to avoid that animal and its actions. Owl's ability here seems bizarre, but it is also awesome in its way; besides, for an owl, a swivelling head is quite an asset!

Owls have both a fighting and a protective instinct. William Hoffman narrates a story of Manabush/Nanabush, who with his grandmother, Nokomis, noticed an owl and a wildcat on the opposite sides of a stream. "Suddenly the Owl said 'Hu-hu-hu-hu, hu-hu-hu-hu; see how I shall strike him; I shall drive him off easily enough.' Then Ma'nabush became alarmed, and said to his grandmother, 'Grandmother, they are going to attack us; let us fly!'" With grandma on his back, Manabush fled the attack of the Manitous "who were ana'maqki'u."[20] These dreaded Manitous are interpreted as antagonistic underwater creatures who gave Manabush "much annoyance at the time of his growing to manhood, and at the establishment of the Mita-wit, or Grand Medicine society." Given, however, that thunderbirds themselves have names cognate with these underwater creatures *(anamaqkiu/inamaqkiu)*, the scare can perhaps be interpreted as coming from both regions of the earth.[21]

Two additional Minnesotan versions of the owl story, told mostly by mothers and grandmothers, involve a little girl. The first version is similar to the previous one, which featured a young boy. In addition to using the owl as a means of making children "be good," the story uses owl "as a threat to keep children close to the wigwam. One old man recalled his mother saying, 'If you go to the sugar bush at night, the owl will come and carry you away in his ear.' [Or 'owls would catch them like mice if they left their dwelling place at night. The fear of owls kept the children home at night.'[22]] Besides the owl, Ojibwe parents used the Sioux and also Frenchman (or any other white man) as a warning or threat. We were told how important it was for children to be taught to be quiet, for sometimes it could be a matter of life or death." Wasseskom/ Eli Thomas of Mount Pleasant in Michigan relates a more general admonition contained in the "Hoot Owl Song": "Long time ago when I was a small boy I was taught after the sun went down I must be quiet. They said to me, 'Don't do that. Owl going to come and get you.'"[23]

The story has a reversal to it, for the owl's abduction of the little girl does not seem to hurt her, nor does it teach her the required lesson; instead it creates anxiety in the mother. In trying to teach her child a lesson, the mother herself had exposed her to the owl, and she thus felt responsible for the kidnapping. During the period of abduction, the owl and the girl share a kindred spirit: the child is never afraid, is nourished and clothed by the bird for four years, and is returned safely to her home. "The little girl said that she had been in a tree and that she was given all kinds of meat to eat, rabbit and other kinds. So the mother thought the owl must have taken her and cared for her."[24]

In the second version of the story involving the little girl, the mother is more assertive, even commanding the owl several times to take the child. Reluctantly, the owl takes her. The mother naturally becomes anxious and lonesome after a while, and searches for the little girl. Imagining that the mother is worried and feeling compassion for her, the owl returns the girl well cared for. This version of the story is a lesson for parents to be temperate in threatening their children, for their actions may prove to be detrimental both to themselves and to their child. "Never again did the mother tell her children that the owl would get them,"[25] the story concludes. So we notice in these stories that the negative qualities of an owl are founded sometimes more in the perception of individual Ojibwe than in the owl itself. In other versions, it is bear who provides kindness to neglected and abused children.[26]

Frances Densmore recalls another incident in which a child, Henry Selkirk, became frightened of an owl when his mother went to a neighbour's wigwam. Seemingly to soothe his nerves and establish a rapport with the owl, he sang a song, "I Am Afraid of the Owl." People in neighbouring wigwams heard the melody and used it in moccasin games, always giving Selkirk credit for its composition.[27]

But the Ojibwe did more than merely frighten children with their owl stories; according to Densmore, they used the medium of an owl to do evil. Densmore outlines a method whereby "the skin of an owl was removed, dried, and filled with 'medicine.' It was said this was sent through the air to the lodge of the person to be affected."[28] In fact, Odenigun sings about this poisonous missive. Persons in the camp nearly starved. Shooting the menacing bird and burning its skin, however, resulted in no harm to the inhabitants.[29]

In his commentary for the section "The Village of Animals," Victor Barnouw discusses the need to be cautious with owls, for their powers can have mesmerizing effects and result in death. In a story, a hunter merely intends to poke a sleeping owl with his gun, when "suddenly the owl opened its eyes and stared at him. 'I couldn't get my eyes off the owl ... I felt something hot go through me, and I felt weak. Then I walked away and could still feel those eyes on my back like a hot rag. I thought of what my grandfather used to tell me about the owl. I haven't gone near one since.'" In another story, from 1942, Pete Martin of Lac Courte Oreilles, Wisconsin, relates that after an owl had been disturbing his sick and grieving wife, the husband shot the bird. The subsequent death of an old man (recounted in this and in another story) is associated with killing this owl. The narrator concludes: "It will be remembered that an owl is encountered on the road to the other world."[30] In an account of a real-life incident on Manitoulin Island, bearwalker is portrayed as a demon "in the form of a hoot-owl."[31] The term "demon," however, has Euro-American affinities; we will examine the complexities of bearwalker later on.

Several stories from the Rama Reserve in Ontario concern owls, witches, maiming, and death. Peter York told a gruesome story of Kuk-oh-chees/Ground Hog, who appropriated the power of owl for evil purposes. She was "an old witch who lived in Rama on the west side of Lake Couchiching [Ontario]. She covered herself with the skin of an owl when she wanted to fly at night for the purpose of taking the first joints off the fingers of children, which she used to string up like old-fashioned, dried apples in her camp. These children would die at once." On one occasion, the Old Witch had forgotten her medicine bag in her camp. Therefore, she could not counteract a young man with her power as he compelled bees to sting her to death. "She said as she died, 'Well, anyway, I never killed any big people, just children.' But the people found joints of fingers of grown-up persons on the strings as well as those of children in her camp." Consequently, she received a new name, Ground Hog, from the place where the young man deposited her body.[32]

In another witch story by Joe Cosh, also from the Rama Reserve, an owl commanded a little boy who was cutting wood that he should cut enough for only two days since his mother would die that evening. The little boy then told his mother and father of the encounter. "About midnight they went out and watched for the old owl. Soon they saw a fire coming toward their camp. It stopped on a cedar tree near the camp, and they shot at it, and they heard a cry. It was the witch. The mother was safe then, and the next day they heard there was an old squaw who had been shot hunting rabbits, but had been trying to kill a squaw. This ends here. The old witch died."[33]

Lottie Marsden's great grandfather told her a male witch story from Georgian Island: When great grandfather's pretty sister became sick, did not respond to treatments, and died shortly afterwards, the family "knew it was the witch that had killed her ... They said that the witch will always come to the grave the first night the person is buried. Well, my grandfather said that he would watch the grave that night, and about twelve o'clock he saw a light coming, and it went right to the grave. This was an owl, which opened the grave and went after the little fingers of the dead person ... My grandfather had his shotgun and shot the owl. The next morning they heard that there was an old man who had died. This was the owl that went to the grave."[34]

In some Algonquian cultures, owls' harmful actions led them to assign a new meaning to these birds. Amy Dahlstrom argues "for a semantic shift in Meskwaki (and elsewhere) by which the word for 'windigo' [cannibal] came to mean 'owl.'"[35] Nodinens of Mille Lacs narrates an event in which he listened to an owl following him. In camp the owl said: "You must preserve every bit of deer. This is a bad sign, and we will not get any more game for a long time." Nodinens concluded: "The hunters went out every day, but could find nothing."[36]

In Northern Ontario, even an Ojibwe recreational activity such as the moccasin betting game portrays owls in a negative way, for an owl confirms a bettor's loss.[37]

In summation, an owl's personality can take many forms and is quite complex. An owl can be both a threatening sinister power and a benevolent advocate. An owl can represent the power of the air but also similar powers in the water. It has mesmerizing powers; it is associated with sickness, grief, and death; it can thwart hunting; and it can signify a loss during a game of chance. The owl's menacing eye, eerie call, and predatory nature serve as a measuring stick for both individual and community self-examination and correction.

Owl on first-degree lodge post. Painted white [black] spots indicate megis shells. Hoffman, "The Midê'wiwin," 182–182a.

Owl as Protector and Healer

In several accounts, owl is regarded as a protector of humans.[38] The principal character in a story from Big Trout Lake in Northern Ontario is covered with an owl skin, is called Owl Skin, and exhorts fellow humans to kill owls in order to use their skin to cover their shelters.[39] Pete Martin of Lac Courte Oreilles spoke of a solicitous owl, an individual's guardian spirit, who referred to a shivering individual as grandson, who in turn referred to him as grandfather. "Then the owl wrapped his big wings around him and sheltered him all the rest of the night."[40]

Other Algonquian people corroborate and add to the owl sagas. Alfred Kiyana of the Fox people presents a rich and varied medicine song text and ceremony in which there is weeping over the killed and wounded. An owl provides blessings and enables people to cross rivers unimpeded and to heal wounds. A girl in the narrative invokes an owl pack or pouch whose power "gladdens the people," makes cliffs passable, widens rivers, mends broken bones, resists the shots of enemies, and provides knowledge about unpredictable and inscrutable events.[41] An owl enters ceremonies and hoots "in the space between the fires."[42] An owl commands people to hoot, and to make an offering to grandfather owl in order to live a long time. The healed begin to sing and smoke a catlinite pipe. There are assurances that grandfather owl will protect and bless both present and future generations as long as the world lasts.[43] There is the promise that an owl's continuous song will oversee the earth through its seasonal changes, and that owl will protect the people by training them to be warriors. In a symbiotic relationship with an owl, people are commanded to sing loudly (women are to hum) and to hold their rattles firmly while sounding them boldly. "The manitou himself listens to all of them and hears how the gourds sound ... If you desire long life for yourselves, that is what you are to do."[44]

Owl's power and presence are manifest in the healing process. Mrs John English of Red Lake, Minnesota, narrated that she was once in a lodge where the medicine men were pounding their medicines on a stone and putting them in little bags. A stuffed owl was placed beside them. After leaving the lodge, she asked about the owl and was told: "They always have to have someone watch to see that they do it right." Densmore wrote that near Vermilion Lake, Minnesota, she visited the remote house of a medicine man and saw two owls (or owl skins) swinging from the branches of trees, suspended by a cord around their necks and drying.[45]

William Jones narrates that Nanabush and his brother created everything in the world, including owls, in order to help humans when they themselves were created.[46]

Gerald Vizenor gives this "pictomyth": "With a large bird above me, I am walking in the sky. I entrust myself to one wind." He comments on birds in general: "Many dream songs of the *anishinaabeg* are dreams of flying as birds and clouds. The singer of this song was watching a bird soaring in the sky above him as he walked and dreamed that he was walking in the sky with the large bird."[47]

Owls play a part in rescue efforts. In "Manabush and the Bear Anamaqkiu," an unnamed young man prepares to save his two older brothers; he makes a small bow and lowers his snowshoes from their hanging perch. "The right snowshoe was called dodo'pa (small saw-whet owl) and the left snowshoe was called the kuku'kuu (horned owl)."[48]

Owls protect humans physically by sheltering them with their skin and feathers. Those protected in an owl-like shelter assume the character and appearance of an owl. In their positive personal relationships with humans, owls provide aid in distressing times and tell the future. An owl's sonorous hoot and its concerned expression reassure the Ojibwe that they will live long lives. The owl is medicinal in many different ways; its healing balm and songs inform and transform both the Ojibwe in general and Mide participants in particular.[49]

Owl as a Teacher of Altruism

Joseph Morris gives a story from Big Trout Lake of Owl Man, who is dependent on Kwokwokwo (Hawk Owl), with whom he has a pact to kill four owls per day, no more, no less. Owl Man's clothes are entirely of feathers and owl parts, and his *matakwan*/lodge is of owl skin. When Owl Man meets someone in great need, he shares his goods with this unfortunate one and also counsels this person to kill only the allotted number of owls each day. Obedience to this regimen and an adaptation to Kwokwokwo's habitat ensure food and shelter. Wisdom consists in helping others.[50]

Desveaux documents two additional stories that limit the hunt. One goes back to the "Old Times"; on this occasion, the limitation pact concerns the killing of grouse. As in many stories, the interdiction to kill only the proper number is violated, with the consequence that the people almost die of hunger. There are allusions to imprudence and greed.[51]

In another story, from John-George Morris, Mingesowash/Eagle's Nest is given the same restricted command as above, which he seems to violate, albeit unconsciously. The woeful result is that his child is swept away in a stream. His wife berates him for his disobedience: "Why do you not now understand what was said to you many times? When they taught you how to live they told you never to kill more than you should!"[52]

In the story "Nanabozho and the Hoot Owl," some owls notice how stingy Nanabush is with the fish he catches. These owls make their "funny noises," frightening Nanabush, who flees, leaving his catch behind and losing all his fish. At home he tries to save face with Nokomis about his failure to bring home any fish by declaring his generosity in letting the Manitous have it all![53] In direct and indirect ways, animals are the teachers of human beings. Animals are often silent metaphors for human foibles and for the qualities for which humans should strive.[54]

In another story, owl is given a pre-eminent position and task. Various animals communed to find a way to inject some colour into their white coats. Hoohoomisseu, the owl, was appointed leader, and sitting very solemnly on a stump, he spoke to the other birds. These birds decided to send owl as a delegate, along with duck and gull, to meet with the Great Spirit to procure the desired colouring.[55]

We have referred to Densmore's citation and song of an owl and bad medicine. To illustrate the virtue of sharing, let us examine it in more detail. A husband and wife came to an old Mide healer, who "gave them food and made them comfortable. Late that night the old Mide got ready to sing, and while he was singing he sent an owl over to the camp where the Indians lived who were trying to starve this man and his wife ... The old rule was that if a man killed an animal he must first divide it among the camps; then he must cook his own share of the meat and invite all the old men to come and eat it with him. If he failed to do this they would be jealous and would 'starve him out,' as was the case with this man and his wife." In addition to protection and sustenance, the owl gave the needy couple medicine to enable them to approach animals in the hunt. "The other camp could get no food after the owl went to the camp. The Indians there nearly starved, but the man and his wife had plenty of game."[56]

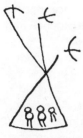

Owl flying. Song scroll. "I am the one, Who is trying to fly, He is making it (the medicine)." "The Midewiwini, the man and his wife, are seen in the wigwam, from which the owl is flying." Densmore, *Chippewa Music*, 1:105–106.

Owls thus provide an example of wise and generous sharing by giving their feathers and skin. They also demand a regular regimen in life as well as judicious limitations in hunting; otherwise, bad medicine will spread, affecting even the animals and thereby jeopardizing the survival of all.

Owl and Directions, Winds, and Seasons

Though thunderbirds are associated more frequently with the four directions, winds, and seasons, owls also have relationships with these. In "Kwokwokwo and the Warm Wind," Solomon Begg narrates that Kwokwokwo and Odijak (crane) decided to search for the warm wind since some people were privileged to experience it and others not. They noticed that the warm wind was kept in the south, in a lodge. Kwokwokwo and others attacked the lodge and freed the warm wind. "That's why today, from time to time, the warm wind blows from the south."[57]

Desveaux notes that ritual celebrations and the winds punctuate regular routines. Winds give the assurance that there is permanence to the seasons – that is, regularity – but they also account for variations.[58] Hawk Owl, as the intelligence and guide of the winds, announces the weather variations. Different seasons result in different conditions and possibilities in the natural environment. For instance, when starvation looms, cold wind and snow may nevertheless presage a successful deer hunt.[59]

Owls direct all of the four winds and mediate with them. This importance is mirrored in the prominence accorded the number four and the cardinal directions/winds in Mide rituals. (The instances of four are very important; there are four (or eight) Mide stages, each with certain ritual instruments, pouches, bags, mats, poles, and variant practices.)[60]

Four winds. Child's moccasin with four winds design. Coleman, *Decorative Designs*, 19.

Owls regulate the winds and thereby usher in the seasons; with other birds and their songs, they also indicate time. Birds enliven the air with their songs and in doing so punctuate and detail each particular season. Their sounds mingle with the wind, enliven it, and name the wind as a carrier of life. As an older Ojibwe remarks, "The songs are alive, more alive than us."[61] Birds other than owl are involved in the seasons; Basil Johnston writes of diver bird whose singing conquers winter and brings summer into being.[62] Death gives way to life. Bob Danley, a recreation planner for the U.S. Fish and Wildlife Service, gives another account of the correlation of owls and warm spring weather: Great Horned Owls have a preferred diet of skunk, which is plentiful in the spring, so "you can tell warm weather is on the way when the nesting trees start to stink."[63]

Begg recounts events in the spring when the rapids are very powerful. Boreal Owl, Kashkejabish, tries so hard to out-shout the roaring rapids that he loses his voice. "So it is that in spring Kashkejabish utters a cry which resembles that of the rapids."[64] In another story, crow and Canada Goose try to out-voice the rapids but cannot mask its competing sounds. Only Boreal Owl's continuous call is equal to the rapids. "That's what he does still today in the spring."[65]

There are several illustrations of the sound environment at the end of winter. At this time of the year the ice begins to melt and the flowing water increases its noise as it gradually frees itself from the ice. One listens to the song of Boreal Owl perched in a tree very close to the encampment, even in the middle of it. Its song, a little wild at first, is as continuous as the reverberations of the waterfall. Thus this owl engages in a consonant but also competitive song with the river. In this story, Boreal Owl loses the competition, but a concurrence of the owl's song and the continuous sound of the river persists so that it is impossible to discern whether the auditory impression is the voice of the owl or that of the river. Finally, the competition ceases altogether and the utterances meld into one.[66]

Owl and spring, owl and spring water, owl and warmth and new life. Desveaux notes that there is even more symbolism here. A continuous sound, except for the wind in the trees, is uncommon in the sub-boreal forest.[67] The wind's subtle and continuous gusts gather all events into its silent embrace. In contrast, an animal's sounds manifest a discontinuous presence. Thus the absolute silence and the seemingly total absence of life on the coldest days of winter are stirred by the least movements and expressions of animal life. Just as animals interrupt the silence of winter, the hunter must act within nature's acoustical sphere of silence to approach game. In making sounds when striking the animal, the hunter, like the animal before him, ruptures the silence for an instant; in the act of ensuring death, he also guarantees his group a livelihood.

The silence–sound interplay is continued in the healing process. To avert the perpetual silence of death, the healer uses the rattle, drum beats, and recitative chant. Life itself is a reciprocity between voices and silence; lullabies and cooing provide a prelude to the stillness of sleep; vision quests are pensive and quiet but also involve listening to sounds. It is Kwokwokwo who speaks and who understands all human conversations directly.[68]

Sylvie Berbaum recounts the role the rattle plays today for the Ojibwe of the Treaty Three region. In the uncreated world there is merely the sound of the shaker/rattle, for not all of the world is manifest as yet.[69] But the shaker's sound is not unrelated to creation, for the seeds of the gourd in a gourd rattle are the elements of regeneration.[70] Sounds and seeds, creation and regeneration. Sound, rattle, and the beginning of the world. Such cosmic reverberations and other influences enter the Midewiwin lodge itself, for as Johnston notes, the "lodge was open at the top, free to receive life, light, and the sound of the whole world and the universe."[71]

Owl on top of one of four painted posts in the fourth-degree lodge. Hoffman, "The Midê'wiwin," 182–182a.

The rattles specifically "were shaken to dispel the spirit of suffering and ill health," Johnston writes. Like the drum, the rattle gathers the people; but while the drum gathers good spirits, the rattle dispels bad spirits.[72] According to Berbaum, "the rattle has this expelling function because of its link with origins; the sound of the rattle, recalling the original one, returns to the source, to a beginning without sickness and bad spirits. The rattle is the reverberating presence par excellence of a therapeutic milieu."[73]

We have already noted that owls were often harbingers of and participants in change through the winds and the seasons. Hoffman writes specifically of the Midewiwin ceremony and the owl. The lodge had ten squared poles, and each of its four parts was oriented to one of the four directions. The colours were a function of this orientation: white for east, green for south, red for west, and black for north. At the top of each pole was "the stuffed body of the white owl." The poles were distributed throughout the four Midewiwin degrees, with owl featured in all four degrees. Also, the pouch of the initiated of the fourth degree contained an owl.[74]

Ojibwe artist Ahmoo Angeconeb writes more generally about the role that birds – one of the Creator's gifts – play as spirits of the air. "The spirit of the air is with us through our cycle of life. It brings greeting to us when we are born, and it is the last element to be with us when we pass on to the spirit world. The bird is also the bearer of messages for the Anishnawbek, because it can fly in the air, walk on the land, swim on the water, and dive underwater, going where we cannot."[75]

Since birds do not seem to be associated with the Mide lodge in the White Earth song scrolls, and bears and otters do, Fulford concludes tentatively that "in the song scrolls birds had become meaningful only in opposition to bears [with the] opposition between earth and sky [as] fundamental while oppositions between earth and water, or sky and water were secondary." In the late nineteenth century, because life on reservations was more sedentary, there was a gradual change in the relationship between earth and water. There came to be less dependence on water transportation; and logging, and the consequent reduction of forest density and coverage, opened vast expanses between earth and sky. With this human-made change in geography came a change in conceptions of animal relationships and of the cosmic areas they inhabited. "In the minds of Hoffman's informants, bears, like otters, may have been associated with two or more elements of the cosmos," Fulford writes, "whereas birds were associated with only one (i.e., the sky)."[76]

In summary, while the owl is closely associated with the south wind, it also has relationships with all four winds and seasons. An owl intelligently mediates with and guides the winds to bring in the appropriate seasons; it breaks winter's silence, and as the ice melts, it sings against and also in unison with the emerging rapids. Silence and sound reciprocate throughout the seasons as well as during hunting rituals, in creation and regeneration, and in healing, sleep and death. In the Midewiwin ceremony, rattles reverberate, recalling mythic times of wholeness and dispelling bad spirits, a ritual directed by the owl's presence and voice in all four Midewiwin degrees. Before colonization, creatures of the sky, earth, and water, while different beings, were integrated into a cosmic whole and not opposed to one another. As colonization advanced, creatures in these three cosmic realms were separated on the scrolls into specific regions, at least conceptually; birds, then, were depicted as inhabiting the skies almost exclusively.

Owl and the Dead

While an owl sings with the spring rapids and heralds the advent of new life, it is also associated with death. In the novel *The Owl's Song*, owl Manitou speaks with an infallible voice of a coming death.[77] An owl's call can presage the death of specific beings, summoning them to a home where they belong.[78] In stories from Lac du Flambeau, Wisconsin, owls guide the dead by placing markers along the way; indeed, owl itself becomes a marker.[79] An owl's visage can be that of death: "The Indians say that the owl's eyes are like a looking glass, and he looks just awful. When he speaks of the owl at the last supper with a dead person, sitting next to the coffin, the Mide priest says, 'When you see your grandfather's eyes shining like glass, don't be afraid of him. Just go up and offer him your tobacco. He'll take it.' They don't say 'the owl.' They speak of him as 'your grandfather.'"[80] One story relates that Nanabush served human beings by using "the eyes of the owl to pass through the land of the sleeping sun."[81] Thus owls were protectors of the dead, but even more, they were the very ancestors themselves who had already passed to the spirit world. Several animals are both aids and impediments to the deceased on their way to the afterlife. Such journeys parallel accounts in the Egyptian *Book of the Dead*, in which funerary hymns, texts, and illustrations on papyrus scrolls are placed in coffins or burial chambers to accompany the dead.[82]

We have already noted the paralysing and haunting effects of an owl's gaze.[83] An owl presents a double mirror with life on one side and death on the other. This is akin to the Mide mediation between life and death: the healing lodge is erected near water, thereby presenting ways to ensure life, but it also includes a death or ghost lodge.[84]

In a story from Lac Courte Oreilles, "the Great Mystery" had instructed various Manitous to be at the service of Nanabush to help his uncles and their descendants. Bear and Daylight came from the east, offering respectively strength and light for meetings. With his drum, Shunien chanted that Kukukuu, the Great Owl, said, "I shall come and sit by the burial place of the dead, to see that their resting place is not disturbed."[85]

"Kokokoo (Owl) passing from the Midewigan [Lodge] to the Land of the Setting Sun, the place of the dead, upon the road of the dead." Hoffman, "The Midê'wiwin," 169a, 171.

The role an owl plays for the dead is more clearly delineated in some Midewiwin birch bark scrolls. Skwekomik's master scroll from Red Lake, Minnesota, shows a circular village of the dead containing a ghost lodge.[86] The path of the dead runs from a Mide lodge to the ghost lodge in the direction of the setting sun. Some master scrolls have varieties of fruits and a tree on the side of the path to lure travellers away from the home of the dead. According to Johann Kohl's drawing,[87] a crooked log stretches across the stream but is too short to reach the opposite shore. Infants and children therefore need help to cross the stream to reach the ghost lodge. In other versions, the log takes the form of a serpentine monster who hinders access unless proper rites are invoked.[88] In Skwekomik's illustration, Kokoko the owl is the guide along this path. He had loaned his eyes to Nanabush when he visited his brother wolf in the afterworld. On another scroll depicting the upper or sky degrees, Red Sky shows a flock of birds; Selwyn Dewdney assumes that owl is among them.[89]

To recapitulate, the owl presents several layers of meaning and several relationships in the Ojibwe world. An owl summons the dead and becomes a relative, a grandfather, who mediates between life and death and who guides by loaning its eyes to travellers on the path to a new home.

Owl and Conservation

In a story, Hawk Owl, representing the older generation, and Boreal Owl, representing the younger generation, contest the origin of the offspring of their mutual lover Wapise, Willow Grouse. Results from the intricate test for paternity indicate that Boreal Owl is the father, much to the dismay of Hawk Owl. But the relationship between the older and the younger does not become hostile; instead, while harbouring tensions, it reflects their interdependence, an alliance, direct concurrence, and cooperation. As the story ends, Hawk Owl encounters Attitamo, the squirrel, who pleads for his life and promises to plant beautiful trees. Also, when North or West Wind is defeated, it changes into a squirrel and thereby continues to be a catalyst in the lives of trees.[90]

Owl and Origin of Day and Night

Shunien narrates a Menomini story that is close to Ojibwe traditions, "The Rabbit and the Saw-whet," on the origins of night and day. Wapus (Rabbit) encountered Totoba (Saw-whet Owl) and in the presence of all the animals in the forest, the two battled for the rule of daylight *(Wabon)* or darkness by repeating the words day and night. Totoba erred and daylight won, but Wapus gave conquered Totoba/darkness a meaningful place, and thus day and night were born.[91] Owl is "the integration of contraries for the sake of enduring, generative harmony," Thomas D. Thompson notes. "Totoba, as dark, happily still has a place in the perpetuating of the fluctuating, generative qualities peculiar to life in all circumstances. That such an uncommonly good truth might be known, *Gook kook'oo'oo*, usually a night-flyer, proves the proper messenger. Her unusual voice indicates light-filled life always visiting everywhere, even the darkest places. She manifests the great mystery that physical objects may be seen in daylight, but the life force itself, unseen as if in darkness, is still to be recognized and respected."[92] In "They Come to Let Us Know," the contemporary Ojibwe artist Roy Morris paints four owls together in one profile. With their big eyes, these birds are attentive and ready to communicate.[93]

Representations of Owl

Representations of owl occur in Ojibwe life in general and on the Midewiwin scrolls and in their ceremonies. These images often join additional avian Ojibwe forms. We have already noted that other birds vie with owl and hawk for the second rung in the Mide rites.

Owls are represented in the form of names and sounds. Place names can vocalize the voices of owls, which are often depicted today as gathering in groups or flocks.[94] According to George Copway, these names are onomatopoetic, that is, based on the sounds that the animals produce.[95] In the seventeenth century, missionary Claude Allouez noted the mutual and reciprocal sounds made by the Odawa and birds.[96] Owls are the good Manitous of the sky realm and of the four winds. Since the owl Manitous are good, their sounds are worthy of imitation.

Grace Rajnovich describes a petroglyph on Picture Rock Island in Lake of the Woods, Ontario, with a hand, bird, and sky communication line, perhaps somewhat distant from direct owl symbolism.[97] Other commentators point to sky contacts: "If the flat hand is pressed to the lips, and thence moved upwards to the heavens, it indicates a prayer or address to Deity," Kohl writes.[98]

Thunderbirds are often depicted in paintings and petroglyphs with power lines from their wings, denoting knowledge and power from above; we have not observed such images of owls. Thunderbird is often the power of Manitou and represents the four winds making things grow. We have seen owls in these capacities as well.[99]

Representations of a foursome are common in Ojibwe designs. Coleman notes that circles or dots are often arranged in groups of fours and eights. The "design is composed of two crossed spirals, forming either a single or double swastika. It represents the four directions or winds, symbolizing universal power and that of owls. It is used in the Midé mnemonic scrolls which the Midé priests interpret as signifying the road of life the Ojibwa should follow if he wishes happiness and long life. According to informants the true Ojibwa swastika always contains a circle in the center, presenting the sun or Kijé manito."[100]

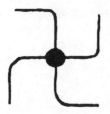

Four winds design. Coleman, *Decorative Designs*, 7.

Representations of real birds (very few owls, however) as well as imaginary ones are "used in decorating fire bags, birch bark baskets, Midé drums and birch bark scrolls."[101] Coleman provides illustrations of birch bark baskets, boxes, and trays on which there are four branches, signifying possibly the directions and winds.[102] In the context of games, she offers two birch bark bitings and other artistic pieces in elaborate designs and patterns of fours.[103]

Somewhat ambiguous dream figures on cloth or hide were carried on the person and were believed to give protection to the bearers. To protect themselves, Ojibwe men wore clothing and moccasins with geometrical patterns, in the belief that Manitou powers dwelled in these abstract representations. While the article manifested the Manitou and animal, the dream itself remained a mystery generally undisclosed to others. Such dream symbols were also found on women's dresses and on head and neck bands.[104] There is a four winds design on a rattle used by the Mide leaders in curing the sick and in a Midewiwin ceremony,[105] indicating that some dreams became public. "One of my informants," Coleman writes, "told of having seen an owl used as a dream symbol embroidered on a man's clothing."[106] In the Minnesota Historical Society Museum are two pieces from the late nineteenth and early twentieth centuries: an "Owl Feather Headdress," and an "Ojibwa Birchbark Owl Charm."[107]

By way of summary: At the beginning of this chapter, we gave informational accounts of owls. Owl was associated with or was the agent of fear, maiming a person and even leading him or her to death. Gradually we noticed owl's positive and humanistic presence, which pervaded all aspects of the Ojibwe life world. We noted owls' nuanced voices, which guide the winds and the seasons of the year. As Vine Deloria states, "Indian knowledge provides a predictive context in which certain prophetic statements can be made."[108]

Owl continues to have an abiding presence in Ojibwe stories and in cultural representations as a creature, as a symbol, and as Manitou. In addition, in the ceremonies of the Midewiwin, owl's presence was indicated by its inclusion on birch bark scrolls. Owl's proclamations and activities transformed Ojibwe lives, with some people appropriating owl so profoundly that they were *called* owls.

Mide leaders were immersed in stories, representations, and celebrations of owls. Stories provided accounts of owls that paralleled those of the Midewiwin rites: on the one hand, the owl was a benevolent advocate, a healer of and protector against sickness, grief, and death; on the other, owl was as a sinister and threatening power that was mirrored in the fifth to eighth steps in the Midewiwin initiation. Owl also displayed contrasting but interrelated spiritual powers, in that it was associated with the air, but also with the earth and water, all concerns of Midewiwin rituals. We have evidence of owls in Midewiwin songs, giving rise to speculation that the owl's sonorous cry permeated the Midewiwin assembly, thus assuring the Ojibwe of long life.

Owl is a wise sharer; it commands a regular regimen in life, and it mediates with the four directions and winds, guiding them vocally to initiate reciprocally both silence and sounds. Such an interplay is evident in hunting rituals, in creation and regeneration, and in healing, sleep, and death, all of which reflect cyclic and cosmic relationships. The owl is visually present during all four stages of spiritual initiation in the Midewiwin ceremonies, and it is acoustically present in the rattle that dispels bad spirits and recalls mythic times of wholeness. On the Midewiwin scrolls, owl is portrayed as a relative, as a grandfather, summoning the dead. Owl thus mediates between life and death, guiding travellers by loaning its eyes to them on the path to death. Just as the Mide ceremonies involve life and death, the owl integrates light and dark, the seen and the unseen. Also, in Ojibwe life in general there are many representations of owl, from vocalizations of its call to depictions on ceremonial and domestic objects.

Ojibwe society in general and the Mide practitioners in particular were steeped in a culture that treasured the owl. These practitioners were active not only in the spiritual domain but also in the political one; these leaders, many of whom came from the lodge, became the voices and messengers of the owl – indeed, they became the owl itself. The owl's formative influence, then, spanned the three ecstasies of time: pre-contact, post-contact, and future.

We arrived at two general conclusions regarding owl and the Ojibwe: first, that owl needed places to dwell, a homeland, both in story and ceremonial form and in territorial locales; and second, that owl and other animals, even in their ambivalent and negative forms, figured profoundly in the lives of the Ojibwe. The Ojibwe, then, could not have willingly ceded proprietorship of their lands, which furnished homes for the owl and which fashioned the very identity of the Ojibwe.[109]

5

Omnipresent and Ambivalent Bears

There are two ways of perceiving and describing bears. One way is to use a Western scientific lens to classify them and recount their actions and characteristics. The second way is to use an Aboriginal lens to narrate episodes of encountering them. We will use both of these lens to describe bears physically. Representational, ceremonial, patterned, and storied approaches to bears will be considered later. Bears are present everywhere in nineteenth-century Ojibwe cultures and have many, often paradoxical characteristics.

Bears' Anatomy, Physiology, and Behaviour

In the scientific and Western way, the bear is perceived in its relatedness to humans and their enterprises. Thus, the bear is popularly seen, in the words of Wayne Lynch, as "as circus clown, roadside beggar, hunting trophy, agricultural pest, zoo entertainer and symbol of the wilderness."[1] Physically, bears, the largest of the carnivores, have heavy bodies and strong limbs. They are indeed monarchs; according to the Naskapi, they are the sole governor and lord of their species, subject to no higher authority.[2]

Some general traits distinguish bears from other carnivores: they walk on the soles of their feet rather than on their toes; their feet are flat and broad with five heavy, curved claws. While walking, the bear's front feet turn inward; "this rotational mobility enables bears to climb and dig better."[3] They have large heads, rounded ears, and very short tails; their small eyes, equipped for depth perception, and their ability to stand on their hind feet are important assets for them as predators.

In the scientific taxonomy, there are eight distinct species of bears, which vary in terms of their behaviour, skeletal formation, and coat colour; the latter changes considerably with location. Let us single out the two species of bears that have associations with the Ojibwe: brown bears *(Ursus arctos)* and the American black bear *(Ursus americanus).* Brown bears, also called grizzlies *(Ursus arctos horribilis)* because of their grizzled or grey silver-tipped hairs, which develop as they get older, are one of the largest and most widely distributed bear species, with the male weighing between 150 and 380 kilograms (330 and 840 pounds) and having a maximum body length of 275 centimetres (110 inches). Brown bears have a heavy, stout body with strong, muscular legs. They are very quick, able to attain speeds of 56 kilometres (35 miles) per hour for a short distance. Brown bears often live longer than twenty-five years. Usually dark-brown in colour, they may actually be "bleached blonds, or brunet, auburn or almost black." They are characterized by a muscle hump over their shoulders.[4]

Brown bears inhabit dense forests, tundra, lower alpine regions, and river valleys. They are largely vegetarian but can be omnivorous, eating a mixed diet of grasses, fruits, bulbs and roots, insects, fish, and small animals. Brown bears are sometimes predators of larger animals such as caribou and moose and can feed on carrion, including whales, walruses, and seals that have washed up on shore. They are solitary except for the females with cubs. They inhabit areas with abundant food sources, such as dump sites, berry patches, and salmon spawning sites. During eating binges, brown bears are able to gain 1.25 to 2.75 kilograms (3 to 6 pounds) of fat each day.

Female brown bears reach sexual maturity at around four-and-a-half years; mating takes place between May and July. There can be a period of delayed implantation of the embryos, and this can be important to the mother's survival: if she does not have enough fat reserves to carry herself through the winter, the embryo will not implant and will simply be reabsorbed by her body. Cubs are born between January and March. A female can give birth to as many as four cubs, who will stay with her for as long as two-and-a-half years. The survival of brown bear cubs depends on the mother's skill at both protecting them and teaching them what to eat, where and how to procure food, where to den, and how to cope with danger.[5]

The most common bear is the black bear, which is highly adaptable and readily associates with people.[6] Black bears are of medium size, weighing 60 to 300 kilograms (130 to 660 pounds) and with a body length of 120 to 180 centimetres (50 to 75 inches); they have a lifespan of twenty-five or more years. Black bears have a heavy body, a short tail, and rounded ears. They can run in excess of 40 kilometres (25 miles) per hour for short distances. They do not have the distinct shoulder hump of the brown/grizzly bear; the claws on their front paws are short, curved, and highly adapted to tree climbing. Fur colour varies from black to chocolate brown, cinnamon brown, pale blue (known as glacier bears), or white. They are the most numerous and widespread of all bear species and can be found in many places in Canada, the United States, and Mexico.

Black bears prefer forested and sometimes meadowy areas, which sequester them from contact with brown bears, which physically are a much larger species. Black bears are generally vegetarians but can be omnivores, eating nuts, berries, fruits, acorns, roots, honey, grasses and other plants, insects (especially ants), deer and moose fawns, carrion, and (in coastal areas) spawning salmon. Black bears are usually solitary except for females with young, and they may feed close together with little interaction. They mark their territories both with scent and by clawing long scratches in tree bark.

Female black bears reach sexual maturity at three or four years of age; mating takes place between June and August. The cubs are born in their mother's winter den in January or February. As with brown bears, the cubs are highly dependent on the mother for survival. For instance, while she is foraging, she often places the cubs under the shelter of a thicket or in a nearby tree. In the event of danger, the cubs will stay in the tree while their mother either stands guard on the forest ground below or climbs the tree after them. Cubs are weaned at around eight months but may remain with their mother for a year and a half.[7]

Lynch writes that while hibernating – which can comprise half their lives – bears "do not eat, drink, urinate, or defecate for months at a time, a metabolic feat unmatched in the animal world."[8] During hibernation, a bear's heart rate drops from the normal 40 to 70 beats a minute, to 8 to 12; its metabolism slows by half; its body temperature, however, drops only slightly. Female bears give birth and nurse during their hibernation. When suckling, the kittens or puppies tread rhythmically on their mother's body with their front paws and produce a loud, continuous humming sound.[9] This sound, called a nursing chuckle, is often loud enough to be heard outside the den. Cubs bond with their mothers in spring and summer, playing with and around them, climbing on their bodies, perching on their heads and sliding or jumping down. The mothers spend considerable time defending and educating their cubs.[10]

"Bears have a rich behavioural repertoire," Lynch writes. "They are intelligent, adaptable creatures"[11] but are generally solitary. They gather "only in small groups in certain seasons at berry patches or fishing grounds."[12] Bears seldom please people: "When bears eat trees, the foresters are unhappy. When they eat fish, the fishermen are unhappy. And when they eat goose eggs, the biologists are unhappy":[13]

"The odours from three ... different sources – urine, feces and body scent – can tell a lot about a bear," Lynch adds. "They can identify an individual, divulge its sex, disclose whether it is an adult or a youngster and reveal whether it is sexually receptive or not. From the smell of another's breath, a bear may even know whether it is fasting or feasting ... Some bears are diurnal, some are nocturnal, and others crepuscular, or active at dusk and dawn."[14]

Black and brown bears delight in two kinds of food: soft mast and hard mast. Soft mast includes soft and juicy foods such as fruits and berries, while hard mast consists of various nuts. Since hard mast has up to twice as much fat content as soft mast, bears ingest it in the fall in order to accumulate as many calories as possible. "A recent study suggests that the bear's digestive physiology may also shift in autumn to increase the animal's ability to digest fat, and this further facilitates rapid weight gain ... The amount of weight that a bear gains in the fall is regulated by its appetite, which in turn is regulated by the amount of fat that it has stored. Once its fat reserves reach a certain level, a feedback mechanism turns off the bear's appetite, and the animal stops feeding." Hormones in the female bear control the incidence of pregnancy, setting it to an optimal time, while "the control of implantation by the size of an animal's fat reserves and the synchronization of implantation with the photoperiod are remarkable refinements in the reproductive biology of bears. They illustrate how sensitively attuned these animals are to their environment."[15]

Bears' fat and bile are carriers of medicine that can prevent gallstones, cure liver and bile duct diseases, and alleviate the symptoms of jaundice and abdominal distention, all without producing side effects. Bear blood can cure osteoporosis.[16] In the Woodland regions of North America, bears were used as the buffalo was used on the prairies and plains. Frances Densmore recounts that this single animal provided most of the needs of the Ojibwe: "The flesh of the bear was cut in strips about 6 inches [15 centimeters] wide and hung on a frame to dry. If intended for winter use, it frequently was put on high racks to freeze. When used it was cut up a little and boiled. Bear meat was liked because it was so fat. All parts of the bear were eaten or utilized. The head was considered a luxury. They singed it, removed the inside, and boiled it whole. The paws were singed, scraped, and boiled. The liver was good to eat and the intestines were so fat that the Chippewa cleaned them and fried them crisp. The stomach was filled with tallow, known as 'bear's grease,' which was used for seasoning ... The gall was dried, mixed with cedar charcoal, and 'pricked into the skin' as a remedy for rheumatism and other ailments."[17]

Ojibwe Relationships with Bears

We have already pointed out the pivotal role that bears played in the Ojibwe Medicine Society. If we count the number of times it appeared in word, representation, and song, bear predominated over all the other animals. Bear, indeed, captured the essence of the Midewiwin.

In many ways, bears were like human beings. Wigwaswátik, chief of the Pekangikum band in Northern Ontario, believed that bears understood human speech. While hunting bears, he spoke to one who had grabbed his gun: "'If you want to live, go away,' and he let go the gun and walked off. I didn't bother the bear anymore."[18] If bears are considered to be merely instinctual beings, the above account is rather bizarre, but if they are regarded as kin to humans, and even superior to them, this behaviour is intelligible and even commonplace.

Paul Shepard writes that human–animal relations can be regarded as metaphorical, for there are shared qualities. But, he adds, something less extrinsic is at work here for Aboriginal peoples. "The animal mask on the body of a person joins in thought that which is otherwise separate, not only representing human change but conceptualizing shared qualities, so that unity in difference and difference in unity can be conceived as an intrinsic truth. And some animals, by their form or habit, are boundary creatures who signify the passages of human life. Finally, in dance these bodies move to deep rhythms that bind the world and bring the humans into mimetic participation with other beings."[19] Ojibwe belief extends further than scientific and factual accounts to include a certain perception of conduct fitting that belief, that is, a belief and perception of human-like characteristics of bear. The actions and vocalizations of bears are then not merely objective qualities, but personal and interrelational properties.

Since there was such a great affinity between bears and humans, some Indians would not eat ursine flesh, according to Landes, "because it would be like eating a man."[20] These inhibitions and prohibitions, however, did not seem widespread. Bears' fat was considered the most delectable and useful of foods; it could be used for frying and seasoning dried meat, as butter or broth, and as oil in the Ojibwe's hair and on their bodies as a defence against mosquitoes. Spiritually, bear fat was believed to be an antidote for cannibalistic spirits.[21]

Many Ojibwe beliefs involved transformation – that is, the idea that bears could be transformed into humans and humans into bears. According to A. Irving Hallowell, a "very old, widespread, and persistent belief [is] that sorcerers may become transformed into bears in order better to pursue their nefarious work." Even in the mid-twentieth century, when Indians themselves questioned the factual nature of many stories of metamorphosis, anecdotal accounts of bearwalkers remained, which, while frightening, were regarded as "highly acculturated."[22] Many accounts, however, attested that transformation was possible not only on the physical level but also, and especially, on the symbolic.

Mide and bear. Song scroll: "I give you medicine, and a lodge, also." "The Mide, as the personator of Makwa [bear] Manido, is empowered to offer this privilege to the candidate." Mallery, *Picture-Writing*, 1:239.

Some efforts to explain these transformative possibilities are based on the premise that human perception can be quite flexible. In this explanation, perception does not definitively establish the identity of the individual, for what is perceived as a bear might remain a human being and vice versa. This transformative possibility is based on an underlying and perhaps unconscious agreement about perceptual ambiguity, as we noted in an earlier chapter.[23]

On the basis of stories and observations, the Ojibwe conclude that humans and bears have close affinities and even, at times, share an identity. David A. Johnson has created an illustration showing this near identity: a profile of two faces, human and bear, which share the same space, with the human hand and bear paw within the interconnected line drawing of the two faces.[24] The conclusion drawn from these affinities, however, presents complex challenges and merits further investigation. The Ojibwe believe that because of this kinship in human/ animal relationships, it is not usually possible to be sure whether a bear is a human being or a human being is a bear. In other words, human perceptions about these beings remain ambiguous most of the time, as we examined earlier.

Some naturalists have shown that a proper human disposition toward bears can help overcome the fear that humans have of them and prevent confrontations and attacks on humans. This disposition is based on an understanding of bears. Charlie Russell from Cochrane, Alberta, demonstrates this close relationship; journalist Mark Stevenson describes Russell's long-time friendship with bears: "He thinks like a bear. He acts like a bear. He fundamentally understands bears."[25]

From his talks with Kitagiguan or Spotted Feather in the mid-nineteenth century, theoretical geographer Johann Kohl learned that bears have the intellectual and volitional capacity to understand the stratagems of others and devise counterploys. Their self-awareness is evident when they chase other animals; and when being stalked, they find places from which to view the hunters while deliberately hiding themselves. When pursued, bears deceive hunters regarding the direction they have taken by running up and down riverbeds. To avoid making tracks in the snow and thereby frustrate hunters, bears jump from one tree stump to another. If they must make tracks in the snow, they take a zigzag route, then turn back or leap off the trail. When they find a hollow tree in which to pass the winter, they will wait and watch for intruders for three days before entering it. Bears have other tricks to fool hunters as well, such as pretending to be dead. As a consequence of this demonstration of intelligence, the Ojibwe respected bears, addressing them not merely as Manitous or spirits but as honoured guests.[26]

For the Ojibwe, the bear was not merely an animal among other animals; it was special in many ways. Rockwell writes that "the bear was the shaggy berry picker, the shambling nut gatherer asleep under the piñon tree, the mysterious herbalist collecting medicines in the dense undergrowth of the wet bottomlands. Using its claws instead of a digging stick, the bear was that wise old animal person digging roots on the sun-baked hillsides."[27] Humans took note of bear's wise medicinal experiments, observed the effects of plants on bear, and imitated bear's practices in maintaining good health. It was bear who presided over the medicine plants and thereby gave humans the power to cure sickness.

In animals, but especially in bear, Indians saw the Great Spirit, a reflection of the seasons of the year, and a reflection of themselves. As Joseph Epes Brown writes: "In them [animals] the Indian sees actual reflections of the qualities of the Great Spirit, which serve the same function as revealed scriptures in other religions. They [animals] are intermediaries or links between human beings and God. This explains not only why religious devotions may be directed to the deity *through* the animals, but it also helps us to understand why contact with, or from, the Great Spirit, comes almost exclusively through visions involving animal or other natural forms."[28]

Besides being a representative of the Great Spirit, bear was an icon of the spring season, as hibernating bear triumphed over the long winter. "It therefore symbolized the rebirth of health, the reawakening of spirit, and the moving from near death to life."[29]

Tree and bear. Song copied by "'Little Frenchman,' an Ojibwa Mide of the first degree": "It stands, that which I am going after." "Tree; showing tracks made by bear spirit. The speaker terms himself equal with this spirit and represents himself seeking remedies." Mallery, *Picture-Writing*, 1:242.

Bear also represented the diversity of the Ojibwe themselves. The bear presented an expansive image, "a host of characters. There are kind and generous bears in the stories, just as there are malicious and perverse bears," Rockwell writes. "There are noble bears willing to sacrifice their lives for their families, and there are selfish, food-hoarding bears. There are cunning bears and bears that are easily duped, bears that threaten and destroy, and benign bears ... Like gods in Greek myths, bears in the Native North American oral tradition possessed all the human fallibilities while retaining their godliness ... Native Americans incarnated the bear in countless rituals. They danced to bring in the spring, to heal the sick, to ensure abundant plant foods, to guard themselves against their enemies."[30]

Ojibwe Gerald Vizenor reinterprets and expands the bear metaphor. There are technological bears and urban bears "as Vizenor moves the human connections with bears and bear metaphors from the spiritual to the secular, from past to present, from the pastoral to the technological, from oral to written, from reservation to city," Nora Baker Barry writes. "[Bears are] the breakers of barriers, they are the beings at the doorways between realism and magical realism, between horror and transcendence. ... [Bears] bridge the gaps between the secular and the spiritual and connect the physical and spiritual."[31] For Vizenor, bears are the repository for unspoken memories in tribal ritual and stories; they are guides and maps, as are the song scrolls, through "death of the old life and resurrection into the new life"; they incorporate traditional portals into contemporary reality, infusing an oral consciousness into the written word. While bears often represent positive values in spiritual ceremonies, erotic bears also represent, like trickster, "gender confusions," "out-of-control sexuality," and "uninhibited animal physicality," all primal passions.[32]

Since the bear image or reality is able to transform itself or be transformed, the signs/symbols of bears cannot be fixed rigidly in the mind or in reality; the symbols themselves are – indeed, need to be – transcended. Both reality and symbols of that reality are flexible, and perceivers note these ambiguities. Thus, there are few limits to human conceptions of animals, or to the conceptions among animals themselves, for in the Ojibwe world animals are not bound by Latin terms and are not limited to a classification by species; their definitions are fluid. With this flexibility, a different world opens up, an expansive world that moves beyond conceptions of humans as the sole foundation for healing and morality, for both humans and animals play a role in healing processes and in moral understanding. If there are any limitations among animals, it is a consequence of their mortality; but even that mortality is eroded by beliefs in transformation and transmigration. There is no completely fixed form to animals' beings, only the possibility of transformation.[33] These transformations involve not only animals but also humans, who can be transformed into animals and back again.

In an interview, Bill Sutton, a rice chief[34] on the Lac Courte Oreilles Reservation, described experiences of sickness and healing, his personal transformations from life to death and back again, and his movement back to the Midewiwin:

[I was first a Catholic and then] I died once, you know. I seen my feet stick out that much in a coffin. And that's when I seen like a big hand like that grab me sitting in there. He set me over there and said, "This is where I put you in the first place." When he let me go over there it was bright daylight over there. [Bill was in the hospital and tore out the tubes the doctors and nurses had inserted into him.] ... And pretty soon the spirits and everything come, it was a drum ... Then I use that good; I bring people back to life, and I talk to my drum all the time. He notify me everything ... So I notice I never sick. I don't take no medication. It's cause I believe that spirit, you know. And every time they sick in wigwam, I go there and that spirit talk to me. And that drum spirit he talk to me. I had some awful cases, man [who committed suicide] ... I completely surrender all into a good spirit. I got back on the trail. Then I went back to Midewiwin, the Indian way of life, religion.[35]

In the Ojibwe world, both humans and animals are personal and not merely sentient beings, things, or machines; humans and animals are interrelated and cohabit the same world. Factors relating to health and causes of disease are also personal; such forces are agents and animated causes. In a technological world, natural causes of health or disease, whether organic or inorganic, are seldom regarded as personal; instead, they are regarded as objective and as natural or unnatural. Yet even scientific perspectives admit that while the agent's personal choice may be a factor, mysterious causes of health and disease often come together through accidental relations. The fusing of mysterious causes is apparent in Ojibwe conceptions. "The Ojibwa believe in a multiplicity of spirits, or manidos, which inhabit all space and every conspicuous object in nature," Hoffman writes.[36] And these Manitou take many forms, including the myriad ones of animals.

Bear often controls other animals and acts vicariously through them. According to Norval Morrisseau, an Ojibwe, many centuries ago the holy bear of the Midewiwin imparted the knowledge of several hundred kinds of medicine through a horned serpent, with the medicines represented by a cup. The cup was kept brim full but never overflowing. The Midewiwin sought medical knowledge through fasting. From the perspective of today's Ojibwe, the cup is overflowing, which indicates, Morrisseau tells us, that "the younger people are not interested in keeping that medicine culture alive." This was a sign long ago. Today, nevertheless, through the horned serpent, the demigod of medicine still gives this knowledge to some, even though they do not fast.[37]

Morrisseau attributes medicine to the horned serpent; however, bear can be a replacement animal because of the fear or taboo surrounding the unmentionable great underwater serpent.[38] He recalls the special relationship that his paternal grandfather had with a bear. While fasting, his grandfather had a dream in which bear promised to be his guardian, to give him special powers – "to do good" and to have good luck. A condition for the promise's fulfilment was that grandfather respect the bear and never kill it. Bear then entered the grandfather's body, with a presence localized in his back or hip. When grandfather's internal bear was poisoned, a medicine man "rubbed and also sucked ... out the affected part at the back."[39]

The near-identification of humans and bears was rather ordinary thinking among the Ojibwe. "An Ojibwa girl about to start her first menstrual period was called *wemukowe*, which means 'going to be a bear.'"[40] Older women also partook of bear spirits. Vizenor wrote a song poem about a brave female warrior who defended her children against the Dakota. She "fought like a great bear, striking the woodland *dakota* warriors and tearing their canoe apart with her hands."[41] In his re-created Ojibwe tales, Vizenor depicts Bagese, a bag lady, as a wild bear who plays roles in trickster stories and who is a trickster herself. She celebrates her descent from stones and bears. Bagese is bear woman, at home in the oral tradition, not the written word, and is not seen with the eyes but is heard in the ears. She plays a *wanaki* game and inhabits the city but also treelines in the mountains. Her stories roar with nature.[42]

Ojibwe called the bear *anijinabe*, which means "people," "an Indian person."[43] After all, bears have anatomical carriages like humans, cuddle their young as human mothers do, and often show moderation in their actions despite their physical strength; they also enjoy sweet foods and liquor! Bears in urban settings have the same weight-gain problems as humans, for retrieving food from dumpsters requires less effort than foraging for berries and carrion.[44]

The Ojibwe, among other Aboriginal peoples, were apologetic when they hunted and killed bears. According to Edwin Higgins, "bears were treated with special respect; when one was killed, several rituals were carried out to placate its spirit and insure continued good hunting. Addressing the bear with such respectful terms as 'Grandmother,' the hunter explained to it his need for its skin and meat. The bear was carried to the lodge which had been cleaned especially for the occasion, and a feast of bear meat was then prepared. The skull was lashed on to a tree and often decorated with a painted design. Such treatment of the bear as a respected fellow being possessing a spirit reflects how the Ojibway saw themselves – as fellow inhabitants sharing the environment with the animal."[45] Indeed, bears transcended the capabilities of humans because they had not only their own powers but those of humans as well.[46] Bears, then, being the most spiritually empowered of animals, merited respect and cooperation from humans.

Bears' human-like, or human, qualities are extraordinary. They partake of an omnivorous diet, can sit or stand, have unique paw prints, and demonstrate emotional and even idiosyncratic behaviour toward fellow bears and toward humans. When they are skinned, their frames and flesh have human proportions.[47] Paul Shepard and Barry Sanders elaborate on this similarity: "Like us, the bear stands upright on the soles of his feet, his eyes nearly in a frontal plane. The bear moves his forelimbs freely in their shoulder sockets, sits on his tail end, one leg folded, like an adolescent slouched on the table, worries with moans and sighs, courts with demonstrable affection, produces excrement similar to man's, snores in his sleep, spanks his children, is avid for sweets, and has a moody, gruff, and morose side ... [Bear is] wily, smart, strong, fast, agile." Shepard and Sanders speculate that this independent being is a replica of humans as they existed in times past and now acts as a reminder of what humans have lost, especially for those in urban life who have difficulty achieving harmony with nature.

Contemporary human life exhibits traces of these bear-like qualities, which, like genetic imprints, are evident "in daily language, religion, literature, folklore, fairy tales, place names, toys, plant and food names, and even surnames." Indeed, vestiges of bear are virtually everywhere, even in contemporary hierarchical structures. When we trace the etymology of the word "bear" in Latin, we find *ferrum*, meaning "iron"; we have the words "fertile" and "ferocious." When we trace the etymology of the word in Greek, we find *arktos/arkhos*, meaning "chief or primary sources," as for example, "archaic," "archbishop," "archaeology."[48] From early contact times to the present, bears have been depicted as related to humans, and their spirit has penetrated cultural and linguistic forms throughout the world.

Representations of Bear in Ceremonial Performances

As portrayed on song scrolls, on pictographs, and in ceremonies, bear is a distinctive being. As we have seen, bear is a kindred being but also a fearsome one physically; its presence is not merely towering, but neither is it merely cuddly. For Norval Morrisseau, the contemporary artist from Sandy Point Reserve, Thunder Bay, Ontario, bear was a special spirit being. Eating its meat was a treat but could also produce unique effects in mere mortals – diarrhea. "To the Indian way of thinking, a person gets shits not through the meat itself but because the bear is sacred, and one cannot eat too much of the meat of a demigod."[49] Visionaries, however, were obliged to eat its empowering meat, paws, and marrow.[50]

For the Ojibwe, killing a bear entailed a ceremony. Some blood was seized in the hand, thanksgiving was made to the animal, and the blood, regarded as a medicine or power, was poured on the ground or dispersed to the four cardinal directions. The proper ritual showed respect for the bear spirit and ensured success in future hunts.[51]

The power of bear continued through private and public ceremonials after its death. Bears' bones were used for sucking rites; its teeth were fashioned into whistles and charms; a fearful power emanated from blowing its teeth.[52] As marks of respect, "clothing and tobacco are tied with one claw in bright-coloured cloth and ribbons and placed in the forest in its honour." Painting the bear's shoulder bones ensured long life; its skull was decorated and painted, with special reverence and prestige accorded an albino bear. To indicate the continued radiation of energy in life and death, Morrisseau created X-ray-like paintings of bears with power lines or waves radiating from them.[53]

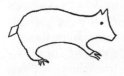

Bear. "Representations of real as well as imaginary animals are common Ojibwa designs. They were used in decorating fire bags, birch bark baskets, Mide drums and birch bark scrolls." Coleman, *Decorative Designs*, 6–7, 9.

John Mink, from Lac Courte Oreilles in northern Wisconsin, wrote of his experiences in the early twentieth century: When he was nursing, his mother's milk tasted like bear's fat, a delicacy. There was a logic to this comparison, for according to Mink, both humans and bears were part of nature and the differences were largely external. "Animals are motivated as men are motivated, live in societies as men live, act as men act, and their fates are intertwined." Thus, when a bear died, the respectful treatment it received was akin to that accorded to humans: "its four paws and head were placed in position on a rush mat and a feast was given." Its head "was decorated with ribbons, beadwork, or a baby's clothes and food and tobacco put nearby." In another tradition, instead of a mat, a pole was the repository for bear.[54] A bowl of wild rice, maple sugar, syrup, and blueberries was placed close at hand. People talked endearingly to the bear "so that its spirit would return to the village of the bears and persuade other bears to allow themselves [and their offspring] to be killed."[55]

Alanson Skinner describes the exceptional veneration accorded to slain bear in some Eastern Cree and Northern Saulteaux traditions. They apologize to the black bear caught in a trap. After it is killed, it is dressed in the best finery obtainable and is laid out to look like a human being. A prayer is offered to the chief of bears to send more of his children to the Indians.[56]

John Tanner mentions that a major consequence of the hunt is or should be hospitality, based on the reality that the animal killed has shared its life. Whatever his charisma in obtaining the animal and his consequent claim, the hunter had to give it to his band, for it was common property. If he met anyone on another hunt, "even a little boy," he was bound to give him his hunt. To maintain possession, however, men sometimes left the animal where they killed it and returned home; they then sent women to bring in the meat, thereby ensuring retention of the game. Another ploy to ensure possession was to hide the hunt and retrieve it later, when no people were around.[57]

Slain bear's power was extended to sounds and images on the song and ritual scrolls of the Midewiwin. Each member of that society possessed a hide or ornamented medicine bag made of otter or bear skin. The Ojibwe believed that during the ceremonies the skins came alive and made various animal sounds. As the medicine bags were pointed at a new member, they "would shoot forth medicine, or magic powers." The power from the bags would fell, paralyse, or kill the initiate. He or she would then be revived.[58]

According to various positions of the sun, this shooting could be a symbol of regeneration. With the sun poised overhead and the medicine bags aimed at his heart, the candidate was transformed into the mythic hero, Nanabush, thus moving the ceremony from the ritual to the mythic world.[59]

In songs and prayers, bear was never "called by the common name, but always che-mahn-duk." These bear songs generally had special authority in the hunt, according to the Red River Ojibwe.[60] Cree stories recall that bear liked to be called one of the following special names: Grandmother, Grandfather, Cousin, Elder Brother, Black Food, The One Who Owns the Chin, Memekwesiw's Little Pup, Chief's Son, Four-legged Human, or Food of the Fire. It angered the bear if a hunter did not call it by one of these names.[61] The Mistassini referred to bear in the following circumlocutory terms in order to avoid its general name: Short Tail, His Great Food, The One Who Owns the Chin, Black Food, and Clown.[62]

Near-Identity of Bears and Ojibwe

The near-identity of lodge and bear flows from values in Ojibwe society that demonstrate a close relationship between that society and bear. Julia Harrison's thesis is that bear and the Ojibwe Medicine Society are replicas of each other. Bear is the guardian of the Midewiwin, and the lodge represents the bear.[63] Harrison maintains that bear retains three traditional themes of Ojibwe ideology: self-orientation, mobility, and divisibility. By examining metaphorical bear, present-day Ojibwe can tap into their culture's threefold nature, can understand their own true being, and, on that foundation, can create new social and political communities.

First, we will examine the theme of self-orientation that Harrison presents. In Canada, especially between 1760 and 1820, the heritage of the Ojibwe peoples was placed in jeopardy. The revival of the Midewiwin, with its emphasis on good health, was a valued response to the ravages of disease, permanent settlements, greatly diminished supplies of food and furs, and the change from French to English control. The Midewiwin ritual, which was strongly communal in its orientation, harnessed the powers of the Manitous, the most powerful of which was the bear, and directed the salutary use of herbal remedies and medicines. For Harrison, the Ojibwe paradigm was "like the bear, like the Midewiwin, and like the Ojibwe themselves." There were not just close links among these three realities; there was a near-identity. Each component in this paradigm achieved its uniqueness through a similar type of separation: the bear differed from other animals, for it avoided "becoming an integral member of any larger group structure ... If the bear was in a group, it was for a specific purpose," such as picking berries. The Midewiwin was separated from other ceremonies; and the Ojibwe were somewhat distinct from other nations, just as individuals in a community differed from the whole. While not atomistic in nature, the Ojibwe people, like bear, were self-dependent, often relying on individual powers rather than on those of the group.

Second, there is the theme of mobility. The Midewiwin ritual scroll depicts bear's paws, which symbolize walking or running, and advancing from one place to the next. In a similar manner, texts recount Ojibwe migrations and various encampments.[64]

Manitou. Song scroll: "Almost, He will listen to us, Manido." "This outline is frequently used to represent a manido." Densmore, *Chippewa Music*, 1:61.

Third, there is the concept of divisibility. The song scrolls depict isolated parts of bear's anatomy, such as paws and head. Such isolated body parts could stand on their own, but when they do, according to

Harrison, they have merely implied and not very definite meanings; the pieces have limited meanings in themselves and require the symbol of the whole for completion. Such is also the case with Ojibwe cultures: they can be divided into parts, but they require a wider context for an adequate understanding. Fitting individual images together on the scrolls and interpreting them requires a wide and penetrating knowledge of Ojibwe life.[65] For Harrison, the metaphors of self-orientation, mobility, and divisibility among bears, within the Midewiwin, and in Ojibwe society were an attempt to create a code for regulating experience.[66]

While the Ojibwe and their ceremonies had affinities with the characteristics and actions of bears, there were also notable differences. Bears were transcendent beings with mysterious capacities beyond human understanding and imitation. One of these transcendent qualities was bear's ability to hibernate and survive the rigours of winter and emerge in the spring alive and well, with offspring in tow. In the Midewiwin ritual, practitioners imitated bears and "became bears" in order to partake in these transcendent qualities. Thus the bear was regarded as the epitome and the essence of Ojibwe culture and became the key to thwarting disintegration, a rallying call for that purpose. Bear represented traditional values and was celebrated in rituals and stories. Like a flag or national anthem, bear was and is a symbol replete with meaning.[67]

Bear in the Midewiwin Ceremonies

Bear is the predominant figure on all levels of the Midewiwin. Bear guards and protects the sweat lodge; Ruth Landes writes that in one of the creation stories, grandfather bear furnished his hide to create the first sweat lodge and to cover the Ojibwe.[68] Images of bear pervade the Midewiwin lodge: its stakes are referred to as bear legs; the ritual pipe is in the form of a bear. The stone carrier is called the "bear's shoulder strap," the water carrier is "our Grandfather's tail," and the two drumsticks are the "forepaws of our Grandfather."[69] Fred K. Blessing records that the *pindjigossan* or medicine bag/pack that was used for the fourth degree of the Mide ceremony was that of either a bear paw or a bear cub.[70] According to Benton-Banai, members of the bear clan kept order in the community; and since they had extensive knowledge of plants, they had a medical leadership role as well. In addition, members of the bear clan guarded the entrance to the Midewiwin lodge, just as individual bears did.[71] Hoffman provides a pictograph of a bear standing over the initiation lodge with his four feet inside both east and west doorways, suggesting his protection of the lodge or, perhaps, the bear's appropriation of the lodge itself.[72]

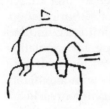

Bear in lodge. "Friends and family … saw through the doorway the approach of a bear." Hoffman, "The Midê'wiwin," 172a-173.

Bear was the "guiding spirit of the Midéwiwin,"[73] and the candidate followed "the bear path"[74] through the initiation ceremonial. During songs, which used bear imagery, and during the procession, both the presider and the candidate walked on their hands and knees like the bear Manitou,[75] although sometimes dog imagery was used in place of bear.[76] The songs in the lodge indicated the predominance of bear: "I give you medicine, and a lodge also"[77] (which Fulford translates as "Somebody is calling the bear").[78] Four good bear spirits often met the candidate at the entrance to the midewigan, guided the candidate around it, and deflected the four malevolent bear spirits who tried to thwart progress in the lodge.

Following initiation into the second degree, Mide candidates had the power to change into bears and could perform good or evil acts, thus either protecting or destroying. Chameleon-like and endowed with many powers, bear could in turn transform himself into different spirits. As well, an evil human power could assume the form of any animal, including bear, and could then retransform into a human form, "innocent of any crime."[79] Later on, we will examine bear as evil spirit independent of the lodge.

While in the lodge, the candidate had to pray and make tobacco offerings to the bear spirit. Three feasts and three prayers moved the bear spirit to allow admission from the first to the second degree. Smaller serpents moved to either side of the path in the lodge, while a larger serpent arched its body to permit the candidate to pass to an ascending degree. Or, alternatively, serpents flattened themselves to permit the candidate's passage, with the bear having power to overcome the snake Manitous.[80]

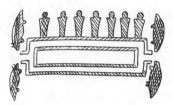

"Four malignant Bear Spirits ... guard the entrance and exit to the second degree." Seven Mide celebrants preside. Hoffman, "The Midê'wiwin," 168, 169a.

In second- and third-degree rites, the candidate impersonated the bear. The Minnesota Ojibwe considered the bear spirit "the tutelary guardian" and became like bear more intensively in the fourth degree. As Mide practitioners ascended the degrees, they were progressively more empowered with the "ability to grasp from the invisible world the knowledge and means to accomplish extraordinary deeds. [These practitioners then became] more confident of prompt response and assistance from the sacred manidos and his knowledge of them becomes more widely extended ... To enter the fourth and highest degree of the society requires a greater number of feasts than before, and the candidate, who continues to personate the Bear Spirit, again uses his sacred drum ... and chants more prayers to Dzhe Manido for his favor."[81]

The sacred drums "which the candidate must use when chanting the prayers, and two offerings must be made" on the first level of the Midewiwin. The bear spirit protects those at the entrance of the lodge (rectangular box). Hoffman, "The Midê'wiwin," 167–169a.

The medicinal themes relating to bear are contained in the ceremonial songs. From White Earth, Minnesota: "I am the strongest medicine, is what is said of me." And as an explanation, "The speaker compares himself to Makwa Manido, the Bear Spirit."[82]

So prominent were bears in Mide Sikassige's day that small clumps of tree structures called bears' nests were erected "where the Bear Manido rested during the struggle he passed through while fighting with the malevolent manidos within [in order] to gain entrance and receive the fourth-degree initiation." Posts were planted on the sides of the east and west entrances, at the bottom of which were laid stones. "These four posts represent the four limbs and feet of the Bear Manido, who made the four entrances and forcibly entered and expelled the evil beings who had opposed him."[83]

Selwyn Dewdney writes that on the four master scrolls from Berens River, Manitoba, bear "straddles the scroll like a colossus, his barrier-penetrating tongue thrust out in full view."[84] On the twenty scrolls that George Fulford selected from the White Earth Reservation, "otters, bears and birds ... constitute 92 per cent of the animal pictographs ... [permitting] meaningful generalizations."[85] In the Redsky birch bark scrolls from Thunder Bay, Ontario, bear has an impressive and all-pervasive presence. On one scroll depicting origins, bear makes four attempts to break through the barriers between himself and the world.[86] Bear successfully carries the Pack of Life through the obstacles and is strengthened in the initiation rite by passing through the Mide lodge itself.[87]

On each of the five classical scrolls that Dewdney examined, bear's tracks enter the lodge and in one case pass through it. This could represent either the presiding Mide who breaks through on the last of the four grades or the candidates themselves during their initiation. On the scrolls that are uterine- or tongue-like, bear is stationed at the entrances, Dewdney tells us; bear is also associated "with a rectangular form which may alternatively represent the sacred drum, or the Bear's Nest."[88]

"The Bear's nest ... are the places where Makwa [bear] Manido takes his station when guarding the doors [of the lodge]." Hoffman, "The Midê'wiwin," 174b, 178.

Bear is not merely the all-encompassing figure of life, however. On Skwekomik's master scroll, bear is a dominant figure along the path of the dead.

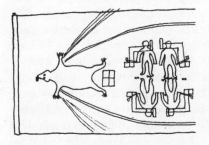

A huge bear "straddles the scroll [and lodge] like a colossus, his barrier-penetrating tongue thrust out in full view." From a scroll near Berens River, Manitoba. Dewdney, *The Sacred Scrolls*, 139, 151.

Also, on the fourth level of the Midewiwin especially, the forces of good and evil clash. As candidates progress toward this level, it becomes increasingly possible for them to attain powers that could be used for evil ends. On Sikassige's scrolls, a senior lodge member with a bow and four arrows helps the candidate drive out malignant monsters in the sacred space. In the fierce clash for power, monsters shoot fire across the lodge entrance and threaten the candidate with disease.[89]

The lodge and its practitioners have broad symbolic meanings for the Ojibwe. Thomas Vennum suggests that the lodge itself represents Lake Superior, with the Sault as its eastern entrance.[90] John Grim regards the lodge's practitioners as trans-individual, trans-clan, and as universal types who can disclose primordial ancestors to all Ojibwe.[91]

Totems/Dodems, Clans

While the Midewiwin mediated the pre-eminent influence of bear, another more common mediation occurred through Ojibwe clans. The clan system typified by animal totems/dodems, including bear, is a complex and for many an ancient tradition.[92] There are at least two ways of understanding clans. First, according to Theresa Schenck, the totemic name "was originally the family or clan name of the people who lived in a given village and was the most important feature of identification of the group. Later, as clans mixed in larger villages, the totemic name and sign were retained, serving in much the same way as a person's family name."[93] Henry Schoolcraft described the totemic name as "the most striking trait in their moral history"[94] and as "a link in the genealogical chain by which the bands are held together."[95] According to the early-nineteenth-century French cartographer Joseph N. Nicollet, "it [the totem] is not a sacred name, neither is it connected with any favors of the spirits. There is no mystery attached to it. The totem being an institution of purely civic nature, they are inclined to quote with pride the name of the great family to which they belong. It is simply a collective name."[96]

The second interpretation of clan or totem, which might be more recent, reflects a more mystical and spiritual approach.[97] The Ojibwe believed, for instance, that the bear totem – one of the more numerous Ojibwe family trees, forming one-sixth of the nation – carried and breathed into its members its variant characteristics and dispositions. William Warren described the role of the bear totem or clan as having characteristics infused by bear itself; bear clan members were war chiefs and warriors, keepers of the war pipe and war club, and were responsible for defending against enemies. In addition to identifying family members, a bear totem indicated physical and psychological characteristics of bear that were traceable to members of the totem.

Thus, members of the bear totem had a disposition similar to that of the bear: "They are ill-tempered and fond of fighting, and consequently they are noted as ever having kept the tribe in difficulty and war with other tribes, in which, however, they have generally been the principal and foremost actors." Members of the bear clan were also viewed as similar to bear in physical characteristics: they had long, thick, black, coarse hair "which seldom becomes thin or white in old age."[98] Black, reminiscent of black bear, was a fitting colour for members of the bear dodem, who placed black marks on their clothing, on their corpses, and as markers on their graves. Human genes and bear genes intermingled to form the clan. In this way, the kinship of clan members determined characteristics and experiences that were quite similar to one another. Physical and dispositional likenesses led to affinities in cognitive powers as well.

Our purpose is not to decide between these meanings of clan or totem, but to discern the meanings of the symbols, especially that of bear, among the representations offered. Fulford theorized that when Ojibwe life was relatively stable and harmonious, bear images were definite and easy to discern. After their identity was challenged, the Ojibwe – on the White Earth Reservation, for example – transformed clan emblems, such as bear, into a "symbolic vehicle for rites of passage traditionally associated with the clans." These symbols or pictographs then became ideas, which were interpreted by songs; these pictographic images then tended to be transformed through repetition into human faces. There is, then, a development in these images. Initially, there were clans with animals as guides, then the animals were depicted on song scrolls, then the animals became transformed into human images, then those images were fashioned into abstract ghostly figures. Thus the clan symbols, while transformed and altered on the song scrolls, nevertheless preserved the identity of the Ojibwe clans and continued to root them in the traditions of their ancestors.[99]

When Fulford placed twenty-four of the song scrolls published by William Hoffman and Garrick Mallery into concordances and examined them, he noticed that "otter, bear and bird [display] distinctive frequencies of distribution throughout the sample of song scrolls as well as [show] a high capacity for transformation." These animal and avian beings were gradually altered into human forms and became symbolic and associative.[100] From concordances of twenty song scrolls, Fulford concluded that "iterative mechanisms of simplification, elaboration, condensation, substitution and inversion" transformed the nature of symbols, including that of bear.[101] In that tradition of transforming images into symbols, George Morrison of the Grand Portage Band has created contemporary abstract totem forms; two among them are Churinga, adorning the Fond du Lac Tribal and Community College's forest campus, and Red Totem, at the Heard Museum in Phoenix, Arizona.[102]

Bear clan members have been portrayed as belligerent in temperament; but there are other portrayals of them featuring hospitable spirits, for the bear clan, along with the crane clan, welcomed the Europeans to Turtle Island. Warren writes that they "received the white strangers, and extended to them the hand of friendship and rites of hospitality, and in remembrance of this occurrence they are said to have been the favorite clans with the old French discoverers."[103]

An example of a group feeling among members of the bear clan, and among clans in general, is that women from the same bear clan in Red Lake, Minnesota, could nurse one another's babies, but mothers from another clan might be scratched and bitten when they nursed children other than those of their own clan; women from the non-specific clan might also regard bear cubs as ugly![104] Human genes mixed with bear genes were believed to compose the bear clan. In these ways, kinship between humans and bears determined experiences that were quite similar to one another. As noted earlier, physical and dispositional likenesses led to affinities in cognitive powers between humans and bears.[105]

"Symbolic Petition of Chippewa Chiefs, Presented at Washington, January 28th, 1849, Headed by Oshcabawis of Monomonecau, Wisconsin." Oshcabawis, right, leads the chiefs; all eyes are directed to and united with him and his eyes envision the future. A line from his eye is also directed backward to a number of small rice lakes, the reason for the journey. "The heart of each animal is also connected by lines with the heart of the Crane chief to denote *unity of feeling and purpose.*" The long parallel lines represent Lake Superior and the small parallel lines "a path ... to the villages and interior lakes [where] the Indians propose ... to commence cultivation and the arts of civilized life." Schoolcraft, *Historical and Statistical Information,* 1:417a.[106]

The bear clan gave a framework for government and ensured strength and order for the Ojibwe. Since members of the clan studied plants, they acquired great knowledge of how to treat the unhealthy and injured. The bear clan was so important socially that its members held important posts in Midewiwin society.

A clan or totem today might denote merely a surname replete with honour and meaning, but it can also convey historical and cultural meanings for the Ojibwe.

Evil Bears

For the Ojibwe, bear was a power to contend with because of its ferocity. It can be difficult to discern or predict the moods and actions of bears; also, there are accounts of bears having an evil disposition and doing dreaded deeds. The Ojibwe could sometimes kill an evil one without being held liable, even if later on this bear was revealed to be human. Such bears were often called bearwalkers.[107] A bearwalker is a human being who is envious of another, who dresses like a bear, and who stalks and/or casts a spell on a subject; this spell is believed to cause strange maladies, paralysis, and eventually death.[108] Children and adults feared bearwalkers, believing that they spread harmful medicine and caused death; also, that they fed on humans dead or alive.[109] Basil Johnston, however, indicates that bearwalkers could also be of assistance to the Anishinaabe.[110]

Warren writes that by the time the Ojibwe were suddenly and completely dispersed from La Pointe, Wisconsin, the "Evil Spirit had found a strong foothold amongst them ... Horrid feasts on human flesh became a custom. [Medicine men] had come to a knowledge of the most subtle poisons, and they revenged the least affront with certain death." Warren recounts an occasion when a bearwalker disinterred an only child; the waiting father shot him.[111]

From his experiences in captivity, John Tanner gives accounts of evil bears: "By some composition of gunpowder, or other means, [those impersonating bears] contrive to give the appearance of fire to the mouth and eyes of the bear skin, in which they go about the village late at night, bent on deeds of mischief, oftentimes of blood ... They are the principal men of the Metai [Midewiwin], who thus wander about the villages, in the disguise of a bear, to wreak their hatred on a sleeping rival ... But the customs of the Indians require of any one who may see a medicine man on one of these excursions, to take his life immediately, and whoever does so is accounted guiltless."[112]

Hoffman refers to the character of the bear and to fire in a Midewi-win pictograph: "The reference to the flame (fire) denotes the class of conjurers or Shamans to which this power is granted, i.e., the Wabeno, and in the second degree [of the Midewiwin] this power is reached."[113]

Contemporary Ojibwe artists illustrate this nefarious power of bear-walker. James Jacko from Wikwemikong Reserve, Ontario, has painted this dreaded curse of bearwalking on a canvas "with jarring blue tones."[114] In an illustrated story by the Woodland artist Carl Ray, a bear towers over two rocks that entomb a man and a woman. Giant bears, as tall as trees and impervious to arrows, shake the earth and strike fear into ordinary people.[115]

But the Ojibwe sometimes view bearwalkers in a somewhat positive light, as benevolent shamans or medicine men. In John Penesi's account from Bois Fort and Mackinac Island, a man transformed himself into a bear by putting on a large bear robe, representing the carrier of evil medicine; he then sang magic and mystic songs, appeared like fire, flashed light beams, aroused fear, "did magic," and struck two people dead. In this case, good consequences followed from the evil deed: since the Ojibwe could not be certain who was an ally or an enemy, "never in any way, therefore, did people speak ill of one another."[116]

Not all transformations involve ursine forms and actions; humans with various characteristics sometimes change into other-than-bear forms. According to Ojibwe missionary Peter Jones, "Witches and wizards ... turn themselves into bears, wolves, foxes, owls, bats, and snakes ... Several of our people have informed me that they have seen and heard witches in the shape of these animals, especially the bear and the fox. They say that when a witch in the shape of a bear is being chased, all at once she will run around a tree or a hill, so as to be lost sight of for a time by her pursuers; and then, instead of seeing a bear, they behold an old woman walking quietly along, or digging up roots, and looking as innocent as a lamb."[117]

Evil bear. Song scroll: "Makes a great noise the bear. The reason I am of flame." "A band about his body [indicates his evil] spirit form. By means of his power and influence the singer has become endowed with the ability of changing his form into that of the bear, and in this guise accomplishing good or evil." Hoffman, "The Midê'wiwin," 228a, 230.

Bears are powerful beings whether their actions lead to evil or good. Carl Ray paints double images of humans and animals, that is, of hybrids that are neither one nor the other. Thus, in one painting, "Medicine Bear," a ferocious animal rushes in one direction while a human, with hair streaming and mouth open, flees in the opposite direction. Ray's painting suggests a tension between the two figures but also a resolution and harmony that balances the equal and opposing forces.[118] Morrisseau's "Sacred White Bear" depicts a powerful but benign bear, with horns, external power lines, divided circles, a pendant medicine bag around his neck, an internal life line, and dot clusters on his feet and ankles.[119]

Bear may continue to exercise his evil powers even when dead. In an episode narrated by Rémi Savard, Tshakapesh's parents were killed by a bear. To avenge their deaths, Tshakapesh killed the bear; his sister ate of the bear's head but got "violent cramps in her jaw and was unable to open her lips."[120]

Bear as Archshadow

According to the contemporary writer Gerald Vizenor, the Midewiwin and bears were mediators in the treaty-making process; and since those treaties remain in force to this day, bears still cast their shadows on the world. Those archshadows loom in Ojibwe memories, stories, and ceremonies and are depicted as song pictures on birch bark, where they are intended as maps for right living. These pictures "are the creation of hundreds of distinctive songs and stories about dreams, love, war, animals, birds, movements, and ceremonial music of the *midewiwin,* the great society of healers, or the Grand Medicine Society." In these media, bears, like tricksters, are symbols of both good and evil. Bear as medicine, and as the keeper of knowledge in vision questing, transforms and renews life. Bear also lends balance and sustains and regulates human existence. In *Summer in the Spring,* Vizenor describes how Great Bear is a means to bring the sun spirit to teach the Ojibwe about the Midewiwin.[121] There is evidence, especially in this ceremony, that bears are guides, guardians of portals to spiritual power, and restorers of life; they have the power of immortality and resurrection. In fact, in this celebration, leaders as well as candidates can impersonate bear.[122] "The bear is an archshadow in the silence of tribal stories," Vizenor offers in summation, "the memories and sense that are unsaid in the name ... [They are] shadow memories."[123]

Anthony Wallace writes that bears have ceased to be the stock of food and trade but are still part of ceremonials; they mostly satisfy a spiritual need rather than a physical one. Bear transcends utilitarian goals such as nourishment; it has become expressly part of a family relationship. The spiritual dimension was evident earlier, in that prayer and petition were part of hunting. Now that the hunting of bear has diminished, new meanings of bear have emerged, beyond that of sustenance, a transference Wallace calls "The Bear Abductor Complex." There was a time when bears could abduct humans; now humans abduct bears for spiritual nourishment. Since bear game is no longer immediately available, "the meaning [of bear] has changed to the prevention of disease, while the 'traits' themselves have remained the same."[124]

Bear as Celestial

A story attributed to the Ojibwe concerns the role that namesakes of bear – father-Big Bear and son-Little Bear – had in the formation of the Big and Little Dippers. "A long while ago," there were two moons and no stars. With his bow and arrows, and guided by his grandfather, a young boy named Little Bear shot at one of the moons, shattering it to form many stars, and then made a home among those stars with his father, Big Bear. Thus we have both the Big Dipper and the Little Dipper, called by the Anishinaabe, Big Bear and Little Bear.[125]

Celestial stories teach that harmonious survival and well-being depend on participating in and respecting the laws of nature – specifically those of the heavens.[126] These stories highlight indigenous peoples' interest in astronomy; that knowledge aided survival by enabling them to tell time, give directions, and forecast weather.[127]

Jonas King provides another Ojibwe story of the creation of constellations that involve bear. There were two men, Bemikkwang and Nigankwam. Nigankwam poked at a mound and out came a bear, which they shot. "The two men skinned the bear, cooked it in the pot, and ate the whole carcass at one meal. Nigankwam then arose, took up the skull of the bear and threw it into the sky, where it became three stars (in the Great Bear?). Bemikkwang arose, took up a vertebrum [sic] and threw it into the sky; it also changed to stars." When Nigankwam threw the breastbone into the air, it became the Milky Way. "Nigankwam and Bemikkwang were the first human beings. Afterwards Nigankwam made a woman and had children, who were the ancestors of the present Indians."[128] Jim Nanibush states that "the first Indian was made of clay by Nigankwam, 'leading thunder,' who created man at the command of the Great Spirit. That is why the Indians are brown."[129]

In some of the Algonquian and specifically Anishinaabe cultures, those with expert knowledge of the astral world are known as the Wabeno-innin, the "Morning Star Men" or "The Men of the Dawn."[130] In one story, a mysterious painter, seemingly tired of summer's greens, used an entire palette to create a new world of colours in deciduous plants. In another story, a mighty bear roamed the countryside wreaking havoc among the encampments. Bear pillaged and destroyed, chased other animals away, and even ate women and children. After meeting as a group, the people sent the bravest hunters and their dogs after the bear. They found the bear and chased him; after one of their arrows wounded him, bear ran so fast he ascended into the sky. Hunters and dogs also ascended in pursuit. The four stars, the bowl of the Big Dipper, represent bear. The three stars in the handle of the dipper represent the hunters chasing the bear, and the dimmer stars around the three hunters are their dogs. The hunters and bear go round and round in the northern sky, and every fall the Big Dipper comes low to the horizon. It is then, according to the story, that the bear's wound leaks a few drops of blood, and this blood changes the colours of the leaves on the trees.[131]

An elderly informant from Big Trout Lake, Ontario, noted that before the advent of calendars, the constellations indicated to observers the time of the year, and especially the end of winter. The apogee of the bear's head in Big Bear (Big Dipper) preceded and announced the end of bear's absence because of his winter hibernation. The Ojibwe from Big Trout Lake knew that after Big Bear disappeared on the nocturnal horizon, terrestrial bear would reappear from his wintry den. So that the terrestrial people could conquer the celestial, a host of animals, especially birds, needed to pierce the sky, master it, and make it their summer abode. Bear would open his cage, and birds would master the sky, their permanent summer. The harshness and uncertainties of winter are in contrast to the steadfastness and faithfulness of the sky, which never abandons humans.[132]

Both large and small bears care for the earth. They do this by immersing themselves in worldly affairs, by being "earthy" – digging for medicinal plants – and by becoming entombed in the earth itself during hibernation. They also care for the earth from their ethereal lodgings in the sky.

Bear creatures also care for the sky, and since humans originated in the sky, those creatures are by extension caring for humans. In one account, Sky Woman gave birth to twins, the parents of the Anishinaabe. The animals were perplexed by these young beings, for they were weak, helpless, and crying. The twins cried even more when Sky Woman's breasts dried up. To sustain her babies, she asked the animals and plants for food, such as honey, seeds, berries, fruit, worms, and flies. After eating these foods, her children remained weak, so Sky Woman asked for solid nourishment, namely, meat. As the animals argued who was to give them flesh, a mother bear felt sorry for Sky Woman and her children and volunteered to give her life to them. "For her sympathy and sacrifice, the twins, when grown up, chose the bear to be a symbol of guardianship and motherhood. From the time of her sacrifice the bear has been regarded as someone special, holy, sacred. When hunters have to kill one out of necessity, they place its skull in a tree above the village so that its spirit continues to watch over the people. It is as well a mark of respect." Bear continues to preside over the Anishinaabe, for in the North dwells a sacred white bear who continues to keep watch by restraining "Winter-Maker from being too harsh or too severe with Mother Earth, the animals, or with people."[133]

Bears and Visions of Sound

The Ojibwe had a strong oral tradition and an inherent gift for music. In this regard, bears played a pivotal role in creating medicinal and ceremonial songs. According to Fred K. Blessing, the Ojibwe on the Red Lake Reservation had innate musical abilities as well as strong musical traditions. Even in the 1950s there were "very few adult Chippewa males who [were] unable to sing at least a few songs." Both men and women knew these songs even though they did not sing publicly. Composers and singers showed remarkable creativity and adaptability; they often "would learn Siouan songs and teach them to their own people … Of all the cultural traits of the Chippewa that have persisted to the present time, the songs seem to have been altered the least with the changing way of life occasioned by contact with the white man." Blessing favourably compared Ojibwe music with Western forms and remarked on the widespread performance of Ojibwe songs: "At least in some respects certain Indian songs are like grand opera which is sung the world over irrespective of the language in which it is written."[134]

Music reaching the heart. Song scroll: "The sound of flowing water, Comes toward my home." "A pointed tipi represents the home of the Midewiwini ... The wavy lines [indicate] the pulsating sound [which reaches] the body or heart of the man, not his ears. When this is sung the members of the Midewiwin rise and dance during the remainder of the series of songs." Densmore, *Chippewa Music*, 1:65.

George Farmer/Nebadaykeshigokay of the Bois Fort Reservation in Minnesota indicates the links among song, prayer, and healing.[135] We have noted that songs were sung during the Midewiwin performances and that "words" were recorded on song scrolls. Michael McNally interprets these Mide songs as largely invocational, "requesting or generating powers of the manidoog. Songs were also occasional, seeking supplication in moments of death, starvation, and danger. Occasional songs even existed for seeking to calm rough water for lake crossings, indeed among the more dangerous aspects of life in the region. Fusing pharmacological and physiological aspects of medicine with the ceremonial and social, the prayers of song, dance, and drum were elemental to Ojibwe." During "one or two days in singing, howling, drumming, dancing and feasting," the sick were healed.[136]

People with a strong oral tradition, such as the Ojibwe, are highly sensitive to sounds. Words are one form of sound; singing and vocalizations are two others. According to Desveaux, the auditory mode manifested the spiritual in sounds such as crackling, hissing, blowing, and whistling, and even in more distinct sounds such as wailing and moaning.[137] Densmore, however, was selective in her recordings of Ojibwe sounds. She tried to exclude some vocalizations from her wax cylinder recordings of Ojibwe music, for they, along with drumming, could have distorted early-twentieth-century technical reproductions of the singing.[138]

Writing about the White Earth Reservation, Densmore noted that each Mide had his or her own set of songs, some of which were composed personally and others which were purchased. "It was not permissible for one man to sing a song belonging to another unless he has purchased the right to sing it." Songs had medicinal power, and by purchasing a song, one received some of its power. A song sung by Odenigun, an old man "especially skilled in medicine," gave the origin of bear songs. A young man lost consciousness after jumping off a cliff into a river. "Four bears came and walked around his body, singing this song. When the young man regained consciousness he heard the bears singing; when he opened his eyes he saw the bears walking around him, and when they had walked around him four times he rose up strong and well. Then the four bears began to walk up the cliff and the young man followed them ... [This young man] became a teacher and leader in the Midewiwin," and he sang empowered bear songs.[139]

Vizenor relies on Densmore to depict in a "pictomyth" the spirit in the heart of a Mide singer.[140] The singer is filled with knowledge relating to sacred medicines from the earth. In the drum song, the sky clears and the waters are smooth; the "fair weather is symbolic of health and happiness ... The words of [the above] song predict health and happiness for the person to be initiated." Regarding this song, Vizenor comments: "The expression *he hi hi hi* is the sound of the feeling of the power of the sacred spirit of the midewiwin. A midewiwin song is completed with the syllables *ho ho ho ho*."[141]

We have observed that all animals, but especially otter and owl, disclose their power through sound. The reverberations of songs, instruments, and pouches in the Mide lodge move through space and establish connections. Through these exchanges of sound, humans and animals interact contextually. We have also seen this interplay where artist and medium engage in a collaborative (often acoustic) manner to create objects. The dream images, whether representational or abstract, coalesce in vision, sound, and image. We have noted that the sonic and the aural lend themselves to a number of meanings and manifestations – visionary, gestural, pictorial, musical, verbal, and printed.[142]

Musicians and attendants in the second-degree lodge. Hoffman, "The Midê'wiwin," 182–182a.

Densmore describes some of the Medicine Society's healing rites with bear as teacher. Maingans/Little Wolf of the White Earth Reservation sang three songs to treat the sick in a ritual based on the Midewiwin. The first and third songs used these words: "I am singing and dreaming in my poor way over the earth, I who will again disembark upon the earth." The third song, recorded by Densmore in 1908, indicated that Maingans, a *tchissakiwinini* or herbal medicine and spirit healer, had received power from a bear: "The big bear, to his lodge I go often."[143] Maingans elaborated: "In my dream I went to the big bear's lodge and he told me what to do. He told me how to swallow bones and I often go back to his lodge that I may learn from him again. This is what I say in this song which I made up myself." Vizenor comments: "Maingans' personal spiritual power comes from his dream songs about the big bear. The big bear is his spiritual teacher."[144]

Bear has a broad symbolic role in many song scrolls. Fulford notes that in his analysis of twenty song scrolls from White Earth, the bird symbol evokes a literal response – "I am the sparrow [i.e., little] hawk" – whereas the bear and otter symbols elicit a different response, "suggesting that their symbolic value is much wider, more diffuse and in Ojibwe terms, powerful." In the scroll songs, bear is invoked as "strong," as "my namesake spirit," as "a meteor," and as "flames." References to bear are oblique instead of explicit, for the Ojibwe strove to avoid the wrath of such a powerful other-than-human person, which a direct citation might inspire.[145]

Bear as Medicine and Healer: Following the Bear Path

In the Preface we narrated an Ojibwe story about the power of bear grease. H.C. Wolfart and Freda Ahenakew recount a contemporary story, "The Priest's Bear Medicine," in which Alice Ahenakew's husband, Andrew, an Anglican priest, mediated a cancer treatment for his brother, Walter. In Andrew's vision, which came to him in The Pas, Manitoba, a bear approached to give his body as a gift. "I have come to give you my body, for since God made the earth, when He made the animals, we, we are still as God has made us in the very beginning, we have no sickness in our bodies … Thus He has sent me hither that I might give you my body, for you to use, for you to make medicine there from my body and to doctor people who are sick."

Bear commanded the priest to make bear medicine, demonstrated the process, and showed him what it would look like. But the priest hesitated, for his Christian and scientific traditions presented different approaches. The bear insisted: "But, in any case, you will do it nevertheless, that which I have come to tell you … You are doubting me, but you will nevertheless do what I have told you! For I have been sent hither from the holy place, that I might come to give you my body for you to use in healing people."

The bear left him and scurried off in mid-air to the north, leaving the priest confused. "What ... will the Bishop say to me about this, for it is like Cree medicine; after all, I am a priest, I would definitely have to see him first." He forgot the dream for a while, but then remembered it and conveyed the ingredients and process to his wife, who told him that the dream was a gift from the spirit powers and that its instructions had to be followed. When Father Andrew learned that a polar bear had been killed at Cochin, Saskatchewan, he procured the appropriate parts and went home to Sandy Lake. He followed the bear's instructions on how to make the medicine: it was to be done in the quiet of late evening, and there was to be no metal involved. He was unsuccessful in his attempt to make it, but his wife succeeded. They drank some of it and were given added strength. Andrew took the medication to the hospital for his brother, who had cancer; the brother drank too much of it and got very sick. But two days later he was cured, and word spread quickly throughout the community. Alice later convinced her husband to include Cree rituals in Christian ceremonies, such as sweet grass for smudging.[146]

In a story by Alfred Fiddler of Sandy Lake, Ontario, the trickster, Wisakachak/Nanabush, believed that bear meat and fat were much prized. To procure these, he killed a bear and cut off the fat, but he lost it in a lake. As a result, it was beaver, not Wisakachak, who benefited from the fat, as is clear from its portly appearance today.[147] Other animals, such as squirrel, provide grease that is much inferior to that of bear. Beneficial grease always has some connection with bear.[148]

Densmore writes about plants that were used as medicines on the White Earth Reservation in Minnesota. Since health and long life represented the highest goods for the Chippewa/Ojibwe, the most highly revered persons among them were those who had the knowledge to bring about both. Those who treated the sick claimed that their knowledge came from Manitous, or spirits. Those who used material means to cure sickness were usually members of the Midewiwin, and the one "who treated the sick without material means was called a *djasakid*" or healer.[149]

While the knowledge and application of herbs was the individual's own, the storehouse of information and practices from which healers drew remained secret among the Midewiwin and was passed from one generation to the next.[150] (Non-Midewiwin, though, also had extensive medical knowledge.) Medical practitioners of the Medicine Society "followed the bear path" as they ascended the degrees of the

Midewiwin, and they received the most powerful remedies from the bear spirit in the lodge. One form of bear medicine was comprised of roots cut into two-inch pieces and strung on a cord when stored for use. "Such a string of roots bore some resemblance to a necklace of bear claws," Rockwell observes. "[The plant is actually] a spreading dogbane. The root is diuretic [increasing discharge of urine], sudorific [causing sweat], emetic [causing vomiting], cathartic [cleansing], and anthelmintic [destroying parasitic worms in the intestine]." The Ojibwe of southern Ontario referred to one of their most potent medicines as "bear medicine ... They used it to treat headaches, earaches, coughs, and heart troubles and chewed it to purify their bodies."[151]

The bear is often regarded as an ill-tempered animal, but it also shows kindness, especially through its gift of bear medicine. Bear is perhaps the only animal that is sensitive to herbs, for it digs them out with well-adapted claws, and eats them. Consequently, says Densmore's collaborator, Siyaka, "if a man dreams of a bear he will be expert in the use of herbs for curing illness."[152]

The Ojibwe's admiration for the bear often centres on their belief that it possesses knowledge of medicine and its practice. This admiration encompasses not only bears but also medicinal plants themselves. Densmore writes of White Earth residents caressing the "straight stalks, delicate leaves and fine white roots" of a plant and demonstrating reluctance to leave it. "An unfailing custom of the Mide in gathering plants for medicinal use is to dig a little hole, speaking meanwhile to the plant. Mr. Gagewin, a Mide, said that when he dug a plant he spoke somewhat thus: 'You were allowed to grow here for the benefit of mankind, and I give you this tobacco to remind you of this, so that you will do the best you can for me.'"[153]

Bear and Nanabush shared the honour of being patrons of the Medicine Society. The Ojibwe in northern Michigan and Wisconsin generally regarded bears as having a positive influence on themselves both individually and communally. In the nineteenth century, Shawondasee related the tale of how ten brothers "conquered" a large bear. The youngest brother, Mudjekewis, wrested from the bear a necklace of wampum, which was an important object for war as well as "the great means of happiness," for it represented the war-like character of the gigantic bear. The young man killed the bear, cut it into small pieces, and scattered them to the four winds. From these pieces emerged smaller bears who were less menacing. The treasured wampum was divided and given to all the warriors; "those grains or shells of the pale hue [were] to be emblematic of peace, while those of the darker hue would lead to evil and to war." Because of his courageous achievement, Mudjekewis "was to direct the west wind. [The other warriors were commanded] to do good to the inhabitants of the earth [and] to give all things with a liberal hand."[154]

Anuqcuag/Richard La Fortune also relates that wampum/necklace had medicinal power. In his account, "Tell Me a Story, Raven Makes a Necklace," a sick grandson who was alone searched for a remedy for his illness. Since Badger was too busy to provide one, Old Man Bear agreed to supply the medicine. But Raven was the one who actually transmitted wisdom and solace to the grandson. Raven related the teaching of the leaders that the unity and strength of "many hearts and hands" would ensure salutary changes. He gave the boy a necklace crafted from many shells that radiated sun-like beams and that reverberated sounds so that the healing party could "hear a different name for this disease." In this story, the shells echo the insight that the grandson's malady is mainly psychological. The words of wisdom that emerge are as follows: "To be alone and afraid is not good for our people. When we stay together, then we feel our strength."[155]

From bear stemmed power over the winds, the wisdom to discern the causes of disease, and a caring spirit that provided solace for the sufferer. However, bear was most frequently associated with the power of medicine to heal physical ailments. While bear fat was generally regarded as medicinal, Claude Lévi-Strauss points to Ojibwe stories in which bear meat and fat are also food for bear lovers and mistresses. One story "warns the hero to be on his guard against a seductive food. This is a transparent, tremulous substance resembling bear-fat, but which is really frogs' eggs."[156]

In an Ojibwe story from the north shore of Lake Nipigon, bear rescues his people from predators. During the cruel winter, a trapper, Windigo, prayed to an evil spirit, which gave him extraordinary powers of rejuvenation, strength, and growth. Using those powers, Windigo turned Ojibwe villagers into beavers and devoured them; with every morsel he grew taller and taller but also hungrier and hungrier. Big Goose found the village that Windigo had ransacked; he prayed to Great Manitou for help and received aid from the Great Bear Medicine Man, who threw his arms around Goose, filled him with immense powers, and provided him with a strong physique to challenge the evil spirits and Windigo. The now mighty goose, Missahba, caught up with Windigo, and a cosmic fight took place during which they hurled mountains and glaciers at each other, shaking the earth. After Big Goose killed Windigo, he shrank from his giant size back to that of an ordinary Ojibwe. The beavers that Windigo had devoured were set free, became humans again, and returned to their village. To illustrate this story, Morrisseau painted Big Goose and Great Bear Medicine Man with many power lines emanating from the medicine bag into the air, into the exterior of Medicine Bear, and into his mind and hands. Power lines proceed from Medicine Bear's mouth and anus and are linked to his heart, then to the mouth and anus of Big Goose.[157]

In the late nineteenth century, Garrick Mallery reproduced a drawing made by Niópet, chief of the Menomini. In it, Niópet depicted a white bear spirit that guarded the deposits of Native copper around and in Lake Superior. In an accompanying story, the white bear "is covered with silvery hair, and the tail, which is of great length and extends completely around the body, is composed of bright, burnished copper. This bear spirit lives in the earth, where he guards the precious metal from discovery."[158] Also allied with copper, Rajnovich tells us, is the great water creature, Mishipizheu, whose power is in copper.[159] In a subsequent volume that will apply these stories to the treaties, we will examine in greater detail both Aboriginal and post-European responses to this precious metal.

Many cultures throughout the ages have respected bears and viewed them as having powerful spirits. Shamans or medicine men/women have often "impersonated" the bear by wearing a bearskin cloak and a necklace fashioned from bear's teeth and claws, in the belief that healing and nourishment emanate from these bear parts, including bear paws.[160] Garments fashioned from bear skin have invoked bear's spirit in order to ensure a good life. Several sports teams today (Boston Bruins, Chicago Bears) use the bear's name and image to identify themselves and to bring them victory.

Bear-otter-lodge. Song scroll: "What am I going around? I am going around the Midewigan." "The oblong structure represents the Midewigan. The otter-skin Mide sack is taken around it ... The Makwa Manido (bear spirit) is shown at the left, resting upon the horizontal line, the earth, below which are magic lines showing his power, as also the lines upon the back of the bear. The speaker compares himself to the bear spirit." Hoffman, "The Midê'wiwin," 238a, 250.

Bear as Patterned

Ojibwe in the nineteenth and twentieth centuries believed that bears had many powers. To ensure the continued presence of those powers, they made representations of real or imagined bears, along with those of moose, deer, beaver, wildcat, buffalo, and wolf. Animal patterns had simple but highly developed geometric and floral forms. Sister Bernard Coleman noted of the northern Minnesota Ojibwe that their artists decorated "fire bags, birch bark baskets, Midé drums and birch bark scrolls."[161] Images of the body parts of humans and animals – a realistic design of the heart, for instance – were used in these designs. Coleman also noted that while the ordinary term for the heart was *odeima*, in Midewiwin ceremonies the word used for it was *gashkendeigun*. The heart had a special name, was used in a specific context, and was given an honoured place – on the Mide drum alone. Practitioners of bad medicine also used the heart image. That image, derived from a dream symbol, also appeared on Mide scrolls and signified bear's kind spirit, the guiding light of the Midewiwin.[162]

On an unpainted drum belonging to John Smith of Walker, Minnesota, there are four hearts, each about 10 centimetres (four inches) high, and equal distances apart. Sister Coleman writes that most old Mide drums were painted and decorated with certain symbolic teachings of the Midewiwin such as a "star, moon, sun, thunderbird, heart, cross, medicine man's eye, hand, bear paw, and other symbols of manitos or enlightened beings both animal and human."[163] Also on the drum were specific images of bear as they appeared in the Mide ceremonies. Another bear image – which was really a part of bear itself – was the medicine bag that a new Mide member received on his or her initiation.[164]

On a Midewiwin birch bark scroll, "a bear, representing the guardian spirit of those to be initiated, stands at the entrance of the Midé lodge, to help the young man in need of his aid," Coleman writes. "His footsteps are seen approaching the lodge and the candidate must follow in his tracks. He must offer sacrificial feasts to the bear, so that it may cause the bad spirits to disperse, and so that the initiate may proceed. Several Midéwiwini, or priests, stand near the entrance ready to perform the ceremony. Animal and fish symbols represent animal spirits which will have to be overcome."[165]

In the second degree of the Minnesota Midewiwin, bear provides the spiritual force for the candidate. Representations of panther, lynx, thunderbird, other birds, turtle, otter, fish, and serpents, in addition to images of bear, are found on objects of the Midewiwin ceremonies and scrolls.[166] In that rite, the candidate furnishes three feasts, represented by three tipis; he or she must also offer three prayers to the bear so that the evil spirits may be overcome and will leave, or, if they remain, so that the candidate may pass over them. In the fourth degree of the ceremony, the candidate must assume the bear spirit itself, breathe on the adverse animals, and use the Mide drum. "The oblong figure at the end of the diagram [on the Mide scroll] represents the path which [the Mide participant] must journey through life. Many side paths may lure him, but he must pay no heed to them, and finally he will reach the end of the world (the circle at the end of the line)."[167]

The skin from a bear's chin, including the lower lip and part of the tongue (called lytta), was an important representation of bear. According to Cath Oberholtzer, Cree women used these bear parts as charms. The chin skin was bound with a fabric and decorated with beads, tassels, and/or yarn and was presented to hunters, who sometimes wore it around the neck. These tassels can be interpreted as power lines of the animal's spirit, for tassels on the hats of children and hunters represent an animal's spirit or soul. "The acquisition and decoration of the bear chin and lytta are bound up in the total bear ceremonialism which is itself a part of the larger complex of hunting rituals," Oberholtzer writes. "Not only was the removal of these parts associated with respect to the bear's spirit, the presentation of these items to the hunter's family was also a way to announce the killing of the animal without mentioning the bear by name."[168] After it was decorated by the hunter's wife or mother, the chin was placed near the head of the hunter's sleeping area. The chin and its placing expressed a growing relationship between bear and hunter – the acquiring of the bear's spirit by the hunter. The hunter sometimes carried the bear chin secretly or tied it on his gun. Respect for the bear and belief in the power of its spirit underpinned these rituals.[169]

Besides aiding the hunt, the bear chin had curative powers. Speaking to a bear hide or chin skin, or covering the sick person with the skin while performing ritual singing, were methods of aiding recovery by transferring the bear's power from the hide to the person.[170] This transference of power is in accordance with pictographic recordings of a bear helper with extended tongue who receives and confers power directly from a bear's mouth. Images in the first four degrees of the Midewiwin depict a vigorous bear tongue breaking "through the barriers between himself and the spirit world.[171] Richard Preston recorded another example of bear chin's curative power, this time for the Eastern Cree. When it became apparent that a girl's illness would not respond to the treatments of nurses, a man "took some bear chins and went around Billy's [father of the ailing girl] house three times singing. And then he put the bear chins under the head of the bed, way down and left them there." And, of course, the girl recovered.[172] Thus the bear's chin is a synergistic metonym of the bear itself, a container of its power. A Cree hunter can attest "to his power and competency as a man, as a hunter, and as a potential curer" when he gathers many bear chins.[173]

Besides bear's chin, bear's hide can bestow hunting and curative powers. A Western Cree story told by Stan Cuthand demonstrates these powers. A wounded man lay dying. When he was just about dead, his father took a bear's hide, began to speak to it, and then covered his son with it, making certain to arrange it so that the two were positioned head to head. And, of course, the dying man lived.[174]

In the use of bear chins and skins, we note the healing power of bear. It is no wonder that bear is the patron of herbalists and medicine men and women, for bear is the mediator between vegetative powers and human health givers and is a facilitator of the transformation and transference of power. Bear, as the great healer, imparts from his tongue the power to heal. Humans are healed or turned into bears by touching or licking a bear's tongue, just as mother bear can lick her amorphous newborn lumps of flesh into bears.[175]

While living bears can empower healers, bears "on the other side of death" can confer unique remedies. Chief Moses Day Daybwaywaindung gives his interpretation of an early-nineteenth-century ritual parchment from Lake of the Woods and Rainy Lake: Bear comes "by a mountain in the land of the dead. If we have done rightly in this world we will see Mokwa [bear] thus journeying in the world on the other side of death. We never see him thus in this life ... Mokwa encircled this 'sick' [person] and overcame it, so now when a medicine man wishes help in doctoring some patient he calls upon Mokwa, and he, having overcome disease, gives him the 'power' he asks, and the patient gets well."[176]

Although accounts vary, the Ritzenthalers list bear – either a bear paw or a bear cub – as symbolizing the fourth rung on the Midewiwin healing ladder.[177] The Lac des Bois community near Kenora, Ontario, acknowledges seven degrees in the Midewiwin, with a bear's paw or claw representing the seventh degree.[178]

We noted earlier that representations of dream figures, generally those of animals, were a challenge in Ojibwe society. The dreamed animal, a Manitou, belonged to the dreamer, and it was believed that the animal's power remained with the animal and the dreamer for as long as the nature and experience of the dream was not made public; when this disclosure happened, the dream's power was diffused and perhaps lost. However, the dreamer might desire that the animal be depicted in some form, as a constant reminder to himself and perhaps to others of the power of the dream and the unfurling of the animal's power, but also as a way of harnessing that power in the hunt or to cure the sick. As a response to the task of depicting the power while keeping the dreamer's experience completely or partly anonymous, the Ojibwe evolved a strategy to depict the dreamed animal abstractly and symbolically. Even though the particularities of the dream experience had been erased, the abstract image would be readily available to the dreamer, albeit ambiguous as to its details. This ambiguity had yet another function – to depict in images the belief that spirits could transform their appearance. Thus an iconographic convention, that of abstract geometric forms, also expressed the transformative possibility of animals. Consequently, this nineteenth-century artistic stylization recorded "multiple levels of reality and also particular visionary perceptions of these realities,"[179] Phillips concludes.

Patterned images, then, either concrete or abstract, were and continue to be the preferred means of communication for the Ojibwe. In *Emotional Expression among Cree Indians* (1999), art therapist Nadia Ferrara observes that the Cree teach their children to express inner emotions through the imagery of dreams and art. Then as people mature, they continue to use narratives, metaphors, and images – more in nonverbal forms and less in verbal imagery – to make sense of their world and to provide meaning and an understanding to their experiences.[180]

As we have discussed with regard to bear's lip, tongue, chin, and hide, the power of bear resided in its actual body part. In a similar way, a representation of the dream figure, made of cloth or hide and carried on the person, gave protection by its presence. The guardian Manitou in a dream often commanded the dreamer to wear the dream article, for "the Ojibwa believed that the essence of the guardian manito dwelt in its representation"[181] and that "crafted objects are animate beings."[182]

The specific dream animal could be incorporated into an abstract pattern or a crafted representation, but future generations might not understand the design's meaning, and indeed, might consider it merely a design or representation to be treasured for its artistic merit alone.

Since the bear was healer and the medicine ceremony was intended to heal, it is conceivable that many motifs that embodied curative properties have been forgotten, for abstractions and images by nature depart from many particularities; these departures can then lead to misunderstandings. We have already observed that design motifs such as the swastika and the dotted circle indicated the four winds and the Great Spirit. These motifs designated universal power, and in the Mide ceremonies, they were interpreted by Coleman's collaborators as signifying the road the Ojibwe should follow if they desired happiness and long life. These collaborators often were not specific about the meanings of the symbols, and it is possible that they were withholding their interpretations; Coleman, however, noted that they cautiously conjectured that such symbols generally emanated from dreams and were to be used for protection.[183] Phillips suggests that many aesthetic and iconographic consistencies in design were linked to linguistic, mythological, and ethnographic information. The abstract geometric designs were symbolic rather than decorative, at least initially; real spirit power – cosmic energy – radiated from these images. The design elements were unspoken words, but nevertheless, "a common vocabulary used to describe spirit power in Great Lakes art from the early contact period through the first part of the 19th century."[184] The focus on communication of the spirit powers, however, does not deny the aesthetic worth of Ojibwe ceremonial objects such as garments, and their crafts that had varied geometric designs and vivid colours.[185]

The crafted piece "takes on its own life and is a living presence in the world," Karen A'Llerio writes. "What is created takes up the characteristics and spirits of the materials which go into it. It takes on and carries with it the attitudes and energy, the spirituality, which the artisan puts into it. And what is created carries all the cultural meanings and traditional knowledge associated with the materials, the artist, and the kind of object it is." In addition, the crafted object as a whole displays its own character and spirituality.[186] Artists write of a symbiotic relationship between themselves and the media they are using. The craftsperson might impose his or her intention on the object, but there is an interaction, a co-creation, between creator and created. For the Aboriginal artist, this mutual and reciprocal creativity takes on a personal form. As A'Llerio narrates, in creating from deer hide the artist "feels as if the deer is there helping him, giving him directions."[187]

Material objects such as woven bags, tattoos, and pouches are containers that merge several agents and energies into a greater collective power.[188] Phillips contends that woven bags from the Great Lakes area became cosmic maps, with the merging of motifs representing the Thunderbird of the Sky World on one side, and the Underwater Panther on the other.[189] Such items in representational form and/or geometric imagery organize and locate the spiritual powers and also record "the relationship of the artistic imagery to personal dream experience."[190]

Human beings themselves became both the recipients and the images of patterned powers. Missionary Francesco Bressani related in 1653 that Hurons commonly wore tattoo-like decorations on their bodies (and sometimes "wore" these decorations alone!); he referred to these as permanent paintings. This tattoo painting "on the face, the neck, or the breast or some other part of the body [depicted] some animal or monster, for instance an Eagle, a Serpent, a Dragon, or any other figure they prefer ... I know not whether a single individual was found, who was not painted in this manner, on some part of the body." These tattooed spirit images were probably derived from dream experiences and had the same significance as pouches and bags later on. Bressani, however, thought that the paintings, made with stoical indifference to pain, were pursued because of "vanity, and a fantastic caprice." He conceded, however, that these images served several purposes: as "a mask against the cold and the ice" in winter, as a way of disguising inward fear at wartime, as a method of making Hurons "more terrible to the enemy, and [as a concealment for the] extremes of youth or age, which might inspire strength and courage in the adversary. It serves an adornment at the public feasts and assemblies." To instil courage in their prisoners who were condemned to death, Hurons burned images into their flesh.[191] We do not know whether all of the images used above arose from dreams, or whether the impetus to torture had the same origin. Ojibwe body imaging resembled that of the Huron, as we shall see when considering thunderbirds.

In Cree narratives, bear is presented as a healer and a mentor. Oberholtzer traces the meaning of the lacing on a moss bag and on the bag's "tikanagan [cradleboard] cover" beyond its practical use to its origins in an atemporal past. In "the episode describing the peopling of the earth, Spider lowers the founding couple in 'a bag-like container' he has woven from his never-ending line of silk." The couple eventually land in an eagle's nest and are rescued by bear and wolverine.[192] Bear then acts as their mentor, "the one who taught them all they needed to know about how to remain alive."[193] Their descent into eagle's nest is cushioned by spider's woven container. "The spider's protective weaving in the mythic episode becomes mirrored in the earth world through the lacing of the infant's bag. And in a parallel manner, the role of earthly parents is to teach their children how to live in their new world just as the bear instructed the original couple."[194] Sarah Preston sees in the ancient use of a bear-skin mattress for the newly delivered mother "the metonymic presence of the bear as both healer and mentor."[195]

Bear as Child Abductor

Many stories portray bear as a beneficent abductor, much like owl. In stories of this kind from the north shore of Lake Superior, the parents are less than kind to their little boy; they whip him and yell at him. The boy is naughty or foolish, and sometimes a grandmother or grandfather intervenes, as in the version related by Norval Morrisseau from the Sandy Lake Reserve. In that telling, the grandparents plead: "He's just a little child, Kitchi-Manitou's gift to you. Don't abuse him."[196] The setting for the child's abduction is berry-picking time or his home. In some versions, the boy runs away from home and gets lost, and a bear intervenes, snatching him. In others, the boy is presented as already ensconced in a bear's den or nest, where he is treated as one of the bear cubs, suckling, eating, hibernating, and forgetting his former existence. Sometimes the parents find the child and take revenge on the kidnapper even though the boy has been well cared for (he has good clothes and is fat, for he has been well fed on crushed dried fish from the bottom of bear's feet and on berries from her front paws). At other times, bear casts from her nest dried, smoked fish, which becomes ruffled grouse, in order to throw the parents off the right path in their search for their son. In yet another variation, the bear perceives that the parents are sorrowing and returns the child after a few months, or even two years, promising that if anyone needs food, a bear will always be available. After the child is returned to his former home, he may retain bear-like characteristics and habits such as avoiding people, skirting fishing traps, and eating and acting like a bear. In some stories, the child desires to stay with his new parents, calling the bear "mother," while she in turn calls him "grandson." Eventually the boy may forget about his abduction or recall it only in the presence of a bear.

Several conclusions can be drawn from these bear abduction stories. Morrisseau draws this one: "Bears take better care of their offspring than do some parents."[197] For the Ojibwe, this care often takes the form of the bear's wise ways, positive qualities, and availability in the hunt.

The bear abductor stories express an affinity between bears and humans, a kinship that humans can acknowledge: when bears speak, humans can understand them and reply; also, humans and bears eat the same foods and drink the same liquids. Morrisseau depicted this interdependence in his art, in which power lines flow from one being to the other. In one illustration, those lines emanate from Grandfather Potan's mouth and address the bear's eyes, indicating either a power directed toward the bear or some type of causal connection between them.[198] In the story that complements this illustration, Grandfather Potan was searching the local garbage dump for magazines and comics so that he might understand the white people better. While walking home through the bush, he "suddenly came face to face with a large brown bear who was busily digging at the roots of a tree at the side of the path." Morrisseau recalled that the Ojibwe have great respect for bears and that in the distant past, bear, as the Ojibwe's ancestor, had a human form. So there was a previously established kinship between bears and humans. In the conversation that followed, Grandfather used polite terms and reminded the bear of their ancestral ties; yet in the end, he had to threaten it with a stick and swear at it in English before it understood and let Grandfather pass.

The incident left Grandfather pensive as he walked home: "Things must be pretty bad with the Ojibwas ... that even our ancestor the Bear no longer understands us. Indeed, since the coming of the white man we have fallen very low, forgetting our ancient legends and ancestral beliefs. The time has come for us all to write and to record the story of our people; not only for ourselves but also for our white brothers so that they will be able to understand and respect us." For the younger Morrisseau, the challenge was to write about and paint the heritage of his people.[199]

Bear as Environmental Guardian, Mother

Bear is an ambivalent animal capable of both evil and heroic deeds. In the above stories, neither of these qualities is omitted, but the image of a beneficent being predominates. Bear is often portrayed as part of nature and as echoing its attributes and characteristics. Humans learn about themselves from nature since nature manifests, in the words of Basil Johnston, "some aspect about life and being, beauty and goodness; birth, growth, decrepitude, death, regeneration, transformation." Because animals live in harmony and purpose with the seasons of the year and therefore within nature's laws, they can provide norms regarding what humans ought and ought not perform. Humans have but to read what is written on these nature–animal scrolls.[200]

Bears are powerful guardian spirits. Since they are the keepers and givers of plant knowledge, "bears are one of the animals represented on the medicine wheel,"[201] says Denise George, gallery coordinator at Wanuskewin Heritage Park, Saskatoon, Saskatchewan. Bears are the guardians of nature, helping control the ice and snow so that it melts at the proper times and does not flood the earth.[202]

Ojibwe believe that keeping "The Great Law" will ensure a sustainable future. To illustrate the need to conform to this law, they relate a commonly told tale: Since rabbit was not fastidious about what he consumed, he ate many kinds of plants without harming any species. One summer, however, he found roses especially tasty. In fact, he ate nothing but roses so that when summer was half over, roses started to become scarce. He was like Windigo, never satisfied. Bee started to complain that the scarcity of roses was impeding his efforts to make the best honey. Other animals became tired of bee's complaining but were too busy with their own tasks to notice anything was awry. Before long, bee could not find any roses at all. He enlisted hummingbird to search for some, but neither of them could find any. In this emergency, both of them called a Great Council of all the animals. Some animals considered the problem to be trivial. As the meeting was about to disband, bear uttered a loud, bellowing moan: "You mean that the reason that I have been finding so little of the honey that I love so much is that you, Bee, haven't been able to find any roses?" Bear's strident observation about the lack of his much prized food made an impact on the other animals. Upon reflection, they too imagined the consequences of this deprivation, especially when bear protested: "If I don't have my honey, I will not sleep the winter away. And if I don't sleep the winter away, I will not be able to find nuts and berries for they will be buried under the snow. And if I cannot eat nuts and berries, I will have to eat some of you, my brother animals, to survive the winter that surely will come."

The animals realized that they themselves or their food sources would be endangered if bear terminated his annual hibernation. Owl was the first to evaluate the situation; he suggested that the animals investigate whether there were any roses left on the earth. Birds flew to the ends of the land, and hummingbird returned with a single, half-dead rose. The rose was so weak she was unable to disclose what had happened. After she was nursed back to health, she told them that rabbit had consumed almost all of the roses. Bear became angry at rabbit, seized him by his ears, stretched them, and then struck him, splitting his upper lip. The animals wanted to kill rabbit, but the sole remaining rose intervened, stating that it was not entirely his fault. It was the fault of everyone. "Bee tried to tell you what was happening, but no one would listen ... In not listening, you all broke the greatest of all the Great Laws and thereby are all at fault. That law tells us that all living things must watch over all other living things and Mother Earth." Nanabush now made the following surmise: "All depend on others to live. The disappearance of any will affect all. In the end, all animals live off of the plants, and the plants live off of Mother Earth. So," he told all the animals, "Rabbit will not be killed so that he can be a sign for all lest we forget the lessons we should have learned from this experience. Rabbit's ears shall remain long to remind us that we must listen, and his lip shall remain split to remind us that we may lie with our silence. And to ensure Rose's future, from this time forward, Rabbit is not to eat roses." In fact, nature would protect itself, for "roses will have thorns to keep them safe from rabbits."[203]

As the above story indicates, bear is a passionate other-than-human person. He can have either an affectionate or an adversarial relationship with many beings, including trees. Generally, bears regard trees positively; they climb them to get a better view of the terrain, and they also hide in them.[204] Bears are themselves sometimes identified as trees or take the form of trees. But trees can also be targets of bears' rancour. In his volume of Ojibwe stories, Desveaux includes one from Big Trout Lake of a bear and a tree. According to Solomon Begg, in the spring bear walked around a small lake and saw some small fish. He left them alone for the time being but wanted to catch and eat them on his return. When he returned, he found that the fish were gone. He became furious, and as he walked along he heard a voice: "When you walk you wiggle your rear end!" A tree had mocked him. To get even, he slashed the tree with his claws and bit it with his teeth, marks evident on the bark of trees today.[205]

Another story expresses the solitary but also somewhat communal nature of bear. Bear wanted someone to live with him and approached turtle, who first refused and then accepted. In the fall, bear planned for the cold winter by building a reasonably warm shelter that was secluded from people. He instructed turtle to find some pine branches for the shelter, and to trim them in such a way that they would not disclose bear's and turtle's presence. They built a fire to keep warm, but the winter was long, and turtle went out to search for more branches. In building the fire, turtle accidentally burned bear's nose, and he became furious. Bear dismembered turtle and was alone again.[206]

Turtle. Song scroll. "He said." "The Turtle Manido will lend his aid in speed. The turtle was one of the swiftest manidos, until through some misconduct, Minabozho deprived him of speed." Hoffman, "The Midê'wiwin," 228a, 239.

Desveaux offers an interpretation of this story. Bear and turtle are protagonists but develop a dysfunctional relationship during the winter as in a previous story involving two owls in conflict.[207] Bear and turtle pursue an insular existence on a temporal plane. Bear lives in his subterranean den for more than half the year; turtle inhabits an underground den for a shorter time.

Several Menomini stories relate how nature – the winds and directions – and many animals summon their unique powers to help destroy evil spirits. In one of these, badger, otter, beaver, mink, and muskrat help create a new earth after a powerful flood.[208] "The island formed in this way was called Mishee Mackinakong, the place of the Great Turtle's back, now known as Michilimackinac."[209]

In another story, bear is a certain Man-from-the-West, the wind of the west, a vector of cold and winter. He quarrels with a woman, and this dispute leads them to the top of a mountain, where bear is defeated, falls to the bottom of a cliff, and is broken on the rocks. "The bear is the periodic mediator between this subterranean world and ours," Desveaux concludes. "He was the depositer of fire. In fact, he lives in association with the more solid elements of the lower world which dominate the aquatic element; he is the master of stones."[210]

Games

A number of animals had roles in Ojibwe games. In one story, for all of his great powers, Nanabush continued to be pursued by dangerous spirits – a chase alluded to in tales of how the ball game originated. According to Shunien and other prominent Mide, Nanabush wanted to avenge the death of his brother, wolf, in a ball game. In this game, the thunderers played against the dangerous spirits, and appeared in the guise of two bear chiefs, one a powerful silvery-white one and the other a grey one.[211]

The ball game is a cosmic stadium for the meeting of spirits, for the revelation of their characteristics, for insights into their powers and actions, and for the resolution of critical problems, including ill health. This game was mandatory for the Ojibwe; during it, terrestrial, extraterrestrial, and underground adversaries, including bear, all played.

A Menomini account gives one of the reasons why a ball game was played. "When a young man fasts and dreams of his manido, he always wears that manido in the shape of a small effigy or as an amulet. His manido helps him to succeed in his undertakings. But if he forgets his manido and does not make offerings to him, then he will lose his power, and his manido will not assist him. Then the man must give a ball game and offer presents to his manido, and thus again receive his favor. The man thus giving the feast selects the leaders of the two sides, which consists respectively of players of the widishianun (or phratry) [brotherhood of clans] of which the leaders are members. The leaders are persons conspicuous for their endurance and skill, and for the possession of special powers conferred by their manidos."[212]

Shunien gives additional instructions and reasons for playing ball. "When one becomes sick through neglecting his manido, and is unable to prepare a ball game, some relation or friend of his widishianun assumes the responsibility of getting up the game, by which the anger of the sick man's manido will be appeased and the sufferer again be taken under his protection."[213]

Wasanganachank and Midasuganj recount another sport, "The Bear Game," "the first game ever." This gambling performance, patterned on stories of creation, was revealed to a boy while he fasted and slept. Instructions for the game are provided: continue for as long as the world lasts, play at night, use four mittens, gamble your entire possessions, provide tobacco, and don't play for trivial reasons. A song from bear is sung. Manitou power possesses the game, and all who play it will live to an old age.[214]

The Huron and Ojibwe philosophies of games appear similar. For Hurons, games were used for healing, as missionary Jean de Brébeuf recorded in 1636 from Ihonatiria in what is now the Georgian Bay region: "There is a poor sick man, fevered of body and almost dying, and a miserable Sorcerer will order for him, as a cooling remedy, a game of [la] crosse. Or the sick man himself, sometimes, will have dreamed that he must die unless the whole country shall play crosse for his health; and, no matter how little may be his credit, you will see then in a beautiful field, Village contending against Village, as to who will play crosse the better, and betting against one another Beaver robes and Porcelain collars, so as to excite greater interest." Since Hurons could consider not just individuals or villages but the entire country to be sick, nation-wide games could avert maladies and misfortune for a great number of people. This ritual, guided by dreams and utilizing songs and cultural symbols, combined betting and healing.[215] We will consider lacrosse more extensively in our chapter on thunderbirds.

Anxiety and excitement during games and gambling took on cosmic proportions, with sky, wind, and rain influencing the outcome. The vision quest could be included in the context of a match.

Bear and Greed

A story from Northern Ontario inveighs against greed. Because the summer was very dry and plant growth was slow, there were only a few berry patches and the berries were small. At such times, it was customary for camp members to band together to pick all the berries they could, so that everyone would have an equal chance to obtain food for their family. But there were always some greedy and grasp-ing individuals who thought only of themselves. One couple went berry picking before sunrise, planning to return quietly with their ber-ries while everyone else was still sleeping. No one would be the wiser, they thought. While they were picking berries, they heard bear's loud crash as he broke down the bushes. The couple was so frightened that they dropped their containers with berries and ran as fast as they could to the camp. They made so much noise during their return that they woke up everyone, who came out and stared at them. The couple was so ashamed of their selfishness that they disappeared into their tipi and didn't show themselves for several days. "After this, every time anyone tried to get ahead of the others in picking berries they were sure they could hear the growls and grunts of the bears, reminding them that they must think of others."[216]

"Chipmunk," a story from what is now the Upper Midwest, begins by recounting a long stretch of prosperity for the people, a time when plants and animals flourished. These riches, however, led to ease and comfort, and laziness also. "Before long the respect for Mother Earth and her plants and animals started to diminish. The hunters began to be wasteful. They left the less desirable parts of animals that they killed to rot in the forest while they carried only the choice parts back to their camps. As a result, many more deer, moose, and caribou were slaugh-tered than was necessary."

The animals noted the waste, disrespect, avarice, and even cruelty, for animals were being killed for entertainment and sport.' They suspected that a Windigo had possessed the people to make them so irresponsible. A council of all the animals decided that the people must die for their reckless behaviour. Chipmunk alone dissented; he argued that the people were a young species undergoing an understandable immature phase; they needed more time to grow up. "This laziness and cruelty will pass," he said. But bear insisted that brother mosquito spread a fatal disease among the people, a fitting punishment. Chipmunk contended, however, that this avenging tactic was contradictory, for it met cruelty with cruelty. Bear remained adamant and even threatened chipmunk with death. When chipmunk pleaded for leniency for these people in order to retain them as friends, bear lunged at chipmunk and scraped his back with his claws. Chipmunk lamented his plight: he did not want to alienate either his fellow animals or humans. He wanted to do something, but what? He was so small.

Meanwhile, mosquitoes were carrying out their task of stinging the people, who began to die. Chipmunk pleaded with Nanabush that justice be done. Nanabush, however, refused to take sides in this event, for after all, most of the animals had decided democratically on the present course of action. Nevertheless, Nanabush gave chipmunk this wise advice: "Enlist the power of the other living things." But who might these other beings be? Chipmunk pondered and listened; he heard rumbling, swishing, and whispering noises, a forest full of sounds. He had been so embarrassed about the previous events that he had forgotten about the plants, for they were living beings also. And other living beings depend on plants. So he asked the plants what they could do to alleviate the disease. The large white pine called a council in which plants spoke with strange voices that chipmunk could not understand. "Bushes rustled; grasses whispered; pines sighed. Sounds came from all directions." White pine spoke: "We have decided to give our barks, our leaves, our roots, and our berries so that the People may live." Plants had provided food in the past, and now they taught chipmunk how to mix potions for medicines to cure this plague and other diseases. Chipmunk in turn would teach the medicinal remedies to the people. But in the nearest village no one would listen to him except Nokomis. She treated her granddaughter with the new medicine and passed the remedy to other women. Knowledge of the treatment spread; the people were cured. "In gratitude, they asked Nanabohzo to give Chipmunk a fitting reward. So he gave Chipmunk the marks of Bear's claws on his back as a sign of his bravery and said, 'Chipmunk

shall from this day on be welcome in every camp and village and shall
have no reason to fear the People.'"[217]

Wasaygahbahwequay/Maefred C. Arey from Cass Lake, Minnesota,
gives a story with a lesson and a reason why bear has a short tail. In the
winter, bear used its long tail as a fishing line, which he inserted into a
hole in the ice. Since bear wanted to catch many fish, he left his tail in
the ice for a long time. As a result, his tail froze into the ice, and when he
walked away he lost most of it and now has a short one. "He knew this
wouldn't have happened if he hadn't been so greedy for those fish."[218]

Let us conclude this chapter on bears. Bears can be seen through two
lenses: a Western, scientific one and an Aboriginal one. Through the
Western lens, bears are popularly regarded as related to humans through
either an engaging likeness or a fearful difference. Bears are different from other carnivores, for they are monarchs, subject to no higher
authority. We singled out for consideration two of the eight species
inhabiting the Great Lakes region: brown and black bears.

Humans have a sense of wonder about bears since they are like themselves in physique, behaviour, and intelligence. Also like humans, they
rely on nature for medicaments. But bears also have admirable qualities
somewhat unique to themselves: they have the ability to hibernate, and
they adapt readily to various terrains and climates.

Through an Aboriginal and specifically an Ojibwe lens, bears are
regarded as personally related to humans: both are boundary creatures
that participate in the animal world and also the human one. Feelings
of awe and fear toward bears pervade the Ojibwe, but so do feelings
of gratitude toward them, for they are gifts of the Great Spirit with
multiple uses, as were the buffalo on the prairies.

Multiple Ojibwe beliefs and perceptions overlay bears, for like
humans they can be transformed into other creatures. Both humans and
bears can be regarded as hunters and hunted, with the same spiritual,
physical, and mental characteristics. The Ojibwe behave respectfully
toward and cooperate with bears, whom they perceive as the most spiritually empowered of animals and as possessing a cosmic presence and
power. Ever since early contact times, Ojibwe have considered bears to
be related to humans. Indeed, bears' spirit has penetrated cultural and
linguistic forms throughout the world.

In ceremonies, especially in those of the Medicine Society or Midewiwin, physical or representational parts of bears are omnipresent. In
addition, there are images of bears on pictographs, on birch bark song
scrolls, on petroglyphs, on ceremonial instruments, and on everyday

objects. Symbols on song scrolls seem to have evolved from actual physical animals, portraying them as guides; then representations of animals were depicted on song scrolls; and, finally, those representations were transformed into humans, which were abstracted into ghostly figures. In some representations, human faces fused with those of animals to assume animal characteristics.

Totems feature bear both as a prized physical being and as an emotionally powerful one. A bear clan or totem today – or *any* clan or totem – may denote merely a surname with honour and meaning, but such a totem can also convey historical and cultural meanings for the Ojibwe. These meanings flow from bear-like characteristics imprinted on totem members. Members of the bear clan may have dispositional, cognitive, and physical capabilities similar to those of bear. In this way, the bear clan may provide a framework for government and ensure strength and order for the Ojibwe. In addition to this, bear clan members studied plants and used the knowledge thereby gained to treat the unhealthy and injured. Because the bear clan was so important socially, its members held important posts in the Midewiwin.

Stories of ferocious bears presented forbidding images and even evil ones; humans as bearwalkers projected mysterious, ghost-like qualities. More prominent, however, were images of bear displaying kindness, healing powers, and a welcoming spirit; this was manifest especially in private and public ceremonials during and after its death. Bears' physical parts were utilized in performances; bearskin bags were regarded as alive; bear's bones were used for sucking out evil spirits; its teeth were fashioned into whistles and charms; a fearful power emanated from blowing its teeth. The Ojibwe treated bear's body parts with great respect; clothing, tobacco, and ribbons were placed in the forest in its honour. Bear's skull and shoulder bones were decorated and painted. In contemporary paintings, bear's X-ray forms and power lines indicate that it radiates constant energy. Today, bear surnames carry bear power.

Bears are no longer readily available as food in many contemporary Ojibwe communities; they have now assumed a more spiritual meaning – they symbolically prevent disease, guard the Ojibwe from psychological harm, and guide moral intentions and actions.

In some Algonquian traditions, there is a reciprocal relationship between Earth Bear and Sky Bear. Terrestrial bear mimics the actions of the Big Bear constellation; this is re-enacted ceremonially. As they are killed, Earth Bears ascend to the sky to descend again at birth, in an analogy of human ascent and descent. The bear constellation represents not only bear but also the hunters and their dogs, with the other stars as guides. Through sympathetic intercommunication, what happens in the heavens also happens on earth. As celestial hunters kill the bear, spill his blood, and gather his grease, earth's leaves turn colour and snow falls. Celestial Bear's seasonal rotation around the North Star parallels bear's seasonal life on earth.

Stories about celestial creatures such as bear teach that harmonious survival and well-being require humans to participate in and respect the laws of nature, specifically those of the heavens. Stories of the Big Dipper/Big Bear underscore indigenous peoples' interest in astronomy, for such knowledge aided their survival: it enabled them to tell time, give directions, and forecast weather. Bears displayed their celestial and terrestrial powers by caring for people, but also by influencing the seasons, especially winter and spring, by creating snow but also restraining it, and by releasing birds in the spring. All of this led to harmony and balance in the cosmos. Since they provided solid physical nourishment, bears symbolized guardianship and motherhood.

Bears were not only food but also "bear medicine." Bears were medicinal models, for they had knowledge of plants and their spirits. They dug for herbs and ate them. Mother bears licked their cubs into life. The Ojibwe who became bears in the lodge acquired this knowledge from bear spirits and also from their own investigations.

In animals, but especially in bear, the Ojibwe saw a reflection of the Great Spirit, a reflection of the seasons of the year, and a reflection of themselves. While bear symbolized positive qualities, it also embodied, like Nanabush, a host of ambivalent ones – it was generous and stingy, kind and perverse, noble and fearful, intelligent and stupid, rational and reckless. Bear was the doorway not only to the ideal but also to the real. Because of its ambiguous nature, it was virtually impossible to confine bear into neat patterns, for it, like humans, often transcended them in its seemingly limitless transformations.

Many geometric designs on Ojibwe cultural objects harboured the omnipresent power of bear. There are images of bears on song scrolls and on medicine bags; essential components of the medicine ceremony involved actual animal parts such as skins of the bear's lower lip and part of its tongue or lytta, as well as bear hides. After these ceremonies, these animal parts were regarded as symbols of power and were often tied to guns; this action carried the bear spirit and symbolized a growing relationship between bear and hunter. Bear chins and bear hides also had curative powers, for healing energy was transferred from them to sick persons.

Dream images of bear were kept personal by the dreamer and were transformed into abstract patterns. In this way, the images could be meaningful and readily available to the dreamer, but their power would not be diluted through manifold sharings. Since these crafted images were symbolic rather than merely decorative, they were believed to be animate beings that carried traditional knowledge and collective powers. Tattooed images on the Ojibwe's bodies charted cosmic forces and channelled them into their beings.

In bear abductor stories, bear surpasses some parents in the care of and wise dealings with their children. Also in these stories, bear evidences an ancestral relationship to humans and cares for them by providing his body in the hunt. In other stories, bear demonstrates power over the winds, the wisdom to discern the causes of disease, and a benevolent spirit to provide physical and psychological solace for the sufferer, particularly through bear grease. Bear is a judge and harmonizer; he guards natural beings, especially copper. Through negative and positive examples, bear demonstrates the consequences of generosity and greed. Bear is also associated with the origins of maple sugar, and of menstruation.[219]

There are stories of bears as evil, and of witch bears that strike fear and kill humans. The greatest menace is bearwalker, a stalker, who can cast spells and cause strange maladies, paralysis, and even death.

But stories of beneficent bears predominate over evil ones. Bears learn from nature, live in harmony with it, and thus can provide norms for human conduct. Bears, as keepers and givers of plant knowledge, are on the medicine wheel. Celestial Great Bear is a keeper and respecter of the beauty of the earth, guides the seasons of the year, and enjoys all elements of nature. Bears mediate between the subterranean and the earth. They help newcomers adjust to new territories. The story of the depletion of the roses illustrates the interconnectedness and interdependence of all life, animal and plant, and the responsibility shared by all not to exploit natural resources. Bear's loud grumbling is a compassionate reminder for the people not to be greedy, although at other times bear wants to exact strict justice on the people for their evil ways.

Ball games are the cosmic context for resolving conflicts. In these and other games, cosmic spirits meet, reveal their powers and actions, and help resolve critical problems, including that of ill health. In these games, terrestrial, extraterrestrial, and underground adversaries, including bear, gamble and regain fortune, health, and protection.

6
Water Creatures

According to nineteenth-century Ojibwe testimonies, there are several dialectical processes in their animal life world. One general dialectic, and quite an obvious tension-laden movement, is between sky birds and sea creatures; another is among the sea creatures themselves; another is between the Great Lakes Ojibwe people and the combined sky world/water world. Each of these dialectics has an oppositional force, and it might be tempting to construe them as dualistic; evidence, however, points to a necessary convergence of these forces – most often a beneficial one for the Anishinaabe. We will begin by examining the water creatures themselves.

From the perspective of mainstream scientists, the study of these water creatures is called cryptozoology and the objects of this study are called cryptids. From the perspectives of the Ojibwe, the sortings are quite different and subtle, for the emphasis is on interrelationships: on these water creatures as cousins; as related to fellow sea dwellers, on copper and silver; on having kinship ties with women; and on waters, the habitat of funny little creatures.

Stylized wild cat. Finger-woven bag used for medicine bundles, Central Great Lakes, late eighteenth century. Phillips, *Patterns of Power*, front cover.

Harmful Creatures

Many cultures regard creatures of the sea in a negative way, and the Ojibwe are no exception. The portrayals of these sinister beings, their habitats, and the names they are given all corroborate this perception. Such creatures are described as wild cats who live in underground caverns or in the vast water; they often have horns and are called evil spirits, devils, and serpents. They are frequently regarded as bad medicine and are associated with catastrophic events. The very dwelling places of such monsters in the sea and in caves evoke a forbidding feeling. One such place was present-day Devil's Warehouse Island in Lake Superior Provincial Park, where Mide scrolls were kept. As spirit eyes followed one's presence, mosses dripped with dew and ferns shivered with the slightest breeze. These beings elicited reverence, awe and fear.[1] Selwyn Dewdney writes that the most dangerous and most powerful sea presence is Mishipeshu, "an underwater monster whose dragon-like tail could lash a lake into a vicious squall, or treacherously shift a current in the rapids, to swamp the canoe of anyone who failed to render the proper respect."[2] Indeed, Garrick Mallery associates the Grand Medicine Society itself with a powerful, horned sea monster that commands attention in the fourth Mide lodge. Such monsters or sea snakes were one of the most common representations on petroglyphs and petroforms.[3] While the medium of expression for these water creatures, and for sky creatures also, might change, they retain a force in contemporary cultural expressions.[4]

Additional negative images appear. William Hoffman describes five serpent spirits that cause illness and are opposed to Nanabush (one of those credited with founding the Grand Medicine Society).[5] According to Sam Snake's story, "Adventures of Nanabush," because of the evil Serpent People, Nanabush created the world.[6] Dewdney writes that "malignant monsters ... invaded the sacred precincts ... enormously powerful beings ... Some sent flames across the entrance; others struck ... with a deadly disease."[7]

Claude Allouez wrote in 1667 that not all of the spirits in Aboriginal worlds were regarded as beneficent. The Ottawa believed "there are many spirits ... some beneficent as the sun, the moon, lakes, rivers and woods; others malevolent, as the adder, the dragon, cold, and storms." Of the spirits that Allouez called malevolent, he added: "During storms and tempests, they sacrifice a dog, throwing it into the Lake. 'That is to appease thee,' they say to the latter; 'keep quiet.' At perilous places in the rivers, they propitiate the eddies and rapids by offering them presents."[8]

But in contemporary contexts, it is difficult to sift the positive aspects of these creatures from the negative. In Ojibwe artist Carl Ray's depiction, "Evil Serpent," a man is caught in the centre of a large, entwining serpent; power lines from the serpent to the man and vice versa connect the serpent's mouth to the man's knee. Not only this man but also bear, fish, and turtle are encircled by the serpent. Another Ojibwe painter, Roy Thomas, has titled a painting unequivocally as "Demon Fish." Blue Sky Woman recounted that such sea creatures had left a permanent impression on the earth: they had clawed birch trees and the bark contained their visible marks.[9] In addition, Nanabush and bear engage in clawing, leaving behind marks on trees.

"Horned serpents were associated with drownings, floods, sorcery, and human sacrifice, and considered a very bad omen in dreams or individual sightings," Arthur Bourgeois writes.[10] To be on the land and view the water was one stance; another was to face the water while on or in it. Water is necessary for life and is symbolically important as well, yet it remained a source of disquietude and mystery for nineteenth-century Ojibwe. The visible swirls of eddies often had menacing undercurrents. The water itself and its mists evoked many representations – some well formed and others quite indefinite – such as monster spirits, mermen and mermaids, Mishipeshu (Water Lynx) and Mamaquishawok (the Little People in the Rocks).[11] In the war between Nanabush and the Great Serpent, the serpent angrily sent a flood over the world and various animals tried to renew life by diving and bringing up earth.[12]

Sea creatures were often unfriendly to the Ojibwe and their hero, Nanabush. Delia Oshogay tells a series of stories interpreted by Maggie Lamorie, "Wenebojo Myths from Lac Courte Oreilles." In one of these, "Wenebojo in the Whale and His Fight with an Ogre," despite his grandmother's expressed doubts that he would catch any fish, Wenebojo/Nanabush went angling anyway, singing, and even taunting the leading fish spirit: "'Misinamegwe, come on and swallow me.' He sang that over and over. The big fish heard him. He was king of the fish." Misinamegwe enlisted his helpers, Sunfish/My Flap Door, and Bass/My Door Step, to determine what Wenebojo wanted. Wenebojo, however, wanted an answer not from the subservient spirits but from influential Misinamegwe himself. When told of this, "the big fish got mad and went up to where Wenebojo was fishing. Wenebojo saw him coming, and his boat began to swirl around when the mouth of the fish came near. Wenebojo couldn't hold the boat back, and the big fish just swallowed him, boat and all." With some modifications, this story resembles the biblical one of Jonah and the whale.[13]

Wild cat's whirlpools. "Bold set of concentric circles suggestive both of the whirlpools created by the Misshipeshu and of its coiled tail which stirs up the waters." Front side of woven bag. Central Great Lakes, late eighteenth century. Phillips, *Patterns of Power*, 43, 67. Also, Phillips, "Zigzag and Spiral," 415, 423.

When Wenebojo regained his wits inside the fish's stomach, he noticed that the bowels of the fish were like a big, long wigwam, with an owl and a squirrel living inside it. Both of them told him how they had been caught and predicted that they were going to die. "Wenebojo started to do everything to that big fish inside. The fish began to feel sick to his stomach. He thought, 'I guess I'll go to the shore and throw up Wenebojo.' But Wenebojo knew what he was trying to do. He put his boat crosswise in the fish's throat so that fish couldn't vomit him up. Misinamegwe next tried to move his bowels to get rid of Wenebojo. Wenebojo could see something at the other end of the wigwam contracting and expanding. He knew it was the fish's rectum, and he tied it so tight that the fish couldn't do anything. Poor Misinamegwe died from all this." Owl, squirrel, and Wenebojo, however, were getting sick. They heard a knock on the fish's back and ascertained that raven was pecking a hole in the dead fish and was feeding on it. Somehow they directed the fish to float to the shore near grandmother's dwelling; she opened the fish with a knife, all of them escaped, and Wenebojo gave some fish to owl and squirrel.[14]

Wenebojo/Nanabush had taunted the great fish and stirred its enmity. Underwater manidos could become jealous of the success of others, Barnouw comments. They killed Wenebojo's nephew because he was successful in hunting. Envy and jealousy were also common among the Ojibwe. If a person was known to have leadership qualities or was adept at gambling, for instance, feelings of inferiority and resentment might develop in others and beating and wounding could follow.[15] In his *Narrative*, Tanner wrote of his experiences of a similar attitude: because he was a good hunter, a fellow hunter became jealous of his success and damaged his gun.[16] Ruth Landes writes that although women were not as prone as men to show jealousy, one woman told her that she had been isolated in the village and was hated by all women because of her skill in beadwork and tanning.[17] These stories and experiences served as warnings that a successful person could attract the jealousy and hostility of others.

"Fabulous serpent." Schoolcraft, *Historical and Statistical Information*, 1:408b.

Snakes and the Afterlife

Sea creatures manifest both positive and negative attitudes toward the afterlife; some snakes are helpful guides while others erect roadblocks. Tom Badger tells a story, interpreted by Julia Badger, "Wenebojo's Brother Makes the Road to the Other World." At four places along the road to the afterlife, the brother planted signs indicating animal spirits – otter and owl at the first two. At the third place he put two signs, one on each side of the road, making it appear that there were two converging hills. "They're not real hills. They're two snakes with their heads together. When those snakes breathe, fire shoots across the road from their mouths. The road runs between them." The brother put a sign at the fourth place and created a modest-sized river. "It wasn't very big or very wide. A man can jump across it, if he's a good jumper. He put a log across the river. It wasn't really a log. It's really a snake. They don't tell this in the story. When it's referred to, it's spoken of as a log; but the Indians know it's a snake. The water is swift there. The log bobs up and down all the time. On the right hand side of the log, the water is clear. Where the river flows, it's as dark as it can be. You can't see the bottom of it. On the left hand side of the log, the water is black." On top of a hill, between two roads, "the devil" had put a strawberry with a spoon in it.[18] This devil invited those on the way to the hereafter to eat strawberries, a multilayered symbol: of spring and new life, and of Ode'imin (which means strawberry), the youth who brought the Mide performances to the Ojibwe. Hence, berries or strawberries symbolize the liminal state between the here and the hereafter, as well as the means to make this transition.[19]

According to the Three Fires Anishinaabe, the turtle and snake petroforms at Bannock Point, Manitoba, also point to the afterlife. The voice of the great snake beckons and carries the person "down to the edge of a river which flows with white water and treacherous currents. Across the river beat the drums from the land where you will reside eventually." Then the snake will disappear and the giant turtle will speak to the deceased.[20]

"Pine Point Snake Petroform. Whiteshell Provincial Park." Pettipas, "Tie Creek Study," 63.

Helpful Creatures

Many people, including the Ojibwe, are apprehensive about the reptilian world, and specifically about serpents and other sea creatures. Water creatures, however, have had an important place in the lives of the Anishinaabe people, who could readily feel, hear, and see water creatures, for they lived in the midst of many rivers and lakes, with the great one, Lake Superior, predominating.

James Tanner, who spent thirty years among the Ojibwe, writes in a generally positive manner about sea creatures. The great underground wild cat sings a song for medicine hunting, illustrated in a line drawing: "I come to change the appearance of the ground: I make it look different each season." Tanner comments: "This is a Manito who, on account of his immensity of tail, and other peculiarities, has no prototype. He claims to be the ruler over seasons. He is probably Gitche-a-nah-mi-e-be-zhew (great underground wild-cat)." About a similar line drawing, Tanner comments: "Under-ground wild cat is my friend."[21] The wildcat "has horns ... is a master, an evil spirit, or devil ... Of this last they speak but rarely."[22] These felines on petroglyphs show lines "projecting from the sides of the face [which] denote a spirit or enlightened animal."[23] Such underground wild cats were believed to guard copper deposits in the Lake Superior region.

Wild cat. Song of Chiahba: "Under-ground wild cat, is my friend." "The wild cat here figured has horns, and his residence is under the ground." Tanner, *A Narrative*, 377–8.

Although the Anishinaabe had an explicit or at least implicit foreboding about these creatures, on some important occasions they were viewed positively. For instance, instead of spelling his full name when he signed the 1836 Manitoulin Island Bond Head Treaty, Pesa Atawish/ Vincent Atawish used the snake totem.[24] Other leaders of Algonquian nations signed nineteenth-century treaties with the Government of Canada using animal pictures of their totems or clans.[25] Still others used snake as a surname,[26] or its skin as a medicine bag.[27] Hoffman depicts a spiral snake on a relic belonging to a Mide.[28] While in the second degree of the Mide ceremony serpent spirits try to harm the candidate from the outside and prevent his progress, in the third degree the serpent plays a positive role; here "the serpent manito helps the candidate by arching its body so he may pass beneath unmolested."[29]

Attentive to the beneficial powers of water creatures, Aboriginal peoples incised images of them on stone and wood in order to record the results of a spiritual quest; these images would exorcise the power of frightening monsters or retain the forces of guardian spirits.

Animals like wild cats sometimes did not help the Anishinaabe directly, but instead banished aquatic evil spirits from their own privileged domain, the water. On other occasions, however, these water creatures became a living and caring presence. When the Ojibwe were at war with the Dakota, for example, these monsters expelled enemies from the waters and, with other water animals, became protectors of the Anishinaabe. In this relationship, waters helped define these people, for water comprised the greatest percentage of their human bodies, was maintained and renewed by the thunderers, and connected the people to their ancestors, as M. Assinewe of the Sagamok Anishinaabeg near Sudbury, Ontario, testifies.[30] The powwow drum originated in the context of water – an account we will pursue later.

Eight wild cats. Powers emanating from eight long-tailed underwater panthers on the back side of a woven bag. Central Great Lakes, late eighteenth century. Phillips, *Patterns of Power*, 43, 67.

Many of North America's petroglyph and petrograph sites have positive medicinal significance. Tanner supports this notion as he comments on the beings called medicine animals: "Snakes and the under-ground wild cat are among his [medicine man's] helpers and friends. The ferocity and cunning as well as the activity of the feline animals have not escaped the notice of the Indians."[31] In the context of songs for the Midewiwin, Tanner provides four figures that have medical implications. The first one, wild cat, sings a song for the Mide only: "I walk about in the night time." Tanner comments: "This first figure represents the wild cat, to whom, on account of his vigilance, the medicines for the cure of diseases were committed. The meaning probably is, that to those who have the shrewdness, the watchfulness, and intelligence of the wild cat, is entrusted the knowledge of those powerful remedies, which, in the opinion of the Indians, not only control life, and avail to the restoration of health, but have an almost unlimited power over animals and birds."

The second image, a human being, speaks: "I hear your mouth, you are an ill (or evil) spirit." Tanner comments: "The wild cat, (or the sensible and intelligent medicine man,) is always awake … If one man speaks evil of another, to bring sickness upon him, the wild cat hears and knows it."

The third figure sings: "Now I come up out of the ground; I am wild cat." Tanner comments: "I am the master of the wild cats; and having heard your talk, I come up out of the ground to see what you do." The fourth wild cat sings: "Behold! I am wild cat; I am glad to see you all wild cats." Tanner comments: "This figure, with open eyes and erect ears, denotes earnestness and attention."[32]

In summary, wild cat embodies the medicinal and healing process in himself. He is also the symbol of many virtues prized by the Ojibwe.

Garrick Mallery relies on Henry Schoolcraft to describe this physical wild cat and its powers. A specific image of the wild cat "was drawn by Little Hill, a Winnebago chief of the upper Mississippi, west. He represents it as their medicine animal. He says that this animal is seldom seen; that it is only seen by medicine men after severe fasting. He has a piece of bone which he asserts was taken from this animal. He considers it a potent medicine and uses it by filing a small piece in water. He has also a small piece of native copper which he uses in the same manner, and entertains like notions of its sovereign virtues."[33]

William Jones tells a story, "The Women and the Great Lynx," in which Great Lynx – *Ginebik* – tried to capsize a canoe filled with three women. By her dream-power, one of the women broke "his tail and beat him off with a paddle. It was this same monster that was later killed near Sault St. Mary [*sic*] for having taken away a babe on a cradle-board and killed it." During this latter incident, an Ojibwe snatched part of Great Lynx's tail and used it as an amulet to counter the monster's power. This object wielded power similar to that of Mide songs sung to calm the waters.[34] Thus the monster was an abductor in the waters but part of its tail was used to pacify those same waters.[35]

Snake. "Song for medicine hunting: 'Long ago, in the old time, since I laid myself down, ye are spirits.'" "This is the figure of a snake running over the ground ... [Some say it is] Mesukkummegokwa, the grandmother of mankind, to whom Nanabush gave in keeping, for the use of his uncles and aunts, all roots and plants, and other medicines derived from the earth ... Hence it is that the medicine men make an address to Mesukkummegokwa whenever they take anything from the earth which is to be used as medicine." Tanner, *A Narrative*, 354–5.

The underwater Manitous and their chief, or *ogimaa*, Mishipeshu,[36] were to be treated with respect. When imprisoned in the water during winter, these spirits were relatively powerless, and their names could safely be mentioned, for such invocations in these cold times did not unleash their powers.[37]

Many Ojibwe stories portray animals that sing, wound, and heal. On the Agawa site in Northern Ontario is a rock painting of a great sea creature that, while menacing, is helpful to the Ojibwe. In the nineteenth century, Chief Chingwauk made bark drawings and interpretations of this pictograph, which features a striking image of a creature with a large, dragon-like head and curved horns that has assumed a talking or striking position. With its long body and tail, and fissures or projecting sawtooth spines along the length of its back, it is a mystifying and dangerous being that controls the deep waters. Two snakes are pictured below the main image, as well as a canoe alongside it. In his drawing of it, Chingwauk attributed the painting to the medicine-warrior, Myeengun (Wolf), "who is skilled in the Meda [Midewiwin] ... [and who] records the aid he received from the fabulous night panther." This night panther is mollified by tobacco and can ensure safe water passage. Its power helped Chingwauk give this interpretation.[38]

"The Mishipizheu (Great Lynx) at Agawa Rock on Lake Superior" with canoe and snakes. Rajnovich, *Reading Rock Art*, 13.

Also beneficial to the Ojibwe are trout and sturgeon, cousins who inhabit relatively shallow waters. These fish join a chorus reminding the Ojibwe to share themselves and their produce. Stories urge the Ojibwe to be grateful and to offer, initially to the Great Spirit, the first fruits of the season (blueberries, maple sugar, and wild rice) or the first animal killed. The order for sharing should include other people before oneself. Above all, both individuals and the group are not to be greedy. Great sturgeon (also called Grandfather), who gives himself in the form of an abundance of food, taught lessons of sharing to boasting and greedy individuals and then to the whole people. One story presents young Winona and cousin Bonnie, who boast that they had caught first 100 fish, then 1,000, and then a trillion. While they are describing having caught a seemingly limitless catch, the narrator states that they had actually caught enough for only two or three households.[39] Boasting about the actual catch led to an exaggeration; a moral commitment led to a confession of only a modest number. This story, like many others, is both descriptive and prescriptive. In "The Gift of Trout," the contemporary Ojibwe artist Roy Morris paints two spirit figures that are joined to trout; trout in turn houses a human who cooks on an open fire.[40]

In another story involving trout, Nanabush and Soaring Eagle went fishing during the long winter and agreed to split their catch. Nanabush, however, absconded to his winter camp with all of the fish that were caught. Since they had no provisions for the long winter, Soaring Eagle and his family were in danger of starvation. Water Spirit discovered their plight and "invited Soaring Eagle to a feast and gave him food to take home to his family. Trout also told Soaring Eagle how to catch more fish, but warned him to stop fishing once he had enough to last through the winter. But he caught enough for three winters." Soaring Eagle got tired and as he ended the fishing task, he tried to pull his son from the water with twine, for he had been fishing in the water; the twine broke and his son drowned. "Trout came to Soaring Eagle in a dream, and told him the Great Sturgeon had taken his son because of his greed. The next morning, Soaring Eagle travelled under the ice to see the Great Sturgeon, who returned his son after warning him to take only what he needed in the future."[41]

The underwater Manitous provided the Ojibwe with medicine and copper and also granted sanctuary to some who had fallen through the winter ice. These water creatures inspired terror and awe but also reverence. Vecsey writes that "without the aid or benign neglect of this being – part snake, part lynx, part mountain lion – the Ojibwas would surely starve or suffer death in raging waters."[42]

Water creatures provided food and protection to Aboriginal peoples around the Great Lakes. The eighteenth-century French Jesuit traveller and historian Pierre-François-Xavier de Charlevoix, who was fascinated with rattlesnakes in the Great Lakes region, wrote: "There are some of them as thick as a man's leg, and sometimes thicker, and long in proportion ... [Their] colour is lively without being dazzling, and a pale yellow, with very beautiful shades ... But the most remarkable part of this animal is its tail; this is scaly like a coat of mail, somewhat flattish, and it grows, say they, every year a row of scales; thus its age may be known by its tail ... It is from this noise, this sort of serpent has obtained the name it bears."

Charlevoix also noted that on the south shore of Lake Superior there were two small islands. "These are called Rattlesnake islands, and we are told they are so infested with these reptiles that the air is infected with them." Of the Niagara region, he wrote: "Indians esteem the flesh of those reptiles a very great dainty. In general, serpents are no way frightful to these people; there is no animal you see oftener painted on their faces and bodies, and they seldom even pursue them, except for food. The bones and skins of serpents are also of great service to their jugglers and wizards in divining; the last of which they make uses of for belts and fillets [headbands?]. It is no less true what we are told of their having the secret of enchanting, or, to speak more properly, stupifying those animals; their taking them alive, handling them, and putting them in their bosom, without receiving any hurt; a circumstance, which contributes not a little towards gaining them the real credit they have amongst these people."[43]

For those who knew how to observe, the waters themselves had their own moods and dangers. Of the Great Lakes, particularly of Lake Superior and its turbulent depths and waves, Charlevoix wrote: "When a storm is about to rise you are advertised of it, say they, two days before; at first you perceive a gentle murmuring on the surface of the water which lasts the whole day, without encreasing in any sensible manner; the day after, the lake is covered with pretty large waves, but without breaking all that day, so that you may proceed without fear, and even make good way if the wind is favourable; but on the third day when you are least thinking of it the lake becomes all on fire; the ocean in its greatest rage is not more tost [tossed], in which case you must take care to be near shelter to save yourself; this you are always sure to find on the north shore, whereas on the south you are obliged to secure yourself the second day at a considerable distance from the water side."

Charlevoix then echoed the observations of previous explorers: "The Indians out of gratitude for the plenty of fish with which this lake supplies them, and from the respect which its vast extent inspires them with, have made a sort of divinity of it, to which they offer sacrifices after their own manner. I am however of opinion, that it is not to the lake itself but to the genius that presides over it, that they address their vows. If we may credit these people this lake proceeds from a divine original, and was formed by Michabou god of the waters, in order to catch beavers." To a god or genius, Charlevoix attributed the creation of a causeway "to dam up the waters of the rivers, and those of the lake."[44]

As noted earlier, serpents figure in present-day Ojibwe paintings. In one of these, "The Shaman's Drum," a serpent that overarches the people appears on the upper part of one side of the drum; on the other side is a medicine person who sits on a bear while beating a red drum.[45]

In his painting "Androgyny," Norval Morrisseau indicates the convergence of snake and sturgeon; thunderbird dominates in the centre and is surrounded by other spirit beings. A serpent lurches upwards and breaks through (as does bear) the middle and upper worlds, where creatures and plants are portrayed in vibrant colours. This interaction is in the context of a shaking tent and drum, a cosmological rendition suggesting a communion of the three worlds: the upper, middle, and lower.[46] In "Spirit of the Water God" and "Goddess of Fish," the contemporary Woodland artist Francis Kagige depicts power relationships or sensory links among sea creatures and others, including humans.[47]

We have noted that the reverential and relational term Grandfather had been given to several animals. George Hamell suggests that for many Aboriginal peoples this term was extended to the keeper[48] of shells, copper, and fur-bearing animals. Grandfather gave the Ojibwe gifts of shell, copper, and animals for use in their daily lives and in their Midewiwin performances. As with the Ojibwe's traditional practice, however, these gifts were not merely to be received and used; they were also to be given away or exchanged. Initially, the Ojibwe gave copper, shells, and furs to other Native groups or used them as trading goods. During the early contact period, Hamell writes, the Europeans who arrived on the ocean were "initially and indirectly perceived as Under(water) World Grandfathers" who, as the keepers of shells, copper, and furs, now exchanged new trade goods such as glassware and copper, brass, and iron items. In the trading process, the Ojibwe perceived that these "European Grandfathers were requesting in exchange for their glass wares and other items only that over which they were also traditionally the keepers." The trading process with Europeans was regarded as an exchange of gifts, as heavily charged symbolically, and as according with traditional Ojibwe practices. The Ojibwe also interpreted the dressing of their own deceased with copper and shells as an exchange. "Such goods were being returned to the Under(water) World and to the Under(water) World Grandfathers from whence they were ultimately derived and from whom more such goods would be received in this grand cyclic exchange between this and the 'other' world."[49]

Women, Water, and Snakes

Amphibious creatures such as serpents demonstrate ambivalent powers for the Ojibwe: on the one hand, they are sources of disease and dread, but on the other, they have curative powers (a claim made by many other cultures as well). Sea serpents are sinister and there are taboos against uttering their names, but they can also offer protection, especially for women. In the following oral narrative, Sandra Corbiere describes how "big animals" prevented the enemies' abduction of Ojibwe women: "A long time ago, when she [Sandra Corbiere's grandmother] was just a baby and her grandmother would speak to her eh, she used to tell me about things that happened a long time ago ... like ah, they're some still in canoes and different ah people coming in, different nations eh, and ah some of the stuff that happened like ah [pause] the Ojibway women used to get stolen and taken to another part, and she used to talk about that and ah ah things that would happen like ah when you're traveling on the lake, there use to be those ah animals ah big animals use to come after you eh ... but ah you used to see them in the water."[50]

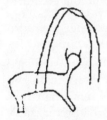

"Round-horned panther that lives in Mokwa's house ... This house was a mountain underneath the ground." Chief Moses Day Daybwaywaindung's Medicine Bark (History Chart) Parchment. Reagan, "A Ritual Parchment," 235, 242.

The sea world harboured kindred spirits. From this world emerged water snakes, who were attracted to women, for women had a likeness to water; they were regarded as keepers of water, for water in their amniotic sacs was the initial home of their children. Water beings often aided women in bringing gifts to the Manitous, since water creatures and women had a curious reciprocal appeal for each other. In fact, in the underworld, water snake was the special helper of women. According to William Bisneshi Baker, the powwow, its songs, and the water drum arose from a Dakota, Tailfeather Woman, in the context of water. In one story, white soldiers attacked the Dakota people and killed four of Tailfeather Woman's sons. The mother escaped by hiding in a pond, under lily pads, for four days. During her hiding, Great Spirit gave her instructions on how to build the water drum and perform its ceremonies, and also directed her to pass this ceremony from community to community. The performance promoted peace as the norm for living instead of war; this was the beginning of the powwow for all Aboriginal peoples.[51]

Health. Bear and manitou restore a person to health.
Chief Moses Day Daybwaywaindung's Medicine Bark
(History Chart) Parchment. Reagan, "A Ritual Parchment,"
235, 242.

The Anishinaabe artist Ahmoo Angeconeb continues this motif
of peace in drawings that depict harmonious relationships of under
world, middle world, and sky world. In "Family Migration," "Man
at Obishikokkang," and "Woman and Guardians," the sky world,
however, is not more important than the middle or the under world.[52]

The following stories illustrate the affinity that amphibious creatures
have with humans, especially with women. In "The Two Squaws and
the Serpent," George Brant of the Rama Reserve recalls that a snake
was initially fascinated by two women who picked berries and who
then slept under a canoe; the snake was attracted to them and crawled
on top of them, but got a whiff of wild onions from their breath and
left. In turn, the breath of the serpent made the women's hair turn
white! Reciprocal odours from both sets of creatures had remarkable
effects.[53]

In "The Tree Serpent," Brant narrates that two travelling women prepared to rest at the end of the day, and broke off cedar branches to make
a bed. While they were sleeping, a large serpent that looked like a man
appeared from a hole in a tree. A woman was with him. The two Indian
women were frightened and ran away.[54] Another story, "The Girl and
the Serpent," by Lottie Marsden, also from the Rama Reserve, tells of a
twelve-year-old girl who befriended a serpent. When the father learned
of this episode, he shot the serpent. "This girl felt awful bad. She would
not eat. She said to her father, 'Why did you kill the best friend that I
had?' ... She died a couple of days afterwards, she was that sorry for the
serpent."[55] In "The Serpent Lover," Mrs Sampson Ingersoll, also from
Rama, narrates that an Indian girl dressed up in the evening, went to a
marsh, and sat in a large patch of cattails. When a serpent approached
and coiled itself around her, she let her hair down. On another occasion,
"the serpent did not say anything to the girl, only made love to her."
After the family learned of the serpent, they killed it.[56]

In "Snake Spirit," Sam Ozawamik offers a variant to these stories. A young woman visited an adder, became pregnant, and gave birth to two children, a boy and a girl. "They were spirits, and for this reason that woman could not stay in the village ... In due course, they [the children] prospered. In time they grew into great numbers. These were the Iroquois, the little Iroquois. They were said to be more than unusually bad tempered. But what was expected? They were spirits."[57] And, after all, what could you expect of serpents and the Iroquois! In "The Serpent and the Squaw," Joe Cosh recounts another story told by an aged man: While the father hunted during the day, the mother dressed in silk and abandoned her children. Some time afterward, the mother revealed to her family that she had been visiting a serpent at a lake. At the wife's request, the father dressed in silk and pretended to be the wife and visited the same lake; he attracted the attention of the serpent and shot it. The family lived happily ever after.[58]

Another story, "The Squaw Who Lived with a Serpent," by Lottie Marsden: A girl decided to leave home because she thought she might be killed. After an absence of two years, she returned with a child who was a little serpent, for the daughter had married a serpent. The new mother was disappointed that her parents were displeased with her baby. The father killed the serpent/granddaughter, but told his daughter one of two stories: that two Mohawks had killed the child, or that the child had fallen out of a tree. Apparently, the young woman believed him and continued to live with her parents.[59]

Kenneth G. Snake from the Rama Reserve tells the story "The Old Woman and the Serpent": In the summer, an old woman bought meat from a store to feed a serpent. She seemed to do this so that the serpent would not eat her cousins. Sometimes she forgot to feed the animal, and eventually all of her cousins were dead. Even though her son and daughter also died, she continued to work hard to feed the serpent. The serpent was always afraid of thunder. One summer she did not see the serpent and then she died.[60]

In these stories of women and snakes, some women are able to transcend their own natural and community feelings of fear. They nurture a wholesome sensitivity toward serpents, understand them, find a kinship with them, and thus move from fear to reverence. In some cases, women live intimately with them. Artists are often the ones who depict this sensitivity. Thus in his Horizon Series, George Morrison paints various faces of Underwater Manitou, some rather obscure, but others that move and change, unrestricted by negative perceptions from individuals and groups.[61]

Woman with medicine bag. Chart from White Earth Reservation: "Denotes that women also have the privilege of becoming members of the Midewiwin. The figure holds in the left hand the Mide sack, made of snake skin." Hoffman, "The Midê'wiwin," 185.

While some women are intimately associated with and rely on water and sea creatures, this is not the case with women generally. On the basis of his evaluation of four Ojibwe stories, J. Randolph Valentine concludes that women are often the ones who have wisdom and a keen sense of proper judgment: "Ookomisan [Nokomis, grandmother] has a preternatural awareness of the future, knows the physical circumstances of everyone, is clearly at some level at least jointly in control, and does not hesitate to set Nenabozho straight for his foolish invention of war, yet in the gracious way of an elder, without passing judgement on him, but on the particular act. And she does so by pointing to the effects of his actions on children."[62]

Women, water and snakes – these are interrelated in many Ojibwe stories. There is an easy interplay among them, with dispositions of fascination, erotic and procreative actions, and mutual protection. Men represent values of humans cohabiting only with fellow humans; men are generally defensive and aggressive towards serpents' relationships with their spouses or with their daughters.

Sea Creatures and Copper

We have already alluded to the water spirit's guardianship and gift of copper, which has medicinal properties. Even when Ojibwe came to realize that selling copper could lead to wealth, they often did not capitalize on this opportunity. Copper was holy and was used symbolically in ceremonies such as those of the Midewiwin. William Warren mentions that non-Aboriginals in the seventeenth century such as Samuel de Champlain, Pierre Boucher, and Jean Talon, and then Alexander Henry in the early nineteenth century, wrote about the value of copper;

unlike them, however, Aboriginals generally did not use it for "common purposes."[63] As Bernard Peters develops in his article, "Wa-bish-kee-pe-nas and the Chippewa Reverence for Copper," copper formed the identity of Great Lakes people;[64] it was "mined, gathered, worked, and used for about six thousand years in the Lake Superior basin."[65]

To protect copper, the Ojibwe were often secretive about its location, which was also considered sacred. Some Ojibwe pointed out relatively unimportant copper deposits to non-Aboriginals to steer them away from sacred places; some planted chunks of copper in obvious locations to deceive prospectors. Copper deposits around the Great Lakes often coincided with places where healers came to dream and hear voices. "Anishinaabeg elders came to the sacred copper sites in the late spring to heal their bones," Gerald Vizenor writes. "Copper held healing spirits, the best energies of the earth. Some healers prescribed the cold river water that ran through the exposed copper stone as a source of health and mythic dreams." In general the Anishinaabe did not like to talk about copper; they especially did not mention by name Mishipeshu, Manitou of the underworld, who controlled copper or *miskwabik*.[66] Copper had value in itself and did not depend on humans to determine its worth; the Ojibwe, therefore, were often content to let it remain where it was.

Like other Europeans, Charlevoix thought that Aboriginal peoples in the Great Lakes region regarded the abundant copper as hallowed; it was "the object of superstitious worship amongst the Indians; they look upon them [pieces of copper] with veneration, as if they were the presents of those gods who dwell under the waters; they collect their smallest fragments which they carefully preserve without however making any use of them. They say that formerly a huge rock of this metal was to be seen elevated to a considerable height above the surface of the water, and as it has now disappeared they pretend that the gods have carried it elsewhere; but there is great reason to believe that in process of time, the waves of the lake have covered it entirely with sand and slime; and it is certain that in several places pretty large quantities of this metal have been discovered, without even being obliged to dig very deep."[67]

Although the Ojibwe had a high cultural regard for copper, they did not initially accord monetary value to it. They wore or carried copper as amulets, which they wrapped carefully and handed down to future generations. Copper glistened, but shells and glass beads also reflected light. All of these items had symbolic worth, offering prestige, status, and wealth. According to George Hamell, "shell, crystal, and native copper were their owner's assurance and insurance of long life (immortality through resuscitation), well-being (the absence of ill-being), and success, particularly in the conceptually related activities of hunting, fishing, warfare, and courtship." Early on, European trade goods were also part of this beneficial structure.[68]

Copper was often viewed as a gift of the water spirits and therefore as rather mysterious and worthy of reverence. Water itself was often viewed as a gift from the Great Spirit. In 1667, missionary François Le Mercier wrote about the high estimation that the Algonquins had for the waters of Lake Superior. They revered the lake "as a Divinity, and offer it sacrifices, whether on account of its size – for its length is two hundred leagues, and its greatest width eighty – or because of its goodness in furnishing fish for the sustenance of all these tribes, in default of game, which is scarce in the neighborhood." Mercier then referred to nuggets of copper at the lake's bottom, some of which were of considerable weight. "They keep them as so many divinities, or as presents which the gods dwelling beneath the water have given them, and on which their welfare is to depend. For this reason they preserve these pieces of copper, wrapped up, among their most precious possessions. Some have kept them for more than fifty years; others have had them in their families from time immemorial, and cherish them as household gods."[69]

Water was a good in itself, but it also produced such beneficial and spirited items as copper, fish, and other sea creatures. Writing in 1667, Claude Allouez pointed to the powers of fish and the gifts from the waters: "[They] believe ... that the souls of the departed govern the fish in the lake; and thus, from the earliest times, they have held the immortality, and even the metempyschosis, of the souls of dead fishes, believing that they pass into other fishes' bodies. Therefore they never throw their bones into the fire, for fear that they may offend these souls, so that they will cease to come into their nets. They hold in very special veneration a certain fabulous animal which they have never seen except in dreams, and which they call Missibizi, acknowledging it to be a great genius, and offering it sacrifices in order to obtain good sturgeon-fishing. They say also that the little nuggets of copper which they find at the bottom of the water in the Lake, or in the rivers emptying into it, are the riches of the gods who dwell in the depths of the earth."[70]

For the Ojibwe, serpents had ambivalent characteristics: on the one hand, they were sources of disease and dread, and on the other, as noted earlier, they exhibited curative powers. An example of this ambivalence is encountered in the narrative of John Tanner, who recalls that a medicine man, "Mukkwah, the bear, heard the sound of bad fire in the breast of the Naudoways [Iroquois]." The healer extracted a small snake; Eshkebukkekoosha, an Ojibwe medicine man, prescribed a continuation of the recovery process – an aide was to go to running water, offer tobacco, bring water to the sick person, and wear a small hoop of wood on his head like a cap. On one-half of the hoop was the figure of a snake and on the other half was the figure of a man. The snake's task was to care for the water while the man represented the Great Spirit. The hoop was "not to be worn on ordinary occasions only when bringing water for the family, friends or one who was sick."[71]

"The wild cat." "Song for the Metai [Mide] only." Tanner, *A Narrative*, 345.

All animals could aid humans, including serpents, who were especially adept at scheming. Ojibwe leader Sahgimah became a wily (and heartless?) strategist for the Ottawa at the Battle of the Blue Mountains near Penetanguishene, Ontario. When the Mohawks were defeated, he said: "By the power of the Great Serpent we shall not slay these craven Mohawks; we shall use them as messengers to go home to bring the news of what a Mohawk defeat means on the shore of the our lake of the Ottawas. Let us first array our glorious battlefield so that it may be well remembered. Let us cut off the heads of all the dead enemies and mount them on poles with faces turned towards our lake, then let these men go home and tell their kindred."[72]

Sea Creatures and Silver

For the Ojibwe, copper held many powers and symbolic meanings. Silver, too, was regarded as a gift of the underworld; it reflected light against the dark and evil spirits.[73] About 1760, wampum and glass beads began to be overshadowed by trade silver. Alexander Henry wrote during his experiences around Michilimackinac, in the context of the growing prevalence of silver, that when the Chippewa killed a bear, its "head was adorned with all the trinkets in the possession of the family, such as silver arm-bands and wrist-bands, and belts of wampum; and then laid upon a scaffold, set up for its reception, within a lodge. Near the nose was placed a large quantity of tobacco."[74] Silver items were a significant part of trade; Matthew Clarkson, an Indian agent at Fort Chartres near present-day St Louis, made the following entry in his diary: "Account of silver truck Captain Long left with me on the 28th February, 1767, the day he went from the Kaskaskias for the boats under Captain Smith's care. One hundred and seventy-four small crosses; eighty-four nose crosses; thirty-three long-drop nose and ear-bobs; eighteen short do.; one hundred and twenty-six small brooches; thirty-eight larger brooches; forty rings; two narrow arm-bands; six narrow scalloped wrist-bands; three narrow plain, do.; four half-moon gorgets [collars protecting the throat]; three large do.; six moon do.; nine hair plates; seventeen hair-bobs."[75] At the beginning of the twentieth century, Densmore described an ornate "chief drum" from Lac du Flambeau, Minnesota, that was decorated with beadwork, silver disks, and thimbles.[76]

Because silver, like copper, was so important to the Ojibwe, they felt the need to protect it. One story recounts that Nanabush, the spirit of the deep sea water, wished to reward the Ojibwe on Isle Royale, near Thunder Bay, Ontario, for their loyalty to the spirits, their peaceful dispositions, and their industrious acts. The Great Spirit revealed to them a tunnel that led to the centre of a rich silver mine. He warned the people that if they disclosed this entrance to the greedy white man, Nanabush would be turned into stone. These Ojibwe used silver from the mine to fashion beautiful adornments, and when Sioux warriors noticed these, they wanted to know the secret location of the silver. At first, torture and death could not make them divulge the source. Then a cunning Sioux scout disguised himself as an Ojibwe, entered their camp, and learned the mine's location. On his way back to his own camp, the scout went to the silver mine and took several pieces of the precious metal. He stopped at a trading post and used a nugget of the stolen silver to buy food. Two white men noticed the silver, plied the scout with liquor, and persuaded him to lead them to the mine. As they sighted Silver Islet, a terrible storm erupted, drowning the two white men; in a stupor, the Sioux scout drifted along in his canoe. Then an extraordinary event happened: a giant sleeping figure appeared in an opening in the bay. The Great Spirit's prophecy, like that of the Greek sybils,[77] had come true: Nanabush had turned into stone, now named the Sleeping Giant, a solidified presence, a landmark guarding the silver and the bay. The

Ojibwe believe that the Great Spirit's curse or that of the deep sea water prevails to this day, for attempts to activate silver mining have failed: waters from Lake Superior continue to flood the silver deposits. Nature itself continues to protect the silver and to thwart the onslaughts of greedy and not so greedy people.[78]

The Little People

There were also strange and unclassifiable sea creatures that had only a tangential relationship to the Midewiwin. Percy Berens recalled hearing the drumming and singing of the "mound builders," the Memegwesiwag, three times in his life. Percy's brother, Gordon, spoke about these late-nineteenth-century mound builders: "There's people living, isolated people like, that could do a lot of things ... They're the people that could do a lot of magic things ... If they want to bless you, you'll hear that drum. First you'll hear that drum and then they'll show in person and give you what you want to know what you want to do in a magical way. They come in dreams too." Percy believed that the Memegwesiwag had given him the rib of an animal not found in that area. "Well he kept that thing, you know," Gordon recalled, "and when he was trapping nobody could beat him. He was always the head trapper. Nobody could beat him. He was always the highest one." The little people continued to bless him.[79]

Creatures under the earth. Song scroll: "I am blessed, My Mide brethren, By the four Mide spirits, Who live in the four layers, Of the earth." The singer explains: "The circle is the earth. These three people live in the fourth layer under the earth; from there they sing." Densmore, *Chippewa Music*, 1:56.

These weird people lived in fittingly strange places, one of which was Michipicoten Island. Visitors to that island today confirm that it is "inhospitable," "dreary and desolate," and "haunted," and feel, like earlier visitors, that it is jinxed, for a mining boom there was brief.[80] To add to its eeriness, ghosts seemed to whisper from the other side of the island.[81]

To the extent that these extraordinary creatures were associated with water, they were perceived as amorphous. To the extent that they were terrestrial, they had more definite contours. Spirits might be limited by their identity with a specific animal, whereas these creatures – often regarded as monsters, but often quite small – never revealed their identities and remained shrouded in mystery. According to Desveaux, beings such as these were immaterial, "abstract entities, prototypes of the species." They lacked substance and became real only by making sounds, by breathing, and by stinking. No one ever saw them in their beings; they were "nothing but metamorphosis, nothing but the sum of every possible and imaginable form." Such creatures left everything to the imagination and did not respond to ordinary human words and actions; they were "neither human ... nor natural." They were at best on the periphery of human perception and analogy and therefore could instil many fears and anxieties.[82] According to ordinary ways of perceiving,[83] since such beings hovered between reality and unreality, responses to them varied, but they could instil uneasiness because their images were too fleeting to grasp.

Associated with the waters and with copper were snakes and monsters that inhabited the hills and other terrain. At the beginning of the twentieth century, Jonas George from the Rama Reserve in Ontario described these creatures in detail, in contrast to the uncertain portrayals given above: they were twelve feet long and eighteen to twenty-four inches thick, had long jaws full of teeth, and appeared to be half fish and half snake. They lived in the hills near lakes and made use of underground passages between hills and water. They could sometimes be seen early in the morning moving around swiftly, forcing weeds and floating sticks high onto the shore. They agitated the water "with so much force that they [left] the small lakes partially dry."[84]

Generally, though, these amphibious creatures remained a mystery. Jim Wenjack wrote about meeting the Maymaygwayshug while fishing with nets in Northern Ontario. One of them was on the water's surface near his net. On being sighted, this creature, which had a face covered in fur, scurried away toward a rocky cliff, laughing hard. As a precaution against provoking unpredictable actions, the Anishinaabe asked Wenjack not to tease or play tricks on them when he was hunting and fishing.[85] Selwyn Dewdney and Kenneth Kidd describe this enigmatic dwarf-like sea creature as an artist, a devil at the foot of a cliff, more to be avoided than feared.[86]

William Jones tells a tale of people paddling at Thunder Cape near Thunder Bay; they became afraid when they sighted water imps living in the rocks of a cliff. "In form they were like human beings. They went out on the lake in a stone canoe, and could raise a thunder-storm by singing a magic song. When observed, they fled at once into the caverns under the water."[87]

John Penesi of Fort William narrated the following story, "The Thunderers," which is similar to the one above. An unidentified and unidentifiable being sang this song three times, not to raise a thunderstorm but to clear it: "A clear sky is verily my firmament, much am I in fear of it." After the song, there was a great calm and a beautiful, cloudless sky appeared.

> And so immediately back home in their canoes went the water-fairies. Many a time have they seen those fairies, and once in a while they have been addressed by them. 'Very fond are they of tobacco,' said the people. And one other time they saw them far out on the lake in a canoe; they tried to head them óff from going into a rock. Of a truth, they did succeed in heading them off; whereupon [the fairies] then flung their heads down low upon their bosoms, covering themselves from above with their arms, and they would not look towards [the people]. But one spoke to them: 'Where do you live?' But one of the fairies spoke, he spoke to his comrade: 'Come, you should look! for as handsome as a human being do you look.' Thereupon up rose [so as to be seen] one of the fairies, he had hair on the face. Thereupon they were released to go peacefully on their way in their canoe. And then straight for the steep cliff [they went]; with a small entrance opened the cliff, and in they went with their canoe. They could be heard laughing, and the sound of their paddles was audible.[88]

Let us summarize this chapter on water creatures: Water was a beneficent being, in that it furnished many gifts to the Ojibwe such as food and also the Medicine lodge with its healing powers. Water also provided warnings against storms and gave lessons against boasting and greed. To ensure the close and ongoing presence of the benevolent water Manitous, the Ojibwe painted their images on their faces and bodies.

Another view of underwater creatures held by nineteenth-century Ojibwe peoples was that they were harmful spirits, or bad medicine. Yet another was that they were inherently good, provided that humans accorded them respect. Still others evaluated these underwater creatures in a dialectical way, as having both qualities: sometimes beneficial and sometimes malevolent, though with the beneficial prevailing; both aspects seemed necessary in an Ojibwe world. Serpents were an example of this interlocking dual relationship, in that they both helped and hindered passages in Midewiwin performances and in the afterlife.

Some women and sea creatures had a curious reciprocal fascination, based perhaps on similar affective dispositions; generally, men did not share in this attraction.

Sea creatures, shells,[89] and copper and silver dispelled the darkness, ensured healing, and indicated origins. These metals had valued symbolic meanings for the Ojibwe, and European fur traders fit very well with that symbolism. The Ojibwe initially regarded those traders as keepers of the deeps and also as gift givers, for they continued the trade in shells, copper, and furs that the Ojibwe had already established with other Aboriginal peoples.

Besides the readily identifiable water creatures, both good and harmful, there were puzzling little creatures who moved in inaccessible places, uttered strange sounds, and remained relatively unclassifiable.

7
Thunderbirds

In this chapter we depart from our general schema, focusing on the actions and symbolism of avian creatures rather than on their physical appearance.

One approach to the existence of creatures of the upper world and those of the waters is to pose them in opposition to each other. Many images and sounds indicate that this is appropriate. According to Richard Dorson, the creatures of the upper world – the thunders – engage in an ongoing battle with the creatures of the under world, the serpents. As a logical continuation of this, Ojibwe regard the creatures of the sky as friendly toward humans since they give protection, and those of the lower world as enemies.[1]

We have already noted that this rigid classification of sea creatures as solely evil misses the mark in Ojibwe orderings. For them, underwater creatures are sometimes beneficial and sometimes malevolent, and the same holds for the thunderbirds.

The Cree and Ojibwe "consider the thunder to be a god in the shape of a great eagle that feeds upon the serpents, which it takes from the earth." Peter Jones observed that the thunderbirds, brothers and sisters to lightning, have their homes on high mountains and that in their nests are the bones of serpents.[2]

Julia Harrison has developed "a hierarchy of power" in the Ojibwe world and has situated thunderbirds within that order. She contends that a belief in a powerful supreme being, Kitche Manitou, was well entrenched in Ojibwe religious thought "by the early 19th century"; such a being was present in the entire cosmos, and he "could take any form that he wanted." At a seemingly lower level than Kitche

Manitou were the four brotherly winds that were his messengers and that "were conceptualized as thunderbirds who lived at the four cardinal points." On the next lower level were the underwater Manitous or panthers, which influenced "the abundance and availability of both land and water animals, thus of great importance to Ojibwa hunters."[3] And at the level below this, according to Harrison, was "the culture-hero Nanabozho who was born of a human mother and sired by a spirit, Epingishmook (the West)."[4] But the conception of a hierarchy of powers does not appear to have been part of early traditional thought and action; this conception could present some problems for contemporary Ojibwe as well.

Thunderbirds as Givers

The Ojibwe and others maintained that earth's energies were exposed on high rock cliffs and along waterways. The large birds that nested on these cliffs gathered these energies and dispersed them, thereby mediating between earth and sky.[5]

Alethea Helbig recounts a story from Lac Vieux Desert in Wisconsin: Nanabush asked the thunders, who were in charge of warm weather, to advance the seasons so that the underground serpents, representing the power of winter, would emerge and could be killed. Thus the seasons began their struggle. From Mount Pleasant, Michigan, Eli Thomas welcomes the thunders as grandfathers and implores them: "Protect us, give us luck!" Thomas notes that if the thunders do not have the power to chase the snakes and sea lions out, it will be end of the world.[6]

Thunderbirds, however, do have a lot of power, which they exercise in various ways and at various times. Mark Sakry and Carl Gawboy from Minnesota offer an adapted story of Nanabush and the thunderbirds. Nanabush's/Naniboujou's father was the wind, and his mother "walked the earth among human beings, alone. She had powers she did not know ... [She] disappeared into the air the instant he was born, so Naniboujou lived with the old woman he called Grandmother. They lived alone on the shore of Lake Superior." Naniboujou became curious about a very large fish in the water that his grandmother warned could do him much harm. He was resolved to kill that powerful fish, and to that end, he fashioned a great bow of ash and an arrow of cedar. The only feathers that would be adequate to make the arrows fly forcefully would have to be plucked, according to his grandmother, from a bird "who lives in the sky beyond that cloud. You would have to go there to get the feathers you want."

Naniboujou wanted those feathers very badly. To get them from the cliff dwellers, he cleverly changed into a small rabbit and pleaded with thunderbird, who swooped down to kill him. "'Thunderbird, stop!' cried Naniboujou. 'Am I not truly an artful little creature? Would I not make a good playmate for your fledglings?'" The "little rabbit" was persuasive, and thunderbird carried him to his children. Thunderbird's wife, however, was suspicious that the rabbit might be a "man-spirit." While both of the mature thunderbirds were hunting for food, the rabbit changed back into Naniboujou and stripped most of the feathers, more than he needed for his arrows, from the young thunderbirds. As he fled the nest, he heard the sky open. "It was his father the Wind. Suddenly, there was horrible lightning. It was the flashing eyes of the thunderbirds. Thunder boomed over the earth. It was the thunderbirds' voices. The thunderbirds sped at Naniboujou with their talons … The booming and flashing, the blowing and crashing, finally caused Naniboujou to tire. He grew perplexed. Then, quickly, Naniboujou crawled inside a hollow birch tree that had fallen. The talons of the thunderbirds almost got him. The hollow birch tree saved his life." Ironically, though, the birch trees were regarded as the children of the thunderbirds. The thunderbirds' "eyes flickered off toward the heavens. Their voices faded. The Wind rolled away the clouds and left Naniboujou in a wake of tears that was rain dripping from the leaves." This harrowing event changed Naniboujou. He said, "From now on, human beings will find the protection of this tree useful in many ways. Anyone standing under it will find shelter from lightning and storms. Its bark will make their lodges. Their food will not spoil in it. And it will have many more uses. But … anyone using the bark of the birch tree will make generous offerings to it." Naniboujou left the feathers that he did not need for his arrows in the hollow log. He then went and killed the great fish. "To this day, human beings will find the marks of Naniboujou in the tree's bark. They are little dashes. They will also find patterns of the little thunderbirds."[7] We have already noted that other beings – bears and sea creatures – also left permanent marks on birch bark.

Mide celebrating. Song scroll: "Verily, The sky clears, When my Mide drum, Sounds, For me, Verily, The Waters are smooth, When my Mide drum, Sounds, For me." "The arch represents the sky from which rain is falling. The two ovals represent quiet lakes. In his left hand the man holds a Mide drum and in his right hand a stick for beating the drum." Densmore, *Chippewa Music*, 1:112.

Jonas George from the Rama Reserve in Ontario tells of Thunderfolk or Mim-mah-kie (or Nim-Mah-Kie) before contact with white people. An Indian went hunting in the bush when a storm arose. For protection, he crawled under a pine tree, which the lightning struck several times. A little man, about two feet tall, stood on one side of the tree and another on the other side. "Both these men were fine little fellows, all black and shining, and were called Mim-mah-kie, Thunder. They climbed up in the air as if they were climbing ladders and disappeared. After they went up, more lightning came down. These little men set the lightning at the trees and made the thunder. Thunder and lightning kept the monsters down on the land and in the lakes."[8]

The above account suggests thunderbirds' beneficial effects for human beings. Other sources point to the thunderbirds having a more ambivalent nature. Sister Bernard Coleman writes that the *animikiig* were great Manitous, and that some informants told her "there were four of these thunderbird manidos, while others referred to four leaders and their families. Two of the leaders were thought to be good and the other two bad. Sometimes, although not usually, we heard that there was just one immense thunderbird." Many terms were used to describe them: "the thunderers, the grandfathers, the old men, or the old men with wings." Thus when there was a thunderstorm out of season, Old Man Thunder could be chastised for being around at the wrong time of the year.[9]

The good thunderbirds aided Nanabush in warfare against evil underwater Manitous. To extend and continue this power, thunderbird designs figured on Mide drums and on nettle fibre bags. Because power in these items flowed from thunderbirds, both the items and the thunderbirds were regarded with awe and reverence. The Ojibwe were admonished "never to speak carelessly about the manidos that bring the rain." Thunderbirds were expected to reveal their presences so that it was "no wonder that when the first airplane flew over Red Lake, some of the Ojibwa thought that it was a thunderbird and ran down to the shore with tobacco and cloth as an offering for protection." When children dreamed, an *animikiig* could reveal new names for them, and these spirit beings in the new names "imparted mystic power" to them. The following four ceremonial names were given to these sky beings: "Thunder Coming from the West, Bird Going Around in the Air, Bird That Dips Up and Down, and Ice Bird."[10]

Sun figure. Peterborough petroglyph. Vastokas and Vastokas, *Sacred Art*, 57.

In a story told by William Jones, "The Thunderers," two youths who were fasting for eight days near Thunder Bay wanted to learn the cause of the rumble upon the clouds of Thunder Cape. As they ascended, the roar of the thunderer grew louder. "And then suddenly it seemed as if something were now opening and now closing, for such was the way the cloud behaved. And then at that place they beheld two big birds, and also two young [birds]; and it was like the play of fire as [the birds] opened and closed their eyes when [the youths] were seeing [them]. Perhaps it was as long as it takes to hold in the breath twice, such was the length of time they had to observe them; then again up closed the cloud." One of the youths was content with this observation alone, but another wanted to see more. "And as he started on his way back [to the place] then came the lightning, striking the place where the youth was standing, whereupon he was killed. And so back home came the other youth." After a time, however, the Ojibwe were no longer afraid of the thunderers and visited the Cape.[11]

Relationships among Humans, Sky, and Water Creatures

The dialectical relationship between humans and animals in the Anishinaabe cosmos is nowhere more evident than in the relations between the sky creatures and the underwater ones. These beings, some of whom seem to be protectors and others to be harmful, formed complex symbols for past Ojibwe and continue to do so in the present. Humans have found themselves immersed in antagonistic forces and are thus aware of their need for help from the powers above and below. Traditional beliefs have changed, yet the thunder and underwater Manitous in their various representations express meanings and values that even today are in harmony with earliest sources.[12]

In Norval Morrisseau's paintings, it is the sky that heals through its colours.[13] In his "Thunderbird and Inner Spirit," a human nestles inside a thunderbird.[14] This close relationship between humans and thunderbirds is also reflected in seventeenth-century accounts. Missionary James Buteux asked a Montagnais why Aboriginal persons fixed their javelins with points in an upward position. The Montagnais replied: "As the thunder had intelligence, it would, upon seeing these naked javelins, turn aside, and would be very careful not to come near their cabins. When the Father [Buteux] asked another one whence came that great clap of thunder, 'It is,' he said, 'the Manitou who wished to vomit up a great serpent he has swallowed; and at every effort of his stomach he makes this great uproar that we hear.' In fact, they have often told me that flashes of lightning were nothing but serpents falling upon the ground, which they discover from the trees struck by lightning. 'For,' say they, 'here is seen the shape of those creatures, stamped, as it were, in sinuous and crooked lines around the tree. Large serpents have even been found under these trees,' they say." To these explanations, Buteux responded: "A new kind of philosophy, truly!"[15] Reuben Thwaites notes from his reading of Ojibwe stories that the lightning (serpents) are the food of the thunderbirds.[16]

Gitche Manitou, centre, and his helpers the thunderbirds. Chief Moses Day Daybwaywaindung's Medicine Bark (History Chart) Parchment. Reagan, "A Ritual Parchment," 235, 241.

Birds and Play

For nineteenth-century Ojibwe, games had a prominent place.[17] According to Robert and Pat Ritzenthaler, the game of lacrosse among the Menomini was "a mimic war game believed to have been given to the men by the Thunderer manidog, whose property it was considered to be." The person who called the game had the thunderbird as his guardian spirit "and the game was played to honor that spirit. He who called the game did not play, but stood on the sidelines offering prayers and sacrifices. He also presented the player with prizes, which were often brightly colored cloth strung on a rack to one side of the playing field."[18]

The Anishinaabe were reputed to be the inventors of the Great Lakes version of the game of lacrosse. It had many merits over other games. "Through this game baaga'adowe, our ancestors took it upon themselves to keep one another strong, not only physically, but spiritually as well," a contemporary Ojibwe lacrosse player, Jeremy Morgan, maintains. "We play to strengthen the circle. We play to keep on surviving" and to ensure a good life.[19]

Another Menomini version of the origin of lacrosse, besides the one given by the Ritzenthalers, involves medicine and truth verification. According to Mitchell Beaupré, a collaborator's grandfather named Ackinit/Uncooked dreamed of being told to go to the top of a bluff where he had once killed a deer. He took his son along with him at the time of sugaring, telling him he was looking for medicine. Ackinit saw a nest and heard a voice commanding him to take a green egg (an imitation of the lacrosse ball) from it and show it to his people. The thunderers had left the egg and wanted tobacco in return. To guarantee the truth of Ackinit and his dream, the grandson then played lacrosse.[20]

Frances Densmore fits games among the Ojibwe/Chippewa of the Great Lakes region into two classes: "(1) Games of chance, including the moccasin, hand, plate, snake, and stick games; and (2) games of dexterity, including the bone, bunch of grass, awl, woman's, and la crosse games."[21]

According to George Flaskerd, the Ojibwe played most games solely for pleasure, and gambling was of secondary importance. Drumming and singing were an essential part of Ojibwe games, and the drummer used to sing.[22] Densmore recounts that Mainans, Akiwaizi, Nitamigabo, Gagandac, Giwitabines, Wabezic, and William Prentice sang moccasin game songs, some without words.[23]

Supplication. Song scroll: "The spirits have pity on me; from on high I see you." "The sky is shown by the upper curved lines, beneath which the Mide is raising his arm in supplication." Hoffman, "The Midē'wiwin," 244a, 284. Fulford translates the song scroll as "I have really wanted to meet him." "Ojibwa Picture Writing," 181.

In the past, the game had several names other than lacrosse, including the healing or medicine game and the Creator's game. The game could be played to resolve disputes or strife among family or clan members; also, tribal leaders or war chiefs would play it to settle their differences. The game could be extended over a whole day or a week, with ceremonies, prayer and feasting. Tensions often ran deep, so when the games were extended, more time was available for healing. Lacrosse could also develop strong men.[24]

For the Ojibwe, lacrosse embodied their culture. The spirits provided ideas for the game and also furnished the equipment, appearing "with a lacrosse stick in one hand, a red, buckskin-covering a ball in the other," Thomas Vennum writes.[25] Lacrosse was more than recreation; it "functioned as a surrogate or little brother of war, a healing ritual, a memorial celebration to settle territorial disputes and, with wagering, as a substitute for the plunder of victory." The game combined spiritual, physical, and performance components. Preparations for it included warm-ups for the athletes and the readying of equipment and the playing field but also spiritual ceremonies. The coach was often a medicine man who gave potions to prevent injuries and overcome cramps. The butt end of the long-handled racket, called a crosse or lacrosse stick, sometimes featured a carving. The racket itself was likened to a drum stick or to a war club, which demonstrated the game's relationship to music and warfare.[26]

Alexander Henry provided an eighteenth-century description of lacrosse: "*Baggatiway*, called, by the Canadians, *le jeu de la crosse*, is played with a bat and ball. The bat is about four feet in length, curved, and terminating in a sort of racket. Two posts are planted in the ground, at a considerable distance from each other, as a mile, or more. Each party has its post, and the game consists in throwing the ball up to the post of the adversary. The ball, at the beginning is placed in the middle of the course, and each party endeavours as well to throw the ball out of the direction of its own post, [and] as into that of the adversary's ... The game of baggatiway, as from the description above will have been perceived, is necessarily attended with much violence and noise."[27] "It is the wildest game extant among the Indians," added William Warren, "and is generally played in full feathers and ornaments ... The great object is to obtain possession of the ball; and, during the heat of the excitement, no obstacle is allowed to stand in the way of getting at it." Because of the mad manner in which it was played, Warren concluded that "the game was very well adapted to carry out the scheme [attacks and wars] of the Indians."[28]

The fusing of elements of play and war was apparent in a 1763 Ojibwe/Sauk lacrosse game, which included a pre-planned surprise attack involving 400 to 600 Aboriginal men. The goal of the attack, directed by chieftain Mihnehwehna,[29] was the capture of Fort Michilimackinac, an English garrison on Lake Michigan.

For the Ojibwe, dreams determined the course of a lacrosse game, which always involved aggression and cunning, a vivid example being the war at Fort Michilimackinac. Dreams could also determine which games either gender must play. Thus, a woman who dreamed of the spirit women in the east would have to play either the bow-and-dice or the double-ball game and follow the rigorous demands of that dream. According to Menomini Beaupré, a man who dreamed of thunderers would have to hold a lacrosse game to receive the help promised by the thunderers; the dream also required that the lacrosse racket be shaped like a war club, for the game should resemble a battle. Thus both the spirit women and the thunderers gave protection to women and men and usually promised health.[30]

Thunderbird and plants. Song from Little Frenchman: "I, who fly." "This is the outline of a Thunder bird, who appears to grasp in his talons some medical plants." Hoffman, "The Midê'wiwin," 292a–293.

Another Menomini story features intergalactic warfare. Beings above the earth challenged those below to a game of lacrosse. Nanabush became curious about this celestial–terrestrial duel, for those animals taking part and those viewing this event had assumed gigantic proportions. As the battle-like game ensued, Nanabush retaliated against the underground creatures, who rallied their resources and created large waves as they chased Nanabush.[31]

John Penesi from Fort William, Ontario, tells of a less violent but nevertheless challenging game, "The First-Born Sons Play Ball." The seasonal birds of summer and winter engaged each other in play. The summer birds had the edge during the summer months, while in winter, the summer ones retreated to the south, leaving the playing field (the air) exclusively to the winter ones.[32] According to Emmanuel Desveaux, "thunderbirds represent the nature of summer par excellence."[33] Games of chance were played for fun, or seriously by professionals. Betting games were not ruled merely by chance, however; many Aboriginal peoples believed that the movements of the cosmic bodies influenced these games.[34]

Some parts of the game are regarded today as spiritual performances flowing from a historical "collective tribal organization";[35] a departing coach may receive an honour song,[36] and games may include drumming, singing, and feasting. An eagle staff[37] often travels with the team. Lacrosse coach Morgan concludes that the richness of the game is that it combines elements of hockey, baseball, football, basketball, and tennis. Lacrosse is now an international game and has an eternal character to it: "We will continue to bring the spirits of our ancestors to the ball field to cheer us on in our game baaga'adowe."[38] Thus, lacrosse links the present with the past, the young with the old, and birds and land animals, as well as songs, dance, and drum, with a rich heritage.[39] This mixture of sports and dance was already evident in the seventeenth century.[40]

Lacrosse. Tracy Thomas of the Wolf Clan of the Mohawk Nation, illus. Vennum, *Lacrosse Legends*, 97.

Thunderbirds and Ojibwe Life

The thunderers, who were among the originators of Ojibwe/Menomini games, influenced Ojibwe life in ways other than through games. Densmore provides this narrative about thunderbirds: "From near the family wigwam on Minnesota Point, an Ojibwe lad of the 1880's watched the storm clouds gather over the steep dark hills that line the north shore of Lake Superior. When the thunder clapped, the boy's mother explained, 'That is the animikig striking their wings against the hills.' And when the lightning cut zigzag lines across the sky, she said,

'That is the flashing of the animikig's eyes.' The mother was instilling in her son Ojibwa beliefs concerning the animikig – the thunderbirds. The strength of such beliefs is illustrated by a comment that we heard an old Indian of northern Minnesota make in 1958: 'The thunder is not made by clouds bumping against each other. It is the animikig.'"[41] Albert Lacombe recounts that Aboriginal peoples ("les sauvages") "imagine that these sublime birds cause lightning by flashing their eyes and their wings create a thunderous noise. They shoot invisible and flaming arrows which become the thunderbolts."[42]

In their actions, the Ojibwe themselves and their cultures resemble the thunderbirds. Peter Jones/Kakiwakwonabi has a thunderbird-like name, Sacred Waving-Feathers; he observes that other Ojibwe, too, have associative names such as Head Thunder and Yellow Thunder. He also notes that thunderbirds, "most powerful [deities]," are like human beings in their use of bows and arrows. They have wings that can be removed and attached again to make sounds.[43] Ceremonial prayer pipes, often clothed with a bird-skin mantle, spew smoke from their stems and fire from their bowls just as real thunderbirds do, "so the ascending smoke appeared to come out of an eagle's or hawk's mouth."[44]

In some stories, thunderbirds' positionings in the air and on the earth account for heat lightning. Sister Coleman writes that "on the reservations at Fond du Lac and White Earth, we were told the story of the young thunderbird who struck the side of a hill and broke his wing. He was then caught between the precipices. When he tried to free himself, he kept on striking against the rocks, and he repeatedly broke his wing as he did so. This explains the continuous flash of heat lightning."[45]

Artist Ahmoo Angeconeb writes about the versatility and importance of the creatures of the air. He alludes to the gifts of the Great Spirit, the Creator; these gifts are birds who are the spirit of the air, fish who are the spirits of the water, and sun who is the spirit of the fire. "The bird represents the air on Turtle Island. The spirit of the air is with us through our cycle of life. It brings greeting to us when we are born, and it is the last element to be with us when we pass on to the spirit world. The bird is also the bearer of messages for the Anishnawbek, because it can fly in the air, walk on the land, swim on the water, and dive underwater, going where we cannot."[46]

Among the Ojibwe, the number four is predominant, as we have noted earlier. According to Sister Bernard Coleman, "of the curvilinear design motifs, the circle is one of the simplest forms used. This design is sometimes called the dot. Arranged around a center circle or space in groups of four it is called the four-bead design unity. This and the eight circle grouping are frequently used in Ojibwa design patterns." This general design pattern is applied to the four principal winds governed by the thunderbirds. The specific design of two crossed spirals forming a single or double swastika, which represents the four directions or winds, indicates power rushing in from all areas. Such designs are present on children's moccasins for protection and on beaded vests,[47] birch bark baskets, boxes, trays, and rattles for curing the sick.[48]

Woman's moccasin with floral motif in fours used at Mille Lacs in the late nineteenth century. Coleman, *Decorative Designs*, 18–19.

Thunderers as Communicators and Protectors

Thunderers can impart knowledge and foretell the future. Encouraged by his father, William Jones fasted on a regular basis beginning in his youth. He dreamed about many things in open places, in the forest, or on mountains, but the focus of his dreams was "the manitou that was above" who spoke to him. "I [was] given the knowledge of what would happen to me. And by all the people of the stars was I blessed. It was then that I constantly dreamed of every sort of observance and of song; of the songs that are on high did I hear. By a great throng of the sky-people was I blessed; everywhere over the earth and on high was I conveyed by them, how it [all] looked I was shown, how it was everywhere in the circle of the heavens that I had dreamed about." Jones was carried to "a soothsaying-lodge," which he entered and then "saw many sky-people there, like human beings they looked. Very pleasing was the sound of their voices when they sang." The large and distant stars that he visited, especially fisher star and eight stars as a group, blessed him. For him, visiting the stars was possible through dreaming about them. Most influential were the soothsaying lodges whose Manitous empowered dreams and the dreamer with visions, songs, and utterances. "In course of time the soothsaying-lodge becomes filled with the people of the sky that have entered in ... And should the presence of some person be desired, he is simply whistled for, whereupon he comes. And then he is asked: 'What kind of life have you lived?'"

Thunderbird. This design is "frequently seen on old Mide bags or on Mide scrolls and drums." Coleman, *Decorative Designs*, 7, 9.

Snapping turtle supervised the soothsaying wigwam, Jones notes. "Whatsoever he may say will truly happen to the [people]. It is his soul that does the talking. Whatsoever language he uses is the one the person speaks when doing his talking in the soothsaying-lodge. All creatures enter the soothsaying-lodge; likewise all the animal-folk that are on earth, also all the birds that are on high, the winds, and every kind of metal that is, and rocks, and all creatures that live and move in the summer-time, enter in. And what the man doing the soothsaying thinks is what the incomers say; they sing, all sorts of songs do they sing."

Thus, the dreaming process with its visions and empowerments precedes and foreshadows predictions for individuals and the group. "Therefore such is the reason why the soothsaying-lodge is called 'the testing-by-dream.' Beforehand is it known how things will come to pass by means of the soothsaying." During another fasting event, Jones interpreted his consequent dream to mean that he would live a long life. During another fast, he dreamed that a Manitou had inspired people to make him a universally esteemed leader.[49]

According to Theresa Smith, the most common thunder name – *animikeek* – characterizes not merely the storm, or the thunderbird *Manitouk*, "but the very sound of the thunder – its voice ... [The Anishinaabe] experience the action of the *animikeek* as speech events." The thunderbird Manitou's actions are manifest in the thunderclaps, which "signal the arrival of powerful visitors and initiate a kind of dialogue. Through verbal and ritual responses, the Anishinaabeg demonstrate their attention to, respect for, and relationship with highly powerful and individualistic Manitous."[50]

Smith continues: "Since the *animikeek* are hunters in search of underground or underwater *manitouk*, Thunder tells humans, who are not the objects of the hunt, to head for cover lest they be struck by stray shots ... These stray shots are normally the misdirected work of young

Thunderers who are still perfecting their skills." The objects of the strikes are selective, singling out the underwater creatures but also non-Aboriginals, for the Anishinaabe have a special relationship with the thunderers, that of assured protection.[51]

"The Thunderers are kept busy with watching over us," William Jones writes of an unidentified Fox Indian's apocalyptic predictions. "They grow angry at the sight of the wrong done to us. With great effort they restrain themselves when they behold the people driven to an extremity, when they behold the people enduring wrongs beyond all endurance. Naturally there must be an end of this thing: it will be on a day yet to come. The Thunder manitous will no longer withhold their patience. In that day they will crack open this earth and blow it to pieces. Where the white man will be hurled, no one knows and no one cares. After this, the manitou will then create this world anew, and put the people back in it to live again. In that day they will no longer be pestered with the white man."[52]

Thunderbirds, especially females, can give warnings to protect the people. Norval Morrisseau's painting, "Man Changing Into Thunderbird," is based on a story of a young man who turns himself into a thunderbird in order to be free to marry the thunderbird maiden he loves.[53] Angeconeb gives a contemporary rendering of the above story in his five-phase work, "Ahneesheenahpay Myth of the Thunder People." In the story accompanying Angeconeb's painting, Ceah Patricia Angeconeb and Lucy Ogemah of Lac Seul First Nation, Ontario, narrate that a young man followed a beautiful young thunder woman into the sky world. Chipmunk and squirrel helped in the ascent. When the young man went hunting on top of the mountain, he noticed a pool of water with beautiful colours. "He took some of this water in the palm of his hand and decorated his moccasins." Young Thunder Woman warned him about the great Water Serpent Spirit in the pool that threatened and frightened the Thunder People. In the past, Giant Water Serpent Spirit had "grabbed several of the young and tried to drag them down. They fought with him and tried to fend him off with their thunderbolts." Despite the warning of Young Thunder Woman, the young man dived into the depths and wrestled a young thunder being away from the Serpent Spirit. In recognition of this deed, the Thunder People accepted the young man; he married Young Thunder Woman and was transformed and became one of the Thunder People.[54]

Three early-twentieth-century stories from Rama Reserve in Ontario indicate a personal and beneficial relationship between Ojibwe and thunderbirds. In "The Indian and the Thunder," Mrs Sampson Ingersoll narrates that during a powerful thunderstorm, an Indian who was hunting in his canoe went ashore and stood against a large pine tree. Thunder struck the tree and the man but did not kill him. "Thunder came down and took the Indian up, saying it was sorry he struck him. Thunder put Indian down in his canoe and took him home. When the Indian got home, he died."

Another Rama Reserve story, "Thunder Power" by Marjorie St Germain: An Indian and a preacher were sceptical about the existence and power of thunderbirds. The preacher called them powerless idols. This "unbelieving Indian" then went hunting and saw within a greenish circle a serpent and a big white bird about the size of an eagle. The serpent asked the Indian to shoot the bird, and the bird asked him to shoot the serpent. "The serpent promised that if the Indian shot the enemy, he would give him power to kill any wild game. The bird promised a better power – anything he wished would happen and would aid him. The Indian shot the serpent. In a thunderstorm, the Indian noticed a big white feather. He picked it up and wished for the storm to cease and it did ... Everything went well in the village and the minister never thought of idols anymore."

John York from Rama narrates in "Thunderbird" that an Indian who went trapping received the admonition in his dream that one should never walk across the ice of any lake at night. As he was coming home at night with a bag of beaver on his back and an ice chisel in his hand, he decided to walk across the ice. "He heard something coming down from above ... [He] fainted and dropped onto the ice, and the next thing he knew he found himself sitting inside the claws of a big bird." The bird carried him into the air and deposited him on a rock; then the Indian got inside another bird. He fainted again as he was wafted to a strange place. He had been away a long time and once in his camp again, he found everything strange and old. His wife reiterated the command, "Never walk across the ice of any lake at night ... This story shows that a long time with Thunderbirds was actually very short."[55] Life was short for the one aided by thunderbirds, but longer for everyone else.

Thunderbird Symbolism

Among the good Manitous, Grace Rajnovich names thunderbirds along with the four winds.[56] Like other animals that played a significant part in individual dreams and lives, thunderbird was incorporated into both ceremonial and everyday material cultural forms. Since the

Ojibwe believed that these avian creatures, as accessed in vision quests, preserved their power only if they were inaccessible to other people, artists represented the thunderbirds in symbolic and abstract ways. One form that artists gave to thunderbird was the zigzag, which depicted their wings, their movements, or the resultant lightning. As we have already seen, abstract depictions of otter's tail and trail also used this zigzag. Thus the referent of the zigzag lines is not always clear. These lines, Rajnovich observes, "could be the pattern of lightning or the path of the otter which, when chased, tries to deceive its enemies by varying its course. The zigzag lines were doubled, tripled and overlapped to form cross-hatching and diamonds."[57] Of course, contemporary zigzag lines on many cultural items may no longer represent either otter or thunderbird; they may be what is now a conventional Ojibwe cultural design.

The zigzag designs that the Ojibwe used on ceremonial and everyday items are interpreted in various ways. Erwin Panofsky delineates three levels of meaning for motifs in general: (1) "Primary or natural subject matter ... [These are] representations of natural objects such as human beings, animals, plants, houses, tools, and so forth ... The world of pure forms thus recognized as carriers of primary or natural meanings may be called the world of artistic motifs. An enumeration of these motifs would be a pre-iconographical description of the work of art"; (2) "Secondary or conventional subject matter ... We connect artistic motifs and combinations of artistic motifs (compositions) with themes or concepts. Motifs thus recognized as carriers of a secondary or conventional meaning may be called images, and combinations of images are what the ancient theorists of art called *invenzioni*; we are wont to call them stories and allegories"; and (3) "Intrinsic meaning or content. It is apprehended by ascertaining those underlying principles which reveal the basic attitude of a nation, a period, a class, a religious or philosophical persuasion – qualified by one personality and condensed into one work."[58]

When we apply these levels of meaning to Ojibwe cultures we find that the first level, the natural or representational, may be embodied in such forms as a human figure, otter, owl, and bear. Individuals both inside and outside these cultures can readily identify these natural and representational forms. A second level of meaning can be ascertained only in the context of the carriers of motifs, such as stories and traditions. One must have at least a minimal understanding of the milieu in which these stories originated. On the third level of meaning, the interpreter must examine these images in relation to their visual form and, most important, in their entire cultural context.

As Joan M. Vastokas applies Panofsky's distinctions, birch bark scrolls – and, we might add, all Ojibwe cultural representations – are subject to the second type of interpretation and meaning. These pictorial images "require detailed knowledge of the oral tradition that belongs to every Midewiwin scroll." Such precise information about each scroll and its images is difficult to obtain, and interpreters like ourselves and Vastokas may therefore appear to be stymied. If we follow a broader perspective, however, such as the one provided by Panofsky's third level, we may have a more immediate access to the meanings of various scrolls. On this level we consider the broader meaning of the scrolls – indeed, of all representations – by immersing them in the history of the Ojibwe in general and in the performances of the Midewiwin in particular.[59]

We have noted one of Ruth Phillips's and Rajnovich's interpretations – that zigzag geometric motifs depict the back-and-forth movements of otter, or thunderbird's wings, interpretations that seem to fall under numbers two and three in Panofsky's pattern. Panofsky's categories require more nuance than this, however, given that artists within or outside a cultural context may provide straightforward interpretations of an image even while withholding – intentionally or not – hidden or opaque meanings that are latent in the design. This opacity may also exist because the nature of the image is such that it does not disclose its real meaning readily or at all. But this opacity may also exist in the perceivers, who may not be culturally conditioned or receptive enough to receive the meanings the images intend to convey.

Phillips attributes the latent meanings of zigzag patterns to both otter and thunderbird but also offers a rationale for the use of geometric patterns, and specifically for applying them to thunderbird: "Zigzags express the chief manifestations of the powers of the sky spirits, lightning and thunder." These representations on bags or as tattoos on the skin, for instance, were the result of visual and acoustic experiences, which needed to take concrete form "in order to retain the blessing of the guardian spirit, yet the vision had, at the same time, to be kept private lest its power be forfeited." Since thunderbirds were unique universal spirits, recognizable and concrete images of them on designs could retain their cosmic energy – something that was not possible for images of most other beings. Those who had visions of guardian spirits other than thunderbird preserved their patterns of power through imagery that was more ambiguous and abstract and that often depicted multiple levels of reality. Thunder-filled humans had a special relationship with their spirit beings, and they mapped this relationship with recognizable and specific design motifs, which then organized the cosmos spatially.[60]

Emmanuel Desveaux maintains, along with Phillips, that there is great power in the abstract form. Concrete beings are localized and limited in number, whereas abstract creations can be readily multiplied and can be spread over an almost limitless number of places. Such depictions were the specialty of women. In fact, Desveaux thinks that the more concrete and representational is masculine and figurative, while the more geometrical and abstract is feminine in character. For the Ojibwe, these abstract motifs embodied spirit powers that were not well defined although they were very expansive in terms of reaching out to multitudes of people.[61]

Artists of the abstract created new images in the world that were not merely aesthetic. They created semantic beings that could now distribute energy in a new way, for these presentations had an internal dynamism. When this art came into contact with European ideas and materials, an invigorated fusion and synthesis could occur, as in the treaties – at least ideally.[62]

Let us examine some Ojibwe cultural items that make reference to thunderbird. In general, the older the objects, the more likely that the motifs embody animal referents. The later the dated objects, the more likely that they have commonly accepted patterns without specific animal references. We have already considered bandolier bags in our chapter on otter. Two bandolier bags in the Minnesota Historical Society Museum, however, are pertinent to our examination. An "Ojibwa Woven Plant Fiber Yarn Bag," dated from the late nineteenth to early twentieth century, has three wide horizontal bands of geometric patterns. Do these squares and rectangles form stylized thunderbirds? An "Ojibwa Beaded Cloth Bandolier Bag," dated c. 1916, and described as a medicine bag made by an Ojibwe of Cass Lake, Minnesota, uses a multicoloured asymmetrical floral pattern. These are the predominant bags in the Minnesota Historical Museum collection. There is also an undated bandolier bag with three wide horizontal bands of geometric patterns. Do the squares and rectangles form stylized thunderbirds and the wavy lines otters in abstract form?

Thunderbird's or otter's zigzag trail. According to Elizabeth Rock, "When an otter is pursued, it tries to deceive the enemy by changing its course," and consequently the zigzag lines. It is also called a lightning pattern occurring "very frequently on Ojibwa quill and beadwork articles." Coleman, *Decorative Designs*, 2–3. We have already used this line drawing in our chapter on otter. There is some ambiguity in the attribution of these wavy lines, for they could also be lightning and refer to thunderbird. See Phillips, "Zigzag and Spiral," 417–18.

Patterns of diamonds and zigzags, however, could relate to thunderbird as well as to otter. Another bandolier bag in the Minneapolis Institute of Arts collection, also from 1870 in the Great Lakes region, has two groupings on the right shoulder strap; one group has ten thunderbirds in red and gold on a rectangular surface; six thunderbirds are in another rectangular area. There are possible stylized wings on both shoulder straps. A bandolier bag with striking shades of blue, green, and yellow, from the 1860s, has "a repeating X pattern on the panel [which] alludes to thunderbirds ... Wavy white lines along the bag's edge represent lightning," the Institute of Arts comments conclude. In another bag from 1830 to 1850, the artisan wove beads into the fabric in a zigzag line pattern using a finger-weaving technique that resembles braiding. A "Knife Sheath" of cotton and leather, judged to be from the nineteenth century, uses glass beads to form diamonds and lines.[63] A panel from the early nineteenth century features emphatic red, orange, and green wavy lines above and below a black thunderbird outlined in gold.[64] A black pipe, dated around 1873, had a long wooden brown-shaded flat stem/handle with seven sets of triangles, and many hollow lines.[65]

The materials on which women artists created these images were not limited to hides or ceremonial items. Representations of dream figures were also carried on an "individual who wished to secure protection by its presence," Sister Bernard Coleman writes. "Often the wearing of the dream article was an injunction given in the vision by the tutelary manito. The Ojibwe believed that the essence of the guardian Manito dwelt in its representation." A dream symbol could be embroidered on clothing, for instance.[66]

Thunderbirds were some of the most powerful Manitous, and since they travelled singly or in pairs, they were depicted singly, as two, and sometimes as four. They represented the four winds created by Kitche

Manitou, and as his messengers, they brought lightning, thunder, and rain to make things grow. Thunderbirds "were sought as spirit protectors in individual vision quests and because of their swiftness, endurance, and ferocity, associated with war." The task of the Manitous was to aid humans by driving off bad spirits from the earth and water.[67]

Thunderbird. Song by Sikassige: "I brought the medicine to bring life." "The Mide Manido, the Thunderer, after bringing some of the plants – by causing the rains to fall – returns to the sky. The short line represents the ... imaginary vault of the sky." Hoffman, "The Midê'wiwin," 203–203a.

Because of their importance as protectors, thunderbirds were displayed in designs available to the public – on fire bags, birch bark baskets, scrolls, and drums.[68] According to Elizabeth Rock, a teacher at the Cass Lake Reservation in Minnesota in the mid-twentieth century, "if the thunderbird design is represented with two heads, it signifies the animikig, which often travel in pairs at the bidding of Mudgikiwis, the leader of the thunder manitos. When the design has only one head and is represented with wings outspread, it symbolizes Mudgikiwis. Both of the designs ... were worked in green beads on a background of orange beads."[69] At White Earth in Minnesota, four designs of thunderbird were worked in various quills on birch bark; plain quills, yellow quills on red bark, and neutral-coloured quills on straw-yellow bark were used. Thunderbird was also depicted on a dream badge, on a birchbark scroll, and on a Mide drum painted half-red and half-blue.[70] According to William Hoffman, thunderbird played a major role in both the Mide and the Jessakkid, for through turtle the practitioner had access to "numerous other malevolent manidos, especially the Animiki, or thunder-bird."[71]

Stylized thunderbird, on reverse side of finger woven bag. Phillips, *Patterns of Power*, back cover.

Designs from dreams were not only carried on one's person, but also sometimes imprinted on the dreamer's own skin. This penchant for displaying designs of animals in such a manner is apparent in the eighteenth-century writing of James Isham, a Hudson's Bay Company factor: "They have severall mark's upon their bodies, face and hands, Which they do by pricking the skin with a Needle in the shap'e and for'm they Design tell the Blood Comes, they then take some gun powder, or Coal beat fine, Wich they Lay on Rubbing itt for a while tell the bleeding is over, w'ch stands good and never washes out."[72]

Sites of rock paintings in the Province of Saskatchewan depict juxtapositions of thunderbirds and serpents, T.E.H. Jones suggests. At the McDonald Bay Site, Pinehouse Lake, Saskatchewan, of the seven to eight figures, four are thunderbirds, which are interspersed with serpents. At this site, a "snake extends downward from the left to the upper left thunderbird, and below the snake is a more-or-less straight, upright line with three 'prongs' at its lower end." Also in Saskatchewan, at the High Rock Narrows Site 2 there is a bird figure with long, sinuous wings alongside a small bird with a long, snake-like line extending downwards from the tip of its right wing. At the Stanley Rapids Site in northern Saskatchewan, a more contemporary site that includes the image of a man using a rifle to shoot a deer, there is a stylized bird-like symbol with outspread arms or wings inside a curved arc, with a snake-like figure above the bird and one on each side of it. Jones suggests that ancestors of the present-day Algonquian peoples created most of the rock paintings on the Canadian Shield during pre-contact periods; many were Cree artists. Jones interprets the rock paintings as following from visions and as a means of seeking spiritual power.[73]

Thunderbird. Song scroll: "I am flying into my lodge." "Represents the Thunder-Bird, a deity flying into the arch of the sky. The short lines denote the (so-called spirit lines) abode of spirits or Manidos." Hoffman, "The Midê'wiwin," 192a, 196.

Woodlands painters are adept and sensitive in fusing modern techniques with traditional images of thunderbird. With his palette, Morrisseau melds forms reminiscent of beadwork, costume design, stained glass windows, and figures from birch bark scrolls.[74] His "Artist and Shaman Between Two Worlds" features a thunderbird with large wings that are tipped with snakes.[75] In "Conflict Between Good and Evil," Carl Ray images a vortex of whirling lines, which converge "into a cluster of flailing claws and paws. A waving line of communication leads from one mouth to the other." Fine communication lines imitate water surface patterns on a northern lake when wind and waters collide.[76]

Two Menomini stories, "Sun Caught in a Snare" and "The Women of the Eastern Sky," gather together and link several beings – the celestial ones, bear in the waters, and women.[77]

Two great cosmic spirits, thunderbird and underwater panther, Mishipeshu, are depicted on early Ojibwe bags. These motifs, represented also on ritual garb, express symbolically the "transition between upper and underworlds ... a mapping of the cosmos and the spirit forces which energize it, [a] ... spatial organization of the cosmos, and the locating of force fields within this spatial model,"[78] Phillips concludes.

The tensions between and interdependence of the creatures in the sky and those in the upper and lower waters are evident in Angeconeb's linocut, "The Pommerngrief Meets the Anishinawbe Thunderspirit."[79] A winged serpent with horns and tail, and with tongue exposed, stands on its hind legs and is about to claw with its front ones. The heads of thunderbird and a human being merge with each other; a human hand is raised and a wing elevated as if to stave off or pacify the serpent.

Early-nineteenth-century Minnesota Ojibwe from White Earth, Leech Lake, and Red Lake felt there was a communion between the upper and lower worlds. A representation from that area, "The Water Birds Will Alight," shows water birds landing on members of the Midewiwin, who are in the form of fish; the "ability to attract water animals is greatly desired by members of the Mide," Densmore writes. To complement the representation, Gegwedjiwebinun sings: "Surely, Upon the whole length of my form, The water birds will alight."[80]

While Ojibwe welcomed sea creatures and water, they also desired the friendship of air creatures, as we have noted in our consideration of owl. Land was also a privileged domain, and beaver's life typified cosy domiciles both in water and on land. When beaver surfaces, he draws the entire water world with him, as suggested in this song picture: "When I appear, the men of the deep will be cast up by seething waters." And the prized objects of the waters, the white Mide shells, also appear: "They are being cast up by seething waters, The white Mide shells."[81] But for land-bound humans, for hunters, a battle continues with water creatures, and especially with rattlesnakes, as given in this hunting song by Becigwiwizans: "Come, Behold, Let us have a contest, O rattlesnake, Most subtle of reptiles, O rattlesnake."[82] This kinship of three worlds is evident in various ways: in Ojibwe cultures, feathers, carried or worn, pointed to the upper avian world; furs were obviously extracted from the middle world, and silver, which reflected light against the evil spirits, represented the under world.[83]

Wild cat with long tail, on front side of woven bag. Thunderbird on back of woven bag. Central Great Lakes, late eighteenth century. Phillips, *Patterns of Power*, 43, 68.

A melancholic mood overcomes singer Gagandac in "Song of the Thunders": "Sometimes, I go about pitying, Myself, While I am carried by the wind, Across the sky." Gagandac becomes part of the storm mystery.[84] In "The Approach of the Storm," he sings: "From the half, Of the sky, That which lives there, Is coming, and makes a noise."[85] It is a noise to warn of the storm's approach. Tobacco is then offered.

A dreamer while fasting saw clouds rising in the south, and Manitou spoke, as sung by Eniwube: "Brother, come here with us."[86] The dreamer went into the clouds and saw the thunderbirds, who taught him "The Approach of the Thunderbirds," sung by Kimiwun: "The sound approaches, the [thunder] birds draw near."[87] And another, "The Thunderbirds," sung by Awunakumigickun: "The [Thunder] birds startle me."[88] Again, by Najobitun in "Song Picture no. 58": "I who live in a cave, Our grandfather, Arms he has, With feathers, I who live in a cave."[89]

In his etching "Thunderbirds in the Métro," Angeconeb captures the contemporary omnipresence of these avian creatures. The thunderspirits, the grandfathers, ride with the artist on the metro.[90] In his linoblock "Ahneesheenahpay Sky World, Middle World, and Under World," Angeconeb connects these three worlds with wavy lines of intercommunication.[91]

The Ojibwe painter Roy Thomas writes about a necessary appreciation for water: It is "one of the four sacred elements, and a life-giver from our Creator. At a very young age we are taught to have a deep respect for water. If it isn't respected it can take life away." His etching "Our Gifts" shows water birds held up by the underwater panther, or lynx, Mishipeshu.[92] Thomas continues: "Our gifts from Keshay-Manitou, the Creator, are the spirit of the air (bird), the spirit of the land (animal), the spirit of the water (fish), and the spirit of the fire (sun). [We] share these with non-Anishnawbe people, our relatives."[93]

Another contemporary Ojibwe painter, Roy Morris, often depicts animals and humans in communion. In his painting "He Talks with Others," bears, a moose, an owl, an underwater creature, and a human being speak with one other. In "We Are Picking Berries," two thunderbirds rest on a bear's back; two humans pick berries; another bear is in the background. All of these constitute the "we" in the title. In "The World I Know Is Different," a round spirit figure connects human beings, a wigwam, and underwater creatures. In "The Earth Watches: She Remembers My Grandfathers," sea, sky, and land creatures watch and remember. In "The Rabbit Is Important to Us," spirits, a falcon, and a panther-like creature are intertwined as they attack a surprised rabbit.[94] Morris paints with bold colour orchestration "demonstrating [the] connectivity" of all cosmic powers, which connectivity, he confesses, he learned from listening "to the trees, grass, wind and waters as they told stories to one another."[95]

According to Thomas Sandy of the Rama Reserve in Ontario, there is an antipathy between two sky creatures, thunderbirds and mosquitoes, as given in "What Lightning Strikes." Both thunderbirds and humans give their blood involuntarily to mosquitoes, thereby nurturing them. Moreover, mosquitoes stay with the thunderbirds during the winter. When the thunderbirds asked the mosquitoes about the source of the copious blood in their stomachs, "they said they got it from the trees. If they had told the Thunderbirds where they had got the blood, all the Indians would have been killed. This is the reason why the trees are struck by lightning" – they are the object of the thunderbirds' wrath.[96]

Among the Ojibwe. the thunders had special roles. "The Crane and Loon Clans were the Chieftain clans and generally recognized as those clans from which the chieftainship emerged … The bird clan were the spiritual leaders, the planters, the cultivators. Among these were the Thunderbird clan, Baldheaded Eagle clan, Golden Eagle clan, the Soaring Eagle clan, the Hawk clan."[97]

Offerings of tobacco to the Manitous were a panacea of sorts. We have noted that tobacco was offered to the sea creatures to acknowledge their presence and to ensure safety and health. Such offerings were also made to thunderbirds so that they would make a lot of noise to terrify the sea creatures and thereby secure "protection against property damage and physical injury during a windstorm." While tossing a pinch of tobacco into the fire, the Ojibwe could speak to the thunderbirds. At other times, an individual might be warned by his non-thunderbird guardian spirit about impending sickness in the community. The Ritzenthalers recall that on one occasion the Ojibwe followed proper protocol to implore immunity from sickness: A runner told the people to assemble at a specific time and place. Food and clothing were "offered to the manidog of the air, especially to the thunderbirds. This was done by the dreamer or by someone he had already designated to speak for him. The dreamer related his dream and told the manidog that this offering of clothing was in their honor, and he implored their intercession in warding off the sickness."[98]

The Midewiwin ceremonies mediate the powers of the Manitou world above and the Manitou world below and synthesize the "dialectical relation between Thunderers and Mishebushu."[99] This mysterious and powerful ceremony is "established as a unique event of cosmic centration and participation by the assembled personalistic powers [and is] ritually presented as the accumulated force of the multilayered cosmos."[100] The tensions between creatures of air and those of sea give way to a constructive dialectic, reflected in their being featured together on designs of fibre nettle bags and in their co-presence in cultural performances.[101]

Thunderbird characterizes sacred sites. Thor and Julie Conway write that there was a time when all pictograph sites had names; the recovered original names of sites in Northern Ontario are those of the following large, cliff-nesting birds of prey: thunderbirds, ravens, eagles, and various hawks. These pictographs form "an ancient art gallery," the Conways observe, one that serves as a source of spiritual enlightenment offered by the resident spirits.[102] "The cliffs, simultaneously soaring into the sky and dropping precipitously into the darkness of northern lakes, provide a figurative bridge between aboriginal worlds." Aboriginal peoples say that the spirits in the sky realm soar down to earth through the hole in the sky and that birds in that realm are links between the physical and the spirit world; they express the ancestry of the Ojibwe and demonstrate a continuity with the present. They also believe that the natural deposits of white calcite coating the cliffs, or guano, originated from a powerful, mystical, and earthy source, the thunderbirds.[103]

To summarize this chapter: In Ojibwe traditions and in related ones, thunderbirds are different creatures than the water beings; they have diverse relationships with humans. Judging by their presence – which is often signalled by spectacular, fireworks-like displays and sounds – these beings are very powerful and as pervasive as the four winds. While some animals perceived during vision quests cannot be represented physically if they are to retain their powers, this is not the case in some traditions with thunderbird. That Ojibwe depict thunderbird not only in abstract zigzag lines but also in stylized images indicates its privileged status. The thunderbird maintains its power when it is portrayed on material and ceremonial items, carried on the person, or tattooed into the skin.

As protectors, thunderbirds drive off bad spirits, be they human or underwater. They have a personal and beneficial relationship with humans, exemplified especially in the provision of rain.

Nineteenth-century and contemporary Great Lakes rock paintings, songs, stories, and painters' representations show both tensions and a profound interdependence among sky creatures, those on the earth, and water beings. Among all these beings, there is a unity within differences.[104]

Thunderbird designs. Coleman, *Ojibwa Myths*, 101.

In imitation of the thunderers, the Ojibwe play many games, the predominant one being lacrosse. This game, an amalgam of many others, combines in intent and action music, war, healing, prophecy, and truth verification. Ojibwe believe that because lacrosse has celestial origins, it is ruled by cosmic forces and not merely by chance.

The Ojibwe bestow reverence on thunderbirds; their sounds and sites are sacred.

Conclusion

Nineteenth-century Ojibwe had a somewhat similar and reciprocal relationship with animals, as contemporary technological-industrial human beings do. Some animals provide companionship and can be enjoyed for their playful natures; some are prized for the protection they provide and for their food value. Some, like dogs in hunter-gatherer societies, can be trained for tasks and can work in coordination with their owners.

Generally, pets can offer loyalty and can be prized for their attractiveness, their songs, their guardianship, and the mental and physical health benefits they provide. Humans who domesticate animals for subsistence or profit, those who use animals for experimentation, and those who train them for sport have a different relationship to animals than the nineteenth-century Ojibwe did.

For the Ojibwe, the human and animal worlds intersected but were also separate. Generally, animals were not domesticated, trained for human tasks, and not subservient to human beings. They were free; they had their own lives, a worth not generally determined by human beings but independent from them. In this non-anthropocentric relationship, animals had meaning in themselves, however mysterious that meaning was and however difficult to understand.

Spirit figure on Midewiwin birch bark scroll. St John's Abbey Archives.

An Ojibwe term that came to be applied to animals – other-than-human persons – suggested a commonality with humans but an otherness as well. That commonality and otherness led many Ojibwe to refrain from categorizing animals and listing their characteristics, since animals had many transformative possibilities, just as humans did. Ojibwe words and stories did not express fixed animal identities; animals were accepted as an enigma. Or, perhaps, humans lacked the cognitive capacity to penetrate the nature of animals. Hence metaphors and stories – more flexible than analytic, mathematical thinking – were used when speaking about them. Humans often perceived ambiguities in the meaning of animals; the same animal could be both helpful and harmful. Humans could begin to understand the nature of animals only after many experiences.

A cognitive movement beyond appearances could affirm continuities in the actions of humans and animals, and the Ojibwe posited some essential characteristics of both humans and animals in their "early stories." In these stories, humans and animals shared many common attributes. Today, many of these universal characteristics have been lost; nevertheless, too rigid distinctions between humans and animals seem unfounded and artificial.

The relationship between Ojibwe and animals is very close, sometimes approximating a shared identity. For their proper names, humans use those of animals, as do the clans; artists portray humans and animals within one another or with power lines joining them; humans use masks and perform dances and other ceremonies to imitate the actions and sounds of animals.

Animals engage in many transformations. Humans do also. But the greatest challenge for humans is to effect a dispositional transformation in cross-cultural understanding. Only when humans strive to enter animal (and plant) worlds can they be open enough to communicate and live with them.

Mide and roses. Song scroll: "Our dwelling, Is royal, Our dwelling, Is widely renowned." "The Midewiwini is seen in his own lodge, roses being introduced to express the idea of beauty or luxury." Densmore, *Chippewa Music*, 1:113.

Midewiwin, the quasi-hierarchical society that is believed to have predated the arrival of Europeans, presented ideals and was formative for Ojibwe leadership. Those who aspired to ascend the rungs of this Medicine Society's ladder were empowered by many animals from the sky, the earth, and the waters. While groups outside the Midewiwin had their own clan structures and moral perspectives, this society served many functions for Ojibwe cultures; the core task for this group was the pursuit of well-rounded health – physical, psychological and spiritual. To ensure that the Ojibwe hunter society remained healthy, Mide practitioners studied the medicinal properties of many plants and learned to administer them. The various animals depicted on the birch bark scrolls, and the songs these scrolls inspired, brought unique powers to the lodge and to the Ojibwe as a whole; bear, however, was the commanding presence both within the lodge and outside it.

Old man. Song scroll: "Those who are spirits, Are making me old, Where I am sitting." "Through the power of the Mide a man lives to be so old that he leans on a staff as he walks." Densmore, *Chippewa Music*, 1:107–8.

From an examination of the moral values of four nineteenth-century Ojibwe, we conclude that the conversion of some Ojibwe to Methodism and Catholicism, and their embrace of Christian missionary activity, occurred within the framework of their Ojibwe cultures. Explicit or implicit in the moral retrievals of these four was a reliance on Midewiwin performances. For Peter Jones, Christianity served the Ojibwe purposes of *bimaadiziwin*, a healthy and long life. A new identity for his people could emerge in which the son of the Great Spirit would protect his people as the guardian spirits had in the past. Andrew Blackbird thought that American education was the only goal for his family and his people, though in the end, however, his twenty-one precepts showed that he could not and would not erase his ancestral past in this educational quest. Cosmic spirits at special times and places would continue to guide and protect his people. For George Copway, the English language and Methodism provided a firm schematic foundation for his life, his teaching and preaching. Like an uncontrollable earthquake, however, there were seismic shifts in this moral program, which included the "sayings of the medicine men" and the purposeful voices of nature. William Warren considered it his moral imperative to record the history of his people before they were assimilated. While he drew parallels between the Mosaic law and that of the Ojibwe, he also pointed to virtues unique to his own people: a special way of forgiving and moral excellence in war and in the hunt.

The first symbol on the Midewiwin's ascending ladder was the playful and entertaining figure of otter. Equally agile on land or water, otter embodied the life and aspirations of the Ojibwe. Those who had visions and heard the various sounds of otter wished to retain his presence without diminishing his spiritual energy; the Ojibwe believed they could do this by fashioning garments and other items that preserved otter's track and tail in geometrical patterns.

Although the Ojibwe often considered the owl's eyes, and its bodily presence and voice in the day and in the night, as sinister, owl was largely a helpful animal. It protected and healed the people; it taught the Ojibwe not to be greedy but to share. In addition, owl displayed cosmic powers in directing the winds and the seasons; it sang with and against the rapids and heralded the advent of new life in the spring. Owl had a cyclic and cosmic relationship with the earth and with the Ojibwe. As a guide to the afterlife, owl mediated between life and death. The Mide lodge was permeated with the voice and presence of owl, and its leaders became the messengers of owl.

Bear – the archshadow of the Ojibwe – was both an ideal, surpassing human possibilities, and a source of sustenance. Stories abound of bear as the bringer, keeper, and practitioner of healing, for bear loomed large in the Midewiwin lodge. Relationships with bears, be they alive or dead, were always both personal and respectful. Bear's power was seemingly unlimited and could be applied for both good and harm. Its cosmic power in the skies served as both a model and a cause of terrestrial happenings.

Wild cat and whirling waters on back side of woven bag. Central Great Lakes, late eighteenth century. Phillips, *Patterns of Power*, 43, 64. "Lower half of a Panther, but the top half of the image dissolves into rows of castellated lines." Phillips, "Zigzag and Spiral," 415, 422.

Water and its creatures were ambivalent symbols and realities in nineteenth-century Ojibwe lives. Water could nourish life or could snuff it out. Sea creatures such as snake and lynx could be frightening and menacing or could be good medicine. In fact, both characteristics were necessary and even complementary, in that sea creatures sometimes gave protection to navigators through their rugged dispositions and powerful actions. There are images in the Midewiwin of snakes preventing entrance both into the lodge and into the afterlife. Yet at the same time, snakes could serve as a bridge or passageway after death. Women and snakes had a curious reciprocal relationship with each other. Silver and copper were also water creatures who dispelled the darkness, ensured healing, and indicated origins.

Thunderbirds on front side of woven bag. Central Great Lakes, late eighteenth century. Phillips, *Patterns of Power*, 43, 64. "A group of thunderbirds ... adjacent to a bold, irregular, zigzag line representing lightning." Phillips, "Zigzag and Spiral," 415, 422.

Thunderbirds had a privileged role among the Ojibwe. They asserted their might in spectacular fireworks displays and through overpowering sounds; they brought the four winds and rain. Thunderbird's power was not diminished, as in the case of other animals, by representational images tattooed on the skin, carried on the person, or portrayed on material and ceremonial items. Thunderbirds were the originators of the predominant Ojibwe game, lacrosse. This game embodied the symbols of war, song, healing, prophecy, and truth verification. In Ojibwe cosmology, earth, water, and sky creatures demonstrated both tensions and interdependence.

At the very least, Ojibwe cultural forms are worthwhile not only in themselves but also as guides for non-Aboriginals. In order to acknowledge that legitimacy, the latter must develop cross-cultural understanding.

An affinity is possible between humans and animals that goes beyond what is expressed in Western cultures. Indeed, for the Ojibwe the very foundation for human existence is a close human–animal relationship in many ways: corporeal, cognitive, creative, linguistic, affective, and that of destiny.

The mere classification of animals, while appearing to be precise, does not capture their essence. Animals elude complete human understanding. Although they attempt to enter animals' worlds and describe those experiences, Ojibwe accept that animals inhabit their own worlds, which are often shared with humans. Hence relationships with and characterizations of animals remain ambiguous, mysterious, and impervious to complete human comprehension. This human inability, however, does not mean that animals cannot influence human life or are not important. As an examination of the ascending rungs of the Midewiwin ladder indicates, animals intersect human lives in many ways. Along with other cultural representations, they embody cultural ideals for humans and teach many lessons. Indeed, they are necessary for survival.

APPENDICES

Appendix A
Leadership among the Ojibwe

For Mide leaders and others, in the past and today, the earth is a source of laws that provides leadership and guidance for humans. This may sound strange, for many peoples believe that only humans as the highest form of earthly beings can be the authors of principles for right living. In this latter view, the earth is often considered as inanimate, as having "no purposes of its own, no discernible thoughts, communication patterns or conscious life-ways," John Borrows writes. But many Anishinaabe people "characterize the earth as a living entity that has thoughts and feelings, can exercise agency by making choices, and is related at the deepest generative levels of existence ... The land's sentience is a fundamental principle of Anishinabek law, one upon which many Anishinabek people attempt to build their societies and relationships."

Both the earth and its creator are consulted and heeded before important decisions are made. The Anishinaabe will listen to the Creator and/or earth through ceremonies "or they will elect to understand the earth's requirements by observing its interactions with wind, water, fire and other beings to which she relates," Borrows notes. There is a reciprocal relationship of responsible stewardship between an item of the earth, between stones, for instance, and human beings. Humans must relate as responsible stewards to these stones and protect them in time of need. In turn, stones will relate to humans as responsible stewards and protect them in certain situations.

Borrows tells of a proposed development that, on one level, promised to be very useful for the community, for the land examined – on the Bruce Peninsula in Ontario – looked empty and was not productive. On another level, however, this proposed development did not respect the 440-million-year-old bedrock, which was a storyteller of the tropical seas and a home to mosses, lichens, and plants. This so-called barren rock or alvar was also a home to spirit trails and spirit power, bearwalkers, and deceased relatives. For Borrows, this largely treeless stretch of land "reveals earth as having being and can be legally recognized." He accords this land political citizenship, for the earth has a place in Ojibwe jurisprudence. According to these Anishinaabe spiritual ways and laws, the earth is "a living being with the power of choice requiring respect for its autonomy, privacy and personal convictions against the liberal framework of post-reformation Europe." This Anishinaabeg directive "provides guidance about how to theorize, practice and order our association with the earth, and could do so in a way [that] produces answers that are very different from those found in other sources."[1]

The blessings that individuals and groups received, and the power of spirits in performances and stories and in the land itself, formed Ojibwe leaders. In theory, anyone who lived these cultures and was open to their formative powers could become a leader. But in reality, an authentic leader had to have something extra, which some called magical powers and others identified as charisma.

Leaders had animal helpers who bestowed both a power on them and a near identity, based on a kinship between humans and animals. Richard Preston notes that such close associations could lead to a sharing of feelings between hunter and the geese hunted, for instance. "Communication may be seen as a transference or bridging of feelings from man to animals or from animals to man. The mechanism of communication may be known only as a deep, strong effort to communicate. A progression from the idea of communication of desires between men and animals to the idea of love between men and animals includes the idea of a *playing relationship* between men and animals."[2] There could also be a kinship between powerful leaders and rocks, including the petroglyphs into which they could transform themselves and thereby achieve permanence.[3]

Those who became leaders either through heredity and/or charisma had to be hard-nosed pragmatists. As with the leaders of the buffalo hunt, their leadership was task-oriented and could be for a limited time. Of the three types of Aboriginal leaders who signed the Robinson Treaty of 1850, the first two were oriented to general tasks for their people, while those of the third type, referred to as inside leaders or chiefs, were specific to bands. The first two types served outside the bands, were the leaders of hunting bands, and were called headmen;

some of them, referred to as trading chiefs, led the trading post bands. In their dealings with European trading post officials, the trading post band organizers were the ones who seemed to be the spokespersons for the band. But even though they often received robes of recognition (chief's clothing),[4] they had only temporary authority and did not actually represent the band itself. The leadership roles of the hunting and trading post bands ceased when their jobs ceased. While the most numerous negotiators of and signatories to the Robinson Treaty were the trading post band leaders, Lisa Hansen thinks that they had to stay in contact with the band chiefs in order to learn which decisions they should take. Some inside band members, therefore, were also represented at this treaty, as well as Mide leaders.

The role of the trading post leaders was a new one at this time, predated by the traditional roles of the hunting leaders and inside band leaders. Hansen writes:

> Within a hunting group, the senior male member was most often recognized as headman of the group. His leadership was based on his age, knowledge and skills as a hunter, perhaps also on his reputation as a shaman, as he fulfilled his role as leader through his ingenuity, personality and his enjoyment of the group's approval ...
>
> [An inside band] chief's authority was based on his age, his oratorical skills and his ability to act as an arbitrator among band members and, following contact, between them and Europeans. Since the Lake Superior Ojibwa spent most of the year scattered in hunting groups ... [hunting] headmen would have had more influence over their daily activities than did chiefs.[5]

Appendix B
The Sweat Lodge

The sweat lodge is not the same as the Midewiwin lodge. The pre-eminent function of the Midewiwin lodge is healing, while the sweat lodge is mainly a purification ceremony, although the roles of these lodges quite often overlap. In one story, the sweat lodge was given to a boy who travelled to the dark side of the moon and met with the seven Grandfathers. This lodge is a means of purifying the mind and body, a powerful experience akin to being born anew. Although the sweat lodge can "cure" some sicknesses, it is more often a first step to other ceremonies. In some traditions, it is open only to men, for women have a natural purification process (i.e., menstruation).[6]

In a more contemporary vein, Michael Relland writes that the different types of lodges – the sweat lodge, the learning lodge, the healing lodge, the men's lodge, and the family lodge – are general and spiritual instruments of healing, with the emphasis on internal healing. Relying on the testimony of Danny Musqua of Saskatoon, Saskatchewan, Relland writes: "They strengthen the connection between the spiritual realm, which is the source of healing, and the physical realm, which is the cause of illness. These ceremonies allow for the power of the spiritual world to be mediated through physical reality by restoring balance and harmony. Such is the case with the sweat lodge where, through the power of prayer, the Grandfathers, or spirits, are evoked to provide healing and guidance to the individuals present as well as [to] the community at large."[7]

Relland records that each lodge

provides an opportunity for prayer and the rejuvenation of the spirit. For those attending the sweat lodge, the experience is healing in a number of ways. For example, through prayer the individual's ability for spiritual expression and forming of closer relationships with the Creator and the spiritual realm is developed. The burden upon the spirit is also lightened during the course of the sweat. This is due to the spiritual and physical nature of the sweat lodge ... The sweat lodge is the womb of mother earth and the lodge's physical darkness and warmth replicates our own experiences within our mother's womb.

[It is a] safe, secure environment where people can express their pain and sorrow without fear of reprisals or the risk of their trust being violated ... [It is also a] sacred place where the Grandfathers are present and often choose to carry our burden for us until we are strong enough to deal with it ourselves. According to this belief, the forces of the world of the unseen are tangible and have the capacity to impact upon and influence the physical world through direct involvement. Finally, the sweat promotes healing through nurturing a sense of connectedness with the spiritual realm, the physical realm and our fellow human beings ... [and] with the earth ... [It] utilizes the four elements of earth, fire, air and water.[8]

Participants commune first with the Grandfathers and then with one another in an honest and sincere way.

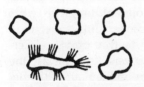

A bathing song by Kitagiguan/Spotted Feather with stones and fire that heat them. Kohl, *Kitchi-Gami*, 287, 289.

Another type of lodge, the learning lodge, fosters an understanding of self and strengthens bonds with the Creator if one deprives oneself of food and water for three or four days and devotes oneself to prayer and reflection. A weaker body loosens "the bonds and constraints that the physical universe places upon our spirit. As our physical body weakens and the bonds to the physical world loosen, the spirit grows in strength and we become more in tune with the spiritual world." Through a deeper understanding of self, individuals realize their role in the cosmos and this connection reveals to them the frailty and vulnerability of life. They receive a glimpse of the cycle of life, death, and rebirth.[9]

Appendix C
Bear as Celestial

The Oklahoma Delaware envision a close relationship between celestial and terrestrial bear. "The stars of the Corona Borealis form the bear's head, which has been separated from its body, and which the bear is forever trying to reach. When the bear catches up with its head, according to legend, the world will come to an end." The bear became ceremonial food in the Bear Sacrifice Ceremony and at funeral feasts, where the eating of bear meat "could easily take on a sacramental character."[10]

An intriguing aspect of bear is its reciprocal sky-to-earth and earth-to-sky influences in some Algonquian traditions, although to what extent this interpretation is also an Ojibwe feature remains conjectural. In the Munsee-Mahican world, for instance, the Bear Sacrifice Ceremony re-enacts on earth the celestial constellations, "specifically the constellation Ursa Major [Big Bear][11] projected upon the floor of the Big House sanctuary. The interior furnishings of the sanctuary and the stations formally occupied by the ceremonial officials correspond to the position of the stars forming the constellation. The acts and movements of the ritual performers parallel the movements of the Ursa Major as the events of the annual life cycle of the earth-bear symbolically rotate with those of the Sky Bear. Furthermore, the earth-bear sacrificed in the ceremony is conceived as a fragment of the celestial bear, and everything done during the ritual is a transcendental reference to him. The sacred performance annually renews the eternal relationship of earth beings and sky beings ... a pantomimic demonstration of an interplay between earth and sky beings temporally and spacially [sic] coordinated."[12]

According to the cultural narrator Nekatcit, in the dialectic between sky and earth, bear is the major actor – Big Bear in the sky with bears in the forest. "The sky bear is eternal, the earth bears perish or are killed by men and return in spirit form to the realm above, whence they descended when born in their dens. And among them was one, who, each year, was destined to become a vicarious sacrifice to attest the devotion of men to the creed of their ancestral priesthood. To them the analogy between the life and death of men and the existence of soul-spirits and the celestial bear was a manifest tent [tenet] in support of their belief in the continuity of all life and its indestructibility."[13]

Also according to Nekatcit, "the constellation Great Bear, or Great Dipper, was believed to represent a 'bear hunt' ... The four stars forming an irregular rectangle marked the body of the bear, the three stars forming the handle of the Dipper, according to popular observation, were three hunters (the bear has no long tail!), the 'little star' ... just visible beside the second one from the body was the dog of one of the hunters. And the entire cluster was the Indians' guide. By watching its position and knowing their bearings in relation to it at given times of the night in different seasons they would never become lost in their wanderings."

In a more detailed one-to-one correspondence between the sky bear and earth bear, the Wabanaki attribute "the autumnal reddening of the forest foliage to the tinting of the leaves by the blood of the celestial bear slain at this turn of the season by the star-hunters, and the white mantle of early winter snow on earth to the coating of white bear's grease falling upon earth when the sky-hunters fry out the fat of the slain bear."[14]

Snow or rain. Song scroll. "Drifting snow, why do I sing." "The horizontal curve denotes the sky, the vertical zig-zag lines indicating the falling snow – though being exactly like the lines employed to denote rain. The drifting snow is likened to a shower of delicate migis shells or spots ... this shower of migis descends from the abode of Kitshi Manido and is ... looked upon as sacred." Hoffman, "The Midê'wiwin," 228a, 229. Fulford's translation of the song scroll is "I wait for him." "Ojibwa Picture Writing," 178.

According to the Oklahoma Delaware, "the Bear's seasonal rotation around the North Star was taken to sympathetically parallel the life cycle of bears on the earth: upright (awake) in summer, prostrate on its back (hibernating) in winter, head up (emerging from its den) in spring, head down (entering its den) in late autumn. This close coordination in life cycle of the Celestial Bear and earthly bears suggested the possibilities of a sympathetic communication between them." The seasonal "killing" of the Celestial Bear was associated with winter hunting on parallel celestial and earthly paths. As Wallace concludes: "In a very general sense, it would almost seem that the ceremony served as a sort of world-renewal rite, as an affirmation of the order of the universe and the human morality appropriate thereto."[15] Those things which transpire in the sky world – its images and principles expressed in the Big Bear star lore and knowledge – complement events on earth, but are prior and are pre-eminent.

Appendix D
Ojibwe Historical Relationship with Copper

We noted ambivalent Ojibwe relationships to copper. One was that of revering it and letting it be, and the other was its utilization for the community's commercial benefit. Some Ojibwe leaders seemed to want miners to exploit this mineral, while others maintained a more reticent, laissez-faire position. According to William Warren, the 1826 treaty reflected these dual positions. Lewis Cass, governor of the Michigan Territory, was delegated by the U.S. federal government to meet with the Ojibwe and negotiate over the copper and other minerals abundant on Ojibwe lands. Shingabawossin, chief of the Crane clan from Sault Ste Marie, Ontario, spoke on behalf of his people, having urged them to "discover [disclose] to the whites their knowledge of the minerals which abounded in their country." Warren comments: "This, however, was meant more to tickle the ears of the commissioners and to obtain their favor than as an earnest appeal to his people, for the old chieftain was too much imbued with the superstition prevalent amongst the Indians, which prevents them from discovering [disclosing] their knowledge of mineral and copper boulders to the whites."[16]

Later, however, in council, Shingabawossin in a seemingly straightforward manner advocated an opposing position: "If you have any copper on your lands, I advise you to sell it. It is of no use to us. They can make articles out of it for our use. If any one has any knowledge on this subject, I ask him to bring it to light."[17]

Yet it is evident that even earlier than the above account, Aboriginal peoples had sold copper. Around 1669, missionary Claude Dablon indicated that he had purchased a slab of copper.[18] Reverence toward this ore remained, however. In 1820, Wabishkipenas/The White Bird, an Ontonagon, guided entrepreneurs in an offhand manner to large bodies of copper in the upper part of Lake Superior. This gesture made him quite unpopular with his band, which banished him from his community for his failure to respect Gitchi Manitou and the sacred substance.[19] Barbara Chisholm and Andrea Gutsche recall that a non-Aboriginal copper miner at Ontonagon on Lake Superior's south shore also stirred up Aboriginals' anger; in 1849, in the aftermath, Shingwauk and Kinebinogojing raided a copper mine at Pointe aux Mines.[20]

Archaeological evidence corroborates Aboriginals' early knowledge of copper. Digs on Isle Royale, at the Minong Mine area, indicate that Aboriginal peoples had mined for copper and used and traded it at a time when stone was the primary material for tools. These Aboriginal miners demonstrated "enterprise and perseverance" with regard to copper[21] and made a very large supply of copper available for use, writes S.A. Barrett.[22] Corroborating this, the following archaeological copper objects have been found on the McCollum Site in a bay on southeastern Lake Nipigon: discs, bracelets, beads, an adze, and socketed and bevelled knives, dated 200 BC–AD 200.[23] There is evidence at another site of tempering, a process that gave copper an edge as good as iron or steel; this art has since been lost.[24] On exhibit at the McCord Museum in Montreal is a Native copper lance crafted 4,000 to 5,000 years ago.[25] Before the contact between indigenous peoples and Europeans, various Aboriginal peoples used copper nuggets for bartering. "Between 5,000 and 1,000 B.C., a copper trade route ran from the Great Lakes to the mouth of the Saguenay River."[26]

Johann Kohl recounts that an Ojibwe reluctantly sold treasured masses of copper that had been buried for three generations in the woods. For the owner, it was a "great treasure," and because of it, the owner says, "I have caught many beavers, killed many bears. Through its magic assistance I have been victorious in all my battles, and with it I have killed many foes. Through it too, I have always remained healthy, and reached that great age in which thou now findest me."[27] Anthony Buchner points out a correlation between the formation of certain archaic copper specimens and pictographic representations of astronomical objects. He finds that consistently, "linear features are correlative with solar while ellipses align with lunar or even planetary events."[28]

Notwithstanding a quasi-entrepreneurial spirit among some Ojibwe regarding copper, reverence for it prevailed. There are stories to support this. One of these, repeated with variations, seems to have first been recorded by missionary Claude Dablon around 1669. It tells of the consequences of not abiding by a taboo that demanded reverence for the ore. Dablon identified an island opposite Missipicouatong [Michipicoten] as the place "where copper is found in abundance." It was a "floating island" that shifted its location with the prevailing winds. In an Aboriginal story, four men in pre-contact times lost their way in the constant fog and ventured into the area. "These men, then, wishing to prepare themselves something to eat, adopted their usual method: taking some stones that they found at the water's edge, they heated them red-hot, and threw them into a bark dish filled with water to make it boil, and by this device to cook their meat. While selecting these stones, they found that they were almost all pieces of copper; accordingly, they made use of some of them, and, after taking their repast, resolved to embark as soon as possible, fearing the lynxes and hares, which are as large as dogs in that region, which were coming to eat up their provisions and even their canoe. Before setting out, they loaded themselves with a good many of these stones, large and small, and even with some slabs of copper; but they had not gone far from the shore when a powerful voice made itself heard to their ears, calling in great wrath: 'Who are those robbers carrying off from me my children's cradles and playthings?'" Apparently there was a strong resemblance between these copper slabs and the cradleboards the Aboriginals used. The small pieces of copper were the "toys and playthings of savage children" whom they were now despoiling.[29]

To continue with Dablon's account: "That voice astonished them greatly, as they knew not whose it was. Some say that it was thunder, because there are many storms there; and others that it was a certain spirit whom they call Missibizi, who passes among these peoples for the god of the waters, as Neptune did among the pagans. Others say it came from Memogovissiouis: these are, they say, marine people somewhat like the fabulous Tritons or the Sirens, who always live in the water and have long hair reaching to the waist. One of our savages told us he had seen one of them in the water, according to what he imagined. However this may be, that astounding voice inspired such terror in our travelers' souls that one of the four died before reaching land. A short time afterward a second was taken off, and then the third; so that only one was left, who, after returning to his country and relating all that had happened, died very soon afterward. The savages, all-timid and superstitious as they are, have never dared to go there since that time, for fear of dying there, believing that there are certain spirits who kill those who approach them. And, in fact, in the memory of man, no one has been known to set foot there, or even to be willing to sail in that direction, although the island seems to be open enough.

While acknowledging the truth value of part of the story – namely, the discovery of copper – Dablon nevertheless provides an interpretation that differs from the Aboriginal one: "There is truth and there is untruth in this whole narrative, and the following is what is most probable: namely, that those four persons were poisoned by the water that they boiled with the pieces of copper, which communicated their poison to it, owing to their very great heat; for we know by experience that this copper, when it is put into the fire for the first time, exhales very malignant vapors, which are thick and infectious and whiten the fireplace. It is not, however, a poison so immediate as not to operate more promptly in some cases than in others, as happened with those of whom we are speaking; who, being already affected by the poison, may have easily imagined that they heard those voices, if they heard, however slightly, some echo, such as is commonly found among the rocks bordering that Island. Perhaps this fable has been invented since the event, from not knowing to what to attribute the death of those savages; and when they say that it is a floating Island, it is not incredible that the mists with which it is often laden, by becoming thin or dense under the sun's rays, make the island appear to the observer sometimes very near, and at other times farther away. What is certain is that, in the common opinion of the savages, there is a great abundance of copper in that Island; but they dare not go there."[30]

Dablon noted that some quantities of copper were in large slabs while others were comparable to grains of sand; some areas were so copper laden that stones thrown on them made a ringing sound. Other claims about the size and abundance of copper merited further investigation, Dablon wrote.[31]

Beaver and one of the men of the deep on song scroll: "When I appear, The men of the deep, Will be cast up by seething waters." Densmore, *Chippewa Music*, 1:65.

Appendix E
Lacrosse and War

The game of lacrosse was closely associated with the successful assault on an English garrison at Fort Michilimackinac on Lake Michigan by the Ojibwe/Sauk in 1763. This garrison, which housed thirty families, "was one of the most important positions on the frontiers," William Warren writes. "It was the place of deposit, and point of departure between the upper and lower countries; the traders always assembled there, on their voyages to and from Montreal."[32]

Alexander Henry, an eyewitness to the Trojan horse–like attack, and a prisoner of the Ojibwe after their victory, provides a background to the ambush: "Meanwhile, the Indians, from every quarter, were daily assembling, in unusual numbers, but with every appearance of friendship, frequenting the fort, and disposing of their peltries, in such a manner as to dissipate almost every one's fears ... In the course of the same day, I observed that the Indians came in great numbers into the fort, purchasing tomahawks, (small axes, of one pound weight,) and frequently desiring to see silver armbands, and other valuable ornaments, of which I had a large quantity for sale."[33]

The English at the fort were celebrating the king's birthday when "the ominous ball was thrown up a short distance in front of the gate of Fort Machinaw, and the exciting game commenced," Warren relates, relying on the accounts of Henry and "old French traders and half-breeds."[34] "The two hundred players, their painted persons streaming with feathers, ribbons, fox and wolf tails, swayed to and fro as the ball was carried backwards and forwards by either party, who for the moment had possession of it ... The game, played as it was, by the young men of two different tribes, became exciting, and the commandant of the fort even took his stand outside of his open gates, to view its progress. His soldiers stood carelessly unarmed, here and there, intermingling with the Indian women, who gradually huddled near the gateway, carrying under their blankets the weapons which were to be used in the approaching work of death.

"In the struggle for its possession, the ball at last was gradually carried towards the open gates, and all at once, after having reached a proper distance, an athletic arm caught it up in his bat, and as if by accident threw it within the precincts of the fort. With one deafening yell and impulse, the players rushed forward in a body, as if to regain it, but as they reached their women and entered the gateway, they threw down their wooden bats and grasping the shortened guns, tomahawks, and knives, the massacre commenced, and the bodies of the unsuspecting British soldiers soon lay strewn about, lifeless, horribly mangled, and scalpless. The careless commander was taken captive without a struggle, as he stood outside the fort, viewing the game, which the Ojibway chieftain had got up for his amusement ... Not a hair on the head of the many Frenchmen who witnessed this scene was hurt by the infuriated savages," Warren concludes.[35] "[They] obtained possession of the fort."[36] Henry was captured, but Wa-wat-am/Wow-yat-ton/Whirling Eddy, his adopted Ojibwe brother, helped him escape.[37]

Notes

Preface

1 This paper was published as "The Concept of the 'Soul' in *The Jesuit Relations:* Were There Any Philosophers among the North American Indians?" *Laval théologique et philosophique* 41 (1985): 57–64.
2 Kant, *Groundwork*, 96.
3 Coleman et al., eds., *Ojibwa Myths*, 82. Midasuganj/Ten Claw gives a related story from the Bois Fort Reservation, Minnesota; Jones, *Ojibwa Texts*, 1:311–15.
4 According to Wub-e-ke-niew from the Red Lake Reservation in Minnesota, the Midewiwin or Mide "is a compilation of the wisdom of my people over the course of about a million years, as well as the tools for understanding reality." *We Have the Right to Exist*, 9.
5 In this context, to bark is to remove the outer layer, the bark, of a tree.
6 Brightman, *Grateful Prey*, 32.
7 Lynch, *Bears*, 2.
8 Lynch, *Bears*, 19.
9 Harrison, "The Midewiwin," 80–1.
10 Morrisseau and Robinson, *Travels*, 60.
11 Morrisseau, "Foreword," 10.
12 Morrisseau and Robinson, *Travels*, 61–2, 64–5, 83, 116–17.
13 Morrisseau and Robinson, *Travels*, "Preface," 9–10.
14 Miller and Jensen, *Questions That Matter*, 46.
15 Stein, "Sacred Emily," 395. See also Stein, "Rose is a Rose," 537–9; in this poem, the term, Rose, refers to a person instead of a flower.
16 Kostelanetz, *The Yale Gertrude Stein*, xiii.
17 Dewdney and Kidd, *Indian Rock Paintings*, 69.

18 Overholt and Callicott, *Clothed-in-Fur*, 29. See Meyer and Ramirez, "'Wakinyan Hotan,'" 92: "Although translation from one disparate way of thinking to another is difficult, coming to understand another way of thinking is not a question of overcoming the difficulties of translation. Coming to understand another world view is 'learning how to reason' in the style of the other world view."
19 Harrison, "The Midewiwin," 80.
20 Black, "Ojibwa," 5 (1977) 97.
21 Lanoue, *Images in Stone*, 80.
22 Hallowell, "Ojibwa Metaphysics." 75.
23 Hallowell, "Ojibwa Metaphysics," 75.
24 Brightman, *Grateful Prey*, 169.
25 Brightman, *Grateful Prey*, 165.
26 Guss, *The Language of Birds*, ix.
27 See Berbaum, *Ojibwa Powwow World*, 17.
28 McPherson and Rabb, "Transformative Philosophy," 209.

Introduction

1 We will use this generally Aboriginal term in several ways in this book: a keeper can be a person who guards, preserves, and cares for a ceremonial object; a keeper can also be a group or nation that conserves values and meanings, or a keeper can be a spirit being in dreams or elsewhere who leads fellow spirits.
2 Hallowell, "Ojibwa Metaphysics," 66–7. Nichols and Nyholm define *aadizookaan/aadizookaanag* as traditional story (stories), legend or myth, or having the character of a legend or myth; *dibaajimowin/dibaajimowinan* is a story (stories) or narrative; *A Concise Dictionary of Minnesota Ojibwe*, 16, 45.
3 Jones, *Ojibwa Texts*, 2:547–59.
4 Warren analyses the name common among the Ojibwe; they called them-selves Anishinaabe. For Warren this name can mean "spontaneous man," "common people," or "original people." *History of the Ojibway People*, 27–8; we will generally use Schenck's edition for references. See Baraga, *Dictionary of the Otchipwe Language*, 2:38; Nichols and Nyholm, *A Concise Dictionary*, 10; *anishinaabe* can mean an Indian in contrast to a non-Indian; Anishinaabeg is the plural form.
5 The two terms, reserve and reservation, are used in Canada and the United States respectively. We will use the one that pertains to the country under consideration.
6 Jones, *Ojibwa Texts*, 1: xi.

7 Thwaites, *The Jesuit Relations,* 45 (1659), 205.
8 Echlin, "The Translation of Ojibway," has given a model to establish the social, cultural, and linguistic context of stories.
9 See Burgess, "Elaboration Therapy," 22–36.
10 Petroglyphs are images carved on rock surfaces. Pictographs are images drawn or painted on rocks. Petroforms are patterns or shapes arranged with small or large rocks on the ground or on rather flat rocky surfaces. These three types of representation are often called rock art. Other forms of communication are the line drawings and images on birch bark scrolls or on other materials indicating ideas, speech, and songs.
11 Black-Rogers, "Foreword," xv–vii.
12 Martin, "Animal Blessings." Animals care for humans; humans care for animals. In a technological and industrial society, it is hard to let animals, even pets, be; Grandin and Johnson make suggestions on how to give animals happy, satisfying lives and humane deaths; *Animals Make Us Human.* Attachment to pets can have a childish side, as shown by cartoon characters and stuffed bears. People can achieve more control over their pets than they do over fellow humans; see Scowen, "The Evolution of 'Fur Kids,'" L3.
13 Brightman writes of the benefactive interrelationship between animals and humans even in the hunt; humans obviously benefit from the hunt, but in Aboriginal perspectives, animals also benefit; this feral reciprocity is evident in the title of his book, *Grateful Prey,* 199–212.
14 Ingold, *The Perception of the Environment,* 48.
15 Black, "Ojibwa Taxonomy," 97. Citing Hallowell, she gives two tables (p. 94) to delineate both the overlapping of the two categories of humans and animals and to demonstrate within the broad category of persons both human persons and other-than-human persons, with the latter including seemingly inanimate things. For a consideration of "non-human animals" in Western philosophy, see Calarco and Atterton, *Animal Philosophy.*
16 Bower, "When Stones Come to Life," 360–2.
17 Steinfels, "Modernity and Belief," 16.
18 Warren, *History of the Ojibway People,* 35.
19 According to Warren, the northern and southern Ojibwe separated eight generations ago, that is, about two hundred years earlier, about 1650; Warren, *History of the Ojibway People,* 50 and 50n26.
20 Karklins, *Trade Ornament Usage,* 21–2.
21 Blessing, "Birchbark Mide Scrolls," 163.
22 Rogers/Chief Snow Cloud reminisces about his early years on the White Earth and Cass Lake Reservations at the beginning of the twentieth

century, and about his father's role as a leader of the Midewiwin. *Red World and White*, 146–53.

23 Hoffman, "The Midê'wiwin," 173. Hoffman claims some authority in understanding the Midewiwin; he writes of "my initiation"; "The Midê'wiwin," 236. Wub-e-ke-niew begs to differ. "What Hoffman wrote was based on the Métis' imitation or misinterpretation of the *Midé*." In addition, Wub-e-ke-niew criticizes Hoffman for being "locked into [his] own culture," especially into a hierarchical way of thinking. *We Have the Right to Exist*, 81, 333, 14n.

24 One of many authors of this close kinship between animals and humans is novelist Sara Gruen in *Ape House*. She demonstrates that bonobos, like others of the ape species, are capable of reason and of carrying on deep relationships; they can learn a sign language. But in spite of their closeness to humans – bonobos share 98.7 per cent of their DNA with humans – they are often treated cavalierly and cruelly. They are vivisected, and shot for food, and their orphaned children are stolen as pets and for sideshows. See also Goodall, *Jane Goodall: 50 Years at Gombe*.

25 See Section 35, *The Constitution Act*. These rights extend to the Indian, Inuit, and Métis peoples.

26 See Finlay, "Debating Phenomenological Research Methods."

27 Ashworth. "Presuppose Nothing!"

28 Finlay, "Debating," 12.

29 Finlay, "Debating," 14.

30 This uniqueness of Aboriginal cultures is now formulated in Canada's *Constitution Act*. As Youngblood Henderson comments: "When Europeans arrived in North America, aboriginal peoples *were already here*, living in communities on the land, and participating in distinctive cultures, as they had done for centuries. It is this fact, and this fact above all others, which separates aboriginal peoples from all other minority groups in Canadian society and which mandates their special legal, and now constitutional status." *First Nations Jurisprudence*, ix.

31 For an elaboration on the unique nature of Aboriginal societies and present-day legal implications, see Henderson, *First Nations Jurisprudence*.

32 Turner, *This Is Not a Peace Pipe*, 72.

33 Turner, *This Is Not a Peace Pipe*, 113.

34 See "Ethical Guidelines for Research," *Report of the Royal Commission*, vol. 5, Appendix E.

35 "Ethical Guidelines." *Report of the Royal Commission*, vol. 5, Appendix E.

36 For extensive considerations of incommensurability and comparability involving individuals and groups, see Chang, *Incommensurability, Incomparability, and Practical Reason*.

37 See Ricoeur, "The Hermeneutics," 193.
38 See Baraga, *A Dictionary of the Otchipwe Language,* 233; Fulford, "Ojibwa Picture Writing," 5n2.
39 For Blessing's use of the names Mide and Midewiwin, see "Medicine Bags," 77. For a consideration of the Midewiwin from the 1880s to the 1930s, see Paap, "The Ojibwe Midewiwin."
40 Hodge, *Handbook of Indians of Canada,* 396–400.
41 The name Saulteaux is derived from the French verb, *sauter,* "to leap over, to jump"; Douglas, *Cassell's French and English Dictionary,* 291. Thus, for the French, Saulteaux described those who lived near the jumping waters, Sault Ste Marie; hence they were known as People of the Falls.
42 Warren, *History of the Ojibway People,* 27–8.
43 Bird-David, "Sociality and Immediacy," 596–7. His analogy is general, but we have applied it to the Ojibwe.
44 See Gill and Sullivan, *Dictionary of Native American Mythology,* 340–1.
45 My thanks to Lawrence Martin for this clarification.

1. The Grand Medicine Society, the Midewiwin

1 Blessing, "Medicine Bags," 127.
2 Jones uses the term "mystic rite" in the headings of several stories; *Ojibwa Texts,* 2:531–609.
3 Wasagunachank or Midasuganj, "Mighty-One, Black Tail-of-a-Fish, and the Mystic Rite." Jones, *Ojibwa Texts,* 2:581–9.
4 Stories from Bois Fort: "The Creation, Origin of Death, and the Mystic Rite," "The Creation," "The Mystic Rite is Tested," "Mighty-One, Black Tail-of-a-Fish, and the Mystic Rite." Jones, *Ojibwa Texts,* 2:547–609.
5 Fulford, "Ojibwa Picture Writing," 179: Fulford's translation. Hoffman's literal translation is: "In your body I put it / the spirit." "The Midê'wiwin," 230.
6 Hilger, "Lac Courte Oreilles: Interviews with Elders," Part 2, Tape 4, 65.
7 Hilger, *A Social Study of One Hundred Fifty Chippewa Indian Families,* 113.
8 There are similarities and differences between the Ojibwe practice of the Midewiwin in general, and that of the Cree; see Bird, *Telling Our Stories,* 87–101.
9 Ritzenthaler, "Chippewa Preoccupation with Health," 182.
10 Cadzow, "Bark Records of the Bungi Midéwin Society," 131.
11 John Pete in the 1930s in Lac Vieux Desert. Kinietz, *Chippewa Village,* 198, 208–10.
12 Blessing, "Medicine Bags," 127.

13 Skinner, "Notes on the Eastern Cree and Northern Saulteaux," 154–5.
    Stewart initially calls this celebration on the east shore of Lake Winnipeg,
    "Feast of the Metawain," but afterwards, "Feast of the Long Life."

14 Harrison, "The Midewiwin," 95, 100.

15 Landes, *Ojibwa Religion and the Midéwiwin*, 97. According to "recent" rites
    from Red Lake and Emo, Dewdney remarks, a similar replacement took
    place. *The Sacred Scrolls*, 112.

16 Redsky, "Unpublished Manuscript," Archives and Collections, Thunder
    Bay Museum.

17 Vastokas and Vastokas judge that the Midewiwin symbols can shed light
    on the petroglyphs. *The Sacred Art of the Algonkians*, 37, 47.

18 Dewdney, *The Sacred Scrolls*, 121.

19 Brehm, "The Metamorphoses of an Ojibwa Manido," 691.

20 In 1634, missionary Paul Le Jeune refers to them as *kichikouai*, the "genii of
    the air or of the light." Thwaites, *The Jesuit Relations*, 6 (1634), 161.

21 Grim, *The Shaman*, 145.

22 Vecsey, *Traditional Ojibwa Religion*, 191.

23 Hoffman, "The Midê'wiwin," 156–7.

24 Gill and Sullivan, *Dictionary*, 325.

25 Jones, *History of the Ojebway Indians*, 144–7, 270–1. See Vennum, *The Ojibwa
    Dance Drum*, 184; and Hallowell, *The Role of Conjuring*, 74.

26 Le Jeune gives an early (1634) and detailed description of the Shaking Tent
    Ceremony; Thwaites, *The Jesuit Relations*, 6:161–71. See Clelland, *Rites of
    Conquest*, 69.

27 Hoffman, "The Midê'wiwin," 157–8.

28 Keesing, *The Menomini*, 48–50.

29 While Jesuit writings do not affirm the pre-contact origin of the Midewi-
    win, in 1674, Jacques Marquette points to an early Mide cross, which he
    mistakenly interprets as a sign of a previous Christian presence; Thwaites,
    The Jesuit Relations, 59 (1669), 103.

30 Harold Hickerson, *The Chippewa and Their Neighbors*, 7, 59, 63.

31 According to Warren the Mide lodge was "here, long before the pale face
    appeared among [the Anishinaabe, and] it was practiced in its purest and
    most original form." *History of the Ojibway People*, 45.

32 Hoffman was familiar with conventional medicine practices since he was
    a medical doctor; he also presented himself as an authority on early- and
    late-nineteenth-century Midewiwin performances, for he states that he ob-
    served Mide practices on Red Lake and White Earth Reservations, Minne-
    sota, between 1887 and 1889. He used diagrams made by Sikassige, a Mille
    Lacs Ojibwe Mide, and scrolls dating to 1830. Although Sikassige was only
    a second-degree Mide, he knew of the fourth degree since he was present

at his wife's fourth-degree initiation. Hoffman copied the birch bark scrolls of Skwekomik, who had received them in 1825 from his father-in-law, Badasan, chief of the Winnibegoshish Ojibwe. Hoffman, "The Midê'wiwin," 165, 172.

33 Kinietz, *The Indians of the Western Great Lakes*, 215–7.

34 Blessing, "Birchbark Mide Scrolls," 122.

35 Dewdney, *The Sacred Scrolls*, 57–80.

36 Vennum, "Ojibwa Origin–Migration Songs," 753.

37 Hall, *An Archaeology of the Soul*, 75.

38 Kidd, "A Radiocarbon Date on a Midewiwin Scroll," 41–3.

39 Hoffman, "Pictography," 217.

40 Bandow, *White Dogs*. Also supporting pre-contact origins of the Midewiwin is William Rex Weekes, "Antiquity of the Midewiwin: An Examination of Early Documents, Origin Stories, Archaeological Remains, and Rock Paintings from the Northern Woodlands of North America," PhD diss., Arizona State University, 2009.

41 Przybilla and Councillor, *Ojibwe Tales*, 21–2.

42 Hamell, "Trading in Metaphors," 7.

43 Landes, *Ojibwa Religion*, 109–10. Cutfoot is at various times a young boy, a grown man, and later an aged man.

44 Johnston, *Ojibway Heritage*, 80.

45 Benton-Banai, *The Mishomis Book*, 64–5.

46 Cleland gives this figure from an ancient birch bark scroll. *The Place of the Pike*, 2; the "original" figure is given by Hoffman, "The Midê'wiwin," 172a.

47 Hoffman, "The Midê'wiwin," 173. Ninety-year-old Day Dodge and Saycosegay narrated a version of this story. Vizenor, *Anishinabe Adisoka*, 71–5.

48 Blessing, "Medicine Bags and Bundles," 80.

49 Warren, *History of the Ojibway People*, 35, 43–4, 46.

50 Blessing, "Medicine Bags and Bundles," 79–80.

51 Vennum, "Ojibwa Origin–Migration Songs," 785, 79n.

52 Fulford, "Ojibwa Picture Writing," 133, 179, 181–3, with Fulford's translations. He retranslated some of Hoffman's materials and checked them with two Ojibwe who taught the language.

53 Barnouw, "A Chippewa Mide Priest's Description of the Medicine Dance," 81.

54 Vecsey, "Midewiwin Myths of Origin," 451–2.

55 Vizenor, *Anishinabe Adisokan*, 77–85.

56 Vizenor, *Summer in the Spring*, 41, 148.

57 Vizenor, *Summer in the Spring*, 50, 150. Densmore's interpretation of the song scroll is of a "white-haired Mide" spirit rather than a burial song. *Chippewa Music*, 1:60.

58 Hoffman, "The Midê'wiwin," 173.
59 Vecsey, "Midewiwin Myths," 454.
60 A section follows on medicine bags.
61 Balikci, "Note sur le midewiwin," 170.
62 Vecsey, "Midewiwin Myths," 454.
63 Densmore, *Chippewa Customs*, 87.
64 Pettipas, "Tie Creek Study: a Commentary." *Tie Creek Study*, Parts 1 and 2: 6, 15, 75, 83.
65 Landes, *Ojibwa Religion*, 112–13.
66 Lévi-Strauss, *From Honey to Ashes*, 460–4.
67 Albom, *Tuesdays with Morrie*, 141.
68 The Ojibwe established their identity and place in the biosphere through the instrumentality of animals and plants; see Martin, *In the Spirit of the Earth*, 103–4.
69 Cardinal, *The Rebirth of Canada's Indians*, 149.
70 Pomedli, "Ojibway Healing and Ordering," 84.
71 Treaty Three comprises an area in northwestern Ontario and the southeastern part of Manitoba. It was signed between the Ojibwe and the representatives of the British Crown and the federal government in 1873.
72 Morris, *The Treaties of Canada*, 59.
73 Warren, *History of the Ojibway People*, 27.
74 Angel, *Preserving the Sacred*, 142–3.
75 Johnston, *Ojibway Heritage*, 19–20. For an analysis of many Nanabush stories, see Wiget, "Cycle Construction."
76 Vecsey, *Traditional Ojibwa Religion*, 85.
77 Densmore, *Chippewa Customs*, 97.
78 Hewitt, "Nanabozho," 2:19.
79 Vecsey, *Traditional Ojibwa Religion*, 86.
80 Highway, *Dry Lips*, 12.
81 Valentine, "Nenabozho," 590–1.
82 Warren, *History of the Ojibway People*, 8.
83 Coleman, Frogner, and Eich, *Ojibwa Myths*, 56.
84 Coleman, Frogner, and Eich, *Ojibwa Myths*, 55–7.
85 Hoffman, "The Midê'wiwin," 241–2.
86 Benton-Banai, *The Mishomis Book*, 74.
87 Ritzenthaler, "Chippewa Preoccupation with Health," 223. People around the world today are preoccupied with long life and health; in 2004, CBC television asked Canadians to choose "The Greatest Canadian"; they chose the "Father of Medicare," Tommy Douglas.
88 Densmore, *Indian Use of Wild Plants*, 322. See Hallowell, "Ojibwa World View and Disease," 391–448.

89 Ritzenthaler, "Chippewa Preoccupation with Health," 223.

90 Thevet, *Les singularitez*, 1–2.

91 Dickason, "For Every Plant There Is a Use," 11.

92 Beltrami narrated his experiences of performances celebrating plant roots in northern Minnesota in the early nineteenth century. *A Pilgrimage in America*, 403–4.

93 Densmore, *Indian Use of Wild Plants*, 286–305, 322–31.

94 Densmore, *Indian Use of Wild Plants*, 322.

95 Harrison, "The Midewiwin," 156.

96 Rajnovich, *Reading Rock Art*, 136.

97 Balikci, "Note sur le midewiwin," 187.

98 Archives and Collections, Royal Ontario Museum, Toronto.

99 Carpenter, *Eskimo Realities*, 70.

100 Harrison, "The Midewiwin," 89. See Vecsey, "Midewiwin Myths," 464.

101 See Blessing, "Birchbark Mide Scrolls," 116–64.

102 Warren, *History of the Ojibway People*, 61.

103 Reagan, "A Ritual Parchment," 233.

104 Vennum, "Ojibwa Origin–Migration Songs," 753.

105 Deleary, "The Midewiwin," 36.

106 Hilger, *A Social Study*, 110.

107 Morrisseau and Johnston, *The Art of Norval Morrisseau*, 20–5; he illustrates the sacred white bear and bear man.

108 Blessing, "Medicine Bags and Bundles," 127.

109 Warren, *History of the Ojibway People*, 186.

110 A totem/dodem is any being that watches over or assists a group of people, such as a family, clan, or tribe. The totem is usually an animal or other natural figure that spiritually represents a group of related people.

111 Warren, *History of the Ojibway People*, 186.

112 Nesper, *The Walleye War*, 32.

113 Benton-Banai, *The Mishomis Book*, 74, 76–7.

114 Relland, "The Teachings of the Bear Clan," 55.

115 Blessing, "Medicine Bags and Bundles," 76–7.

116 In Ojibwe performances, the water drum is regarded as an other-than-human person. It is generally made of wood, animal skin, and water. See Berbaum, *Ojibwa Powwow World*, 52, 54, 56.

117 Deleary, "The Midewiwin," 78.

118 Haefer, "Foreword," 13.

119 Vecsey, "Midewiwin," 461.

120 Blessing, "Medicine Bags and Bundles," 78.

121 Deleary, "The Midewiwin," 26.

122 Blessing, "Medicine Bags and Bundles," 78–83. The bags Blessing describes are from Cass Lake, Squaw Point on Leech Lake, Inger Village, Red Lake, Possford on the White Earth Reservation, and Mille Lacs.

123 Deleary, "The Midewiwin," 36.

124 Blessing, "Birchbark Mide Scrolls," 118, 126, 162. According to Blessing, "approximately 60 percent of the symbols or hieroglyphs were a true likeness of the object represented … Approximately 40 percent were invented forms which needed interpretation."

125 Barry-Arredondo, "The 'Talking Paper,'" 7. While Schoolcraft maintained that the mnemonic symbols on the birch bark scrolls always had the same meaning, Hoffman noted that the symbols might have variant ones. Thus, a bear might refer to the guardian spirit, to a singer impersonating the bear Manitou, to exorcism of an evil bear spirit, or to the hope of capturing a bear. The person who owned the chart was the one who could single out the intended meaning; see Mason, *Schoolcraft's Expedition to Lake Itasca*, 94; Hoffman, "The Midê'wiwin," 287.

126 Corbiere, "Exploring Historical Literacy," 78.

127 Desveaux, "De l'interdite," 220–1.

128 Chatfield of Cass Lake, Minnesota, "The Midewiwin Songs of Fine-day," 1–2.

129 Barry-Arredondo, "The 'Talking Paper,'" 34. Rajnovich claims that the representations of bear on rock formations are the equivalent of the figures on birch bark scrolls; *Reading Rock Art*, 160.

130 Conway, *Painted Dreams*, 154.

131 Conway, *Painted Dreams*, 9.

132 Conway, *Painted Dreams*, 9, 15, 59.

133 Lanoue, *Images in Stone*, 64.

134 Lévi-Strauss, *The Savage Mind*, 204.

135 Brightman, *Grateful Prey*, 188–95.

136 Lanoue, *Images in Stone*, 65.

137 Lanoue, *Images in Stone*, 65–6.

138 Lanoue, *Images in Stone*, 64.

139 Michelson, "What Happened to Green Bear," 174–5.

140 Dewdney and Kidd, *Indian Rock Paintings*, 46.

141 Desveaux, "De l'interdite," 220–1.

142 Conway, *Painted Dreams*, 151.

143 Hoffman, "The Midê'wiwin," 173. For a contemporary audio of the Mide songs on piano, flute, and drum, as adapted from Hoffman, see Archives and Collections, Carlo Traverso and the Online Distributed Proofreading Team. Thanks to J. Douglas Rabb for this reference.

144 Densmore, *Chippewa Music*, 1:38.
145 Fulford, "Ojibwa Picture Writing," 139.
146 Landes, *Ojibwa Religion*, 97, 103–4. See Pomedli, "Ojibway Healing and Ordering," 77–86.
147 Hoffman, "The Midê'wiwin," 164.
148 Warren, *History of the Ojibway People*, 43–4.
149 See Hoffman, "The Midê'wiwin," 224, 240, 255.
150 Kohl, *Kitchi-Gami*, 49.
151 Theresa S. Smith, *The Island of the Anishnaabeg*, 184.
152 Harrison, "The Midewiwin," 150.
153 Hoffman, "The Midê'wiwin," 169–70.
154 Hoffman, "The Midê'wiwin," 197.
155 Landes, *Ojibwa Religion*, 103–4.
156 Landes, *Ojibwa Religion*, 98–104.
157 Tourangeau, "Visual Art as Metaphor," 135–7.
158 Fulford, "Ojibwa Picture Writing," 126–7.
159 Fulford, "Ojibwa Picture Writing," 186.
160 Fulford, "Ojibwa Picture Writing," 189, 191, 195, 196, 197, 198, 199, 203. Hoffman, "The Midê'wiwin," 248.
161 Schoolcraft, *The Literary Voyager or Muzzeniegun*, 86.
162 Personal communication with Lawrence Martin.
163 Angel, *Preserving the Sacred*, 182.
164 Angel, *Preserving the Sacred*, 12–13.
165 Angel, *Preserving the Sacred*, 205–32. For additional remarks on Ojibwe leadership, see Appendix A.
166 Miller, "Ojibwe Leadership," iii–iv.
167 Angel, *Preserving the Sacred*, 44–5.
168 Bird, *Telling Our Stories*, 101.
169 Chute, "A Unifying Vision," 55–80.
170 Chute, *The Legacy of Shingwaukonse*, 255.
171 Bird, *Telling Our Stories*, 101.
172 Warren, *History of the Ojibway People*, 22–3, and Lovisek, "The Political Evolution," 288.
173 Lovisek, "The Political Evolution," 291.
174 Personal communication with Joan Lovisek, Treaty Three research consultant.
175 Lovisek, "The Political Evolution," 301.
176 Lovisek, "The Political Evolution," 300.
177 See Angel, *Preserving the Sacred*, 42–5.
178 Angel, *Preserving the Sacred*, 56–8.

2. "Paths of the Spirit": Moral Values in the Writings of Four Nineteenth-Century Ojibwe in the Spirit of the Midewiwin

1 Blessing, "Birchbark Mide Scrolls," 127.
2 Blessing, "Birchbark Mide Scrolls," 132.
3 Desveaux thinks that the name "vision quest" might be a misnomer, for the quest involves not only seeing but also fasting and perhaps hallucinations. The quest may not be primarily of the visual type but, in an oral society, that of hearing and following these voices. "Les Grands Lacs," 106.
4 Kugel provides examples of Ojibwe religious/spiritual traditions woven into the political. "Religion Mixed with Politics," 126–37.
5 Jones/Kahkewaquonaby, *History of the Ojebway Indians*, 94–8, 105, 143, 152–3.
6 Jones, *History of the Ojebway Indians*, 84–7.
7 Jones, *History of the Ojebway Indians*, 141–3.
8 Jones, *History of the Ojebway Indians*, 141.
9 See Jones, *History of the Ojebway Indians*, 57, 62.
10 Devens, *Countering Colonization*, 102–4, 107–10, 113.
11 Peterson, "Review of *Many Tender Ties* [1980] and *Strangers in Blood*," 344.
12 Jones, *History of the Ojebway Indians*, 104.
13 Jones, *Life and Journals*, 82–3.
14 Jackson, *The Works of the Rev. John Wesley*, 8:340.
15 Jones, *Life and Journals*, 43–5.
16 Donald B. Smith, *Sacred Feathers*, 74.
17 Donald B. Smith, *Sacred Feathers*, 97.
18 Thanks to Joan Halmo for these observations.
19 A bag of shot or pellets is generally accompanied with a powder horn; Archives and Collections, Trent University Archives.
20 Donald B. Smith, *Sacred Feathers*, 242–3.
21 Axtell, *After Columbus*, 120. Jones was able to create a new identity from two different forces; see Wahpeconiah, "This Once Savage Heart of Mine."
22 Jones, *Life and Journals*, 174. One way of regarding the intelligence and planning that a squirrel exhibits in storing nuts is to consider these attributes as metaphorical. Another approach is to attribute to mammals, such as squirrels, real powers of imagination and foresight. Marc Bekoff and Jessica Pierce do just that; they emphasize that mammals have a broad range of faculties from which flow moral behaviours including those of fairness, compassion, empathy, cooperation, trust, and reciprocity. For these authors, morality is a trait that animals share with humans; *Wild Justice*.
23 See Hele, "'By the Rapids,'" i–ii.

24 Stoehr, "Salvation from Empire," iii.

25 His name actually means black hawk. Blackbird, *History*, 27.

26 We use Odawa and Ottawa interchangeably.

27 See Feest, "Andrew J. Blackbird," 114–23; Cappel, *Odawa Language and Legends*.

28 Blackbird, *History*, 15, 27, 45, 72, 74, 76–7, 102.

29 Blackbird, *History*, 10.

30 Bissell and Blackbird, *Education of Indian Youth*, 7, 9.

31 Blackbird, *History*, 88.

32 Blackbird, *History*, 11.

33 Blackbird, *History*, 24.

34 Blackbird, *History*, 38.

35 Blackbird, *History*, 20.

36 The French were the first Europeans to apply the term *algoumequin* to the people they met in eastern Canada. According to Day, the term may be derived from the Maliseet *elakomkwik*, "they are our relatives." "The Name 'Algonquin,'" 228.

37 Blackbird, *History*, 81–2.

38 Blackbird gives Odawa/Chippewa translations of the Ten Commandments, The [Apostles] Creed, and the Lord's Prayer; *History*, 105–6.

39 Blackbird, *History*, 9; precepts, 88–90.

40 Early Hebrew writers as well as other sages of the past gathered wise and helpful proverbs and precepts. A contemporary compilation, "Native American Values (English and Ojibwe)," comprises thirty-six sayings; thanks to Lawrence Martin for this list of sayings, which has recently circulated quite widely in Anishinaabe country. Jenness, *The Ojibwa Indians of Parry Island*, 80–2, also gives thirty-six directives, which he labels taboos; to these he adds "some curious superstitions" and omens.

41 Blackbird, *History*, 9.

42 Blackbird, *History*, 9–10.

43 Blackbird, *History*, 11.

44 Blackbird, *History*, 85–6.

45 Blackbird, *History*, 9–10. Blackbird quotes the Golden Rule in *The Indian Problem*, 17.

46 Blackbird, *History*, 20. In his *History*, Blackbird is sometimes ambivalent, but generally positive, regarding the worth of the tradition of his ancestors; in his earlier work, Bissell and Blackbird, *Education*, he saw those traditions which upheld the authority of past chiefs as impediments for Indians to succeed as American citizens; they must now embrace a new chief: "We have abandoned our laws, manners and customs, having renounced our

chiefdoms under the most solemn declaration to uphold and support the government of the United States as directed by the *President*, the *head Chief of the Nation.*" Bissell and Blackbird, *Education*, 7–8.

47 Proverbs 13:24: "He that spareth the rod hateth his son; but he that loveth him correcteth him betimes." Proverbs 29:15: "The rod and reproof give wisdom: but the child that is left to his own will bringeth his mother to shame." *The Holy Bible*, Douay Version. This translation of the Bible was the one common among Roman Catholics in Blackbird's day. See Donald B. Smith, *Sacred Feathers*, 74.

48 Blackbird's references are to Boudinot, *A Star in the West*, 216, 225.

49 Boudinot, *A Star in the West*, 225–6.

50 Warren, *History of the Ojibway People*, 62.

51 Blackbird, *History*, 42.

52 Edmunds, *The Shawnee Prophet*, 37.

53 Blackbird, *History*, 9.

54 Blackbird, *History*, 41.

55 Blackbird, *History*, 51. Blackbird, *From the Indian's Standpoint*, 14.

56 Blackbird, *History*, 51–2. By the Treaties of 1836 and 1855, the Little Traverse Bands ceded most of their ancestral lands in Michigan and thereby lost their political and cultural autonomy. At the end of his life, Blackbird reminisced about this painful time: "Their existence as a tribe was extinguished by a treaty with the United States, in the year 1855. Then they were attached to this government, just as you see them now and never again will they have their own government as in former times." Blackbird, *The Indian Problem*, 10.

57 Bissell and Blackbird, *Education*, 13.

58 Blackbird, *The Indian Problem*, 12.

59 We have already underscored the pre-eminence that Blackbird accorded to education for Indians. His appeal was both for the proper use of funds already allocated by the treaties and for additional monies. He is critical of those who did not value educational resources: "But our old men were so blind they could not see nor appreciate this subject." Bissell and Blackbird, *Education*, 12.

60 Blackbird, *History*, 43, 83: Blackbird refers to the Indians as "unwilling parties" in the treaties.

61 Blackbird, *History*, 35.

62 Blackbird, *History*, 84.

63 Walz, "Andrew Jackson Blackbird," 42.

64 Blackbird, *History*, 90.

65 Walz adds that Blackbird's associations with white missionaries were also major influences in his life; "Andrew Jackson Blackbird," 14.

66 Blackbird's father, J.-B. Assiginack, held in tension traditional and European/post-European values; as King, "J.-B. Assiginack," 48, states: "Assiginack had become a symbol of the irretrievable loss of the old ways … His story personifies the dilemma of those individuals from traditional societies who must confront the consuming force of a persistent and ruthless society overwhelming their own." See Leighton, "Assiginack, Jean-Baptiste," 9-10.

67 Bissell and Blackbird, *Education*, 12.

68 Blackbird, *The Indian Problem*, 18–20; this "Lamentation" is reproduced at the end of his life almost word for word from his *History*, 70–1.

69 Blackbird, *The Indian Problem*, 16–17.

70 Walz, "Andrew Jackson Blackbird," 60–1.

71 Walz, "Andrew Jackson Blackbird," 2, 46.

72 Hedrick, *The Land of the Crooked Tree*, 27.

73 Phillips, "Foreword," vii.

74 Copway, *Running Sketches*. For the sorting out of Copway's various reprintings, republishings, and retitlings of his works, see Ruoff, *Life, Letters, and Speeches*.

75 Schmalz, *The Ojibwa of Southern Ontario*, 152.

76 Copway, *The Life, History, and Travels*, 144–5, 295.

77 Copway, *Indian Life and Indian History*, 245.

78 See Pomedli, "True Confessions," 434–56. Conversion to Roman Catholicism remained Baraga's principal aim, however.

79 Copway, *Running Sketches*, 130, 165.

80 Copway, *The Traditional History*, 53: "The law of the nation, like that of ancient Greece, has been enacted with a view to the health of its subjects." Copway also wrote a book of poems about Ojibwe life: *The Ojibway Conquest*. For a contemporary Ojibwe consideration of health, see Norrgard, "Bimaadiziwin: A Healthy Way of Life," (videocassette), Episode 4.

81 Copway, *Life, History, and Travels*, 14–17.

82 Copway, *Life, History, and Travels*. x, 17.

83 Copway, *Indian Life and Indian History*, 97–8.

84 Copway, *Life, History, and Travels*, 20.

85 Copway, *The Traditional History*, 175.

86 Copway, *Life, History, and Travels*, 17.

87 Copway, *Running Sketches*, 331.

88 Copway, *Life, History, and Travels*, 42, 101.

89 Copway, *Life, History, and Travels*, 23–5.

90 Copway, *Life, History, and Travels*, 32–3; *Recollections of a Forest Life*, 159–62.

91 Rex, "Survivance and Fluidity," 25.

92 See Gross, "*Bimaadiziwin*, or the 'Good Life,'" 15–32.

93 Dockstader, *Great North American Indians*, 322. See Warren, *History of the Ojibway People*, 7.
94 Schenck, *William W. Warren*, 109.
95 Warren, *History of the Ojibway People*, 9; we will generally use Schenck's edition for references. See Schenck, "Identifying the Ojibwa," 395–405.
96 Schenck, *William W. Warren*, xi, 30, 32, 52, 98.
97 Schenck, *William W. Warren*, viii.
98 Warren, *History of the Ojibway People*, xx.
99 Warren, *History of the Ojibway People*, 6.
100 Schenck, *William W. Warren*, 167.
101 Warren, *History of the Ojibway People*, 34.
102 Buffalohead, "Introduction." In Warren, *History of the Ojibway Nation*, xiv–xv.
103 Warren, *History of the Ojibway People*, 10. This passage is from the Book of Genesis, 4:9–10.
104 Warren, *History of the Ojibway People*, 35.
105 Warren, *History of the Ojibway People*, 35–6.
106 Warren, *History of the Ojibway People*, 34.
107 Although Warren did not have direct access to Boudinot's writings, the latter's message must have been current, for Warren wrote that he knew of its existence "from hearsay"; *History of the Ojibway People*, 32.
108 Warren, *History of the Ojibway People*, 33.
109 Warren, *History of the Ojibway People*, 61.
110 Warren, *History of the Ojibway People*, 62.
111 For the socio-political centrality of this patrilineal totemic band, see Schenck, *"The Voice of the Crane Echoes Afar."*
112 Warren, *History of the Ojibway People*, 80.
113 Schenck, "William Warren's *History*," 199.
114 Warren, *History of the Ojibway People*, 17.
115 Warren, *History of the Ojibway People*, 137.
116 Henry, *Travels and Adventures in Canada*, 44–5. Warren, *History of the Ojibway People*, 137.
117 Warren, *History of the Ojibway People*, 248–9. See Schoolcraft, *Historical and Statistical Information*, 5:524–7. Schenck notes that "Schoolcraft's mother-in-law, who was Waubojeeg's daughter, was no doubt the source of his information." Warren, *History of the Ojibway People*, 173n8.
118 Warren, *History of the Ojibway People*, 174–5.
119 Warren, *History of the Ojibway People*, 176.
120 Warren, *History of the Ojibway People*, 177–8.

121 Warren, *History of the Ojibway People*, 178. See Schoolcraft, *The Indian in His Wigwam*, 133–45.
122 Warren, *History of the Ojibway People*, 251.
123 Warren, *History of the Ojibway People*, 182–3.
124 Warren, *History of the Ojibway People*, 187–9.
125 Warren, *History of the Ojibway People*, 249. See Schoolcraft, *The Indian in His Wigwam*, 143.
126 Schenck, *William W. Warren*, 107, 109.
127 Warren, "Sioux and Chippewa Wars," in Babcock, "William Whipple Warren," 96.

3. Otter, the Playful Slider

1 According to Landes, *Ojibwa Religion*, 145, "otter, in particular, seemed to guard the first-grade entrance; Weasel, the second; Mink, the third; and Bear, the fourth. Sometimes Bear was said to supervise generally all the grades." Nelson, "Midewiwin Medicine Bags of the Ojibwa," 403, notes that the first-degree skins in his collection include weasel, mink, marten, and otter.
2 For an engaging presentation of many animals, including otter, see Episode 3, "Living Water," *Planet Earth* (TV Series).
3 Cahalane, "Preface," 7.
4 Personal communication with Chief Ron Manitowabi, Wikwemikong, Manitoulin Island, Ontario.
5 Personal communication with Ojibwe researcher, Joan Lovisek.
6 See Paine, *The Nature of Sea Otters*, 5, 11, 107.
7 Haley, *Sleek and Savage*, 12, 106.
8 Haley, *Sleek and Savage*, 110–12.
9 Liers, *An Otter's Story*, cover.
10 Leonard and Briscoe, *Sleeky the Otter*, 79.
11 Rajnovich, *Reading Rock Art*, 58.
12 Chanin, *The Natural History of Otters*, 102–5.
13 Haley, *Sleek and Savage*, 109.
14 Harris, *Otters*, 4–5, 40–1.
15 Desveaux, "Metamorphosis," 39–47; Desveaux, "Les Grands Lacs," 108.
16 See Buffalohead, "Farmers, Warriors, Traders," 236–44; Goulding, "Traditional Role of Aboriginal Women," 1, 10.
17 Harrison, "'He Heard Something Laugh,'" 51

18 Vennum, "Ojibwa Origin–Migration Songs," 784–5. See Warren, *History of the Ojibway People,* 46.
19 Rajnovich, *Reading Rock Art,* 71. See Hoffman, "The Midê'wiwin," 175–7.
20 See Berbaum, *Ojibwa Powwow World,* 45–6.
21 Hoffman, "The Midê'wiwin," 166, 175.
22 Hoffman, "The Midê'wiwin," 282.
23 Hoffman, "The Midê'wiwin," 253.
24 Fulford, "Ojibwa Picture Writing," 120.
25 Rajnovich, *Reading Rock Art,* 98, 100, 101; see Hoffman, "The Midê' wiwin," 208.
26 Vennum, "Ojibwa Origin–Migration Songs," 777–8.
27 Densmore, *Chippewa Music,* 1:23, 47. Johnston, *Ojibway Ceremonies,* specifies otter's presence in the rituals of the Midewiwin.
28 Blessing, "Birchbark Mide Scrolls," 162.
29 Morrisseau, *Legends of My People,* 43.
30 Otter's song is "When I come out the sky becomes clear." Hoffman, "The Midê'wiwin," 203.
31 "Clan System," *Council Fires,* 12. Thanks to Cynthia Bell for this reference.
32 Birch bark bitings involve biting with an eye tooth thin layers of birch bark. The emerging symmetrical designs, done mostly by women, were originally templates for quill-work but are now artworks in themselves. For examples of bitings, see Densmore, *Indian Use of Wild Plants,* 394 and Plate 59.
33 Blessing, "Some Use of Bone," 51, 52.
34 Phillips, "Zigzag and Spiral," 418–19.
35 Desveaux, "Metamorphosis," 41.
36 Hallowell, "Some Empirical Aspects," 390–2.
37 Phillips, "Zigzag and Spiral," 409–19.
38 Coleman, *Decorative Designs,* 2–3. Thanks to Cath Oberholtzer for this reference.
39 Coleman, *Decorative Designs,* 3–4.
40 Skinner, "Medicine Ceremony," 176a and 178a.
41 Phillips, "Zigzag and Spiral," 415.
42 Phillips, "Dreams and Designs," 54, 55, 61. As we will see later, Phillips is not definitive about attributing the zigzag patterns to otter exclusively; that wavy feature can pertain to thunderbirds also.
43 Phillips, "Quilled Bark," 122.
44 Although often considered as trinkets and of not great worth by Europeans, glass beads were treasured alongside and in place of traditional

ornaments in ceremonial contexts. Miller, "A New Perspective on Indian–White Contact," 316.

45 Anderson and Hussey-Arntson, "Ojibwe Bandolier Bags," 46–57. "Pouch. Anishnawbek, Great Lakes, Ontario. Dyed hide, porcupine quills, hemp. Late 18th century–early 19th century." Royal Ontario Museum, Toronto.

46 Whiteford, "The Origin of Great Lakes Beaded Bandolier Bags," 33. Thanks to Marcia Anderson for this reference.

47 Native American Art section of the Minneapolis Institute of Arts, October 2008: 1870 bandolier bag, 2001.62; 1860 bag, 2005.43.

48 Vigorelli, *Gli Oggetti Indiani Raccolti da G. Constantino Beltrami*, 13, 16, 83.

49 Archives and Collections, Minnesota Historical Society Museum.

50 Personal communication, Stan Cuthand, Saskatoon. For international considerations of otters, see Duplaix, *Otters*.

51 Fulford, "Ojibwa Picture Writing," 120.

52 Harrison, "He Heard Something Laugh," 52.

53 Densmore, *Chippewa Customs*, 93. Harrison, "He Heard Something Laugh," 46–53.

54 Densmore, *Chippewa Customs*, 97. See Harrison, "The Midewiwin," 84.

55 Blessing, "Medicine Bags and Bundles," 76–9, 87–8.

56 Blessing, "Medicine Bags and Bundles," 88. See Redsky, *Great Leader of the Ojibway*, 105–8.

57 Deleary, "The Midewiwin," 78.

58 Angel, *Preserving the Sacred*, 44–5.

59 See Pomedli, "Treaties: Rights or Relationships?"

60 Harrison, "He Heard Something Laugh," 52.

61 Desveaux, "De l'interdite," 210; "elles domine toutes les arcanes"; otters govern all mysteries.

62 Hoffman, *The Menomini Indians*, 91–2.

63 This is the depiction on the scroll of James Red Sky of Lac Seul, Ontario. Dewdney, *The Sacred Scrolls*, 62.

64 Pomedli, "Preface," iii–vi.

65 Skinner, "Medicine Ceremony," 179. Since the otter-skin bag has a phallic shape and the cowrie shell a vaginal appearance, for Fulford they signify genital-like activity and are symbols of regeneration. "Manabus and Mitawin," 67–8.

66 Fulford, "Ojibwa Picture Writing," 136.

67 Helbig, *Nanabozhoo*, 72.

68 Redsky, *Great Leader of the Ojibway*, 108.

69 Helbig, *Nanabozhoo*, 104–5.

70 Vizenor, *Anishinabe Adisokan*, 82–3.
71 "Being-in-the-world," a notion from Martin Heidegger, *Being and Time*.
72 Penney, "Great Lakes Indian Art," 17.
73 See Desveaux, "Les Grands Lacs," 104-112.
74 Phillips, *Patterns of Power*, 25, 26.

4. Owls: Images and Voices in the Ojibwe and Midewiwin Worlds

1 Ritzenthaler and Ritzenthaler, *The Woodland Indians*, 87, list snake, fox, or wildcat claw as a third-degree bag.
2 Blessing, "Medicine Bags," 111. Harrison, "'He Heard Something Laugh,'" 51.
3 According to Hoffman, "Notes on Ojibwa Folk-Lore," 218–19, thunderbird or thunder god played a major role for both the Mide and the Jessakkid. It was in charge of the first-degree lodge of the Midewiwin as well as the Jessakkid's Shaking Tent.
4 Landes, *Ojibwa Religion*, 145.
5 See Kinietz, *Chippewa Village*, 207.
6 Blessing, "Birchbark Mide Scrolls," 128.
7 Many birds, including owls, are prominent in everyday experiences and imaginings; see Keen, *Sightings*.
8 The OWL Pages.
9 Armstrong, *The Folklore of Birds*, 113.
10 The OWL Pages.
11 The OWL Pages. Boreal owl is similar to the Saw-whet owl but is somewhat larger.
12 Sparks and Soper, *Owls*, 7.
13 Sparks and Soper, *Owls*, 12–14.
14 Snake, "Nanabush Meets Owl and Rabbit," 49–52. See a similar story edited by Colombo and Laidlaw, *Voices of Rama*, 53. Laidlaw collected these Ojibwe stories from the Rama Reserve, Lake Couchiching, Ontario, between 1915 and 1928.
15 The OWL Pages.
16 The OWL Pages; Sparks and Soper, *Owls*, 23, 27, 29.
17 Ritzenthaler and Ritzenthaler, *The Woodland Indians*, 34.
18 Corbiere, *Ko-ko-ko the Owl*, 2.
19 Corbiere, *Ko-ko-ko the Owl*, 12–24.
20 Hoffman, "The Travels of Manabush," in *The Menomini Indians*, 173.
21 Hoffman gives the name *anamaqkiu* for the underwater creatures and

inamaqkiu for the thunderbirds. He defines the thunderbirds as "deities of the air, who cause the spring rains to come to produce vegetation." *The Menomini Indians,* 296. We will examine the sea creatures in more detail later.

22 Vizenor, *Summer in the Spring,* 149.
23 Kurath, "Chippewa Sacred Songs," 312–13.
24 Coleman, Frogner, and Eich, *Ojibwa Myths,* 40.
25 Coleman, Frogner, and Eich, *Ojibwa Myths,* 41. See Theresa S. Smith, *Island of the Anishnaabeg,* 41n10. A Carrier story accounts for the reason that owls hunt for rabbits and why they have very little down and feathers under their wings and inside their legs. Rossetti, *Musdzi Udada, the Owl,* 4–34.
26 Johnston, *Honour Earth Mother,* 121–2.
27 Densmore, *Chippewa Music,* 1:135.
28 Densmore, *Chippewa Customs,* 114.
29 Odenigun, "Song of the Owl Medicine." Densmore, *Chippewa Music,* 1:105–6. Thanks to Lawrence Martin, Ojibwe, Eau Claire, WI, who shared an Ojibwe owl song from Michigan that gives voice to the spirits of the woods and waters.
30 Barnouw, *Wisconsin Chippewa Myths,* 141–2.
31 Myers, "The Bear-walk (Muck-wa-bim-moo-say)," 17.
32 York, "Kuk-Oh.Chees," in Colombo and Laidlaw, *Voices of Rama,* 41–2.
33 Cosh, "The Owl and the Squaw," 43–4.
34 Marsden, "The Owl Witch," 47–8.
35 Dahlstrom, "Owls and Cannibals Revisited," 92.
36 Densmore, *Chippewa Customs,* 121.
37 Berbaum, *Ojibwa Powwow World,* 74.
38 Molly Loonsfoot, Ojibwe leader, Assinins, MI, referred to owl as protector; personal communication.
39 Morris, "L'homme à-la-peau-de-hibou," "Man with an Owl Skin," 178–9.
40 Barnouw, "The Village of Animals," in *Wisconsin Chippewa Myths,* 141.
41 Michelson, *The Owl Sacred Pack,* 47.
42 Michelson, *The Owl Sacred Pack,* 49.
43 Michelson, *The Owl Sacred Pack,* 55.
44 Michelson, *The Owl Sacred Pack,* 59.
45 Densmore, *Indian Use of Wild Plants,* 326.
46 Jones, *Ojibwa Texts,* 2:531–59.
47 Vizenor, *Summer in the Spring,* 35, 146.
48 Hoffman, *The Menomini Indians,* 179.

49 For an account of the relationship between healing, the Midewiwin, and Treaty Three, see Pomedli, "Ojibway Healing and Ordering," 77–86.

50 Morris, "L'homme au hiboux," 180.

51 Morris, "L'homme aux lagopedes," 181–2; the story is from "Old Times, before human years – a time of great balance." According to the Rock Cree in the neighbouring area of Manitoba, the "good-hearted" share meat and fish while the "bad-hearted" hoard it; the latter action is a violation of trust in the Great Spirit; Brightman, *Grateful Prey,* 158, 377n2.

52 Morris, "Mingesowash (nid d'aigles)," 183–6.

53 Coleman, Frogner, and Eich, *Ojibwa Myths,* 81.

54 A Korean Buddhist film, "Spring, Summer, Fall, Winter ... and Spring," depicts animals as metaphors; a frog, snake, fish, cat, and rooster reveal human frailty and become the instruments of human transcendence. Aesop uses "talking animals in order to make a sharp critique of human foolishness," Gibbs states in Aesop, *Aesop's Fables,* xviii.

55 "How the Sapsucker Got his Colours," 20.

56 Densmore, *Chippewa Music,* 1:105–6; the Mide sings the "Song of the Owl Medicine" in which the medicine is in the form of food to nourish the couple and make them comfortable.

57 Begg, "Kwokwokwo et le vent chaud," 195.

58 Desveaux, *La mythologie,* 1:270.

59 Desveaux, *La mythologie,* 1:272.

60 Desveaux, *La mythologie,* 1:271.

61 Berbaum, *Ojibwa Powwow World,* 47.

62 Johnston, *Ojibway Heritage,* 161.

63 Danley, "When Spring Comes," L6.

64 Begg, "Kashkejabish (chouette de tengmalm)," 2:196.

65 Morris, "Kakabish (chouette de tengmalm) et le rapide," "Kakabish (Boreal Owl) and the Rapids," Desveaux, *La mythologie,* 2:196.

66 In Montagnais accounts, Kukukeshis (Kwokwokwo) engages in a loud, protracted, vocalized see-saw battle with the rapids. In these accounts, Hawk Owl loses his part, just as in the previously recounted story Boreal Owl of Big Trout Lake loses. However, a parallel exists, for in both accounts the competitive owl song and the continuous noise of the river form a consonance of voices. Savard, *Contes indiens,* 33–7.

67 The boreal forest is a vast area of forest and forested area, the largest in the world, extending from Alaska and British Columbia in the west to Newfoundland in the east. The sub-boreal forest is the southern part of this region, from our perspective, in northern Saskatchewan, Manitoba, and Ontario. It is a dense, closed forest that can thin out into open prairie. Marsh, "Forest Regions," 2:670–1.

68 Desveaux, *La mythologie*, 1:269.
69 Berbaum, *Ojibwa Powwow World*, 45.
70 Diamond, Cronk, and von Rosen, *Visions of Sound*, 68.
71 Johnston, *Ojibway Heritage*, 85. The Pantheon in Rome, constructed in the first century, has an opening in its dome so that people can contemplate the heavens.
72 Johnston, *Ojibway Heritage*, 84.
73 Berbaum, *Ojibwa Powwow World*, 46. See Densmore, "The Use of Music in the Treatment of the Sick," 67–76.
74 Hoffman, "Notes on Ojibwa Folk-Lore," 218–19. The transformative possibilities of all beings are evident here. In other accounts, the sacred pole can be viewed as a person. Reviving such sacred emblems as the pole can lead to a re-creation of tribal identity, for the pole spanned many generations, and Aboriginals revering the pole may come to know past traditions, and their deceased who cared for them; thereby they may rediscover a common center. Through the person of the pole, present generations "may carry a blessing forward to their children and grandchildren." Ridington, *Blessing for a Long Time*, 240. We have already noted that the coloured trees typify the four stages of the Midewiwin. James Redsky, "Unpublished Manuscript." Archives and Collections, Thunder Bay Museum.
75 Angeconeb, Debassige, and Thomas, *The Art of the Anishnawbek*. See Archives and Collections, Personal Collection, Ahmoo Angeconeb.
76 Fulford, "Ojibwa Picture Writing," 120, 122n9.
77 "But the owl's song … Manitou's telling of a coming death, speaking with the owl's voice. Manitous don't change their minds, or make mistakes!" Hale, *The Owl's Song*, 147.
78 See the film *I Heard the Owl Call My Name*, based on Craven's novel, *I Heard the Owl Call My Name*. Stan Cuthand, Cree Academic Consultant, Saskatoon, affirms this link between owl and death; personal communication.
79 Badger and Badger, "The Wenebojo Myth from Lac du Flambeau." Barnouw, *Wisconsin Chippewa*, 15–18.
80 Badger and Badger, "Wenebojo's Brother Makes the Road to the Other World," 18. In two additional stories from Lac Courte Oreilles, "Wenebojo in the Whale and his Fight with an Ogre" and "An Old Man in the Form of a Bear," owl is swallowed by a big fish and sings near a boy's burial plot. Barnouw, *Wisconsin Chippewa*, 77–82, 138–40.
81 Vizenor, *Summer in the Spring*, 149.
82 See *The Book of the Dead: The Hieroglyphic Transcript of the Papyrus of Ani*.
83 Barnouw, *Wisconsin Chippewa*, 141–2.
84 Thanks to Joan Lovisek, Ojibwe treaty researcher, Vancouver, BC, for these thoughts.

85 Hoffman, *The Menomini Indians*, 91.
86 Dewdney, *The Sacred Scrolls*, 103.
87 Kohl, *Kitchi-Gami*, 215.
88 Dewdney, *The Sacred Scrolls*, 103–4.
89 Dewdney, *The Sacred Scrolls*, 104–5, 112.
90 Winter, "Kwokwokwo (chouette épervière)," 191–4. In a more complex Swampy Cree story by Joby Maskunow, "Why Owls Die with Wings Out-spread," Horned Owl is both a provider and a prophet; the story involves examining urine and spit to determine paternity. Guss, *The Language of the Birds*, 24-30.
91 Shunien, "The Rabbit and the Saw-whet," 200–3.
92 Thompson, Anishinaabe, Torrance, California; personal communication.
93 Archives and Collections, Thunder Bay Art Gallery. Morris is a member of Muskrat Dam First Nation, now from Sioux Lookout, Ontario.
94 See Morrisseau, "Group of Four Owls;" Sinclair and Pollock, *The Art of Norval Morrisseau*, 169.
95 Copway, *The Traditional History*, 127.
96 In writing about the Ottawa, Claude Allouez notes: "and some other birds are spirits or Manitous, and speak as well as we do; and that there are even people among them who understand the language of birds, as some people understand a little that of the French." Thwaites, *The Jesuit Relations*, 50 (1667), 288–9; Nichols and Nyholm give the Ojibwe terms, "gookooko'oo" for owl, and "gaakaabishiinh" for screech owl. *A Concise Dictionary of Minnesota Ojibwe*, 224.
97 Rajnovich, *Reading Rock Art*, 82.
98 Kohl, *Kitchi-Gami*, 141.
99 Coleman, *Decorative Designs*, 68.
100 Coleman, *Decorative Designs*, 6, 19, displays the swastika design on a child's moccasins suggesting the protection of the four winds.
101 Coleman, *Decorative Designs*, 7.
102 Coleman, *Decorative Designs*, 29. Carrie Lyford points out such designs on an Ojibwe woven bag and bark bags. *The Crafts of the Ojibwa*, Plates 43, 46, 83, 86.
103 Coleman, *Decorative Designs*, 56. See Densmore, *Indian Use of Wild Plants*, 394a, 359b, 359c. See prior chapter on otter for a consideration of birch bark bitings.
104 Coleman, *Decorative Designs*, 71.
105 Coleman, *Decorative Designs*, 82.
106 Coleman, *Decorative Designs*, 70.
107 The "Ojibwa Birchbark Owl Charm" is made of birch bark sewn together with light green embroidery thread; eyes and wings are coloured purple;

it is labelled as a tourist souvenir. Archives and Collections, Minnesota Historical Society Museum.

108 Deloria, *Spirit and Reason*, 147.

109 We are adapting a conclusion that Harold Cardinal made concerning the spiritual stewardship the Cree people had toward timber and the spirit they brought to the treaties. *The Rebirth of Canada's Indians*, 149.

5. Omnipresent and Ambivalent Bears

1 Lynch, *Bears*, x.

2 Webber, *The Bear*, 6–7.

3 Lynch, *Bears*, 2.

4 Lynch, *Bears*, 8–9.

5 www.brownbear.org.

6 Lynch, *Bears*, 19.

7 www.americanbear.org / blackbearfacts.htm.

8 Lynch, *Bears*, 24–34, 51; Herrero, *Bear Attacks*, 149–51.

9 The sounds that animals make recur in songs and stories; see Cavanagh, "Les mythes et la musique naskapis," 5–18.

10 Lynch, *Bears*, 24–34, 51.

11 Lynch, *Bears*, 56.

12 Harrison, "The Midewiwin," 72.

13 Lynch, *Bears*, 109.

14 Lynch, *Bears*, 142, 145.

15 Lynch, *Bears*, 151, 162–3.

16 Lynch, *Bears*, 213–14.

17 Densmore, *Chippewa Customs*, 44.

18 Hallowell, "Some Empirical Aspects," 397, and "Bear Ceremonialism," 1–175.

19 Shepard, "A Post-Historic Primitivism," 285.

20 Landes, *Ojibwa Religion*, 27. For a story about the refusal to eat bear meat, see Marsden, "The Girl and the Bear," 70.

21 Brightman, *Grateful Prey*, 142. See Harrison, "The Midewiwin," 74.

22 Hallowell, "Ojibwa Metaphysics," 74. For accounts of bearwalkers, see Dorson, *Bloodstoppers*, 26–37. For a recounting of the fused identities of bears and humans, see Helbig, *Nanabozhoo*, 33, and Speck, *Myths and Folk-lore*, 28–38.

23 Hallowell, "Ojibwa Metaphysics," 75. For a consideration of the Ojibwe and their use of ambiguities in "etiquette," see Black, "Ojibwa Questioning Etiquette," 13–29.

24 Johnston, *The Bear-Walker*, 9. For a contemporary perception of the plasticity of animal forms, see Geyshick and Doyle, *Stories by an Ojibway Healer*, 62–3.

25 Stevenson, "The Bear Whisperer," F7.

26 Kohl, *Kitchi-Gami*, 35.

27 Rockwell, *Giving Voice to Bear*, 6.

28 Brown, *The Spiritual Legacy*, 28.

29 Rockwell, *Giving Voice to Bear*, 89.

30 Rockwell, *Giving Voice to Bear*, 145, 161.

31 Barry, "Postmodern Bears," 95.

32 Barry, "Postmodern Bears," 99–100.

33 Desveaux, "Metamorphosis as a Limit," 39–47.

34 Chiefs were leaders of their communities in various tasks such as that of ricing.

35 Hilger, "Lac Courte Oreilles: Interviews with Elders," Part 2, Tape 6, 98–9.

36 Hoffman, "The Midê'wiwin," 163.

37 Morrisseau, *Legends of My People*, 55.

38 Martin, "Animal Forms of Manidog," 249–50.

39 Morrisseau, *Legends of My People*, 45.

40 Rockwell, *Giving Voice to Bear*, 16.

41 Vizenor, *Summer in the Spring*, 45, 149.

42 Vizenor, *Dead Voices*, 5–42, passim. The *wanaki game* that Bagese, the bear bag lady, plays is like tarot cards. In the *wanaki game*, words and pictures evoke the presence of animals that reveal associative personal possibilities; see *Dead Voices*, 80–9.

43 Kohl, *Kitchi-Gami*, 408.

44 Griffin, *Animal Minds*, 274–5.

45 Higgins, *Whitefish Lake Ojibway Memories*, 14.

46 Hallowell, "Ojibwa Metaphysics," 74.

47 Hallowell, "Bear Ceremonialism," 148. Preston, *Cree Narrative*, 215–18.

48 Shepard and Sanders, *The Sacred Paw*, xiii–xiv.

49 Morrisseau, *Legends of My People*, 39. According to Skinner, bear paws and marrow were forbidden in the diet of children "lest they should acquire the savage nature of the brute while young and impressionable." "Political Organization," 510. Eating the marrow of bears could make children lazy; Harrison, "The Midewiwin," 73.

50 Skinner, "Bear Customs," 203–9.

51 Tanner, *A Narrative*, 351, 354; the words to the ritual symbol are "That which I take (is) blood, that which I take."

52 Morrisseau, *Legends of My People*, 39.

53 Morrisseau, *Legends of My People*, 41.
54 Skinner, "Notes on the Eastern Cree and Northern Saulteaux," 162.
55 Casagrande, "John Mink," 480, and "Ojibwa Bear Ceremonialism," 113–14.
56 Skinner, "Notes on the Eastern Cree and Northern Saulteaux," 162.
57 Tanner, *A Narrative*, 362.
58 Morrisseau, *Legends of My People*, 43; see Mandelbaum, *The Plains Cree*, 165.
59 Fulford, "Manabus and Mitawin," 67–9. See Skinner, "Medicine Ceremony," 88; and Hoffman, *The Menomini Indians*, 75.
60 Tanner, *A Narrative*, 361. According to Emerson, "*Chemung* is an Indian word for *soul*, literally *shadow* – a figure of speech, or metaphoric word, like the ghost (*geist*) of the Saxon." *Indian Myths*, 380n1.
61 See Hallowell, "Bear Ceremonialism," 43–7; Speck, *Naskapi*, 100; and Tanner, *Bringing Home Animals*, 138–9, 145–6.
62 Speck, *Naskapi*, 97.
63 Harrison, "The Midewiwin," 80–1, 104.
64 See Warren, *History of the Ojibway People*, 43–4.
65 See Fulford, "Ojibwa Picture Writing," 2.
66 Harrison, "The Midewiwin," 11–12, 21–30, 72–6, 102. Harrison studied fifty scrolls in three main collections from Saskatchewan, Manitoba, Ontario, and Minnesota; she analysed twenty-one scrolls in detail.
67 For technological and oral approaches to symbols, see Pomedli, "Foreword," iii–vi.
68 Landes, *Ojibwa Religion*, 118. For a consideration of the sweat lodge, see Appendix B.
69 Landes, *Ojibwa Religion*, 121–2.
70 Blessing, "Medicine Bags and Bundles," 111.
71 Benton-Banai, *The Mishomis Book*, 77.
72 Hoffman, "The Midê'wiwin," 172a; Dewdney, *The Sacred Scrolls*, 148–51.
73 Coleman, *Decorative Designs*, 65.
74 Densmore, *Indian Use of Wild Plants*, 323.
75 Hoffman, "The Midê'wiwin," 262.
76 Landes, *Ojibwa Religion*, 136; Morrisseau, *Legends of My People*, 43.
77 Hoffman, "The Midê'wiwin," 196.
78 Fulford, "Ojibwa Picture Writing," 180.
79 Hoffman, "The Midê'wiwin," 168.
80 Landes, *Ojibwa Religion*, 145–6; Hoffman, "The Midê'wiwin," 168; Johnston, *Ojibway Heritage*, 86.
81 Hoffman, "The Midê'wiwin," 169.
82 Hoffman, "The Midê'wiwin," 211.

83 Hoffman, "The Midê'wiwin," 256. "Among all the animals with which
they are familiar, there is none more impressive to the minds of the Eastern Cree than the black bear"; Skinner, "Bear Customs," 203. "The Ojibwa
considered the bear the most sacred of animals"; Coleman, "The Religion
of the Ojibwa," 54.

84 Dewdney, *The Sacred Scrolls*, 150–1.

85 Fulford, "Ojibwa Picture Writing," 116.

86 Redsky, *Great Leader of the Ojibway*, 102.

87 Dewdney, *The Sacred Scrolls*, 31–2.

88 Dewdney, *The Sacred Scrolls*, 31, 97.

89 Hoffman, "The Midê'wiwin," 262.

90 Vennum, "Ojibwa Origin–Migration Songs," 784. Warren, *History of the
Ojibway People*, 44–5.

91 Grim, "The Shaman," 83.

92 Bishop argues for the existence of Aboriginal clans before European historic times. "The Question of Ojibwa Clans," 44.

93 Schenck, "William W. Warren's History," 199. We have already noted this
in Warren's moral plan.

94 Mason, *Schoolcraft's Expedition to Lake Itasca*, 94.

95 Williams, *Schoolcraft's Indian Legends*, 190.

96 Bray, *The Journals of Joseph N. Nicollet*, 187.

97 See Schenck, "The Algonquian Totem and Totemism," 341–53.

98 Warren, *History of the Ojibway People*, 23. See "The Legend of the Bear
Family," *Wawatay News*, July 30, 1998, 10, about a Penobscot boy who had
bristles on his upper back and shoulders, and who exhibited bear manners that continued into his marriage and were manifest in his children.
The anonymous author, however, does not indicate whether the boy
belonged to the bear clan.

99 Fulford, "Ojibwa Picture Writing," 3–4, 130–1. Fulford examined twenty-
six song scrolls recorded by Hoffman from the White Earth Reservation.
Mallery provided Fulford with four additional song scrolls; *Picture-
Writing*, 1:232a.

100 Fulford, "A Structural Analysis of Mide Song Scrolls," 135.

101 Fulford, "Ojibwa Picture Writing," 126.

102 Peacock, *Ojibwe Waasa Inaabidaa*, 36–7.

103 Warren, *History of the Ojibway People*, 80.

104 Hilger, *Chippewa Child Life*, 154.

105 Animals provided one basis for Ojibwe placement in society; land was
another; see Turnbull, "Indicating Alliance."

106 This "delegation of 11 Chippewa from Lake Superior … asked the government for a retrocession of some portion of the lands which the nation

had formerly ceded to the United States [in 1842]." Schoolcraft, *Historical and Statistical Information*, 1:414–15.

107 See Tanner, *A Narrative*, 343.

108 Myers, "The Bear-walk,"12–18. For more twentieth-century experiences of bearwalkers, see Dorson, *Bloodstoppers*, 26–37, and Tanner, *A Narrative*, 343.

109 Harrison, "The Midewiwin," 79; Vecsey, *Traditional Ojibwa Religion*, 172; Warren, *History of the Ojibway People*, 68–69.

110 Johnston, *The Bear-Walker*, 8.

111 Warren, *History of the Ojibway People*, 67–69.

112 Tanner, *A Narrative*, 343. See also Barnouw, *Wisconsin Chippewa Myths*, 138–9.

113 Hoffman, "The Midé'wiwin," 230. A great fomenter of terror was a bear-walker on Manitoulin Island, Ontario. In 1945, James Nahwaikezhik from the Sheguiandah Reserve killed his father and threatened his mother because he believed they were "bear-walking" him, although at his trial he "said the demon was in the form of a hoot-owl." Myers, "The Bear-walk," 12–18. See Jones, "The Man Who Took Revenge in the Form of a Bear," in "Ojibwa Tales," 387; Hallowell, "Ojibwa Metaphysics," 75.

114 Southcott, *The Sound of the Drum*, 72–4: "Envy is at the root of bearwalking … To be outstanding in any way is not culturally approved by the Anishnabec"; see James Jacko's painting, "Bearwalk," 102.

115 Stevens, *Sacred Legends*, 109–10.

116 Penesi, "The Man Who Transformed Himself into a Bear," Jones, *Ojibwa Texts*, 249–51.

117 Jones, *History of the Ojebway Indians*, 145.

118 Archives and Collections, Art Gallery of Ontario. Andrea Carlson, an Ojibwe painter, not of the Woodland School, gives interactive renditions with animals, while James Denomie gives surrealistic ones; Archives and Collections, Minnesota Artists Exhibition Program Gallery. See McLuhan and Hill, *Norval Morrisseau*, 87, 90, and Ryan, *The Trickster Shift*.

119 McLuhan and Hill, *Norval Morrisseau*, 56, 58.

120 Savard, *Contes indiens*, 4, 70. Several images are given of Tshakapesh: hero-transformer, young man who draws a line behind himself, spider, and perfect man.

121 Vizenor, *Summer in the Spring*, 91–2.

122 Barry, "Postmodern Bears," 93. See Vizenor, *Fugitive Poses*, 170, and "The Midewiwin," 71–5; Johnston, *Ojibway Heritage*, 86.

123 Vizenor, "The Ruins of Representation," 144.

124 Oily meat was well suited for insulation in harsh winters, was very appetizing, and was used in many recipes. Bear skins were used for footwear

and clothes. Wallace, "The Role of the Bear," 38–9, 41. See Pomedli, "Treaties: Rights or Relationships?"

125 Ojibway Sharing Circle, "The Bear, Part of the Big Dipper." For more on bears as celestial, see Appendix C.

126 Callahan, "Interpreting the Pictographs of North Hegman Lake, Minnesota;" http://www.tc.umn.edu/~call0031/Hegman.html.

127 For ways that the Anishinaabe name celestial beings, consult Callahan, "Interpreting the Pictographs." See Jones, *Ojibwa Texts,* 1:193n1.

128 Jenness, *The Ojibwa Indians of Parry Island,* 37.

129 Jenness, *The Ojibwa Indians of Parry Island,* 37n1.

130 For the leadership role of the Dawn Men, see Morrison, "Dawnland Directors," 495–517.

131 Miles and Peters, "The Big Dipper and Colors of Autumn;" http://starryskies.com/articles/dln/9-97/dipper.colours.html. A children's story tells and illustrates the Anishinaabe's changing seasons: Scribe, *Murdo's Story.*

132 Desveaux, "Mythologie et astronomie," 205–17. In Greek stories, the Pleiades, the seven daughters of Atlas who were changed into stars, are called in Ojibwe *makostekwaan/maddodisson,* which means bear's head; Kohl, *Kitchi-Gami,* 118–19. See Claude Lévi-Strauss, *The Origin of Table Manners,* 362–3, for a Menomini account of the role of bears in the origin of the alternation of the days and seasons.

133 Johnston, *Honour Earth Mother,* 122. For an account of the sky creature, Little Image, who slew monster bears and protected human beings, see Jones, "Ojibwa Tales," 370.

134 Blessing, *The Ojibway Indians Observed,* 249. Veteran music historian Vennum observed the remarkable continuity of the rhythms and melodies of Ojibwe song structures from earliest recordings to present usage in powwows; "Indexing Ojibwe Melody."

135 Reagan, "Medicine Songs of George Farmer," 332–69.

136 McNally, *Ojibwe* Songs, 32.

137 Desveaux, "De l'interdite," 224.

138 Densmore writes of harsh and discordant songs; *Chippewa Music,* 1:4.

139 Densmore, *Chippewa Music,* 1:27. There was more recorded music of the Ojibwe at the turn of the twentieth century than for any other Aboriginal group; Vennum, "A History of Ojibwa Song Form," 44. Parthun concludes that the Ojibwe "are a musical people historically and presently." "Ojibwe Music," 297.

140 Vizenor, *Summer in the Spring,* 26, 143.

141 Vizenor, *Summer in the Spring*, 37, 147.

142 Diamond, Cronk, and von Rosen, *Visions of Sound*, 63, 90, 103.

143 Densmore, *Folk Music of the United States*, 7.

144 Vizenor, *Summer in the Spring*, 39, 148. For these songs on "a long-playing vinyl record, duplicated from original wax cylinders," see Densmore, *Folk Music of the United States*.

145 Fulford, "Ojibwa Picture Writing," 135–6, 178.

146 Wolfart, *Âh-âyîtaw isi ê-kî-kiskêyihtahkik maskihkiy*, 62–81.

147 Fiddler, "Legend of Wisakachak and the Bear's Fat." *Wawatay News*, 22 August 1991, 15, and 19 September 1991, 11.

148 Midasuganj/Ten Claw, "Nanabushu is Miraculously Fed Bear-Grease," in Jones, *Ojibwa Texts*, 1:311–15; Wasagunackank/He-that-Leaves-the-Imprint-of-His-Foot-Shining-in-the-Snow, from Pelican Lake, near Bois Fort Reservation, narrates another version of this story; 1:xvii, 341–9. For a narrative of bear as a source of food, see Danziger, *The Chippewas of Lake Superior*, 21, and Densmore, *Chippewa Customs*, 100–1.

149 Densmore, *Indian Use of Wild Plants*, 322. For a contemporary story of illness, specifically diabetes, and health, see McLeod, "Nanabush and the Pale Stranger," *Wawatay News*, 24 April 1992, 14.

150 There is a secretiveness about the Midewiwin, judging by the hesitancy to speak about the ceremonies. Balikci, "Note sur le midewiwin," 192.

151 Rockwell, *Giving Voice to Bear*, 77.

152 Densmore, *Indian Use of Wild Plants*, 324.

153 Densmore, *Indian Use of Wild Plants*, 325.

154 Williams, *Schoolcraft's Indian Legends*, 46–55.

155 Anuqcuag/Richard La Fortune, "Tell Me a Story … Raven Makes a Necklace." *Wawatay News*, 28 July 1994, 28.

156 Lévi-Strauss, *The Origin of Table Manners*, 66–7.

157 Schwarz, *Windigo*, 11–13.

158 Mallery, *Picture-Writing*, 2:481.

159 Rajnovich, *Reading Rock Art*, 103.

160 Hoffman, *The Menomini Indians*, 169–73.

161 Coleman, *Decorative Designs*, 6–7, 44.

162 Coleman, *Decorative Designs*, 11–12, 65.

163 Coleman, *Decorative Designs*, 82.

164 Coleman, *Decorative Designs*, 76; there is a photograph of a bear-paw Mide bag in the Cass Lake Museum. See Densmore, *Chippewa Music*, 1:38. Kohl mentions Mide bags made of skins of wildcats, bears, otters, and snakes; *Kitchi-Gami*, 44. Densmore found that bear paws, wildcat paws, and skins

of the weasel, mink, owl, and rattlesnake were used for medicine bags; Densmore, *Chippewa Customs*, 93. See Lyford, *The Crafts of the Ojibwa*, 102, and Leenbach, "Crafts and Cultural Contact."

165 Coleman, *Decorative Designs*, 79–80.

166 Coleman, *Decorative Designs*, 89.

167 Coleman, *Decorative Designs*, 80.

168 Oberholtzer, "If Bears Could Talk," 270. See Speck, *Naskapi*, 110.

169 Oberholtzer, "If Bears Could Talk," 270. See Preston, "Ritual Hangings," 143, Tanner, "Outlines of the Geography," 688, Speck, *Naskapi*, 237, and Howey and O'Shea, "Bear's Journey," 261–82.

170 Oberholtzer, "If Bears Could Talk," 270–1. See Brown and Brightman, *The Orders of the Dreamed*, 190.

171 Dewdney, *The Sacred Scrolls*, 32.

172 Preston, *Cree Narrative*, 82; Dewdney, *The Sacred Scrolls*, 32, gives images of the bear's tongue.

173 Oberholtzer, "If Bears Could Talk," 272. See Ewers, "The Awesome Bear," 37–8.

174 Brown and Brightman, *The Orders of the Dreamed*, 190.

175 Oberholtzer, "If Bears Could Talk," 272. See Charlevoix, *Histoire*, 118. For women as healers, see Burnett, *Taking Medicine*.

176 Reagan, "A Ritual Parchment," 242. In another account, both bear and snake minister to those on the other side of death and dance in the mornings; Balikci, "Note sur le midewiwin," 176.

177 Ritzenthaler and Ritzenthaler, *The Woodland Indians*, 87.

178 Balikci, "Note sur le midewiwin," 172.

179 Phillips, "Zigzag and Spiral," 418–19. See Hallowell, "The Role of Dreams," 267–89.

180 Ferrara, *Emotional Expression*," 44, 47.

181 Coleman, *Decorative Designs*, 70.

182 A'Llerio, "Craft, Ritual, and World View," iii.

183 Coleman, *Decorative Designs*, 6, 19–22.

184 Phillips, "Zigzag and Spiral," 409, 416–17.

185 See Balikci, "Note sur le midewiwin," 195.

186 A'Llerio, "Craft, Ritual, and World View," 112.

187 A'Llerio, "Craft, Ritual, and World View," 106.

188 See Oberholtzer, "Are Diamonds a Cree Girl's Best Friend?" 351.

189 Phillips, "Dreams and Designs," 58–62.

190 Phillips, "Zigzag and Spiral," 417–18.

191 Bressani, "A Brief Account of Certain Missions," 38 (1653), 251–3.

192 Oberholtzer, "A Womb with a View," 269.
193 Ellis, *"Now then, still another story,"* 7–8; see Jones, *Legends of the James Bay Lowlands,* 9–10.
194 Oberholtzer, "A Womb with a View," 270.
195 Preston, "Competent Social Behavior," 212. Oberholtzer, "A Womb with a View," 270.
196 Morrisseau and Johnston, *The Art of Norval Morrisseau,* 22.
197 Morrisseau and Johnston, *The Art of Norval Morrisseau,* 22. Jones, "The Boy and the Bear," in "Ojibwa Tales," 387. A Bois Fort story by Penesi, "The Boy That Was Carried Away by a Bear," in Jones, *Ojibwa Texts,* 2:271–8. Rae, "The Bearchild," 35–6.
198 Schwarz, *Windigo,* 9. Preston sees this communication in a more affective way; *Cree Narrative,* 212.
199 Morrisseau, "Foreword." Schwarz, *Windigo,* 10.
200 Morrisseau and Johnston, *The Art of Norval Morrisseau,* 16–17.
201 Chartier, "Exhibit Focuses on the Bear Facts." *Saskatoon Sun,* 31 August 2003, 3.
202 Benton-Banai, *The Mishomis Book,* 42–4.
203 Przybilla and Councillor, *Ojibwe Tales,* 27–30.
204 Pete, "Winabijou Looks for the Wolf," 99.
205 Begg, "Makwa (ours) et l'arbre," 2:213. In another story, Old Man calls bear many names such as homely, stub-tail, humped-up big fool, and slow; at first, industrious bear ignores the rhetoric, but eventually gives chase. Linderman, "Old-Man and his New Weapons," in *Indian Old-Man Stories,* 71–80. See "How the Bear Lost His Tale," in Colombo and Laidlaw, *Voices of Rama,* 4–7.
206 Barkman, "Makwa et makikinak (ours et tortue)," 2:216–19.
207 In our section on owls, we noticed that they are in conflict with elements of nature and with one another. Thus, Boreal Owl's voice competes with the roaring river, and Boreal Owl and Hawk Owl vie with each other in a paternity suit.
208 Hoffman, *The Menomini Indians,* 91–2, 131–6. There are many earthdiver stories such as those recorded by Schoolcraft from Sault Ste Marie, Ontario; Williams, *Schoolcraft's Indian Legends,* 67–83. Vizenor focuses on earthdivers in the present clash of civilizations; *Earthdivers,* 9; modern earthdivers are the mixed bloods, "tribal tricksters and recast cultural heroes, the mournful and whimsical heirs and survivors of that premier union between the daughters of the woodland shamans and white fur traders."

209 Johnston, *Ojibway Heritage*, 14.
210 Desveaux, *Sous le signe de l'ours*, 215. For the "reason" that bear is somewhat of an isolated character, see Sandy, "The Man and the Bears," 7–8.
211 Hoffman, *The Menomini Indians*, 131–6.
212 Hoffman, *The Menomini Indians*, 135.
213 Hoffman, *The Menomini Indians*, 135.
214 Jones, *Ojibwa Texts*, 2:507–13.
215 Brébeuf, "Hurons," 185–7. See Adamski, "An Upstream Battle," 31.
216 "Musqua and the Greedy Ones." *Wawatay News*, 21 June 1990, 24.
217 Przybilla and Councillor, *Ojibwe Tales*, 31–5. In another account, "Chipmunk Gets his Stripes," owl gave those marks to chipmunk; Dunn, *Winter Thunder*, 95–6.
218 "How Bear Lost his Tail," in Dunn, *Winter Thunder*, 89–90.
219 "The Origin of Maple Sugar and of Menstruation," in Hoffman, *The Menomini Indians*, 173–5.

6. Water Creatures

1 Chisholm and Gutsche remark about this site: "Reverence is drawn out of you." *Superior*, 77.
2 Dewdney, "Ecological Notes," 21.
3 Mallery, *Picture-Writing*, 2:481–2.
4 See Gile, "The Thunderbird and Underwater."
5 Hoffman, "The Midê'wiwin," 168–169a.
6 Snake, "Tell Me the Story," *Wawatay News*, 14 July 1994, 24–5.
7 Dewdney, *The Sacred Scrolls*, 110.
8 Thwaites, *The Jesuit Relations*, 50 (1667), 285–9.
9 Private conversation with Blue Sky Woman, guide, National Museum of the American Indian, New York, 2007. See Archives and Collections, National Museum of the American Indian, Carl Ray and Roy Thomas.
10 Bourgeois, *Ojibwa Narratives*, 42, editor's note.
11 Asikinack, "Anishinabe (Ojibway) Legends," 157–8.
12 Edmonds and Clark, "The Great Serpent and the Great Flood," in *Voices of the Winds*, 247–50.
13 Delia Oshogay, "Wenebojo Myths from Lac Courte Oreilles," in Barnouw, *Wisconsin Chippewa Myths*. See also "The Prophecy of Jonas," 2:1–11, in *The Holy Bible*, Douay Version.
14 Barnouw, *Wisconsin Chippewa Myths*, 78–9.
15 Barnouw, *Wisconsin Chippewa Myths*, 254.
16 Tanner, *A Narrative*, 95.

17 Landes, *The Ojibwa Woman*, 115–16.
18 Barnouw, *Wisconsin Chippewa Myths*, 18.
19 See Przybilla and Councillor, *Ojibwe Tales*, 21–2; Hamell, "Trading in Metaphors," 7. Penesi of Fort William narrates in "The Spirit-world" that one who died and rose from the dead found in the land of the dead "some large blueberries hanging aloft, some raspberries too. If any one ate them, not again would one return home." Jones, *Ojibwa Texts*, 2:311.
20 Roseau River Chapter, *Tie Creek Study*, 33–4.
21 Tanner, *A Narrative*, 367, 377. Mallery, *Picture-Writing*, 2:182. Rajnovich, *Reading Rock Art*, 103.
22 Tanner, *A Narrative*, 378.
23 Coleman, *Decorative Designs*, 65.
24 Corbiere, "Exploring Historical Literacy," 6.
25 Rajnovich, *Reading Rock Art*, 9.
26 Chief Snake of the Coldwater Reserve in Ontario; Schmalz, *The Ojibwa of Southern Ontario*, 161.
27 Rajnovich, *Reading Rock Art*, 71.
28 Hoffman, "The Midê'wiwin," 291a. Steinbring notes that in the boulder art in Whiteshell Provincial Park, Manitoba, turtle and snake effigies predominate; "Boulder Art in Eastern Manitoba," 3.
29 Coleman, *Decorative Designs*, 80.
30 Private communication in 1999. Toulouse, "Bimaadziwin (the Good Life)," 50, 87, 174, 182.
31 Mallery relies on a figure drawn by Little Hill, a Winnebago chief from the Upper Mississippi, who with his people represent wild cat "as their medicine animal"; *Picture-Writing*, 2:482.
32 Tanner, *A Narrative*, 345–6. See Chisholm and Gutsche, *Superior*, 117.
33 Mallery, *Picture-Writing*, 2:482.
34 Jones, "Ojibwa Tales," 387.
35 Theresa S. Smith, "Oral Traditions," 2:676.
36 Conway and Conway, *Spirits on Stone*, 91, note that the generic term, *peshu*, meaning lynx or cat, was often translated as lion once the Ojibwe learned about lions from the British coat of arms and other sources.
37 Theresa S. Smith, "Oral Traditions," 2:675–6. Apprehensive feelings about snakes might be generally prevalent, but such was not the case for many/most cultures in the past. Even today serpents are associated positively with medicine and history. Many military medical corps and the medical profession itself use the symbolism of the sceptre of Aesculapius, the Greco-Roman god of medicine and healing; this sceptre is also called the

caduceus, a winged staff with two serpents twined about it. Snakes came to be associated with Aesculapius because of their wisdom and ability to cure illness. "Their skin-shedding ability represented healing, longevity, and immortality – the ability to slough off old age and become young again. They symbolized convalescence in their ability to change from lethargy to rapid activity ... Serpents in ancient myths are often said to have knowledge of life-restoring plants." Serpents also have a relationship to phallic symbolism, eroticism, and fertility. Today some cultures employ snakes in various forms of burlesque dances and as aphrodisiacs. Ritter and Ritter, "Prehistoric Pictography," 206. In pre-Inca and Inca cultures, the snake par excellence represented the underworld, one of the three levels of the world. In these cultures, eagle or condor represented the upper world, and puma or cat the middle world; see Osborne, *South American Mythology*, 26.

38 Dewdney and Kidd, *Indian Rock Painting*, 81–2. See Rajnovich, *Reading Rock Art*, 13, 98, 103. Chisholm and Gutsche, *Under the Shadow*, 65.

39 "Great Sturgeon Teaches a Lesson about Greed," *Wawatay News*, Nov. 4, 1993, 21. According to Hannibal-Paci, sturgeon had a complex and varied place in Ojibwe cosmology; "'His Knowledge and my Knowledge,'" 215.

40 Morris, "The Gift of Trout," 2006.

41 "Great Sturgeon Teaches a Lesson about Greed," 21.

42 Vecsey, *Traditional Ojibwa Religion*, 75.

43 Charlevoix, *Journal of a Voyage*, 1:243, 356; 2:5.

44 Charlevoix, *Journal of a Voyage*, 2:44.

45 Archives and Collections, Collection of Gabe and Michele Vadas and Norval Morrisseau. The New York exhibit in which this drum appeared was titled, "Norval Morrisseau: Shaman Artist."

46 Morrisseau, "Androgyny." Blue Sky Woman, interpreter for the New York exhibition, sugggested that generally Morrisseau was inspired by rock paintings.

47 Menitove and Danford, *Woodlands*, 25.

48 We discussed the term "keeper" in the Introduction.

49 Hamell, "Trading in Metaphors," 26–8. See Miller and Hamell, "A New Perspective on Indian–White Contact," 176–93.

50 Toulouse, "Bimaadziwin (the Good Life)," 13.

51 See Vennum, *The Ojibwa Dance Drum*, 44–5, and Barrett, *The Dream Dance*, 256–7.

52 Green, *Ahmoo Angeconeb*. For the unitive ties that Ojibwe art creates, see Tourangeau, "Visual Art as Metaphor."

53 Colombo and Laidlaw, *Voices of Rama*, 23.

54 Colombo and Laidlaw, *Voices of Rama*, 20–1.

55 Colombo and Laidlaw, *Voices of Rama*, 21.

56 Colombo and Laidlaw, *Voices of Rama*, 21.

57 Johnston, *Mermaids and Medicine Women*, 67–71.

58 Colombo and Laidlaw, *Voices of Rama*, 22–3.

59 Colombo and Laidlaw, *Voices of Rama*, 23–4.

60 Colombo and Laidlaw, *Voices of Rama*, 24–5.

61 Martinez, "Along the Horizon a World Appears," 256–62. See Morrison, *Morrison's Horizon*, 174–5.

62 Valentine, "Nenabozho and the Ojibwa Woman," 605.

63 Warren, *History of the Ojibway People*, 60.

64 Peters, "Wa-bish-kee-pe-nas," 53–60. For comments on pre-contact archeological finds of copper, silver, lead, pigments, dyes, clays, and pipestone, see Zedeño, *Traditional Ojibway Resources*, 65–70.

65 Warren, *History of the Ojibway People*, 61n6. See Martin, *Wonderful Power*, 153–80.

66 Vizenor, *The People Named the Chippewa*, 58–9.

67 Charlevoix, *Journal of a Voyage*, 2:45, 208. Charlevoix apparently relies on the seventeenth-century account of Le Mercier; *The Jesuit Relations*, 50 (1667), 265–7.

68 Hamell, "Trading in Metaphors," 25.

69 Thwaites, *The Jesuit Relations*, 50 (1667), 265–7. In a note to this section, Thwaites states: "The copper of Lake Superior was well known among the Algonkin tribes when the French began to settle in Canada, and early writers frequently mention the mines of that region." He adds that two of the difficulties in the copper mining operation were getting access to the copper deposits and then transporting the ore on the lakes; Thwaites, *The Jesuit Relations*, 50 (1667), 327n28. For further remarks on the Ojibwe relationship to copper, see Appendix D.

70 Allouez, *The Jesuit Relations*, 50 (1667), 285–9.

71 Tanner, *A Narrative*, 179–80.

72 Leighton, "Assiginack," 9–10. This account is recorded by Francis Assiginack, who in other places signs himself as "A Warrior of the Odahwahs." See Schmalz, *The Ojibwa of Southern Ontario*, 25, 273n17.

73 Kohl, *Kitchi-Gami*, 62.

74 Henry, *Travels and Adventures in Canada*, 137.

75 Schoolcraft, *Historical and Statistical Information*, 4 (1854) 266–7, 277–8.

76 Densmore, *Chippewa Music*, 2:145.

77 Flacelière, *Greek Oracles*, 4.

78 Villeneuve, *Nanna Bijou*, 225–6.

79 Gray, "I Will Fear No Evil," 27–30.

80 Chaput, "Michipicoten Island Ghosts," 218–21. Chisholm and Gutsche, *Superior*, 101, points to the pitiful conditions of the mines and their failures leading to declarations of bankruptcy.

81 Long, *Ghosts of the Great Lakes*, 143.

82 According to some psychologists and philosophers, the proper term for a disposition toward the relative nothingness exhibited by these peculiar beings/appearances is anxiety, not fear, for fear is engendered by something/someone specific. In references that are initially internal and psychological, and that pertain to anxiety, philosopher Bollnow writes: "Precisely because a man is not threatened from a specific quarter, he is also unable to turn away from this threat … The threat appears to come in an intangible manner from all sides at once, so that one cannot defend oneself against it … The world which formerly surrounded him so warmly and intimately is suddenly snatched away from him … [Anxiety] can be neither larger nor smaller than fear, but is essentially infinite." *Existenz-philosophie*, 67. For phenomenologist Heidegger, anxiety [*angst*] engenders a mood, "uncanniness (*unheimlichkeit*)." One is not at home in, and out of sorts with, any attraction. *Being and Time*, 176; Writing about the disposition of anxiety, Freud notes that the individual loses his grasp on objects and feels helpless: "The patients cannot say what it is they are afraid of." According to Freud, internal psychic anxiety is then replaced by phobias. "Introductory Lectures," 16:402. For Kierkegaard, one form of anxiety is the "dizziness of freedom." *The Concept of Anxiety*, 61.

83 Desveaux, "Metamorphosis," 41, 46–7.

84 Colombo and Laidlaw, *Voices of Rama*, 20.

85 Wenjack, "A Meeting with the Maymaygwayshug," 3.

86 Dewdney and Kidd, *Indian Rock Painting*, 12, 71.

87 Jones, "Ojibwa Tales," 384.

88 Penesi, "The Thunderers."

89 "These shells are thought by some to be the scales … of the Underwater panther"; Howard, "The Plains Ojibwa or Bungi," 125, and *The Plains-Ojibwa or Bungi*, 112–14.

7. Thunderbirds

1 Dorson, *Bloodstoppers*, 53.

2 Jones, *History of the Ojebway Indians*, 85–6. See Chamberlain, "The Thunder-Bird," 51–4.

3 Harrison, "The Midewiwin," 82–3.

4 Harrison, "The Midewiwin," 83. We have previously given a description of Nanabush.

5 Chisholm and Gutsche, *Superior,* 63.

6 Helbig, *Nanabozhoo,* 96–7.

7 Sakry, "Naniboujou and the Thunderbirds," 59, 84, 102.

8 Colombo and Laidlaw, *Voices of Rama,* 36.

9 Coleman, Frogner, and Eich, *Ojibwa Myths,* 102.

10 Coleman, Frogner, and Eich, *Ojibwa Myths,* 102–3.

11 Jones, *Ojibwa Texts,* 2:191–3. Also, Jones, "Ojibwa Tales," 383–4.

12 Theresa S. Smith, *Island of the Anishnaabeg,* 2, 187. See Theresa S. Smith, "The Island of the Anishnaabeg."

13 See, for example, Morrisseau, "The Great Migration." Morrisseau and Robinson, *Travels,* 30–1.

14 Morrisseau, "Thunderbird and Inner Spirit."

15 Le Jeune writes of the Montagnais. Thwaites, *The Jesuit Relations,* 12 (1637), 25–7.

16 Thwaites, *The Jesuit Relations,* 12 (1637), 269n2.

17 For the Abenaki, the Northern Lights were the origin of lacrosse as the lights' shifting movements depicted their ancestors playing this game. Ritzenthaler and Ritzenthaler, *The Woodland Indians,* 109.

18 Ritzenthaler and Ritzenthaler, *The Woodland Indians,* 109.

19 Morgan, *Baaga' adowe, Play LaCrosse,* 5–6. Though initially very popular, lacrosse gave way in its appeal to baseball after the First World War. This new game became encoded in the Ojibwe language and seemed not to change Ojibwe culture significantly, Rhodes argues; "Baseball, Hotdogs, Apple Pie, and Chevrolets," 373–88. Even Nanabush is now depicted as playing baseball; Joe Auginaush, "Gii-pakitejii'iged Wenabozho / When Wenabozho Played Baseball," Treuer, *Living our Language,* 163.

20 Densmore, *Menominee Music,* 36–40. Vennum, *American Indian Lacrosse,* 209.

21 Densmore, *Chippewa Customs,* 114.

22 Flaskerd, "The Chippewa or Ojibway Moccasin Game," 87.

23 Densmore, *Chippewa Music,* 1:157–9.

24 Vennum, *Lacrosse Legends.*

25 Vennum, *Lacrosse Legends,* 1.

26 Vennum, *American Indian Lacrosse,* xii. For additional considerations of lacrosse and war, see Appendix E.

27 Henry, *Travels,* 77–78, 83.

28 Warren, *History of the Ojibway People,* 140. According to a story, "Wakaya-bide Is Killed Playing Lacrosse and Later Takes Revenge," Indians risked death by playing the game; Barnouw, *Wisconsin Chippewa Myths,* 142–8. Henry provides an eighteenth-century description of lacrosse; *Travels,* 77–8, 83.

29 According to Warren (and Henry), the plotter of this "mischief" was Matchikiwish/Madjekewis; Warren, *History of the Ojibway People,* 150.

30 Densmore, *Menominee Music,* 35–7.

31 Skinner and Satterlee, *Menomini Folklore,* 255–7.

32 Jones, *Ojibwa Texts,* 2:167–71.

33 Desveaux, *La mythologie,* 1:215.

34 Archives and Collections, Musée des Beaux Arts, "The Mesoamerican Ball Game."

35 Holzkamm, Waisberg, and Lovisek, "'Stout Athletic Fellows,'" 172.

36 Berbaum writes about contemporary honour songs: "The Grand Entry Songs (Grand Entry as such, the Flag Song, and the Veterans Song), and those honouring someone in particular [a birthday, the memory of some-one revered], are considered Honour Songs. These are accompanied by a specific attitude; the public is invited at that time to stand and the men to remove their caps, 'unless there is an eagle feather attached to them' (Wabigoon powwow, September 1993)." *Ojibwa Powwow World,* 31, 83.

37 Berbaum gives this description of a contemporary eagle staff: "This ban-ner is a tube of cloth, often red, to which is attached a variable number of eagle feathers. When in use, this tube is unwound and placed on a stand of about 1.5 to 2.3 metres high, and bent back to its end. The feathers are on the straight right side of the stand, perpendicular to it … Today, this ban-ner is the first item entering the powwow's dance space during the Grand Entry. The second song of the Grand Entry, the Flag Song, is dedicated to it." *Ojibwa Powwow World,* 36n6. Densmore describes the eagle staff as a "war banner," for it was used in wars with the Sioux. *Chippewa Music,* 2:91.

38 Morgan, *Baaga' adowe, Play LaCrosse,* 6, 18.

39 Vennum, *The Ojibwa Dance Drum,* 15, 33. Land animals play/contest with birds; Skinner and Satterlee, *Menominee Folklore,* 255–7.

40 Massicotte, "La danse chez les Indiens," 51.

41 Coleman, Frogner, and Eich, *Ojibwa Myths,* 101–2.

42 Lacombe, *Dictionnaire de la Langue des Cris,* 262–3; note on "Tonnerre": "Les sauvages s'imaginent que les oiseaux divins font, avec leurs yeux des éclairs, avec leurs ailes font le bruit du tonnerre, et lancent des flèchés invisibles et enflammées qui sont la foudre."

43 Jones, *History of the Ojebway Indians*, 85.
44 Conway and Conway, *Spirits on Stone*, 12, 15, 90–1.
45 Coleman, Frogner, and Eich, *Ojibwa Myths*, 102.
46 Angeconeb Debassige, and Thomas, *The Art of the Anishnawbek*.
47 Archives and Collections, A.T. Newman Collection. The swastika design is identified as pre-Columbian.
48 Coleman, *Decorative Designs*, 6–7, 19–21, 56, 82.
49 Jones, *Ojibwa Texts*, 2:295–301.
50 Manitous are "the power beings of the Anishinaabe cosmos. Thunderbird manitouk refer to the causal agents of the metereological phenomenon"; Theresa S. Smith, "Calling the Thunder," 19.
51 Theresa S. Smith, "Calling the Thunder," 22, 27n12.
52 Jones, "Notes on the Fox Indians," 213–14.
53 Archives and Collections, Private Collection. Morrisseau.
54 Ahmoo Angeconeb, "Ahneesheenahpay Myth of the Thunder People," artist's collection.
55 Columbo and Laidlaw, *Voices of Rama*, 32–3.
56 Rajnovich, *Reading Rock Art*, 36.
57 Rajnovich, *Reading Rock Art*, 58.
58 Panofsky, *Meaning in the Visual Arts*, 28–32.
59 Vastokas, "Interpeting Birch Bark Scrolls," 433–4.
60 Phillips, "Zigzag and Spiral," 417–18.
61 Desveaux, "Les Grands Lacs," 104–12.
62 Desveaux, "Les Grands Lacs," 108–11. See A'Llerio, "Craft, Ritual, and World View," 106, 112.
63 Archives and Collections, Minneapolis Institute of Arts.
64 Archives and Collections, Royal Ontario Museum, "Panel. Anishnawbek, Great Lakes."
65 Archives and Collections, Royal Ontario Museum, "Pipe and 'Puzzle' Stem."
66 Coleman, *Decorative Designs*, 70.
67 Bourgeois, *Ojibwa Narratives*, 41, editor's note.
68 Coleman, *Decorative Designs*, 7, 68.
69 Coleman, *Decorative Designs*, 68.
70 Coleman, *Decorative Designs*, 7, 68–70. See Mallery, *Picture-Writing*, 2:487–8.
71 Hoffman, "The Midê'wiwin," 158. Nichols and Nyholm give the spelling *animikii* and *animikiig* for thunderbird and thunderbirds. *A Concise Dictionary of Minnesota Ojibwe*, 9.
72 Isham, *James Isham's Observations on Hudsons Bay*, 102.

73 Jones, *The Aboriginal Rock Paintings of the Churchill River,* 12–13, 22, 30, 70, 78.
74 Menitove, *Woodlands: Contemporary Art of the Anishnabe,* 7.
75 Archives and Collections, National Gallery of Canada.
76 Carl Ray in Southcott, *The Sound of the Drum,* 17, 22–3, 35, 38.
77 Lévi-Strauss, *The Origin of Table Manners,* 391.
78 Phillips, "Zigzag and Spiral," 417–18.
79 Angeconeb, "The Pommerngrief Meets the Anishinawbe Thunderspirit."
80 Densmore, *Chippewa Music,* l:111.
81 Densmore, *Chippewa Music,* 1:65.
82 Densmore, *Chippewa Music,* l:84–5. Skinner, "Notes on the Eastern Cree and Northern Saulteaux," recounts the fight between two powerful snakes – rattlesnake and natawa. See Simms, "Myths of the Bungees," 334.
83 Archives and Collections, Chateau Ramezay Museum.
84 Densmore, *Chippewa Music,* l:127.
85 Densmore, *Chippewa Music,* 1:129.
86 Densmore, *Chippewa Music,* 2:198.
87 Densmore, *Chippewa Music,* 2:264.
88 Densmore, *Chippewa Music,* 2:274.
89 Densmore, *Chippewa Music,* 1:77.
90 Archives and Collections, Private Collections, Angeconeb.
91 Archives and Collections, Private Collections, Angeconeb.
92 Archives and Collections, Private Collections, Angeconeb. Thomas. See Angeconeb, Debassige, and Thomas, *The Art of the Anishnawbe.*
93 Archives and Collections, Royal Ontario Museum, Thomas. On the Ojibwe culture of gift giving, see Sims, "Algonkian–British Relations in the Upper Great Lakes Region."
94 Archives and Collections, Thunder Bay Art Gallery, Morris.
95 Morris, *Newsletter of Thunder Bay Art Gallery.*
96 Columbo and Laidlaw, *Voices of Rama,* 33–4.
97 "Clan System Played an Important Role in Government," 12.
98 Ritzenthaler and Ritzenthaler, *The Woodland Indians,* 104–6.
99 Theresa S. Smith, *Island of the Anishnaabeg,* 187.
100 Grim, *The Shaman,* 79.
101 Lyford, *The Crafts of the Ojibwa,* 140.
102 Conway and Conway, *Spirits on Stone,* 7–8, give reasons for the creation of these pictographs.
103 Conway and Conway, *Spirits on Stone,* 12, 15, 90–1.
104 For the nineteenth-century philosopher, Hegel, opposites in ideas or in sensory experiences can be thought through, can be resolved, and can be brought to a new unity that preserves the differences. *The Phenomenology of Mind,* 207.

Appendices

1 Borrows, *Living Law on a Living Earth*, 3–6, 10–13, 24, 38.
2 Preston, *Cree Narrative*, 212.
3 Snow, "The Solon Petroglyphs," 285.
4 Schenck writes about Warren's stand on the appointment of chiefs: He "was vehemently opposed to the creation of chiefs by outsiders, believing it to be a disruption to traditional Ojibwe polity. The British and the Americans made chiefs by bestowing flags, medals, and coats in order to have someone in authority who would support them. The French did so less frequently and generally accepted traditional chiefs. The Ojibwe did not respect made chiefs; chieftainship had to be inherited or earned." Warren, *History of the Ojibway People*, 89n16.
5 Hansen, "Chiefs and Principal Men," 243–4. See Chute, "Ojibwa Leadership during the Fur Trade Era," 153–72.
6 Benton-Banai, *The Mishomis Book*, 83–8.
7 Relland, "The Teachings of the Bear Clan," 105–6.
8 Relland, "The Teachings of the Bear Clan," 105–7.
9 Relland, "The Teachings of the Bear Clan," 107–8.
10 Wallace, "The Role of the Bear," 43–5.
11 Ojibwe Chief Peter Tobasonakwut Kelly notes that this Big Dipper is the Northern Thunderbird for the Ojibwe people; "Presentation by Chief Peter Kelly." Unpublished paper.
12 Speck and Moses, *The Celestial Bear*, 32–3.
13 Speck and Moses, *The Celestial Bear*, 55.
14 Speck and Moses, *The Celestial Bear*, 57.
15 Wallace, "The Role of the Bear," 44.
16 Warren, *History of the Ojibway People*, 284.
17 Neill, "History of the Ojibways," 470–1.
18 Dablon, *The Jesuit Relations*, 54 (1670), 163.
19 Peters, "Wa-bish-kee-pe-nas and the Chippewa Reverence for Copper," 53–60.
20 Chisholm and Gutsche, *Superior*, xxiii.
21 Holmes, "Aboriginal Copper Mines," 688–9.
22 Barrett, "Aboriginal Copper Mines," 25–31.
23 Griffin and Quimby, "The McCollum Site," 92–100. See Holzkamm, "Ojibwa Knowledge of Minerals," 89–97.
24 Griffin, "Old Copper Specimens," 120.
25 Archives and Collections, McCord Museum.
26 Archives and Collections, McCord Museum.
27 Kohl, *Kitchi-Gami*, 62.

28 Buchner, "Survey of Southeastern Manitoba Petroforms," 25.
29 Stories involving copper generally include the difficulties experienced in the process of procuring it. Clark and Martin, "A Risky Business," 110.
30 Dablon, *The Jesuit Relations*, 54 (1670), 153–9.
31 Dablon, *The Jesuit Relations*, 54 (1670), 159. Of the Superior Islands, the most fabled for copper were Michipicoten Island and Isle Royale. Caribou Island was often obscured by dense fog; Ojibwe avoided this "Island of the Yellow Sands," believing it was guarded by a huge monster; Gutsche and Bisaillon, *Mysterious Islands*, 268, 273.
32 Warren, *History of the Ojibway People*, 138. See Vennum, *American Indian Lacrosse*, x, xii, 31, 104; and Fisher, *Lacrosse*.
33 Henry, *Travels and Adventures in Canada*, 73, 76.
34 Warren, *History of the Ojibway People*, 141.
35 Warren, *History of the Ojibway People*, 141.
36 Henry, *Travels and Adventures in Canada*, 84–5.
37 Warren, *History of the Ojibway People*, 143.

Archives and Collections

Art Gallery of Ontario, Toronto
Carl Ray, "Medicine Bear," 1979

A.T. Newman Indian Artifacts Collection, University of Wisconsin–Eau Claire
"Swastika Design," A001–48–93

Carlo Traverso and the Online Distributed Proofreading Team
Louise Hope, "Mide Songs from Hoffman, 'The Midê'wiwin,' on Piano, Flute and Drum," http://www.gutenberg.org/files/19368/19368-h/19368-h.htm

Chateau Ramezay Museum, Old Montreal
"Costumes Exhibit," March 2008

Collection of Gabe and Michele Vadas and Norval Morrisseau. Nanaimo, BC
"The Shaman's Drum." No painter given

Feheley Fine Arts, Toronto
Ahmoo Angeconeb, "The Pommerngrief Meets the Anishinawbe Thunder-spirit," 2003

Indian and Northern Affairs Canada, Gatineau, Quebec
Norval Morrisseau, "Androgyny," 1983

McCord Museum, Montreal
"Simply Montréal: Glimpses of a Unique City." Permanent exhibition
"Copper Lance"

McMichael Canadian Art Collection, Kleinburg, Ontario
Norval Morrisseau, "Thunderbird and Inner Spirit," 1978

Minneapolis Institute of Arts
"Bandolier Bag," undated
"Bandolier Bag," 1830–50, 2003.32
"Bandolier Bag," 1860, 2005.43
"Bandolier Bags," 1870s, 2001.62, 2002.166
"Knife Sheath," nineteenth century, 94.4

Minnesota Artists Exhibition Program Gallery
"New Skins, New Paintings by Andrea Carlson and Jim Denomie," 2007

Minnesota Historical Society Museum, St Paul
"Ojibwa Birchbark Cutout Pattern," 10000.1
"Ojibwa Birchbark Owl Charm," 1900–9, 67.199.3
"Ojibwa Loom-woven Beadwork Band," uncertain date, 10000.862
"Ojibwa Woven Nettle and Yarn Bag," early twentieth century, 1981.4.44
"Ojibwa Woven Plant Fiber Yarn Bag," mid-twentieth century, 67.199.3
"Owl Feather Headdress," c. 1890, 2330.E229

Musée des Beaux Arts de Montréal, Montreal
"The Mesoamerican Ball Game"

National Gallery of Ottawa
Norval Morrisseau, "Artist and Shaman Between Two Worlds," 1980

Private Collections
Ahmoo Angeconeb
   "Ahneesheenahpay Myth of the Thunder People," 1986
   "Ahneesheenahpay Sky World, Middle World, and Under World," 1989
   "Thunderbirds In the Métro," 1984

Roy Thomas, "Our Gifts," 1995
Norval Morrisseau
   "The Great Migration," 1992
   "Man Changing Into Thunderbird," six panels, 1977

Royal Ontario Museum, Toronto
Acquisitions of New Contemporary First Nations Art, 2011

Jane Anne Poitras, "Potato Peeling 101 to Ethnobotany 101," mixed media,
2004
Roy Thomas, "Nipe: Waterlife," 1974

Permanent Collection
"Knife Sheath"
"Panel. Anishnawbek," early nineteenth century
"Pipe and 'Puzzle' Stem." Collected by Verner at Treaty Three. Ojibway, c.
1873, Manitoba or Ontario
"Pouch." Anishnawbek, Great Lakes, Ontario, late 18th century–early 19th
century

Smithsonian National Museum of the American Indian, New York
"Retrospective: Norval Morrisseau: Shaman Artist," 2008
Carl Ray, "Evil Serpent"
Roy Thomas, "Demon Fish"

St John's Abbey Archives, Collegeville, Minnesota
"Spirit Figure on Midewiwin Birch Bark Scroll," c. 1939, Cass Lake, Minnesota

Thunder Bay Art Gallery, Thunder Bay, Ontario
Roy Morris
"The Earth Watches: She Remembers My Grandfathers," 2008
"The Gift of Trout," 2006
"He Talks With Others," 2008
"The Rabbit Is Important to Us," 2007
"They Come to Let Us Know," 2007
"We Are Picking Berries," 2006

Thunder Bay Museum, Thunder Bay, Ontario
James Redsky, "Unpublished Manuscript with Copy of a Late-nineteenth-
century Song Scroll"

**Trent University Archives, Native Slides Collection, Peterborough.
Ontario**
"Hudson Bay Region: Indian Boy Holding a Powder Horn and a Shot Bag,"
80-035, 177; O. A. Reference: Acc. 6440 S 11705

Triple K Cooperative Inc., Red Lake, Ontario
Norval Morrisseau, "Group of Four Owls," 1976

Bibliography

Abram, David. *The Spell of the Sensuous: Perception and Language in a More-Than-Human World*. New York: Vintage, 1996.

Adamski, Barbara K. "An Upstream Battle: One of Canada's Oldest Lacrosse Clubs Attempts to Reclaim History." *The Walrus*, May 2007.

Aesop. *Aesop's Fables*. Laura Gibbs, trans. New York: Oxford University Press, 2002.

Albom, Mitch. *Tuesdays with Morrie*. Toronto: Doubleday, 1997.

A'Llerio, Karen. "Craft, Ritual, and World View." MA thesis, Lakehead University, 1999.

Allouez, Claude. In Thwaites, *The Jesuit Relations*, 50 (1667).

Anderson, Marcia, and Kathy Hussey-Arntson. "Ojibwe Bandolier Bags in the Collection of the Minnesota Historical Society." *American Indian Art Magazine* 11 (1986).

Angeconeb, Ahmoo. "Family Migration," 2000. In Green, *Ahmoo Angeconeb*.

– "Man at Obishikokkang," 2000. In Green, *Ahmoo Angeconeb*.

– "Woman and Guardians," 2000. In Green, *Ahmoo Angeconeb*.

Angeconeb, Ahmoo, Blake Debassige, and Roy Thomas. *The Art of the Anishnawbek: Three Perspectives*. Toronto: Royal Ontario Museum, 1996.

Angel, Michael. "The Ojibwa–Missionary Encounter at Rainy Lake Mission, 1839–1857," MA thesis, University of Manitoba, 1986.

– *Preserving the Sacred: Historical Perspectives on the Ojibwa Midewiwin*. Winnipeg: University of Manitoba Press, 2002.

Armstrong, Edward A. *The Folklore of Birds: An Enquiry into the Origin and Distribution of Some Magico-religious Traditions*. London: Collins, 1958.

Arteaga, Alfred, ed. *An Other Tongue: Nation and Ethnicity in the Linguistic Borderlands*. Durham: Duke University Press, 1994.

Ashworth, P.D. "Presuppose Nothing! The Suspension of Assumptions in Phenomenological Psychological Methodology." *Journal of Phenomenological Psychology* 27 (1996).

Asikinack, William. "Anishinabe (Ojibway) Legends through Anishinabe Eyes." In *The First Ones: Readings in Indian/Native Studies*, ed. David R. Miller et al. Craven: Saskatchewan Indian Federated College, 1992.

Auginaush, Joe. "Gii-pakitejii'iged Wenabozho / When Wenabozho Played Baseball." In *Living Our Language: Ojibwe Tales and Oral Histories*, ed. Anton Treuer. St Paul: Minnesota Historical Society, 2001.

Avery, Kathi. "Highlights of a History of Treaty #3." In *Socio-Economic Impact Evaluation Framework for Treaty #3 Development Program*, ed. Fred Kelly. Winnipeg: University of Manitoba Press, 1977.

– "Manito Gitgaan Governing in the Great Spirit's Garden: Wild Rice in Treaty Number 3. An Example of Indigenous Government Public Policy-Making and Intergovernmental Relations between the Boundary Waters Anishinaabeg and the Crown, 1869–1994." PhD diss., University of Manitoba, 1995.

Axtell, James. *After Columbus: Essays in the Ethnohistory of Colonial North America*. New York: Oxford University Press, 1988.

Babcock, Willoughby, ed. "William Whipple Warren and his Chippewa Writing." *Minnesota Archaeologist* 12 (1946).

Badger, Tom, and Julia Badger. "The Wenebojo Myth from Lac du Flambeau." In Barnouw, *Wisconsin Chippewa*.

– "Wenebojo's Brother Makes the Road to the Other World." In Barnouw, *Wisconsin Chippewa*.

Balikci, Asen. "Note sur le midewiwin." *Anthropologica* 2 (1956).

Bandow, James B. "White Dogs, Black Bears and Ghost Gamblers: Two Late Woodland Midewiwin Aspects from Ontario." In *Gathering Places in Algonquian Social Discourse*, ed. Regna Darnell and Peter Hele. New York: SUNY Press, 2008.

Baraga, Frederic. *A Dictionary of the Otchipwe Language, Explained in English.* Montreal: Beauchemin and Valois, 1878.

– *A Theoretical and Practical Grammar of the Otchipwe Language for the Use of Missionaries and Other Persons Living Among the Indians*. Montreal: Beauchemin and Valois, 1878.

Barkman, Katie. "Makwa et makikinak (ours et tortue)," "Bear and Turtle." In Desveaux, *La mythologie*, vol. 2.

Barnouw, Victor. "A Chippewa Mide Priest's Description of the Medicine Dance." *Wisconsin Archeologist* 41 (1960).

– "Reminiscences of a Chippewa Mide Priest." *Wisconsin Archeologist* 54 (1935).

– ed. *Wisconsin Chippewa Myths and Tales and their Relation to Chippewa Life: Based on Folktales Collected by Victor Barnouw, Joseph B. Casagrande, Ernestine Friedl, and Robert E. Ritzenthaler.* Madison: University of Wisconsin Press, 1977.

Barrett, S.A. "Aboriginal Copper Mines at McCargoe's Cove, Isle Royale." *Yearbook of the Public Museum of the City of Milwaukee*, no. 4 (1924).

– *The Dream Dance of the Chippewa and Menominee Indians of Northern Wisconsin.* Milwaukee: Bulletin of the Public Museum of the City of Milwaukee, 1911.

Barry, Nora Baker. "Postmodern Bears in the Texts of Gerald Vizenor." *Melus* 27 (2002).

Barry-Arredondo, Christopher. "The 'Talking Paper': Interpreting the Birch-Bark Scrolls of the Ojibwa Midéwiwin." MA thesis, SUNY Buffalo, 2006.

Beardy, L. *Pisiskiwak ka-pikiskwecik: Talking Animals.* H.C. Wolfart, ed. and trans. Winnipeg: Algonquian and Iroquoian Linguistics, 1988.

Begg, Solomon. "Kashkejabish (chouette de tengmalm)," "Kashkejabish (Boreal Owl)." In Desveaux, *La mythologie*, vol. 2.

– "Kwokwokwo et le vent chaud," "Kwokwokwo and the Warm Wind." In Desveaux, *La mythologie*, vol. 2.

– "Makwa (ours) et l'arbre," "The Bear and the Tree." In Desveaux, *La mythologie*, vol. 2.

Bekoff, Marc, and Jessica Pierce. *Wild Justice: The Moral Lives of Animals.* Chicago: University of Chicago Press, 2009.

Beltrami, J.C. *A Pilgrimage in America: Leading to the Discovery of the Sources of the Mississippi and Bloody River, with a Description of the Whole Course of the Former, and of the Ohio.* Chicago: Quadrangle, [1828] 1962.

Benton-Banai, Edward. *The Mishomis Book: The Voice of the Ojibway.* St Paul: Red School House, 1988.

Berbaum, Sylvie. *Ojibwa Powwow World.* Michael M. Pomedli, ed. and trans. Thunder Bay: Centre for Northern Studies, 2000.

Bird, Louis. *Telling Our Stories: Omushkego Legends and Histories from Hudson Bay.* Jennifer S.H. Brown, Paul W. DePasquale, and Mark F. Ruml, eds. Peterborough: Broadview, 2005.

Bird-David, Nurit. "Sociality and Immediacy: or, Past and Present Conversations on Bands." *Man* 27 (1994).

Bishop, Charles A. "The Emergence of Hunting Territories among the Northern Ojibwa." *Ethnology* 9 (1970).

– "The Northern Chippewa: An Ethnohistorical Study." PhD diss., SUNY
   Buffalo, 1969.
– "The Question of Ojibwa Clans." In *Actes du vingtième congrès des algonquin-
   istes,* ed. William Cowan. Ottawa: Carleton University Press, 1989.
Bissell, Samuel, and Andrew J. Blackbird. *Education of Indian Youth: Letter
   of Rev. Samuel Bissell, and Appeal of A.J. Blackbird, a Chippewa Indian.*
   Philadelphia: William F. Geddes, 1856.
Black, Mary B. "Ojibwa Questioning Etiquette and Use of Ambiguity." *Studies
   in Linguistics* 23 (1973).
Black, Mary R. "An Ethnoscience Investigation of Ojibwa Ontology and World
   View." PhD diss., Stanford University, 1967.
– "Ojibwa Taxonomy and Percept Ambiguity." *Ethos* 5 (1977).
Black-Rogers, Mary B. "Foreword." In Overholt and Callicott, *Clothed-in-Fur.*
Blackbird, Andrew J. *History of the Ottawa and Chippewa Indians of Michigan; a
   Grammar of their Language, and Personal and Family History of the Author, by
   Andrew J. Blackbird, Late U.S. Interpreter, Harbor Springs, Emmet Co., Mich.*
   Ypsilanti: Ypsilantian Job Printing House, 1887.
– *The Indian Problem, From the Indian's Standpoint.* Ypsilanti: Scharf Tag, Label
   and Box Co., 1900.
Blessing, Fred K. "Birchbark Mide Scrolls." In *The Ojibway Indians Observed:
   Papers of Fred K. Blessing, Jr, on the Ojibway Indians from The Minnesota
   Archaeologist.* John J. Kammerer, illus. St Paul: Minnesota Archaeological
   Society, 1977.
– "Medicine Bags and Bundles of Midewiwin." In *The Ojibway Indians
   Observed.*
– "Some Use of Bone, Horn, Claws, and Teeth by Minnesota Ojibwa Indians."
   In *The Ojibway Indians Observed.*
– "A Visit to an Ojibway Dream Dance." *Minnesota Archaeologist* 23 (1961).
Bloomfield, Leonard. *Eastern Ojibwa, Grammatical Sketch, Texts and Word List.*
   Ann Arbor: University of Michigan Press, 1957.
Bollnow, Otto. *Existenz-philosophie.* Norbert Schwinghammer, trans. Stuttgart:
   W. Kohlhammer Verlag, 1969.
The Book of the Dead: The Hieroglyphic Transcript of the Papyrus of Ani. E.A. Wallis
   Budge, trans. New Hyde Park: University Books, 1960.
Borrows, John. *Living Law on a Living Earth: Aboriginal Religion, Law, and the
   Constitution.* Toronto: University of Toronto Press, 2006.
Boudinot, Elias. *A Star in the West, or, A Humble Attempt to Discover the Long
   Lost Ten Tribes of Israel, Preparatory to their Return to their Beloved City,
   Jerusalem.* Trenton: D. Fenton, S. Hutchinson, and J. Dunham, 1816.

Bourgeois, Arthur, ed. *Ojibwa Narratives of Charles and Charlotte Kawbawgan and Jacques LePique, 1893–1895*. Detroit: Wayne State University Press, 1994.

Bower, Bruce. "When Stones Come to Life." *Science News* 155, no. 23 (1999).

Brant, George. "The Two Squaws and the Serpent." In Colombo and Laidlaw, *Voices of Rama*.

Brass. Eleanor. "Musqua and the Greedy Ones." *Medicine Boy and Other Cree Tales*. Henry Nanooch, illus. Calgary: Glenbow, 1978.

Bray, Martha Coleman, ed. *The Journals of Joseph N. Nicollet. A Scientist on the Mississippi Headwaters with Notes on Indian Life, 1836–37*. St Paul: Minnesota Historical Society, 1970.

Brébeuf, Jean de. "Hurons." In Thwaites, *The Jesuit Relations*, 10 (1636).

Breck, James Lloyd. *Chippeway Pictures from the Territory of Minnesota*. Hartford: [1857] 1910.

Brehm, Victoria. "The Metamorphoses of an Ojibwa Manido." *American Literature* 68 (1996).

Bressani, Francesco. "A Brief Account of Certain Missions." In Thwaites, *The Jesuit Relations*, 38 (1653).

Brightman, Robert. *Grateful Prey: Rock Cree Human–Animal Relationships*. Berkeley: University of California Press, 1993.

Brill, Charles. *Red Lake Nation: Portraits of Ojibwe Life*. Minneapolis: University of Minnesota Press, 1992.

Broker, Ignatia. *Night Flying Woman: An Ojibway Narrative*. St Paul: Minnesota Historical Society, 1997.

Brown, Jennifer S.H. "A.I. Hallowell and William Berens Revisited." In *Papers of the Eighteenth Algonquian Conference*, ed. William Cowan. Ottawa: Carleton University Press, 1987.

– *Strangers in Blood: Fur Trade Company Families in Indian Country*. Vancouver: UBC Press, 1980.

Brown, Jennifer S.H., et al. *The Ojibwa of Berens River, Manitoba: Ethnography into History*. New York: Harcourt College, 1992.

Brown, Jennifer S.H., and Robert Brightman. *The Orders of the Dreamed: George Nelson on Cree and Northern Ojibwa Religion and Myth, 1823*. Winnipeg: University of Manitoba Press, 1988.

Brown, Jennifer S.H., and Laura L. Peers. "The Chippewa and Their Neighbors: A Critical Review." In Hickerson, *The Chippewa and Their Neighbors*.

Brown, Jennifer S.H., and Elizabeth Vibert, eds. *Reading beyond Words: Contexts for Native History*. Peterborough: Broadview, 2003.

Brown, Joseph Epes. "Modes of Contemplation through Action: North American Indians." *Main Currents in Modern Thought* 30 (1973–4).

– *The Spiritual Legacy of the American Indian.* Marina Brown Weatherly, et al., eds. Bloomington: World Wisdom, [1964] 2007.

Brundige, Lorraine. "The Continuity of Native Values: Cree and Ojibwa." MA thesis, Lakehead University, 1997.

Buchner, Anthony P. "Survey of Southeastern Manitoba Petroforms, 1974." In *Studies in Manitoba Rock Art: I, Petroforms.* Winnipeg: Department of Cultural Affairs and Historical Resources, 1983.

Buffalo, Chief. "Speech of the Buffalo Chief of La Point at Sault Ste Marie, July 1830." In Neill, "History of the Ojibways."

Buffalohead, Priscilla K. "Farmers, Warriors, Traders: A Fresh Look at Ojibway Women." *Minnesota History* 48 (1983).

Buffalohead, Roger W. *Against the Tide of History: The Story of the Mille Lacs Anishinabe.* Cass Lake: Minnesota Ojibwa Tribe, 1985.

– "Introduction." In William W. Warren, *History of the Ojibway Nation.* St Paul: Minnesota Historical Society, [1885] 1984.

Burgess, Benjamin V. "Elaboration Therapy in the Midewiwin and Gerald Vizenor's *The Heirs of Columbus.*" *Studies in American Indian Literatures* 18, no. 1 (2006).

Burnett, Kristin. *Taking Medicine: Women's Healing Work and Colonial Contact in Southern Alberta, 1880–1930.* Vancouver: UBC Press, 2011.

Cadzow, D.A. "Bark Records of the Bungi Midéwin Society." *Indian Notes and Monographs.* New York: Museum of the American Indian, Heye Foundation no. 3 (1926).

Cahalane, Victor H. "Preface." In Haley, *Sleek and Savage.*

Calarco, Matthew, and Peter Atterton, eds. *Animal Philosophy: Essential Readings in Continental Thought.* London: Continuum, 2004.

Callahan, Kevin L. "Interpreting the Pictographs of North Hegman Lake, MN." http://www.tc.umn.edu/~call0031/Hegman.html.

Callicott, J. Baird. *In Defense of the Land Ethic: Essays in Environmental Philosophy.* Albany: SUNY Press, 1989.

– "Traditional American Indian and Western European Attitudes Toward Nature: An Overview." *Environmental Ethics* 4 (1982).

Cappel, Constance, ed. *Odawa Language and Legends: Andrew J. Blackbird and Raymond Kiogima.* Philadelphia: Xlibris, 2006.

Cardinal, Harold. *The Rebirth of Canada's Indians.* Edmonton: Hurtig, 1977.

– *The Unjust Society: The Tragedy of Canada's Indians.* Edmonton: Hurtig, 1969.

Carpenter, E. *Eskimo Realities.* Arnold J. Skolnick, design. Eberhard Otto, Fritz Spiess, and Jorgen Meldgaard, photos. New York: Holt, 1973.

Casagrande, Joseph B. "John Mink, Ojibwa Informant." In *the Company of Man: Twenty Portraits by Anthropologists*, ed. Casagrande. New York: Harper and Brothers, 1960.

– "Ojibwa Bear Ceremonialism: The Persistence of a Ritual Attitude." In Tax, *Acculturation in the Americas*.

Cavanagh, Beverley. "Les mythes et la musique naskapis." Robert Larocque and Nicole Beaudry, trans. *Recherches amérindiennes au québec* 15 (1985).

Chamberlain, A.F. "The Thunder-Bird among the Crees." *American Anthropologist* 3 (1890).

Chanin, Paul. *The Natural History of Otters*. New York: Facts on File, 1985.

Chaput, Donald. "Michipicoten Island Ghosts, Copper and Bad Luck." *Ontario History* 6 (1969).

de Charlevoix, Pierre-François-Xavier. *Histoire et description générale de la Nouvelle France*. Paris: Chez Rollin Fils, Libraire, 1744.

– *Journal of a Voyage to North-America, Undertaken by Order of the French King*. 2 vols. London: R. and J. Dodsley, 1761.

Chartier, Danielle. "Exhibit Focuses on the Bear Facts." *Saskatoon Sun*, 31 August 2003.

Chatfield, William. "The Midewiwin Songs of Fine-day." *Museum News* 15, no. 10 (1954).

Chisholm, Barbara, and Andrea Gutsche. *Superior: Under the Shadow of the Gods*. Toronto: Lynx Images, 1998.

Christenson, Rosemary. "Anishinaabeg Medicine Wheel Leadership: The Work of David F. Courchene, Jr." PhD diss., University of Minnesota, 1999.

Chute, Janet. *The Legacy of Shingwaukonse: A Century of Native Leadership*. Toronto: University of Toronto Press, 1998.

– "Ojibwa Leadership during the Fur Trade Era at Sault Ste Marie." In Fiske, Sleeper-Smith, and Wicken, *New Faces of the Fur Trade*.

– "Preservation of Ethnic Diversity at Garden River: A Key to Ojibwa Strength." In *Papers of the Twenty-Eighth Algonquian Conference*, ed. David H. Pentland. Winnipeg: University of Manitoba Press, 1997.

– "Pursuing the Great Spirit's Plan: Nineteenth Century Ojibwa Attitudes towards the Future of Logging and Mining on Unsurrendered Indian Lands North of Lakes Huron and Superior." In *Social Relations in Resource Hinterlands: Papers from the 27th Annual Meeting of the Western Association of Sociology and Anthropology*, ed. Thomas W. Dunk. Thunder Bay: Lakehead University, Centre for Northern Studies, 1991.

– "A Unifying Vision: Shingwaukonse's Plan for the Future of the Great Lakes Ojibwa." *Journal of the Canadian Historical Association* 7 (1997).

"Clan System Played an Important Role in Government." *Council Fires,* February 1993.

Clark, Caven P., and Susan R. Martin. "A Risky Business: Late Woodland Copper Mining on Lake Superior." In *The Cultural Landscape of Prehistoric Mines,* ed. Peter Topping and Mark Lynott. Oxford: Oxbow Books, 2005.

Cleland, Charles. "Indian Treaties and American Myths: Roots of Social Conflict over Treaty Rights." *Native Studies Review* 6 (1990).

– *The Place of the Pike (Gnoozhekaaning): A History of the Bay Mills Indian Community.* Ann Arbor: University of Michigan Press, 2001.

– *Rites of Conquest: The History and Culture of Michigan's Native Americans.* Ann Arbor: University of Michigan Press, 1992.

Clements, William M. "Schoolcraft as Textmaker." *Journal of American Folklore* 103 (1990).

Closs, Michael P. "Tallies and the Ritual Use of Numbers in Ojibway Pictography." In *Native American Mathematics,* ed. Closs. Austin: University of Texas Press, 1986.

Coatsworth, Emerson, and David Coatsworth. *The Adventures of Nanabush: Ojibway Indian Stories.* Sam Snake, Chief Elija Yellowhead, Alder York, David Simcoe, and Annie King, narrators. Francis Kagige, illus. Toronto: Doubleday, 1979.

Coleman, Sister Bernard. *Decorative Designs of the Ojibwa of Northern Minnesota.* Washington: Catholic University of America Press, 1947.

– "The Religion of the Ojibwa in Northern Minnesota." *Primitive Man* 10 (1937).

Coleman, Sister Bernard, Ellen Frogner, and Estelle Eich, eds. *Ojibwa Myths and Legends.* Minneapolis: Ross and Haines, 1971.

Colombo, John Robert, and George Edward Laidlaw, eds. *Voices of Rama: Traditional Ojibwa Tales, Lake Couchiching, Ontario.* Toronto: Colombo, 1994.

Constitution Act, 1982: Amended by Constitution Amendment Proclamation, 1983. Ottawa: Supply and Services Canada, 1990.

Conway, Thor. *Painted Dreams: Native American Rock Art.* Minocqua: NorthWord, 1993.

Conway, Thor, and Julie Conway. *Spirits on Stone: The Agawa Pictographs.* San Luis Obispo: Heritage Discoveries, 1990.

Copway, George. *Indian Life and Indian History by an Indian Author: Embracing the Tradition of the North American Indians Regarding Themselves, Particularly of that Most Important of all the Tribes, the Ojibways.* Boston: Colby, 1858.

– *The Life, History, and Travels of Kah-ge-ga-gah-bowh (George Copway): A Young Indian Chief of the Ojebwa Nation.* Philadelphia: James Harmstead, 1847.

– *The Ojibway Conquest: A Tale of the Northwest.* New York: George P. Putnam, 1850.

– *Recollections of a Forest Life, or, The Life and Travels of Kah-ge-ga-gah-bowh, or, George Copway.* London: Charles Gilpin, 1851.

– *Running Sketches of Men and Places in England, France, Germany, Belgium, and Scotland.* New York: Riker, 1851.

– *The Traditional History and Characteristic Sketches of the Ojibway Nation.* London: Charles Gilpin, 1850.

Corbiere, Alan. "Exploring Historical Literacy in Manitoulin Island Ojibwe." In *Papers of the Thirty-Fourth Algonquian Conference*, ed. H.C. Wolfart. Winnipeg: University of Manitoba Press, 2003.

Corbiere, Howard. *Ko-ko-ko the Owl, an Ojibwe–Odawa Legend.* Mary Lou Fox, ed. Martin Panamick, illus. M'Chigeeng: Ojibwe Cultural Foundation, 1977.

Cosh, Joe. "The Owl and the Squaw." In Colombo and Laidlaw, *Voices of Rama.*

– "The Serpent and the Squaw." In Colombo and Laidlaw, *Voices of Rama.*

Councillor, Randy, et al. *Ojibwe Tales: Stories of the Ojibwe People.* International Falls: Lake States Interpretive Association, 2004.

Craven, Margaret. *I Heard the Owl Call My Name.* New York: Doubleday, 1973.

Crawford, Suzanne J., and Dennis F. Kelley, eds. *American Indian Religious Traditions: An Encyclopedia*, vol. 2. Santa Barbara: ABC–CLIO, 2005.

Culkin, W.E. "Tribal Dance of the Ojibway Indians." *Minnesota Historical Society Bulletin* 1 (1915).

Cyr, Kathy Ann Schimke. "Dress of the Chippewa (Ojibwa) Indians: An Analysis of Change from 1640–1940." MA thesis, University of Michigan, 1978.

Dablon, Claude. In Thwaites, *The Jesuit Relations*, 54 (1670).

Dahlstrom, Amy. "Owls and Cannibals Revisited: Traces of Windigo Features in Meskwaki Texts." In *Papers of the Thirty-Fourth Algonquian Conference*, ed. H.C. Wolfart. Winnipeg: University of Manitoba Press, 2003.

Danley, Bob. "When Spring Comes." *Globe and Mail*, 8 October 2009.

Danziger, Edmund Jefferson. *The Chippewas of Lake Superior.* Norman: University of Oklahoma Press, 1990.

Darnell, Regna. "Rethinking the Concepts of Band and Tribe, Community and Nation: An Accordion Model of Nomadic Native American Social Organization." In *Papers of the Twenty-Ninth Algonquian Conference*, ed. David Pentland. Winnipeg: University of Manitoba Press, 1998.

Davidson, John F. "Ojibway Songs." *Journal of American Folklore* 58 (1945).

Day, Gordon M. "The Name 'Algonquin.'" *International Journal of American Linguistics* 38 (1972).

Deleary, Nicholas. "The Midewiwin, an Aboriginal Spiritual Institution. Symbols of Continuity: A Native Studies Culture-Based Perspective." MA thesis, Institute of Canadian Studies, Carleton University, 1990.

Deloria, Vine. *Spirit and Reason: The Vine Deloria, Jr, Reader,* ed. Barbara Deloria, Kristen Foehner, and Sam Scinta. Golden: Fulcrum, 1999.

Denny, J. Peter. "Rational Thought in Oral Culture and Literate Decontextualization." In *Literacy and Orality,* ed. David R. Olson and Nancy Torrance. Cambridge: Cambridge University Press, 1991.

Densmore, Frances. *Chippewa Customs.* St Paul: Minnesota Historical Society, [1929] 1979.

– *Chippewa Music,* vol. 1. Washington: Bureau of American Ethnology, 1910.

– *Chippewa Music,* vol. 2. Washington: Bureau of American Ethnology, 1913.

– *Dakota and Ojibwe People in Minnesota.* St Paul: Minnesota Historical Society, 1977.

– *Folk Music of the United States: Songs of the Chippewa: From the Archive of Folk Song.* Washington: Library of Congress, 1950.

– *Indian Use of Wild Plants for Crafts, Food, Medicine, and Charms.* Washington: Smithsonian Institution, 1928.

– *Menominee Music.* New York: Smithsonian Institution, 1932.

– "The Study of the Indian Music in the Nineteenth Century." *American Anthropologist,* 29 (1927).

– "The Use of Music in the Treatment of the Sick." In Hoffman, *Frances Densmore and American Indian Music.*

Desveaux, Emmanuel. "Les Grands Lacs et les Plaines, le figuratif et le géométrique, les hommes et les femmes," In *Papers of the Twenty-Fourth Algonquian Conference,* ed. William Cowan. Ottawa: Carleton University Press, 1993.

– "De l'interdite de dire au besoin de peindre: l'art iconique Ojibwa." In *Mémoires de la tradition,* ed. Aurore Becquelin and Antoinette Molinie. Nanterre: Société d'Ethnologie, 1993.

– "La métamorphose comme limite de l'animalité symbolique." *Cahiers de littérature orale* 22 (1987).

– "Metamorphosis as a Limit to the Symbolic Values of Animals." In *Papers of the Nineteenth Algonquian Conference,* ed. William Cowan. Ottawa: Carleton University Press, 1988.

– "Mythologie et astronomie des indiens de Big Trout Lake." In *Actes du quatorzième congrès des algonquinistes,* ed. William Cowan. Ottawa: Carleton University Press, 1983.

– *La mythologie des indiens de Big Trout Lake, Ethnolographie analyse des mythes,* 2 vols. Paris: Écoles des Hautes Études en Sciences Sociales, 1984.

– *Sous le signe de l'ours: mythes et temporalité chez les Ojibwa Septentrionaux.* Paris: Éditions de la Maison des Sciences de l'Homme, 1988.

Devens, Carol. *Countering Colonization: Native American Women and Great Lakes Missions, 1630–1900.* Berkeley: University of California Press, 1992.

Dewdney, Selwyn. "Ecological Notes on the Ojibway Shaman Artist." Eberhard Otto, photographer. *Artscanada* 27 (1970).

– *The Sacred Scrolls of the Southern Ojibway.* Toronto: University of Toronto Press, 1975.

Dewdney, Selwyn, and Kenneth E. Kidd. *Indian Rock Paintings of the Great Lakes.* Toronto: University of Toronto Press, 1962.

Diamond, Beverly, M. Sam Cronk, and Franziska von Rosen, *Visions of Sound: Musical Instruments of First Nations Communities in Northeastern America.* Chicago: University of Chicago Press, 1994.

Dickason, Olive Patricia. "'For Every Plant There Is a Use': The Botanical World of Mexica and Iroquoians." In *Aboriginal Resource Use in Canada: Historical and Legal Aspects*, ed. Kerry Abel and Jean Friesen. Winnipeg: University of Manitoba Press, 1991.

Dockstader, Frederick J. *Great North American Indians: Profiles in Life and Leadership.* New York: Van Rostrand Reinhold, 1977.

Doherty, Joanna. "An Examination of the Sources of Ojibwa and Non-Ojibwa Elements in Norval Morrisseau's Art." MA thesis, Carleton University, 1982.

Dorson, Richard. M. *Bloodstoppers and Bearwalkers: Folk Traditions of the Upper Peninsula.* Cambridge, MA: Harvard University Press, 1952.

Douglas, J.H., Denis Girard, and W. Thompson. *Cassell's French and English Dictionary.* New York: Macmillan, 1968.

Downes, Randolph C. *Council Fires on the Upper Ohio.* Pittsburgh: University of Pittsburgh Press, 1940.

Duk, Kim Ki, writer, director. "Spring, Summer, Fall, Winter … and Spring." Sony Pictures Classics, 2004.

Dumont, James. "Journey to Daylight-Land: Through Ojibwa Eyes." *Laurentian University Review* 9 (1976).

Dunn, Anne M., ed. *Winter Thunder: Retold Tales.* Cynthia Holmes, illus. Duluth: Holy Cow!, 2001.

Duplaix, Nicole, ed. *Otters: Proceedings of the First Working Meeting of the Otter Specialist Group, Paramaribo, Suriname, 1977.* Morges: International Union for Conservation of Nature and Natural Resources, 1978.

Echlin, Kimberly Ann. "The Translation of Ojibway: The Nanabush Myths." PhD diss., York University, 1982.

Edmonds, Margot, and Ella E. Clark, eds.. *Voices of the Winds.* Molly Brown, illus. New York: Facts on File, 1989.

Edmunds, R. David. *The Shawnee Prophet.* Lincoln: University of Nebraska Press, 1983.

Eliade, Mircea. *Shamanism: Archaic Techniques of Ecstasy.* Princeton: Princeton
     University Press, [1951] 1964.
Elliott, Richard Robert. "The Chippewas of Lake Superior." *American Catholic
     Quarterly Review* 21 (1896).
Ellis, C. Douglas. *"Now then, still another story –" Literature of the Western James
     Bay Cree—Content and Structure.* Winnipeg: Voices of Rupert's Land, 1989.
Emerson, Ellen Russell. *Indian Myths or Legends, Traditions, and Symbols of
     the Aborigines of America Compared with Those of Other Countries.* London:
     Trübner, 1884.
"Ethical Guidelines for Research." In *Report of the Royal Commission on
     Aboriginal Peoples*, vol. 5, Appendix E.
Ewers, John C. "The Awesome Bear in Plains Indian Art." *American Indian Art
     Magazine* 7, no. 3 (1982).
– "The Bear Cult among the Assiniboine and Their Neighbors of the Northern
     Plains." *Southwestern Journal of Anthropology* 11 (1955).
– *Plains Indian Sculpture: A Traditional Art from America's Heartland.*
     Washington: Smithsonian Institution, 1986.
Feest, Christian F. "Andrew J. Blackbird and Ottawa History." *Yumtzilob* 8,
     no. 2 (1996).
– ed., *Studies in American Indian Art: A Memorial Tribute to Norman Feder.*
     Vienna: Adolf Holzhausens Nachfolger, 2001.
Ferrara, Nadia. *Emotional Expression among Cree Indians: The Role of Pictorial
     Representations in the Assessment of Psychological Mindedness.* London: Jessica
     Kingsley, 1999.
Fiddler, Alfred. "Legend of Wisakachak and the Bear's Fat." *Wawatay News,*
     22 August 1991.
Fine-Day / Dedate Bange / Fast Flutter of Wings. "The Midewiwin Songs of
     Fine-Day," ed. William Chatfield. *Museum News* 15, no. 10 (1954).
Finlay, Linda. "A Dance between the Reduction and Reflexivity: Explicating
     the 'Phenomenological Psychological Attitude.'" *Journal of Phenomenological
     Psychology* 39 (2008).
– "Debating Phenomenological Research Methods." *Phenomenology and
     Practice* 3 (2009).
Fisher, Donald M. *Lacrosse: A History of the Game.* Baltimore: Johns Hopkins
     University Press, 2002.
Fiske, Jo-Anne, Susan Sleeper-Smith, and William Wicken. *New Faces of the
     Fur Trade: Selected Papers of the Seventh North American Fur Trade Conference,
     Halifax, Nova Scotia, 1995.* East Lansing: Michigan State University Press,
     1998.
Flacelière, Robert. *Greek Oracles.* Douglas Garman, trans. London: Elek, 1965.

Flaskerd, George A. "The Chippewa or Ojibway Moccasin Game." *Minnesota Archaeologist* 23 (1961).

Fogelson, Raymond D., et al., eds. *Contributions to Anthropology: Selected Papers of A. Irving Hallowell.* Chicago: University of Chicago Press, 1976.

Freud, Sigmund. *Introductory Lectures on Psycho-Analysis*, ed. James Strachey. London: Hogarth, 1963. Vol. 16 of *The Standard Edition of the Complete Psychological Works of Sigmund Freud.*

Friedl, Ernestine. "An Attempt at Directed Culture Change: Leadership among the Chippewa, 1640–1948." PhD diss., Columbia University, 1950.

Fulford, George. "Manabus and Mitawin." In *Papers of the Nineteenth Algonquian Conference*, ed. William Cowan. Ottawa: Carleton University Press, 1988.

– "Ojibwa Picture Writing: A Study in the Process of Symbol In-formation." PhD diss., University of Western Ontario, 1988.

– "A Structural Analysis of Mide Chants." In *Papers of the Twenty-First Algonquian Conference*, ed. William Cowan. Ottawa: Carleton University Press, 1990.

– "A Structural Analysis of Mide Song Scrolls." In *Actes du vingtième congrès des algonquinistes*, ed. William Cowan. Ottawa: Carleton University Press, 1989.

Getty, Ian A.L., and Donald Boyd Smith, eds. *One Century Later: Western Canadian Reserve Indians Since Treaty 7.* Vancouver: UBC Press, 1977.

Geyshick, Ron, and Judith Doyle. *Stories by an Ojibway Healer, Te Bwe Win, Truth.* Toronto: Summerhill, 1989.

Ghezzi, Ridie W. *Ways of Speaking: An Ethnopoetic Analysis of Ojibwe Narratives.* Philadelphia: University of Pennsylvania Press, 1990.

Gile, Marie. "The Thunderbird and Underwater Panther in the Material Culture of the Great Lakes Indians: Symbols of Power." PhD diss., Michigan State University, 1996.

Gill, Sam D., and Irene F. Sullivan. *Dictionary of Native American Mythology.* New York: Oxford University Press, 1992.

Gilman, Rhoda R. "Last Days of the Upper Mississippi Fur Trade." *Minnesota History* 42 (1970).

Goodall, Jane, with the Jane Goodall Institute. *Jane Goodall: 50 Years at Gombe: A Tribute to Five Decades of Wildlife Research, Education, and Conservation.* New York: Stewart, Tabori, and Chang, 2010.

Goulding, Warren. "Traditional Role of Aboriginal Women Has Great Relevance in Modern Society." *Eagle Feather News* 5 (March 2002).

Goulet, Keith N. "Oral History as an Authentic and Credible Research Base for Curriculum: The Cree of Sandy Bay and Hydroelectric Power Development 1927–67, an Example." MA thesis, University of Regina, 1986.

Gowdy, John M., ed. *Limited Wants, Unlimited Means: A Reader on Hunter-Gatherer Economics and the Environment.* Washington: Island, 1998.

Graham, Loren R. *A Face in the Rock.* Washington: Island, 1995.

Grand Council Treaty #3. "'We Have Kept Our Part of the Treaty.' The Anishinabe Understanding of Treaty #3." Kenora: Lake of the Woods Ojibway Cultural Centre, 1995.

Grandin, Temple, and Catherine Johnson. *Animals Make Us Human: Creating the Best Life for Animals.* Boston: Houghton Mifflin Harcourt, 2009.

Gray, Susan Elaine. *"I Will Fear No Evil": Ojibwa–Missionary Encounters along the Berens River, 1875–1940.* Calgary: University of Calgary Press, 2006.

Great Lakes Indian Fish and Wildlife Commission. *Chippewa Treaty Rights: Hunting ... Fishing ... Gathering on Ceded Territory.* Odanah: Great Lakes Indian Fish and Wildlife Commission, 1988.

– "Chippewa Treaty Rights: An Overview." *Masinaigan* [Talking Paper], January–February 1990.

"Great Sturgeon Teaches a Lesson about Greed." *Wawatay News,* 4 November 1993.

Green, Spencer. *Ahmoo Angeconeb: The Healing and Returning Home Series.* Thunder Bay: Thunder Bay Art Gallery, 2001.

Greene, Jacqueline Dembar, et al. *Manabozho's Gifts: Three Chippewa Tales.* Boston: Houghton Mifflin, 1994.

Griffin, Donald R. *Animal Minds: Beyond Cognition to Consciousness.* Chicago: University of Chicago Press, 2001.

Griffin, James B., ed. *Lake Superior Copper and the Indians: Miscellaneous Studies of Great Lakes Prehistory.* Ann Arbor: University of Michigan Press, 1961.

– "Old Copper Specimens from Near Brockville, Ontario." In Griffin, *Lake Superior Copper.*

Griffin, James B., and George I. Quimby. "The McCollum Site, Nipigon District, Ontario." In Griffin, *Lake Superior Copper.*

Grim, John A. "The Shaman: An Interpretation of This Religious Personality Based on Ethnographic Data from the Siberian Tribes and the Woodland Ojibway of North America." PhD diss., Fordham University, 1980.

– *The Shaman: Patterns of Religious Healing among the Ojibway Indians.* Norman: University of Oklahoma Press, 1983.

– *The Shaman: Patterns of Siberian and Ojibway Healing.* Norman: University of Oklahoma Press, 1983.

Grollig, Francis X., and Harold B. Haley, eds. *Medical Anthropology.* The Hague: Mouton, 1976.

Gross, Lawrence W. "Bimaadiziwin, or the 'Good Life,' as a Unifying Concept of Anishinaabe Religion." *American Indian Culture and Research Journal* 26 (2002).

Grough, Phyllis W. *Our Sacred Gifts: An Ojibwe Perspective in the Preparation of Parenthood; An Ojibwe Perspective on Embryo and Fetal Development; An Ojibwe Perspective on Infant Development; An Ojibwe Perspective on Toddlerhood.* Minneapolis: Minnesota Indian Women's Resource Center, 1990.

Gruen, Sara. *Ape House.* Toronto: Bond Street Books / Doubleday Canada, 2010.

Guss, David M., ed. *The Language of the Birds.* San Francisco: Net Point, 1985.

Guthrie, Gail. "A Study of the Theatrical Elements in the Grand Medicine Society (Midewiwin) Religious Cult as Practiced by the Northern United States Chippewa Indians." MA thesis, Cornell University, 1966.

Gutsche, Andrea, and Cindy Bisaillon. *Mysterious Islands: Forgotten Tales of the Great Lakes.* Toronto: Lynx Images, 1999.

Haefer, J. Richard. "Foreword." In Vennum, *The Ojibwa Dance Drum.*

Hale, Janet Campbell. *The Owl's Song.* New York: Doubleday, 1974.

Haley, Delphine. *Sleek and Savage: North America's Weasel Family.* Seattle: Pacific Search, 1975.

Hall, Robert L. *An Archaeology of the Soul: North American Indian Belief and Ritual.* Urbana: University of Illinois Press, 1997.

Hallowell, A. Irving. "Bear Ceremonialism in the Northern Hemisphere." *American Anthropologist* 28 (1926).

– *Culture and Experience.* Philadelphia: University of Pennsylvania Press, [1955] 1974.

– *The Ojibwa of Berens River, Manitoba.* Forth Worth: Harcourt Brace Jovanovich, 1992.

– "Ojibwa Metaphysics of Being and the Perception of Persons." In *Person Perception and Interpersonal Behavior*, ed. Renato Tagiuri and Luigi Petrullo. Stanford: Stanford University Press, 1958.

– "Ojibwa Ontology, Behavior, and World View." In *Culture and History*, ed. S. Diamond. New York: Columbia University Press, 1960.

– "Ojibwa Personality and Acculturation." In Tax, *Acculturation in the Americas.*

– "Ojibwa World View and Disease." In Fogelson, *Contributions to Anthropology.*

– "The Passing of the Midewiwin in the Lake Winnipeg Region." *American Anthropologist* 38 (1936).

– *The Role of Conjuring in the Saulteaux Society.* Philadelphia: University of
   Pennsylvania Press, 1942.
– "The Role of Dreams in Ojibwa Culture." In *The Dream and Human Societies,*
   ed. G. von Grunebaum and R. Caillois. Berkeley: University of California
   Press, 1966.
– "Some Empirical Aspects of Northern Saulteaux Religion." *American
   Anthropologist* 36 (1934).
Hamell, George R. "A New Perspective on Indian–White Contact: Cultural
   Symbols and Colonial Trade." *Journal of American History* 73 (1986).
– "Trading in Metaphors: The Magic of Beads, Another Perspective upon
   Indian–European Contact in Northeastern North America." In *Proceedings
   of the 1982 Glass Trade Conference,* ed. Charles F. Hayes. Rochester: Rochester
   Museum and Science Center, 1983.
Hannibal-Paci, Christopher James. "'His Knowledge and My Knowledge':
   Cree and Ojibwe Traditional Environmental Knowledge and Sturgeon
   Co-Management in Manitoba." PhD diss., University of Manitoba, 2000.
Hansen, Lise C. *The Anishinabek Land Claim and the Participation of the Indian
   People Living on the North Shore of Lake Superior in the Robinson Superior Treaty
   of 1850.* Toronto: Ministry of Natural Resources, Office of Indian Resource
   Policy, 1985.
– "Chiefs and Principal Men: A Question of Leadership in Treaty
   Negotiations." *Anthropologica* 29 (1987).
Harris, C.J. *Otters, a Study of the Recent Lutrinae.* London: Weidenfeld and
   Nicolson, 1968.
Harrison, Julia. "'He Heard Something Laugh': Otter Imagery in the
   Midewiwin," ed. David W. Penney. *Bulletin of the Detroit Institute of Arts* 62
   (1986).
– "The Midewiwin: The Retention of an Ideology." MA thesis, University of
   Calgary, 1982.
Hay, Thomas H. "The Development of Some Aspects of the Ojibwa Self and
   Its Behavioral Environment." *Ethos* 5 (1977).
Hedrick, Ulysses P. *The Land of the Crooked Tree.* New York: Oxford University
   Press, 1948.
Hegel, G.W.F. *The Phenomenology of Mind.* J.B. Baillie, trans. New York: Harper
   Torchbooks, [1807] 1967.
Heidegger, Martin. *Being and Time: A Translation of Sein und Zeit.* Joan
   Stambaugh, trans. Albany: SUNY Press, 1996.
Helbig, Alethea K., ed. *Nanabozhoo, Giver of Life.* Brighton: Green Oak, 1987.
Hele, Karl. "'By the Rapids': The Anishinabeg–Missionary Encounter at
   Bawating (Sault Ste Marie), c. 1821–1871." PhD diss., McGill University, 2002.

Henderson, James Youngblood. *First Nations Jurisprudence and Aboriginal Rights: Defining the Just Society.* Saskatoon: Native Law Centre, University of Saskatchewan, 2006.

Henry, Alexander. *Travels and Adventures in Canada and the Indian Territories between the Years 1760 and 1776.* Rutland: Charles E. Tuttle, [1809] 1969.

Herrero, Stephen. *Bear Attacks: Their Causes and Avoidance.* New York: Lyons and Burford, 1985.

Herzog, George. "Special Song Types in North American Indian Music." *Zeitschrift für Vergleichende Musikwissenschaft* 3 (1935).

Hester, Lee, Dennis McPherson, Annie Booth, and Jim Cheney. "Indigenous Worlds and Callicott's Land Ethic." *Environmental Ethics* 22 (2000).

Heth, Charlotte, ed. *Selected Reports in Ethnomusicology.* Los Angeles: University of California Press 3, no. 2 (1980).

Hewitt, J.N.B. "Nanabozho." In *Handbook of American Indians North of Mexico*, vol. 2, ed. Frederick W. Hodge. New York: Pageant, [1905] 1959.

Hickerson, Harold. *The Chippewa and Their Neighbors: A Study in Ethnohistory.* Prospects Heights: Waveland, [1970] 1988.

– "The Feast of the Dead among the Seventeenth-Century Algonkians of the Upper Great Lakes." *American Anthropologist* 62 (1960).

– "Notes on the Post-Contact Origin of the Midewiwin." *Ethnohistory* 9 (1962).

– "The Socio-Historical Significance of Two Chippewa Ceremonials." *American Anthropologist* 65 (1963).

– "The Southwestern Chippewa: An Ethnohistorical Study." *American Anthropological Association, Memoir 92,* 64 (1962).

Higgins, Edwin J., with the Whitefish Lake Indian Reserve No. 6. *Whitefish Lake Ojibway Memories.* Cobalt: Highway Book Shop, 1982.

Highway, Tomson. *Dry Lips Oughta Move to Kapuskasing.* Saskatoon: Fifth House, 1989.

Hilger, M. Inez. *Chippewa Child Life and Its Cultural Background.* St Paul: Minnesota Historical Society, [1951] 1992.

– *Chippewa Families: A Social Study of White Earth Reservation, 1938.* St Paul: Minnesota Historical Society, 1998.

– *A Social Study of One Hundred Fifty Chippewa Indian Families of the White Earth Reservation of Minnesota.* Washington: Catholic University of America Press, 1939.

Hilger, Michael, ed. "Lac Courte Oreilles: Interviews with Elders." Janine Strunk et al., transcribers. Eau Claire: University of Wisconsin Press, 1991, part 2, tape 4.

Hinshaw, Robert, ed. *Currents in Anthropology: Essays in Honor of Sol Tax.* The Hague: Mouton, 1979.

Hodge, F.W. *Handbook of Indians of Canada*. Ottawa: Geographic Board of Canada, 1913.

Hoffman, Charles, ed. *Frances Densmore and American Indian Music*. New York: Museum of the American Indian, Heye Foundation, 1968.

Hoffman, William J. *The Menomini Indians*. New York: Johnson Reprint, [1896] 1970.

– "The Midê'wiwin or 'Grand Medicine Society.'" In *Seventh Annual Report of the Bureau of Ethnology*, ed. J.W. Powell. Washington: Smithsonian Institution, 1891.

– "Notes on Ojibwa Folk-Lore." *American Anthropologist* 2 (1889).

– "Pictography and Shamanistic Rites of the Ojibwa." *American Anthropologist* 1 (1888).

– "The Travels of Manabush." In *The Menomini Indians*.

Holmes, William H. "Aboriginal Copper Mines of Isle Royale, Lake Superior." *American Anthropologist* 3 (1901).

The Holy Bible. Douay Version. London: Catholic Truth Society, [1609] 1956.

Holzkamm, Tim. "Ojibwa Horticulture in the Upper Mississippi and Boundary Water." In *Actes du dix-septième congrès des Algonquinistes*, ed. William Cowan. Ottawa: Carleton University Press, 1986.

– "Ojibwa Knowledge of Minerals and Treaty #3." In *Papers of the Nineteenth Algonquian Conference*, ed. William Cowan. Ottawa: Carleton University Press, 1988.

Holzkamm, Tim E., Leo G. Waisberg, and Joan. A. Lovisek. "'Stout Athletic Fellows': The Ojibwa during the 'Big Game Collapse.'" In *Papers of the Twenty-Sixth Algonquian Conference*, ed. David Pentland. Winnipeg: University of Manitoba Press, 1995.

House, Robert. "Preface." In Morrisseau and Robinson, *Travels*.

"How the Sapsucker Got his Colours," *Wawatay News*, 5 October 1989.

Howard, James H. "The Plains Ojibwa or Bungi." *Anthropological Paper no. 1, South Dakota Museum*. Vermillion: University of South Dakota Press, 1965.

– *The Plains-Ojibwa or Bungi: Hunters and Warriors of the Northern Prairies*. Lincoln: J and L Reprints, 1977.

– *Shawnee! The Ceremonialism of a Native Indian Tribe and Its Cultural Background*. Athens: University of Ohio Press, 1981.

– "When They Worship the Underwater Panther: A Prairie Potawotami Bundle Ceremony." *Southwestern Journal of Anthropology* 16 (1960).

Howey, Meghan C.L., and John M. O'Shea. "Bear's Journey and Study of Ritual in Archaeology." *American Antiquity* 71 (2006).

Hoyt, L.F. "Bear Grease." *Oil and Soap* 11 (1934).

I Heard the Owl Call My Name. Daryl Duke, dir. Tomorrow Entertainment, 1973.

Ihde, Don. *Listening and Voice: A Phenomenology of Sound*. Athens: University of Ohio Press, 1976.

– *Sense and Significance*. Pittsburgh: Duquesne University Press, 1973.

Ilko, John A. *Ojibwa Chiefs, 1690–1890: An Annotated Listing*. Albany: Whitston, 1995.

Ingersoll, Mrs Sampson. "Nanabush and the Flood." In Colombo and Laidlaw, *Voices of Rama*.

Ingold, Tim. "Hunting and Gathering as Ways of Perceiving the Environment." In *Redefining Nature: Ecology, Culture, and Domesticating*, ed. Roy F. Allen and K. Fujui. Oxford: Berg, 1996.

– *The Perception of the Environment: Essays on Livelihood, Dwelling, and Skill*. London: Routledge, 2000.

Irwin, Lee, ed. *Native American Spirituality: A Critical Reader*. Lincoln: University of Nebraska Press, 2000.

Isham, James. *James Isham's Observations on Hudsons Bay, 1743*, ed. E.E. Rich. Toronto: Champlain Society, 1949.

Jacko, Esther. "Traditional Ojibwa Storytelling." In *Voices: Being Native in Canada*, ed. Linda Jaine and Drew Taylor. Saskatoon: University of Saskatchewan Extension, 1992.

Jacko, James. "Bearwalk." In Southcott, *The Sound of the Drum*.

Jackson, T., ed. *The Works of the Rev. John Wesley*, vol. 8. London: Wesleyan Conference, 1866.

Jameson, Fredric. *The Political Unconscious: Narrative as a Socially Symbolic Act*. Ithaca: Cornell University Press, 1981.

Janke, Terri. *Our Culture, Our Future: Proposals for the Recognition and Protection of Indigenous Cultural and Intellectual Property*. Sydney: Australian Institute of Aboriginal and Torres Strait Island Studies, 1997.

Jenness, Diamond. *The Ojibwa Indians of Parry Island: Their Social and Religious Life*. Ottawa: National Museum of Canada, 1935.

Jilek, Wolfgang. "Altered States of Consciousness in North American Indian Ceremonials." *Ethos* 10 (1982).

Johnston, Basil. *The Bear-Walker and Other Stories*. David A. Johnson, illus. Toronto: Royal Ontario Museum, 1995.

– "History of the Ojibway People." *Tawow: Canadian Indian Cultural Magazine* 6, no. 1 (1978).

– *Honour Earth Mother = Mino-audjaudauh Mizzu-Kummik-Quae*. Wiarton: Kegedonce, 2003.

– *The Manitous: the Supernatural World of the Ojibway*. New York: Harper, 1995.

– *Mermaids and Medicine Women: Native Myths and Legends*. Toronto: Royal Ontario Museum, 1983.

– "The Midewiwin." In Helbig, *Nanabozhoo*.

– *Ojibway Ceremonies*. Toronto: McClelland and Stewart, 1982.

– *Ojibway Heritage: The Ceremonies, Rituals, Songs, Dances, Prayers, and Legends of the Ojibway*. Toronto: McClelland and Stewart, 1976.

– *Tales of the Anishinaubaek: Ojibway Legends*. Toronto: University of Toronto Press, 1993.

Jones, Blackwolf, et al. *The Healing Blanket: Stories, Values, and Poetry from Ojibwe Elders and Teachers*. Salt Lake City: Hazelden, 1998.

Jones, Ivor T., ed. *Legends of the James Bay Lowlands*. Moosonee: James Bay Education Centre, 1976.

Jones, Peter (Kahkewaquonaby). *History of the Ojebway Indians: With Especial Reference to Their Conversion to Christianity*. London: A.W. Bennett, 1861.

– *Life and Journals of Kah-ke-wa-quo-na-by, (Rev. Peter Jones), Wesleyan Missionary*. Toronto: Anson Green, at the Wesleyan Printing Establishment, 1860.

Jones, T.E.H. *The Aboriginal Rock Paintings of the Churchill River*. Regina: Department of Culture and Youth, 1981.

Jones, William. "Notes on the Fox Indians." *Journal of American Folklore* 24 (1911).

– "Ojibwa Tales from the North Shore of Lake Superior." *Journal of American Folklore* 29 (1916).

– *Ojibwa Texts*, ed. Truman Michelson, vols. 1 and 2. Leyden: E.J. Brill and G.E. Stechert, 1917, 1919.

de Josselin de Jong, J.P.B. "A Few Otchipwe Songs." *Internationales Archiv für Ethnographie* 20 (1912).

– "Original Odzibwe-Texts." *Beiträge zur Völkerkunde*, Bd 5. Leipzig und Berlin: Herausgegben aus Mitteln des Baessler-Instituts (1913).

Kant, Immanuel. *Groundwork of the Metaphysics of Morals*. H.J. Paton, trans. New York: Harper and Row, 1964.

Karklins, Karlis. *Trade Ornament Usage among the Native Peoples of Canada: A Source Book*. Ottawa: Supply and Services Canada, 1992.

Keen, Sam. *Sightings: Extraordinary Encounters with Ordinary Birds*. Mary Woodin, illus. San Francisco: Chronicle, 2007.

Keesing, Felix M. *The Menomini Indians of Wisconsin: A Study of Three Centuries of Cultural Contact and Change*. Philadelphia: American Philosophical Association, 1939.

Kegg, Maude, et al. *Portage Lake: Memories of an Ojibwe Childhood*. Minneapolis: University of Minnesota Press, 1993.

Kelly, John. "We Are All in the Ojibway Circle." In *From Ink Lake*, ed. Michael Ondaatje. Toronto: Lester and Orpen Denys, 1990.

Kelly, Chief Peter Tobasonakwut. "Presentation by Chief Peter Kelly." Unpublished paper.

Kidd, Kenneth E. "A Radiocarbon Date on a Midewiwin Scroll from Burntside Lake, Ontario," *Ontario Archaeology* 35 (1981).

Kierkegaard, Soren. *The Concept of Anxiety: A Simple Psychologically Orienting Deliberation on the Dogmatic Issue of Hereditary Sin.* Reidar Thomte and Albert B. Anderson, eds. and trans. Princeton: Princeton University Press, [1844] 1980.

Kinew, Kathi Avery. "Manito Gitigaan: Governance in the Great Spirit's Garden: Wild Rice in Treaty #3 from the Pre-Treaty to the 1990s." In *Papers of the Twenty-Sixth Algonquian Conference,* ed. David Pentland. Winnipeg: University of Manitoba Press, 1995.

King, Cecil. "J.-B. Assiginack: Arbiter of Two Worlds." *Ontario History* 86 (1994).

Kinietz, W. Vernon. *Chippewa Village: The Story of Katikitegon.* Bloomfield Hills: Cranbrook Institute of Science, 1947.

– *The Indians of the Western Great Lakes, 1615–1760.* Ann Arbor: University of Michigan Press, 1965.

Kinsey, Mabel C. "An Ojibwa Song." *Journal of American Folklore* 46 (1933).

Kohl, Johann. *Kitchi-Gami: Wanderings Round Lake Superior.* Lascelles Wraxall, trans. St Paul: Ross and Haines, [1866] 1956.

Kostelanetz, Richard, ed. *The Yale Gertrude Stein.* New Haven: Yale University Press, 1980.

Kugel, Rebecca. "Of Missionaries and Their Cattle: Ojibwa Perceptions of a Missionary as Evil Shaman." In *American Encounters: Natives and Newcomers from European Contact to Indian Removal, 1500–1850,* ed. Peter C. Mancall and James H. Merrell. New York: Routledge, 2000.

– "Religion Mixed with Politics: The 1836 Conversion of Mang'osid of Fond du Lac." *Ethnohistory* 37 (1990).

– *To Be the Main Leaders of Our People: A History of Minnesota Ojibwe Politics, 1825–1898.* East Lansing: Michigan State University Press, 1998.

Kurath, Gertrude P. "Blackrobe and Shaman: The Christianization of Michigan Algonquians." *Papers of the Michigan Academy of Science, Arts, and Letters* 44 (1959).

– "Chippewa Sacred Songs in Religious Metamorphosis." *Scientific Monthly* 79 (1954).

– "Songs and Dances of Great Lakes Indians." Folkways FE 4003 with disc notes.

La Fortune, Anuqcuag/Richard. "Tell Me a Story … Raven Makes a Necklace," *Wawatay News,* 28 July 1994.

Lacombe, Albert. *Dictionnaire de la Langue des Cris.* Montreal: C.O. Beauchemin et Valois, 1874.

Lafleur, Laurence J. "On the Midé of the Ojibway." *American Anthropologist* 42 (1940).

Landes, Ruth. *Ojibwa Religion and the Midéwiwin.* Madison: University of Wisconsin Press, 1968.

– *Ojibwa Sociology.* New York: AMS, 1969.

– *The Ojibwa Woman,* Lincoln: University of Nebraska Press, [1938] 1997.

Lanoue, Guy. *Images in Stone: A Theory on Interpreting Rock Art.* Rome: Art Center, 1989.

Le Jeune, Paul. In Thwaites, *The Jesuit Relations,* 12 (1637).

Le Mercier, François. In Thwaites, *The Jesuit Relations,* 50 (1667).

Leary, James Russell. "Cultural Variation, Personality, and Values among the Chippewa." PhD diss., Harvard University, 1960.

Leenbach, Richard Benton. "Crafts and Cultural Contact: The Effects of Donor Cultures on the Crafts Production of the Chippewa Indians of Michigan." MA thesis, Pennsylvania State University, 1978.

Leighton, Douglas. "Assiginack, Jean-Baptiste." *Dictionary of Canadian Biography,* vol. IX: *1861 to 1870.* Toronto: University of Toronto Press, 1976.

Leonard, Rhoda, and William S. Briscoe. *Sleeky the Otter.* Joseph Capozio, illus. Toronto: Addison-Wesley, 1964.

Lévi-Strauss, Claude. *From Honey to Ashes: Introduction to a Science of Mythology 2.* John and Doreen Weightman, trans. New York: Harper and Row, 1973.

– *The Naked Man.* John and Doreen Weightman, trans. New York: Harper and Row, 1981.

– *The Origin of Table Manners: Introduction to a Science of Mythology 3.* John and Doreen Weightman, trans. New York: Harper and Row, [1968] 1978.

– *The Raw and the Cooked: Introduction to a Science of Mythology 1.* New York: Harper Torchbooks [1964] 1970.

– *The Savage Mind.* Chicago: University of Chicago Press, 1966.

Liers, Emil E. *An Otter's Story.* Tony Pallazo, illus. New York: Viking, 1953.

Linderman, Frank Bird. *Indian Old-Man Stories.* Lincoln: University of Nebraska Press, 1996.

"Living Water." Episode 3 of *Planet Earth* (TV series). David Attenborough, narrator; Alastair Fothergill, producer. British Broadcasting Corporation, 2006.

Long, Megan. *Ghosts of the Great Lakes: More Than Mere Legend.* Toronto: Lynx Images, 2003.

Lovisek, Joan A. "The Political Evolution of the Boundary Waters Ojibwa." In *Papers of the Twenty-Fourth Algonquian Conference,* ed. William Cowan. Ottawa: Carleton University Press, 1993.

Lowden, Stephanie. *Time of the Eagle: A Story of an Ojibwe Winter.* Fredericton: Partners, 2004.

Lowenthal, David. "Past Time, Present Place: Landscape and Memory." *Geographical Review* 1 (1975).

Lukes, Steven. *Liberals and Cannibals: The Implications of Diversity.* London: Verso, 2003.

Lund, Duane R. *The Lives and Times of Three Powerful Ojibwe Chiefs: Curly Head, Hole-In-the-Day the Elder, and Hole-In-the-Day the Younger.* Silver Spring: Adventure House, 2003.

Lyford, Carrie. *The Crafts of the Ojibwa.* Washington: U.S. Office of Indian Affairs, 1942.

Lynch, Wayne. *Bears, Monarchs of the Northern Wilderness.* Vancouver: Greystone, 1993.

Mallery, Garrick. *Picture-Writing of the American Indians,* vols. 1 and 2. Washington: Bulletin of American Ethnology, [1893] 1972.

Mandelbaum, David G. *The Plains Cree: An Ethnographic, Historical, and Comparative Study.* Regina: Canadian Plains Research Center, 1979.

Marsden, Lottie. "The Girl and the Bear." In Colombo and Laidlaw, *Voices of Rama.*

– "The Owl Witch." In Colombo and Laidlaw, *Voices of Rama.*

– "The Squaw Who Lived with a Serpent." In Colombo and Laidlaw, *Voices of Rama.*

Marsh, James. H., ed. "Forest Regions." *The Canadian Encyclopedia,* vol 2. Edmonton: Hurtig, 1985.

Martin, Calvin. *In the Spirit of the Earth: Rethinking History and Time.* Baltimore: Johns Hopkins University Press, 1992.

– *Keepers of the Game: Indian–Animal Relationships and the Fur Trade.* Berkeley: University of California Press, 1978.

Martin, Lawrence T. "Animal Blessings," *YouTube,* 2007. http://www.youtube.com/watch?v=T5I2GG7e_gk.

– "Animal Forms of Manidog in the Anishinabe Earth-Diver Story." In *Papers of the Twenty-Sixth Algonguian Conference,* ed. David Pentland. Winnipeg: University of Manitoba Press, 1995.

– "J.J. Enmegahbowh and the Christian Anishinaabeg of White Earth." In *Christianity and Native Cultures: Perspectives from Different Regions of the World,* vol. 13, ed. Cyriac K. Pullapilly et al. St Mary's College, Notre Dame: Cross Cultural Publications, 2004.

– "Native American Values (English and Ojibwe)." Unpublished paper.

– "Simon Pokagon: Charlatan or Authentic Spokesman for the 19th-Century Anishinaabeg?" In *Papers of the Twenty-Ninth Algonquian Conference,* ed. David Pentland. Winnipeg: University of Manitoba Press, 1998.

Martin, Susan R. *Wonderful Power: The Story of Ancient Copper Working in the Lake Superior Basin*. Detroit: Wayne State University Press, 1999.

Martinez, David. "Along the Horizon a World Appears: George Morrison and the Pursuit of an American Indian Esthetic." In *American Indian Thought: Philosophical Essays*, ed. Anne Waters. London: Blackwell, 2004.

Maskunow, Joby. "Why Owls Die with Wings Outspread." In Guss, *The Language of the Birds*.

Mason, Philip P., ed. *Schoolcraft's Expedition to Lake Itasca: The Discovery of the Source of the Mississippi*. East Lansing: Michigan State University Press, [1834] 1958.

– *Schoolcraft's Ojibwa Lodge Stories: Life on the Lake Superior Frontier*. East Lansing: Michigan State University Press, 1997.

Massicotte, Jean-Paul, and Claude Lessard. "La danse chez les Indiens de la Nouvelle France aux XVIIe et XVIIIe siècles." *Revue d'ethnologie du Québec* 11 (1980).

Maynard, Daniel P. "Marquette's Kawbawgams." *Michigan History* 74 (1990).

McCellan, Catharine. *The Girl Who Married the Bear*. Ottawa: National Museum of Canada, 1970.

McClellan, Joseph. *The Birth of Nanabosho*. Winnipeg: Pemmican, 1987.

McClurken, James M. *A Visual Culture History of the Little Traverse Bay Bands of Odawa, Gah-Baeh-Jhagwah-Buk, The Way It Happened*. East Lansing: Michigan State University Museum, 1991.

McDermott, P.W. "Snake Stories of the Lake Erie Island." *Inland Seas* 3 (1947).

McEntire, Nancy Cassell, et al. *Discourse in Ethnomusicology III: Essays in Honor of Frank J. Gillis*. Bloomington: Ethnomusicology Publications Group, 1991.

McLeod, John. "Nanabush and the Pale Stranger." *Wawatay News*, 24 April 1992.

McLuhan, Elizabeth, and Tom Hill. *Norval Morrisseau and the Emergence of the Image Makers*. Toronto: Methuen, 1984.

McNally, Michael D. *Ojibwe Songs: Hymns, Grief, and a Native Culture in Motion*. New York: Oxford University Press, 2000.

McPherson, Dennis. "A Definition of Culture: Canada and First Nations." In Jace Weaver, ed., *Native American Religious Identity: Unforgotten Gods*. Maryknoll: Orbis, 1998.

McPherson, Dennis H., and J. Douglas Rabb. "Heteronomy and Autonomy in Canadian Native Policy." Paper presented at the Seventh Annual Meeting of the Ontario Philosophical Society, Carleton University, Ottawa, 1991.

– *Indian from the Inside: Native American Philosophy and Cultural Renewal*. Jefferson: McFarland, 2011.

– *Indian from the Inside: A Study in Ethno-Metaphysics*. Thunder Bay: Lakehead University, Centre for Northern Studies, 1993.

– "Transformative Philosophy and Indigenous Thought: A Comparison of Lakota and Ojibwa World Views." In *Papers of the Twenty-Ninth Algonquian Conference*, ed. David Pentland. Winnipeg: University of Manitoba Press, 1999.

Menitove, Marcy, and Joanne Danford, eds. *Woodlands: Contemporary Art of the Anishnabe*. Janet Anderson, photography. Thunder Bay: Thunder Bay Art Gallery, 1989.

Meyer, Leroy, and Tony Ramirez, "'Wakinyan Hotan,' 'The Thunder Beings Call Out': The Inscrutability of Lakota/Dakota Metaphysics." In *From Our Eyes: Learning from Indigenous Peoples*, ed. Sylvia O'Meara and Douglas A. West. Toronto: Garamond, 1996.

Michelson, Truman. "What Happened to Green Bear Who Was Blessed With a Sacred Pack." *Anthropological Papers, Bulletin 119*. Washington: Government Printing Office, 1938.

– ed. *The Owl Sacred Pack of the Fox Indians*. Washington: Smithsonian Institution, 1921.

Midasuganj/Ten Claw. "Nanabushu Is Miraculously Fed Bear-Grease." In Jones, *Ojibwa Texts*, vol. 1.

Miles, Kathy A., and Charles F. Peters II. "The Big Dipper and Colors of Autumn." http://starryskies.com/articles/dln/9-97/dipper.colours.html.

Miller, Cary. "Gifts as Treaties: The Political Use of Received Gifts in Anishinaabeg Communities, 1820–1832." *American Indian Quarterly* 26 (2002).

– "Ojibwe Leadership in the Early Nineteenth Century." PhD diss., University of North Carolina, Chapel Hill, 2003.

Miller, Christopher L., and George R. Hamell. "A New Perspective on Indian–White Contact: Cultural Symbols and Colonial Trade." In *American Encounters: Natives and Newcomers from European Contact to Indian Removal, 1500–1850*, ed. Peter C. Mancall and James H. Merrell. New York: Routledge, 2000.

Miller, Ed. L., and Jon Jensen. *Questions That Matter: An Invitation to Philosophy*. New York: McGraw-Hill, 2004.

Mihesuah, Devon A. "Suggested Guidelines for Institutions with Scholars Who Conduct Research on American Indians." *American Indian Culture and Research Journal* 17 (1993).

Momaday, N. Scott. "A First American Views His Land." *National Geographic* 150 (1976).

Morgan, Jerry. *Baaga' adowe, Play LaCrosse*. Leech Lake: Leech Lake Band of Ojibwe, Youth Division, 2004.

Morin, Gail. *Chippewa Half-Breeds of Lake Superior*. Orange Park: Quintin, 1998.

Morito, Bruce. *Thinking Ecologically: Environmental Thought, Values, and Policy.* Halifax: Fernwood, 2002.

Morris, Alexander. *The Treaties of Canada with the Indians of Manitoba and North-West Territories Including the Negotiations on Which They Were Based.* Saskatoon: Fifth House, [1880] 1991.

Morris, Billy. "Kakabish (chouette de tengmalm) et le rapide," "Kakabish (Boreal Owl) and the Rapids." In Desveaux, *La mythologie,* vol. 2.

Morris, David. "L'homme à-la-peau-de-hibou," "Man with an Owl Skin." In Desveaux, *La mythologie,* vol. 2.

Morris, John-George. "Mingesowash (nid d'aigles)," "Mingesowash (Eagles' Nest)." In Desveaux, *La mythologie,* vol. 2.

Morris, Joseph. "L'homme au hiboux," "Owl Man." In Desveaux, *La mythologie,* vol. 2.

– "L'homme aux lagopedes," "Grouse Man." In Desveaux, *La mythologie,* vol. 2.

Morris, Roy. In *Newsletter of Thunder Bay Art Gallery.* Summer 2008.

Morrison, Alvin H. "Dawnland Directors: Status and Role of Seventeenth-Century Wabanaki Sagamores." In *Papers of the Seventh Algonquian Conference,* ed. William Cowan. Ottawa: Carleton University Press, 1976.

Morrison, George, et al. *Morrison's Horizon: New Paintings from the Horizon Series.* Minneapolis: Minneapolis Institute of Arts, 1998.

Morrisseau, Norval. "Foreword." In Schwarz, *Windigo and Other Tales of the Ojibways.*

– *Legends of My People, the Great Ojibway.* Selwyn Dewdney, ed. Toronto: Ryerson, 1965.

Morrisseau, Norval, and Basil H. Johnston. *The Art of Norval Morrisseau, the Writings of Basil H. Johnston.* Calgary: Glenbow Museum, 1999.

Morrisseau Norval, and Donald Robinson. *Travels to the House of Invention.* Toronto: Key Porter, 1997.

Murray, David. *Indian Giving: Economies of Power in Indian–White Exchanges.* Amherst: University of Massachusetts, 2000.

Myers, Frank A. "The Bear-Walk (Muck-wa-bim-moo-say): A Witchcraft Belief Still Current among the Great Lakes Indians." *Inland Seas* 9 (1953).

Neill, Edward D. "History of the Ojibways, and their Connection with Fur Traders, Based upon Official and Other Records." In Warren, *History of the Ojibway Nation.*

Nelson, Richard E. "Fond du Lac Treaty Portraits: 1826." In *Papers of the Eighteenth Algonquian Conference,* ed. William Cowan. Ottawa: Carleton University Press, 1987.

– "Inscribed Birch Bark Scrolls and Other Objects of the Midewiwin." In *Actes du quatorzième congrès des algonquinistes*, ed. William Cowan. Ottawa: Carleton University Press, 1983.

– "Midewiwin Medicine Bags of the Ojibwa." In *Papers of the Fifteenth Algonquian Conference*, ed. William Cowan. Ottawa: Carleton University Press, 1984.

Nesper, Larry. *The Walleye War: The Struggle for Ojibwe Spearfishing and Treaty Rights.* Lincoln: University of Nebraska Press, 2005.

– "Waswagoninniwug: Conflict, Tradition, and Identity in the Lac du Flambeau Band of Lake Superior Chippewa Indians' Spearfishing the Ceded Territory of Wisconsin." PhD diss., University of Chicago, 1994, vols. 1 and 2.

Nibenegenesabe, Jacob. "Why Owls Die with Wings Outspread." In *The Wishing Bone Cycle: Narrative Poems from the Swampy Cree Indians*, ed. Howard A. Norman. Santa Barbara: Ross-Erikson, 1982.

Nichols, John D. *An Ojibwe Text Anthology.* London: Centre for Research and Teaching of Canadian Native Languages, University of Western Ontario, 1988.

Nichols, John, and Earl Nyholm. *A Concise Dictionary of Minnesota Ojibwe.* Minneapolis: University of Minnesota Press, 1995.

Nishnawbe-aski Nationa. A History of the Cree and Ojibway of Northern Ontario. Timmins: Ojibway–Cree Cultural Centre, 1986.

Norggard, Lorrain, director. *"Bimaadiziwin:* A Healthy Way of Life." In *Waasa Inaabidaa: We Look in All Directions.* Winona LaDuke, narrator. PBS Eight, WDSE-TV, Duluth, 2002, Episode 4.

Norman, H.A. "Modern Algonkin Songs Using Mide Symbols." *Alcheringa* 3 (1971).

Oberholtzer, Cath. "Are Diamonds a Cree Girl's Best Friend? Preliminary Musings." In *Actes du trente-deuxième congrès des algonquinistes*, ed. John D. Nichols. Winnipeg: University of Manitoba Press, 2001.

– *Dream Catchers: Legend, Lore, and Artifacts.* Richmond Hill: Firefly, 2012.

– "If Bears Could Talk." In *Actes du vingtième congrès des Algonquinistes*, ed. William Cowan. Ottawa: Carleton University Press, 1989.

– "A Womb with a View: Cree Moss Bags and Cradleboards." In *Papers of the Twenty-Eighth Algonquian Conference*, ed. David Pentland. Winnipeg: University of Manitoba Press, 1997.

Odenigun. "Song of the Owl Medicine." In Densmore, *Chippewa Music*, 1.

Ones, Charles Frederick. "Social and Cultural Change in Three Minnesota Chippewa Indian Communities." PhD diss., Yale University Press, 1962.

Osborne, Harold. *South American Mythology*. Feltham: Hamlyn House, 1970.

Oshogay, Delia. "Wenebojo Myths from Lac Courte Oreilles." Maggie Lamorie, interpreter. In Barnouw, *Wisconsin Chippewa Myths*.

Overholt, Thomas W., and J. Baird Callicott. *Clothed-in-Fur and Other Tales: An Introduction to an Ojibwa World View*. New York: University Press of America, 1982.

The OWL Pages, http://www.owlpages.com, 1994.

Ozawamik, Sam. "Snake Spirit." In Colombo and Laidlaw, *Voices of Rama*.

Paap, Howard Dorsey. "The Ojibwe Midewiwin: A Structural Analysis." PhD diss., University of Minnesota, 1985.

Paine, Stefani. *The Nature of Sea Otters: A Story of Survival*. Vancouver: Greystone, 1993.

Palazzo-Craig, Janet. *The Ojibwe of Michigan, Wisconsin, Minnesota, and North Dakota*. New York: Rosen, 2005.

Panofsky, Erwin. *Meaning in the Visual Arts: Papers in and on Art History*. New York: Doubleday, 1955.

Paper, Jordan. *Offering Smoke: The Sacred Pipe and North American Religion*. Moscow: University of Idaho Press, 1988.

Paredes, J. Anthony, ed. *Anishinabe: Six Studies of Modern Chippewa*. Tallahassee: University Presses of Florida, 1980.

Parker, Seymour. "Motives in Eskimo and Ojibwa Mythology." *Ethnology* 1 (1962).

– "The Wiitiko Psychosis in the Context of Ojibwa Personality and Culture." *American Anthropologist* 62 (1960).

Parthun, Paul. "Ojibwe Music in Minnesota." PhD diss., University of Minnesota, 1976.

Peacock, Thomas, ed. *A Forever Story: The People and Community of the Fond du Lac Reservation*. Cloquet: Fond du Lac Band of Lake Superior Chippewa, 1998.

Peacock, Thomas, and Marlene Wisuri. *Ojibwe Waasa Inaabidaa: We Look in All Directions*. Afton: Afton Historical Society, 2002.

Pelletier, Julie Anne. "The Role of Ritual in a Contemporary Ojibwa Tribe." PhD diss., Michigan State University, 2002.

Pelug, Melissa A. "Pimadaziwin: Contemporary Rituals in Odawa Community." *American Indian Quarterly* 20 (1996).

Penesi/Kagige Penasi/Forever Bird, John. "The Boy That Was Carried Away by a Bear." In Jones, *Ojibwa Texts*, vol. 2.

– "The Man Who Transformed Himself into a Bear." In Jones, *Ojibwa Texts*, vol. 2.

– "Nanabush Is Miraculously Fed Bear-Grease," In Jones, *Ojibwa Texts*, vol. 1.

– "The Spirit-World." In Jones, *Ojibwa Texts*, vol. 2.

– "The Thunderers." In Jones, *Ojibwa Texts*, vol. 2.

Penney, David W. "Great Lakes Indian Art: An Introduction." In Penney, *Great Lakes Indian Art*.

– *Great Lakes Indian Art*. Detroit: Wayne State University Press, 1989.

– ed. *Bulletin of the Detroit Institute of Arts* 62 (1986).

Pete, John. "Winabijou Looks for the Wolf." In Helbig, *Nanabozhoo*.

Peters, Bernard C. "The Origin and Meaning of Chippewa and French Place Names along the Shoreline of the Keweenaw Peninsula." *Michigan Academician* 17 (1985).

– "Wa-bish-kee-pe-nas and the Chippewa Reverence for Copper." *Michigan Historical Review* 15 (1989).

Peterson, Jacqueline. "Review of *Many Tender Ties* [1980] and *Strangers in Blood*." *Minnesota History* 48 (1982).

Pettipas, Katherine. "Tie Creek Study: A Commentary." In Roseau River Chapter, *Tie Creek Study*.

Pfaff, Tim, et al. *Paths of the People: The Ojibwe in the Chippewa Valley, 1993*. Eau Claire: Chippewa Valley Museum, 1993.

Phillips, Ruth B. "Dreams and Designs: Iconographic Problems in Great Lakes Twined Bags." In Penney, *Great Lakes Indian Art*.

– "Foreword." In McClurken, *A Visual Culture History*.

– *Patterns of Power, Vers la force spirituelle: The Jasper Grant Collection and Great Lakes Indian Art of the Early Nineteenth Century*. Kleinburg: McMichael Canadian Collection, 1984.

– "Quilled Bark from the Central Great Lakes: A Transcultural History." In Feest, *Studies in American Indian Art*.

– "Zigzag and Spiral: Geometric Motifs in Great Lakes Indian Costume." In *Papers of the Fifteenth Algonquian Conference*, ed. William Cowan. Ottawa: Carleton University Press, 1984.

Pine, Frank. *Two Chippewa Stories from Baraga-L'Anse, Michigan*. Lac du Flambeau: Great Lakes Inter-Tribal Council, 1975.

Pitezel, John. H. *The Life of Rev. Peter Marksman, an Ojibwa Missionary, Illustrating the Triumphs of the Gospel among the Ojibwa*. Cincinnati: Western Methodist Book Concern, 1901.

– *Lights and Shades of Missionary Life*. Cincinnati: Western Methodist Book Concern, 1869.

Pomedli, Michael M. "The Concept of the 'Soul' in *The Jesuit Relations:* Were There Any Philosophers among the North American Indians?" *Laval théologique et philosophique* 41 (1985).

– "Eighteenth-Century Treaties: Amended Iroquois Condolence Rituals." *American Indian Quarterly* 19 (1995).

– "Foreword." In Berbaum, *Ojibwa Powwow World*.

– "The Ojibwa and Bishop Frederick Baraga: Mutual Influences through the Confessional." *Dve Domovini / Two Homelands* (Slovenia) 17 (2004).
– "Ojibwa Influences on Virgil Michel." *Worship* 72 (1996).
– "Ojibway Healing and Ordering in Treaty Number Three." In *Sacred Lands: Aboriginal World Views, Claims, and Conflicts*, ed. Jill Oakes et al. Edmonton: Canadian Circumpolar Institute, and Winnipeg: University of Manitoba Press, 1998.
– "The Otter: Laughter and Treaty Three." In *Actes du trente-deuxième congrès des Algonquinistes*, ed. John D. Nichols. Winnipeg: University of Manitoba Press, 2001.
– "Owls: Windows and Voices on the Ojibwa and Midewiwin Worlds." *American Indian Culture and Research Journal* 26 (2002).
– "Treaties: Rights or Relationships?" In *Papers of the Thirtieth Algonquian Conference*, ed. David Pentland. Winnipeg: University of Manitoba Press, 1999.
– "'Trick or Treaty'? – Treaty Three, Rice, and Manitous." In *Papers of the Twenty-Ninth Algonquian Conference*, ed. David Pentland. Winnipeg: University of Manitoba Press, 1998.
– "True Confessions: The Ojibwa, Bishop Baraga, and the Sacrament of Penance." In *Christianity and Native Cultures: Perspectives from Different Regions of the World*, ed. Cyriac K. Pullapilly. St Mary's College, Notre Dame: Cross Cultural Publications, 2004.
Porter, Frank W. *The Chippewa – Great Lakes*. New York: Chelsea House, 1995.
Preston, Richard. *Cree Narrative: Expressing the Personal Meaning of Events*. Ottawa: National Museums of Canada, 1975.
– "Ritual Hangings: An Aboriginal 'Survival' in a Northern North American Trapping Community." *Man* 64 (1964).
Preston, Sarah. "Competent Social Behavior within the Context of Childbirth: A Cree Example." In *Papers of the Thirteenth Algonquian Conference*, ed. William Cowan. Ottawa: Carleton University Press, 1982.
Przybilla, Art, and Randy Councillor. *Ojibwe Tales: Stories of the Ojibwe People*. International Falls: Lake States Interpretive Association, 2004.
Rabb, J. Douglas. "From Triangles to Tripods: Polycentrism in Environmental Ethics." *Environment Ethics* 14 (1992).
Radin, Paul. "Some Aspects of Puberty Fasting among Ojibwa." *Museum Bulletin* 2 (1914).
– *Some Myths and Tales of the Ojibwa of Southeastern Ontario*. Ottawa: Geological Survey of Canada, 1914.
Rae, Edward. "The Bearchild." In Stevens, *Legends from the Forest*.
Raines, Paula M. "Drumming the Journey Home: Exploring Shamanic Consciousness." PhD diss., Union for Experimenting Colleges and Universities, Antioch College, 1988.

Rajnovich, Grace. *Reading Rock Art: Interpreting the Indian Rock Paintings of the Canadian Shield.* Toronto: Natural Heritage / Natural History, 1994.

Reagan, Albert B. "Medicine Songs of George Farmer." *American Anthropologist* 24 (1922).

– "A Ritual Parchment and Certain Historical Charts of the Bois Fort Ojibwa of Minnesota." *Americana* 29 (1935).

– "The Society of Dreamers and the O-ge-che-dah or Head-Men Dance of the Bois Fort (Ojibwe) Indians of Nett Lake, Minnesota." *Wisconsin Archaeologist* 13 (1934).

Redsky, James. *Great Leader of the Ojibway: Mis-quona-queb.* Toronto: McClelland and Stewart, 1972.

Reid, C.S. Paddy. "The Tranquil Channel Petroglyphs: Cultural Continuities in the Lake of the Woods Rock Art." *Heritage Record* 8 (1977).

Reid, Dorothy. *Tales of Nanabozho.* Toronto: Oxford University Press, 1963.

Relland, Michael Roger. "The Teachings of the Bear Clan: As Told by Saulteaux Elder Danny Musqua." MA thesis, University of Saskatchewan, 1998.

Report of the Royal Commission on Aboriginal Peoples. Ottawa: Minister of Supply and Services Canada, 1996. 5 vols.

Rex, Cathy. "Survivance and Fluidity: George Copway's *The Life, History, and Travels of Kah-ge-ga- gah-bowh.*" *Studies in American Indian Literatures* 18 (2006).

Rhodes, Richard. "Baseball, Hotdogs, Apple Pie, and Chevrolets." In *Papers of the Fifteenth Algonquian Conference*, ed. William Cowan. Ottawa: Carleton University Press, 1984.

– *Eastern Ojibwa–Chippewa–Ottawa Dictionary.* Berlin: Walter De Gruyter, 1993.

– "Some Aspects of Ojibwa Discourse." In *Papers of the Tenth Algonquian Conference*, ed. William Cowan. Ottawa: Carleton University Press, 1979.

Rhodes, Richard, and Evelyn Todd. "Subarctic Algonquian Languages." In Sturtevant, *Handbook of North American Indians.*

Ricoeur, Paul. "The Hermeneutics of Symbols and Philosophical Reflection." *International Philosophical Quarterly* 2 (1962).

Ridington, Robin. "Voice, Representation, and Dialogue: The Poetics of Native American Spiritual Traditions." In Irwin, *Native American Spirituality.*

Ridington, Robin, and Dennis Hastings. *Blessing for a Long Time: The Sacred Pole of the Omaha Tribe.* Lincoln: University of Nebraska Press, 1997.

Ritter, Dale W., and Eric W. Ritter. "Prehistoric Pictography in North America of Medical Significance." In Grollig and Haley, *Medical Anthropology.*

Ritzenthaler, Robert E. "Chippewa Preoccupation with Health: Change in a Traditional Attitude Resulting from Modern Health Problems." *Bulletin of the Public Museum of the City of Milwaukee* 19 (1953).

– "Chippewa Preoccupation with Health: Change in a Traditional Attitude Resulting from Modern Health Problems." PhD diss., Columbia University, 1950.

Ritzenthaler, Robert E., and Pat Ritzenthaler. *The Woodland Indians of the Western Great Lakes.* Prospect Heights: Waveland, 1991.

Rockwell, David. *Giving Voice to Bear: North American Indian Rituals, Myths, and Images of the Bear.* Toronto: Roberts Rinehart, 1991.

Rogers, E.S. *The Round Lake Ojibwa.* Toronto: Royal Ontario Museum, 1962.

Rogers, John/Chief Snow Cloud. *Red World and White: Memories of a Chippewa Boyhood.* Norman: University of Oklahoma Press, 1996.

Rokala, Dwight Allen. "The Anthropological Genetics and Demography of the Southwestern Ojibwa in the Greater Leech Lake–Chippewa National Forest Area." PhD diss., University of Minnesota, 1971.

Ronnander, Chad Delano. "Many Paths to the Pine: Mdewakanton Dakotas, Fur Traders, Ojibwes, and the United States in Wisconsin's Chippewa Valley, 1815–1837." PhD diss., University of Minnesota, 2003.

Roseau River Chapter, Three Fires Society. *Tie Creek Study: An Anishinabe Understanding of the Petroforms in Whiteshell Provincial Park.* Winnipeg: Manitoba Department of Natural Resources, 1990, Parts 1 and 2.

Rosinsky, Natalie M. *The Ojibwe and Their History.* North Mankato: Compass Point, 2005.

Rossetti, Bernadette. *Musdzi Udada, the Owl: A Carrier Indian Legend.* Roman Muntener, illus. Vancouver: Yinka Dene Language Institute, 1991.

Roufs, Tim, and Bernard J. James. "Myth in Method: More on Ojibwa Culture." *Current Anthropology* 15 (1975).

Ruoff, A. LaVonne Brown. "Gerald Vizenor: Compassionate Trickster." *American Indian Quarterly* 9 (1985).

Ruoff, A. LaVonne Brown, and Donald B. Smith, eds. *Life, Letters, and Speeches: George Copway (Kahgegagahbowh).* Lincoln: University of Nebraska Press, 1997.

Ryan, Allan J. *The Trickster Shift: Humour and Irony in Contemporary Native Art.* Vancouver: UBC Press, 1999.

Sah-Kah-Odjew-Wahg-Sah (Fred Pine). "Preface." In Conway, *Painted Dreams.*

Sakry, Mark, ed. "Naniboujou and the Thunderbirds, Trickster of Ojibway Legends." Carl Gawboy, illus. *Lake Superior Magazine,* October-November 1992.

Sandy, Thos. "The Man and the Bears." In Colombo and Laidlaw, *Voices of Rama.*

Savard, Rémi. *Contes indiens de la Basse Côte Nord du Saint Laurent.* Ottawa: National Museum of Man, 1979.

Schell, James P. *In Ojibway Country: A Story of Early Missions on the Minnesota Frontier.* Walhalla: Charles H. Lee, 1911.

Schenck, Theresa. "The Algonquian Totem and Totemism: A Distortion of the Semantic Field." In *Papers of the Twenty-Eighth Algonquian Conference,* ed. David·H. Pentland. Winnipeg: University of Manitoba Press, 1997.

– "Continuity and Change in the Sociopolitical Organization of the Lake Superior Ojibwa." PhD diss., New Brunswick–Rutgers, State University of New Jersey, 1995.

– "Identifying the Ojibwa." In *Actes du vingt-cinquième congrès des algonquinistes,* ed. William Cowan. Ottawa: Carleton University Press, 1994.

– *"The Voice of the Crane Echoes Afar": The Sociopolitical Organization of the Lake Superior Ojibwa, 1640–1855.* New York: Garland, 1997.

– "William Warren's History of the Ojibway People: Tradition, History, and Context." In *Reading beyond Words: Contexts for Native History,* ed. Jennifer S.H. Brown, and Elizabeth Vibert. Peterborough: Broadview, 2003.

– *William W. Warren: The Life, Letters, and Times of an Ojibwa Leader.* Lincoln: University of Nebraska Press, 2007.

Schlesier, Karl. "Rethinking the Midewiwin and the Plains Ceremonial Called the Sun Dance." *Plains Anthropologist* 35 (1990).

Schmalz, Peter S. *The Ojibwa of Southern Ontario.* Toronto: University of Toronto Press, 1991.

– "The Role of the Ojibwa in the Conquest of Southern Ontario, 1650–1701." *Ontario History* 76 (1984).

Schoolcraft, Henry Rowe. *Historical and Statistical Information Respecting the History, Condition and Prospects of the Indian Tribes of the United States.* Seth Eastman, illus. Philadelphia: Lippincott, Grambo, 1851–7 (1969). 6 vols.

– *The Indian in his Wigwam, or Characteristics of the Red Race of America.* New York: W.H. Graham, 1848.

– *The Literary Voyager or Muzzeniegun.* Philip P. Mason, ed. East Lansing: Michigan State University Press, 1962.

– *Personal Memoirs of a Residence of Thirty Years with the Indian Tribes on the American Frontier A.D. 1812 to A.D. 1842.* New York: Arno, 1975.

Schwarz, Douglas O. "Plains Indian Theology: As Expressed in Myth and Ritual, and in the Ethics of the Culture." PhD diss., Fordham University, 1981.

Schwarz, Herbert T. *Windigo and Other Tales of the Ojibways.* Norval Morrisseau, illus. Toronto: McClelland and Stewart, 1969.

Scowen, Peter. "The Evolution of 'Fur Kids'." *Globe and Mail,* 14 December 2012.

Scribe, Murdo. *Murdo's Story: A Legend from Northern Manitoba.* Terry Gallagher, illus. Winnipeg: Pemmican, 1985.

Serafine, Mary Louise. *Music as Cognition: The Development of Thought in Sound.* New York: Columbia University Press, 1988.

Servais, Olivier. *Des jesuites chez les Amerindiens ojibwas*. Paris: Karthala, 2005.

Shepard, Paul. "A Post-Historic Primitivism." In Gowdy, *Limited Wants, Unlimited Means*.

Shepard, Paul, and Barry Sanders. *The Sacred Paw: The Bear in Nature, Myth, and Literature*. New York: Viking, 1985.

Shields, Norman D. "Anishinabek Political Alliance in the Post-Confederation Period: The Grand General Indian Council of Ontario, 1870–1936." MA thesis, Queen's University, 2001.

Shunien. "The Bear and the Eagle." In Hoffman, *The Menomini Indians*.

– "The Rabbit and the Saw-whet." In Hoffman, *The Menomini Indians*.

Simms, S.C. "Myths of the Bungees or Swampy Indians of Lake Winnipeg." *Journal of American Folklore* 19 (1906).

Sims, Catherine A. "Algonkian–British Relations in the Upper Great Lakes Region: Gathering to Give and to Receive Presents, 1815–1843." PhD diss., University of Western Ontario, 1992.

Sinclair, Lister, and Jack Pollock. *The Art of Norval Morrisseau*. Toronto: Methuen, 1979.

Skinner, Alanson. "Bear Customs of the Cree and Other Algonkin Indians of Northern Ontario." *Papers and Records / Ontario Historical Society* 12 (1914).

– *Medicine Ceremony of the Menomini, Iowa, and Wahpeton Dakota: With Notes on the Ceremony among the Ponca, Bungi Ojibwa, and Potawatomi*. New York: AMS, 1984.

– "Notes on the Eastern Cree and Northern Saulteaux." *Anthropological Papers of the American Museum of Natural History*. New York: American Museum of Natural History 9, no. 1 (1911).

– "Political Organization, Cults, and Ceremonies of the Plains-Ojibway and Plains-Cree Indians." *Anthropological Papers of the American Museum of Natural History* 11, no. 6 (1914).

Skinner, Alanson, and John V. Satterlee. "Menomini Folklore." *Anthropological Papers of the Museum of American History* 13 (1913).

Smith, Donald B. *Sacred Feathers: The Reverend Peter Jones (Kahkewaquonaby) and the Mississauga Indians*. Toronto: University of Toronto Press, 1987.

Smith, Donald B., ed. *Life, Letters, and Speeches: George Copway (Kahgegagahbowh)*. Lincoln: University of Nebraska Press, 1997.

Smith, James. "Leadership in Ojibwa Society." In Hinshaw, *Currents in Anthropology*.

Smith, Theresa S. "Calling the Thunder, Part One: Animikeek: The Thunderstorm as Speech Event in the Anishinaabe World." *American Indian Culture and Research Journal* 15 (1991).

– "The Island of the Anishnaabeg: An Interpretation of the Relationship between the Thunder and Underwater Manitouk in the Traditional Ojibwe Life-World." PhD diss., Boston University, 1990.

– *Island of the Anishnaabeg: Thunderers and Water Monsters in the Traditional Ojibwe Life-World.* Moscow: University of Idaho Press, 1995.

– "Oral Traditions, Ojibwe." In Crawford and Kelley, *American Indian Religious Traditions.*

Snake, Kenneth G. "Adventures of Nanabush." *Wawatay News*, 14 July 1994.

– "The Bears and the Turtles." In Colombo and Laidlaw, *Voices of Rama.*

– "Nanabush Meets Owl and Rabbit." In Snake, et al, *The Adventures of Nanabush.*

– "Nanabush and the Owl." In Colombo and Laidlaw, *Voices of Rama.*

– "The Old Woman and the Serpent." In Colombo and Laidlaw, *Voices of Rama.*

– "Tell Me the Story." *Wawatay News*, 14 July 1994.

Snake, Sam, Chief Elijah Yellowhead, Alder York, David Simcoe, and Annie King, eds. *The Adventures of Nanabush: Ojibway Indian Stories.* Francis Kagige, illus. Toronto: Doubleday, 1979.

Snow, Dean R. "The Solon Petroglyphs and Eastern Abnaki Shamanism." In *Papers of the Seventh Algonquian Conference*, ed. William Cowan. Ottawa: Carleton University Press, 1976.

Southcott, Mary E. *The Sound of the Drum: The Sacred Art of the Anishnabec.* Erin: Boston Mills, 1985.

Sparks, John, and Tony Soper. *Owls: Their Natural and Unnatural History.* Robert Gillmor, illus. New York: Facts on File, 1989.

Speck, Frank G. *Myths and Folk-lore of the Timiskaming Algonquin and Timagami Ojibwa.* Ottawa: Government Printing Bureau, 1915.

– *Naskapi: The Savage Hunters of the Labrador Peninsula.* Norman: University of Oklahoma Press, [1935] 1977.

Speck, Frank G., and Jesse Moses. *The Celestial Bear Comes Down to Earth.* Reading: Reading Public Museum, 1945.

Spielmann, Roger Willson. *You're So Fat!: Exploring Ojibwe Discourse.* Toronto: University of Toronto Press, 1998.

Stan, Susan. *The Ojibwe.* Vero Beach: Rourke, 1989.

Steckley, John. *Beyond Their Years; Five Native Women's Stories.* Toronto: Canadian Scholars' Press, 1999.

Stein, Gertrude. "Sacred Emily." In Stimpson and Chessman, *Gertrude Stein: Writings, 1903–1932.*

– "Rose is a Rose." In Stimpson and Chessman, *Gertrude Stein: Writings, 1932–1946.*

Steinbring, J.H. "Boulder Art in Eastern Manitoba." In *Studies in Manitoba Rock Art. I. Petroforms.* Winnipeg: Department of Cultural Affairs and Historical Resources, 1983.

Steinfels, Peter. "Modernity and Belief: Charles Taylor's 'A Secular Age.'" *Commonweal* 135, no. 9 (9 May 2008).

Stevens, James R. *Sacred Legends of the Sandy Lake Cree.* Carl Ray, illus. Toronto: McClelland and Stewart, 1971.

– ed. *Legends from the Forest, Told by Chief Thomas Fiddler.* Edtrip Fiddler, trans. Moonbeam: Penumbra, 1985.

Stevenson, Mark. "The Bear Whisperer." *Globe and Mail,* 5 October 2002.

Stimpson, Catharine R., and Harriet Chessman, eds. *Gertrude Stein: Writings, 1903–1932,* and *Gertrude Stein: Writings, 1932–1946.* New York: Library of America, 1998.

Stoehr, Catherine Murton. "Salvation from Empire: The Roots of Anishinabe Christianity in Upper Canada, 1650–1840." PhD diss., Queen's University, 2008.

Sturtevant, William C., ed. *Handbook of North American Indians.* Washington: Smithsonian Institution, 1981.

Tanner, Adrian. *Bringing Home Animals: Religious Ideology and Mode of Production of the Mistassini Cree Hunters.* St John's: Memorial University of Newfoundland, 1979.

Tanner, John. *A Narrative of the Captivity and Adventures of John Tanner.* Edwin James, ed. New York: G. and C. and H. Carvili, 1830.

Tanner, V. "Outlines of the Geography, Life, and Customs of Newfoundland–Labrador." *Acta Geographica* 8 (1944).

Tax, Sol, ed. *Acculturation in the Americas.* New York: Cooper Square, 1967.

Thevet, André. *Les singularitez de la france antarctique.* Paul Gaffarel, ed. Paris: Maisonneuve, [1557] 1878.

Thwaites, Reuben Gold, ed. *The Jesuit Relations and Allied Documents,* 73 vols. New York: Pageant Books, [1896–1901] 1959.

Toulouse, Pamela Rose. "Bimaadziwin (the Good Life): Sharing the Living Teachings of the People of Sagamok Anishnawbek: Implications for Education." PhD diss., University of British Columbia, 2001.

Tourangeau, Ron. "Visual Art as Metaphor: Understanding Anishinabe Spirituality and Christianity." PhD diss., University of California, Berkeley, 1989.

Treuer, Anton. *Living Our Language: Ojibwe Tales and Oral Histories.* St Paul: Minnesota Historical Society Press, 2001.

Tuhiwai Smith, Linda. *Decolonizing Methodologies: Research and Indigenous Peoples.* London: Zed, 1999.

Turnbull, Molly. "Indicating Alliance: Kinship Terms in Discourse among the Ojibwe and Potawatomi in Southwestern Ontario." MA thesis, University of Western Ontario, 1997.

Turner, Dale. *This Is Not a Peace Pipe: Towards a Critical Indigenous Philosophy.* Toronto: University of Toronto Press, 2006.

Valentine, J. Randolph. "Nenabozho and the Ojibwa Woman." In *Actes du trente-deuxième congrès des algonquinistes*, ed. John D. Nichols. Winnipeg: University of Manitoba Press, 2001.

– *Ojibway Dialogues and Riddles.* Thunder Bay: Lakehead University, Centre for Northern Studies, 1991.

Valentine, Lisa P. *Making It Their Own: Severn Ojibwe Communicative Practices.* Toronto: University of Toronto Press, 1995.

– *Ojibway Creek and Micmac Plays.* Thunder Bay: Lakehead University, Centre for Northern Studies, 1984.

Van Kirk, Sylvia. *Many Tender Ties: Women in the Fur-Trade Society, 1670–1870.* Winnipeg: Watson and Dwywer, 1980, 1999.

Vannote, Vance. *Women of White Earth.* Minneapolis: University of Minnesota Press, 1999.

Vansina, Jan. *Oral Tradition as History.* Madison: University of Wisconsin Press, 1985.

Vastokas, Joan M. "Interpeting Birch Bark Scrolls." In *Papers of the Fifteenth Algonquian Conference*, ed. William Cowan. Ottawa: Carleton University Press, 1984.

Vastokas, Joan M., and Romas K. Vastokas. *The Sacred Art of the Algonkians: A Study of the Peterborough Petroglyphs.* Peterborough: Mansard, 1973.

Vecsey, Christopher. "Midewiwin Myths of Origin." In *Papers of the Fifteenth Algonquian Conference*, ed. William Cowan. Ottawa: Carleton University Press, 1984.

– *Traditional Ojibwa Religion and Its Historical Changes.* Philadelphia: American Philosophical Society, 1983.

Vennum, Thomas. "The Alice C. Fletcher Ojibwe Indian Recordings." In McEntire et al., *Discourse in Ethnomusicology III.*

– *American Indian Lacrosse: Little Brother of War.* Washington: Smithsonian Institution, 1994.

– "A History of Ojibwa Song Form." In Heth, *Selected Reports in Ethnomusicology.*

– "Indexing Ojibwe Melody." In *Papers of the Fortieth Algonquian Conference*, ed. Karl S. Hele and J. Randolph Valentine. Albany: SUNY Press, 2012.

– *Lacrosse Legends of the First Americans.* Baltimore: Johns Hopkins University Press, 2007.

– *The Ojibwa Dance Drum, Its History and Construction.* Washington: Smithsonian Institution, 1982.

– "Ojibwa Origin-Migration Songs of the *mitewiwin.*" *Journal of American Folklore* 91 (1978).

– "Ojibway Music from Minnesota: A Century of Song for Voice and Drum." Audio cassette, compact disc, mixed media. Minneapolis: Minnesota Historical Society. 1997.

– "Southwestern Ojibwa Music." 2 vols. PhD diss., Harvard University, 1975.

– *Wild Rice and the Ojibway People.* St Paul: Minnesota Historical Society, 1988.

Vigorelli, Leonardo. *Gli Oggetti Indiani Raccolti da G. Constantino Beltrami.* Bergamo: Civico Museo E. Caffi, 1987, Contentiore in corteccia di betulla, 13 (no. 32); Tamburo da medicine doppio, 16 (no. 52); Sporta in corteccia di betulla dotata di bretella in cuoio, 83 (no. 31).

Villeneuve, Jocelyne. *Nanna Bijou: The Sleeping Giant.* Moonbeam: Penumbra, 1981.

Vizenor, Gerald. *Dead Voices: Natural Agonies in the New World.* Norman: University of Oklahoma Press, 1992.

– *Earthdivers: Tribal Narratives on Mixed Descent.* Minneapolis: University of Minnesota Press, 1981.

– *Fugitive Poses: Native American Indian Scenes of Absence and Presence.* Lincoln: University of Nebraska Press, 1998.

– "The Midewiwin." In Vizenor, ed., *Anishinabe Adisokan.*

– *The People Named the Chippewa: Narrative Histories.* Minneapolis: University of Minnesota Press, 1984.

– "The Ruins of Representation: Shadow Survivance and the Literature of Dominance." In Arteaga, *An Other Tongue.*

– *Summer in the Spring: Anishinaabe Lyric Poems and Stories.* Norman: University of Oklahoma Press, 1993.

– *Touchwood: A Collection of Ojibway Prose.* Minneapolis: New Rivers, 1987.

– ed. *Anishinabe Adisokan: Tales of the People.* Minneapolis: Nodin, 1970.

Wabasse, Peter. *Hymns in Ojibway and Oji-Cree.* Prince Albert: Northern Canada Mission Distributors, 1999.

Wahpeconiah, Tammy J. "This Once Savage Heart of Mine: Rhetorical Strategies of Survival in Early Native American Writing." PhD diss., Michigan State University, 2004.

Waisberg, Leo G., and Tim E. Holzkamm, "'Their Country Is Tolerably Rich in Furs': The Ojibwa Fur Trade in the Boundary Waters Region, 1821–71." In *Actes du vingt-cinquième congrès des Algonquinistes,* ed. William Cowan. Ottawa: Carleton University Press, 1994.

– "'We Have One Mind and One Mouth. It Is the Decision of All of Us.' Traditional Ahnishinaabe Governance of Treaty #3." Kenora: Working Paper for Grand Council Treaty #3, 2001.

Wallace, Anthony F.C. "The Role of the Bear in Delaware Society." *Pennsylvania Archaeologist* 19 (1949).

Walz, Grace. "Andrew Jackson Blackbird of L'Arbre Croche." MA thesis, Western Michigan University, 1964.

Warren, William W. "Sioux and Chippewa Wars." In Babcock, "William Whipple Warren."

– *History of the Ojibway Nation.* St Paul: Minnesota Historical Society, [1885] 1957.

– *History of the Ojibway People.* Theresa Schenck, ed. St Paul: Minnesota Historical Society, 2009.

– "Oral Traditions Respecting the History of the Ojibwa Nation." In Schoolcraft, *Historical and Statistical Information,* vol. 2.

Wasagunachank or Midasuganj. "Mighty-One, Black Tail-of-a-Fish, and the Mystic Rite." In Jones, *Ojibwa Texts,* vol. 2.

Watrin, François Philibert. "Banishment of the Jesuits from Louisiana." *The Jesuit Relations,* 70 (1764).

Webber, Alika Podolinsky. *The Bear, a Lord Unto Himself,* private publication, n.d., n.p.

Weekes, William Rex. "Antiquity of the Midewiwin: An Examination of Early Documents, Origin Stories, Archaeological Remains, and Rock Paintings from the Northern Woodlands of North America." PhD diss., Arizona State University, 2009.

Wenjack, Jim. "A Meeting with the Maymaygwayshug." *Wawatay News,* April 1985.

Wheeler-Voegelin, Erminie. *Chippewa Indians I: Red Lake and Pembina Chippewa.* New York: Garland Publishing, 1974.

– "Notes on Ojibwa-Ottawa Pictography." In Getty and Smith, *One Century Later.*

White, Bruce. "Ojibwa Fur Trade Protocol." *Minnesota History* 50 (1987).

White, Richard. *The Middle Ground: Indians, Empires, and Republics in the Great Lakes Region, 1650–1815.* Cambridge: Cambridge University Press, 1991.

Whiteford, Andrew Hunter. "The Origin of Great Lakes Beaded Bandolier Bags." *American Indian Art Magazine* 11 (1986).

Wiget, Andrew. "Cycle Construction and Character Development in Central Algonkian Trickster Tales." *Oral Tradition* 15 (2000).

Williams, Mentor L., ed. *Schoolcraft's Indian Legends.* East Lansing: Michigan State University Press, 1991.

Winter, Jeremiah. "Kwokwokwo (chouette épervière)," "Kwokwokwo (Hawk Owl)." In Desveaux, *La mythologie*, vol. 2.

Wisdom and Vision: The Teachings of Our Elders. Report of the National First Nations Elders Language Gathering. Manitoulin Island, West Bay / Ottawa: Ojibway Cultural Foundation / Assembly of First Nations, 1993.

Wolfart, H.C., and Freda Ahenakew, eds. *Âh-âyîtaw isi ê-kî-kiskêyihtahkik maski-hkiy, They Knew Both Sides of Medicine: Cree Tales of Curing and Cursing Told by Alice Ahenakew.* Winnipeg: University of Manitoba Press, 2000.

Woolworth, Nancy L. "Miss Densmore Meets the Ojibwe: Frances Densmore's Ethnomusicology Studies among the Grand Portage Ojibwe in 1905." *Minnesota Archaeologist* 38 (1979).

Wright, Robert H. *Legends of the Chippewas.* Munising: Wright Printing, 1927.

Wub-e-ke-niew. *We Have the Right to Exist.* New York: Black Thistle, 1995.

www.americanbear.org/blackbearfacts.htm

www.brownbear.org

York, Peter. "Kuk-Oh.Chees." In Colombo and Laidlaw, *Voices of Rama.*

Zedeño, M. Nieves, et al. *Traditional Ojibway Resources in the Western Great Lakes.* Tucson: Bureau of Applied Research in Anthropology, University of Arizona in Tucson, 2001.

Index

Marsden, Lottie, 101, 182–3;
Martin, Pete, 100, 102; Midasuganj/
Ten Claw, 3, 161; Mink, John,
127; Morgan, Jerry, 199, 202;
Morris, Joseph, 103; Morris, John-
George, 104; Nanibush, Jim, 140;
Nawajibigokwe, 16; Nekatcit,
232; Ogemah, Lucy, 206; Oshogay,
Delia, 170; Ozawamik, 183; Penesi,
John/Kagige Penasi/Forever Bird,
138, 191, 201; Pete, John, 5, 94; Pine,
Fred/Sah-Kah-Odjew-Wahg-Sah,
31; Rock, Elizabeth, 89, 211–12;
Rogers, Will, 36; St Germain,
Marjorie, 207; Sakry, Mark, 194;
Sandy, Thomas, 216; Saycosegay,
15; Shawondasee, 147; Sikassige,
11, 14, 34, 37, 84–5, 89, 132, 134, 212;
Siyaka, 147; Snake, Kenneth G.,
183; Snake, Sam, 169; Tailfeather
Woman, 181; Thomas, Eli/
Wasseskom, 98; Wasanganachank,
3, 161; Wenjack, Jim, 190;
Wigwaswátik, 119; York, John, 207;
York, Peter, 100

Tanner, John, xxxviii, 24, 72, 127, 137,
171, 173–6, 186–7
Thevet, André, 24
Thwaites, Reuben Gold, 198
totems/dodems, clans, 134–7;
definition of, 249n110
transformation, metamorphosis, xv,
xvii, xix–xx, xxv, 21, 37, 120, 123,
135, 138, 152, 157, 166, 190, 220,
242n18, 263n74
treaty, treaties, xxii, xxx–xxxi, xxxiv,
xxxvi, 17–20, 33, 38–9, 42–4, 47, 49,
62–3, 78, 91, 107, 139, 149, 174, 210,
228–9, 235

Turner, Dale, xxxv–xxxvi
turtle, 8, 29, 72, 151, 159–60, 170, 173,
205, 212

Valentine, J. Randolph, 184
Vastokas, Joan M., 209
Vastokas, Joan M., and Romas K., 7,
27, 197
Vecsey, Christopher, 7, 14–15, 28,
178
Vennum, Thomas, 10, 26, 84, 134,
200, 202
vision quest, xxi, xxvi, 8, 31, 48–9,
52, 107, 139, 162, 208, 212, 218;
misnomer of, 252n3
Vizenor, Gerald, 15, 92, 103, 122,
124–5, 139, 144–5, 185

Wallace, Anthony F.C., 139–40,
234
Walz, Grace, 63–4
Warren, William W., xxvii, xxxviii,
9, 12–13, 20, 22, 26–7, 35, 61,
69–79, 134, 136–7, 184, 200, 221,
235, 239–40; Ojibwe beliefs as an
"Indian Bible," 69
Water creatures, *anamaqkiu,* 98,
261n21; and copper, 184–7, 192,
235–8, 277n69; and Little People,
189–191, 278n82; and silver,
168, 187–9; and women, 180–4;
harmful, 169–72; helpful, 173–80;
earthdiver, 273n208; snakes: and
afterlife, 172–3; and snakeskin,
6, 23, 29, 31, 90, 94, 131, 138, 169,
172–8, 180–4, 187, 190, 194, 199,
212–15, 222–3; symbolism of,
207–18, 275n37
Whiteford, Andrew Hunter, 88
Wolfart, H.C., 145